# COMMUNICATION

A series of volumes edited by:
**Dolf Zillmann** and **Jennings Bryant**

# Audience Responses

# to

# Media Diversification

*Coping With Plenty*

Edited by

Lee B. Becker
*The Ohio State University*

Klaus Schoenbach
*Academy for Music and Theater, Hannover*

**LEA** LAWRENCE ERLBAUM ASSOCIATES, PUBLISHERS
1989    Hillsdale, New Jersey                    Hove and London

Lawrence Erlbaum Associates, Inc., Publishers
365 Broadway
Hillsdale, New Jersey 07642

**Library of Congress Cataloging in Publication Data**

Audience responses to media diversification: coping with
plenty / edited by Lee B. Becker and Klaus Schoenbach.
p.     cm.
Includes indexes.
ISBN 0-8058-0229-0
1. Mass media—Audiences.     I. Becker, Lee B., 1948–
II. Schoenbach, Klaus.
P96.A83A94     1989
302.2'34—dc19

88–16485
CIP

Printed in the United States of America
10  9  8  7  6  5  4  3  2  1

# Contents

**8    France: Experimenting with Pay TV
and Viewdata**    **159**
*Isabelle Pailliart*

**9    Federal Republic of Germany:
Social Experimentation with Cable
and Commercial Television**    **167**
*Elisabeth Noelle-Neumann and Ruediger Schulz*

# List of Contributors

**Lee B. Becker** is a Professor in the School of Journalism and Department of Communication, The Ohio State University, Columbus, Ohio, U.S.A. (BA, University of Kentucky, 1969; MA, University of Kentucky, 1971; PhD, University of Wisconsin, Madison, 1974.) He has written and published in the areas of political communication, audience uses of the media, and media personnel practices.

**R. Warwick Blood** is a Principal Lecturer in Communication, School of Communication and Liberal Studies, Mitchell College, Bathurst, Australia. (BC, University of Sydney, 1969; MS, Syracuse University, 1978; PhD, Syracuse University, 1981.) He has written and published in the areas of politics and mass media, audiences uses of the media, and political polling.

**Heinz Bonfadelli** is a Researcher and Lecturer at the Institute for Mass Communication, University of Zurich, Switzerland. (PhD, University of Zurich, 1980.) He has conducted research and published in the areas of mass media and youth, uses and effects of mass media, and new media.

**Pamela J. Creedon** is an Assistant Professor in the School of Journalism, The Ohio State University, Columbus, OH, U.S.A. (BA, Mount Union College, 1969; MA, University of Oregon, 1970.) She has done research and written in the areas of audience uses of the media and public relations issues.

**Roselyne Bouillin-Dartevelle** is a Professor, Institute of Sociology, Universite Libre, Brussels, Belgium. (PhD, Universite Libre, Brussels.) She has conducted research and published in the areas of methods of mass communication research, audience uses of the media, and cultural practices.

**Jeffrey P. Delbel** is an Associate Professor of telecommunications at Cayuga Community College, Auburn, NY, U.S.A. (Doctoral work, Syracuse University; MS, Syracuse University, 1978; BA, University of Miami, 1974.) His major research interest is new telecommunications technologies.

**Eric S. Fredin** is an Assistant Professor in the School of Journalism, The Ohio State University, Columbus, OH, U.S.A. (BA, Oberlin College, 1969; PhD, University of Michigan, 1980.) His research interests are political communication and the development and use of new communication technology.

**Barrie Gunter** is Head of Research, Independent Broadcasting Authority, London, U.K. (PhD, North East London Polytechnic; degrees in psychology from the University of Wales and the University of London.) He has written 11 books and nearly 150 book chapters, journal papers and newspaper or magazine articles on various psychological and mass communication research topics.

**Walter Haetterschwiler** is a Researcher and Lecturer at the Institute for Mass Communication, University of Zurich, Switzerland. (Lic. Phil., University of Zurich, 1981.) He has done research and published in the areas of mass media and youth, audience analysis, and new media.

**Nick Jankowski** is a Senior Researcher, Institute of Mass Communication, University of Nijmegen, the Netherlands. (BA, University of California, Berkeley, 1967; MA, University of Oregon, 1973.) He has conducted research and published on new cable services and community radio and television and is working on books on community media and on qualitative methodology in communications research.

**Albrecht Kutteroff** is a Researcher in Mass Communication, Social Science Department, University of Mannheim, Mannheim, West Germany. (Diploma in Sociology, Social Psychology and Political Science, University of Mannheim, 1977.) He has conducted research on political elites, mass media elites, news shows in cable and satellite programs, and the social impact of cable television.

**Geoff Lealand** is Research Officer, New Zealand Council for Educational Research, Wellington, New Zealand. (BA, University of Canterbury, 1978; MA, University of Canterbury, 1980; PhD, Bowling Green State University, 1983.) He has worked in audience research in the United Kingdom and New Zealand. His research interests include audience use of the media, children and television, and popular culture studies.

**Paolo Martini** is Senior Editor for the Mass Media Section of *Panorama*, Italy's leading newsweekly magazine. (Attended courses in Political Science, University of Bologna.) He has written and published in the areas of history of media policies, evolution of television systems, and media content.

**Gianpietro Mazzoleni** is a Professor of Sociology of Knowledge, Department of Sociology and Political Science, University of Salerno, Italy. (BA, St. Anselm's College, Manchester, NH, 1969; PhD, University of Rome, 1974.) He has done research and published in the fields of political communication, elections, mass media, and media policies.

**Elisabeth Noelle-Neumann** is Director, Institut fuer Demoskopie Allensbach, West Germany, Professor Emeritus, Institut fuer Publizistik, University of Mainz, and, since 1978, Visiting Professor in the Department of Political Science at the University of Chicago. (PhD, University of Berlin, 1940; Honorary doctorate, Hochschule St. Gallen, 1978.) She has done research and published primarily in the fields of methods of survey research, public opinion theory, and media effects. She has directed the Allensbach public opinion polls and media research since 1947.

**Frank Olderaan** is a Research Fellow, Institute of Mass Communication, University of Nijmegen, the Netherlands. (Drs., University of Nijmegen, 1979.) He has been involved in research on the introduction of interactive cable television in the Netherlands.

**Isabelle Pailliart** is Maitre de Conferences associe, en Sciences de L'information et de la Communication de l'Universite Stendhal, Grenoble, France. (Doctorate de Troisieme Cycle en Sciences de l'Information et de la Communication, 1982.) She has written and published in the areas of local communication administrations, uses of new media, communication networks and communication policy.

**Barbara Pfetsch** is a Researcher in Mass Communication, Social Science Department, University of Mannheim, Mannheim, West Germany. (MA, University of Mannheim, 1985.) She has researched agenda building processes and is currently working on time budget research for media use and research on audience reactions to the introduction of cable television.

**Klaus Schoenbach** is a Professor for Mass Communication, School of Journalism, Academy for Music and Theater, Hannover, West Germany.

(PhD, University of Mainz, 1975. *Habilitation,* University of Muenster, 1982.) He has done research and published primarily in the areas of political communication, methods of mass communication research, and entertainment through the media.

**Ruediger Schulz** is Project Director, Institut fuer Demoskopie Allensbach, West Germany. (PhD, University of Mainz, 1974.) He has done research and published primarily in the areas of television audience analysis, readership research, and communicator research.

**Ulla Johnsson-Smaragdi** is a Project Director and faculty member in the Department of Sociology, University of Lund, Sweden. (PhD, University of Lund, 1983.) She has conducted research and published on children's and adolescents' uses of the media.

**Vernone M. Sparkes** is a Professor, Radio-Television-Film, S. I. Newhouse School of Public Communications, Syracuse University, Syracuse, NY, U.S.A. (MA, Indiana University, 1972; PhD, Indiana University, 1974.) He has conducted research and published in the areas of international communications, communications law, media management, and diffusion of new communications technologies.

**Joseph Mallory Wober** is Deputy Head of Research, Independent Broadcasting Authority, London, U.K. (BA, Cambridge, 1974; MSc, London, 1961; PhD, London, 1967.) His research interests and publications are on psychology and culture, psychology in Africa, and television and social control.

# Preface

The idea for this book grew out of a discussion between the two editors in Munich in the summer of 1985. It matured over the next months, taking shape during the spring and summer of the following year.

During the spring of 1986, Lee Becker was a visiting professor in the Institute of Mass Communication at the Catholic University of Nijmegen, the Netherlands. The support of Professor James Stappers of that institute is particularly acknowledged. During the summer of 1986, the two editors were able to work together in Hannover in West Germany with the support of the German National Science Foundation.

The editors were able to come together in the final stages of the project as a result of support given to Klaus Schoenbach by the Department of Theatre Arts at San Jose State University in the United States. The assistance of the chairman of this department, Professor Stanley Baran, is acknowledged.

The editors also acknowledge the support provided by their home institutions, The Ohio State University and The Academy for Music and Theater, Hannover. Lee Becker was given special assistance as part of the Distinguished Research Award program at his university.

All of the contributors for this volume were recruited to write specifically for this project. Contributors were provided with an outline of the project and a draft of the first chapter to the book and asked to fashion their contributions along the lines specified. Several of the contributors were able to meet with the editors in the summer of 1987 at the conference of the World Association for Public Opinion Research in Montreux, Switzerland, to discuss a preliminary draft of the concluding chapter.

The editors extend their thanks to the contributors for their hard work and their suggestions as the project matured. They submitted their work to tough questioning and editing with the expected grace. The editors alone accept responsibility for the introductory chapter and the conclusions reached in the final chapter.

Many people provided assistance in a variety of ways during the various phases of this project. Marianne Schoenbach deserves particular mention for her assistance in translating two of the chapters in the volume.

Finally, the editors thank three people who tolerated professional conversations when they probably were inappropriate and provided the smiles and other encouragement needed to make this volume possible. Thank you, Ann, Jessica, and Marianne.

*Lee Becker*
*Klaus Schoenbach*

# 1

# When Media Content Diversifies: Anticipating Audience Behaviors

**Lee B. Becker**
*The Ohio State University*
**Klaus Schoenbach**
*Academy for Music and Theater, Hannover*

The 1980s have seen significant changes in the media environments of many Western societies. New delivery technologies or new uses of old technologies have altered the media landscape. New organizations have developed in competition with the old, and the old have employed various strategies of either defense or adaptation.

Although the technologies have played different roles in the various Western societies due to historical and legal constraints placed on them, the common outcome has been an increase in the options available to audience members. Although the choices have not always been those hoped for by critics, or possibly even desired by audiences, the thrust toward content diversification in at least a limited form has been the common denominator in the Western societies.

Communication historians may look back on the 1980s as a critical time in the development of media systems. Cable television, expanded forms of broadcast television, videocassette recorders (VCRs), direct broadcast satellites, viewdata, and teletext all entered into competition with the existing media for attention, time, space, and money. Whether the new media should be allowed to and would be able to obtain those resources was one of the major questions. Where the resources would come from was another.

## THE RESEARCH PROJECT AND THE BOOK

This project began with that simple observation of change. The established ways of doing things were under challenge in the 1980s. In the United States, for example, television programming was proliferating, and the three broadcast television networks, which once held a stranglehold on the flow of broadcast audiovisual materials, were under serious challenge. Television was becoming "pay" television. The vast media empires and smaller, entrepreneurial companies were experimenting with new ways of delivering new materials to the home. In Europe, cable led to increased pressure for expansion of television, and experimentation with viewdata (videotext) and teletext was even more advanced than in the United States, perhaps because the governments or the postal and telephone authorities were putting lots of money into efforts to gain or hold leads in the prophesied communications revolution. Even more importantly, there was significant discussion about dissolving national broadcast media systems that had been protected from domestic and foreign competition. The new means of message distribution did not respect borders as neatly as did the old. The video recorder filled the shelves of stores, and video rental shops were appearing on every corner.

In the political debate, the commercial dialogue, the writings in the popular press, and in academic circles, much was speculated about audience responses to these changes in the media landscape. Some observers said the audiences would be corrupted by the invasion of commercial and culturally debasing content, often coming from elsewhere (usually from the United States). Europeans particularly would be drawn from the uplifting materials of their own media systems to the degrading materials of the marketplace. But audiences, so the alternative (largely commercial, often American) voice would say, would finally get a chance to decide for themselves what kinds of contents they wanted. True democracy would come to the media environment and the public would rejoice in it.

Data to support either of these positions, or any of their variants (generally more articulately presented than heretofore), rarely were available in a single location. The goal of the project we describe here was to assemble evidence, although not necessarily to referee among these various perspectives. Not everyone engaged in the dialogue, of course, has felt a need for facts or is likely to find the data that we have assembled valuable to them. It remains our bias, we clearly admit, that understanding audience reactions to media content diversification resulting from the new media is essential for this debate. We also feel that meaningful responses can be adequately measured. The data assembled here are not believed to be definitive and clearly should not be treated as ends in themselves. The goal of the project, however, was *data-based* interpretation and evaluation.

To that end, we sought to assemble a group of researchers who either currently were engaged in research relevant to our goal or had, in the past, done work pertaining to it. We were aware of some of these individuals. Others became known to us as we talked with colleagues and pursued leads given to us.

We decided early in the project to limit the focus of our search in a very significant way: We only wanted to examine audience responses to media content diversification in societies with Western media systems and cultures. By this we meant capitalistic societies with traditions of media freedom. But we also only wanted to examine societies with cultures having mostly common principles in the area of media habits, orientations to entertainment, and leisure in general.

Among the Western countries, we identified those that had experienced at least some minimal level of change in media content. We never felt that it would be possible to be exhaustive even within this framework, and we did not seek one report from each country fitting our classification. Rather, we sought reports from countries where we knew some information was available and where we felt that something new could be learned by the type of change being experienced. Precise information on media content change in these societies, unfortunately, was not readily available. As a result, we had to make estimates based on our knowledge of changes taking place in the media system. We then inferred that these system changes should produce content change and diversification. Regardless, in many countries it became difficult to select from among the many researchers doing relevant work; in others, it was a matter of identifying the few. The evidence that some of our researchers were able to assemble is quite impressive. In other cases, the data were quite limited.

Because of some good planning and some good fortune, we ended with 11 countries studied by 14 different researchers or teams of researchers. The countries ranged from as far north as Sweden to as far south as New Zealand, and from as large as the United States and Australia to as small as Belgium, the Netherlands, and Switzerland. Included were countries experiencing a great deal of structural change and those with, at the point of writing, relatively little. The individual reports reflect to a considerable extent the concerns and issues facing the country being discussed.

The countries studied vary along two rather important dimensions. The first dimension is the *amount* of new types of material that has become available and the *amount* of choice within those types. By this we mean (a) that fairly significant proportions of the people have access to media delivery systems that (b) offer large numbers of programming or content options. The second dimension is probably more important and clearly more complex: the *diversity* of that material. The complexity results from the fact that there is very little agreement about what is true diversity in content. For instance, some critics hold that increased entertainment offerings result in more of the same, not diversity, whereas others argue that an increased number of choices—even within the entertainment classification—is a form of diversity. Some go even further and argue that all products of capitalistic media systems are without real distinction. Despite these differences of opinion about the meaning of diversity, there is much agreement that a country receiving materials from other cultures is experiencing some form of content diversification. Our countries vary significantly in that regard.

When we crossed these dimensions and roughly located the countries, we came up with four clusters. The first consisted of countries with relatively little new content to date but most of that content coming from outside. We placed New Zealand, Australia, and Sweden in that category, although there were clear differences even among them. In the contrasting cluster was the United States, a country with a great deal of new content but comparatively little of it coming from outside the culture. In between were two clusters, one made up of Italy, France, the United Kingdom, and West Germany, the other including Switzerland, the Netherlands, and Belgium. The former cluster had been experiencing relatively large amounts of new content, comparatively little of which came from outside. The latter were receiving a somewhat lesser amount of new material, most of which came from outside.

Any such classification scheme is open to challenge. For example, one can note that there are many isolated communities in the United States (where three quarters of the households are passed by cable) in which there is little diversity, certainly less than in an urban center in Australia. And in most of our countries, including the United States, those households not passed by cable have fewer television choices than almost all Belgian or Dutch households. It remains the case nonetheless that most American households at this writing have more content options open to them than the typical household in the other countries studied. In addition, the classification scheme tried to anticipate change expected to occur in the countries under examination. For example, the German research site examined in this volume is one of those with a prototypical cable system offering a large amount of content. Before the end of the 1980s, about half of the households in West Germany will have the same access to cable. Thus,Germany was classified according to the community studied rather than the objective situation in the middle of the 1980s.

Nonetheless, the tentative nature of this scheme is worth reinforcing. As we have noted heretofore, there are several different ways of classifying countries. The focus here was on *content* differences (amount and diversity). Other dimensions clearly exist. Even where content diversity is concerned there are options not taken. The use of amount of foreign programming as our sole index of diversity was reasonable, although not exhaustive.

## MEDIA, MASS MEDIA, AND "NEW MEDIA"

In this book, the term *media* is defined as all the ways human beings use to convey symbols to one another—from language to telefax machines. "Mass media", then, are regarded as a specific kind of media. They are technical instruments spreading symbols to a potentially unlimited audience—an audience that, for instance, does not have to gather in one place and at one time (Maletzke, 1963). Mass media range from handwritten newsletters to television.

An often-used term, *new media*, needs further clarification: How "new" must a "new medium" be? First of all, we have to take into account that there are different perceptions of what is "new" and what is not. The mass medium of cable television, for example, may not be considered a "new" medium by its audience. It could simply be viewed as more "plain old television." The same may apply to what the audience thinks of satellite television. This audience may, however, regard the VCR as something "new," although media experts would probably call the use of VCRs a way to delay the watching of television shows. So, in communication research, VCRs, video discs, and compact discs (CDs) are often only called "new *storage* media."

A veritable "new *mass* medium," for some experts, has to address new senses or new combinations of senses. It has to use new channels of information. In that definition, for instance, radio was "new" because it was the first mass medium to transmit live sounds as opposed to the earlier ones that either had to be read (newspapers, magazines) or contained only sound that had been recorded some time before (records). FM or stereo radio then would be only an improvement of what is still the mass medium of radio.

From the standpoint of the *industry*, on the other hand, everything may be "new" that requires new production lines—CDs, for instance. Although, for media experts, CDs may still be nothing but records, only with less background noise.

In this book, we use a pragmatic definition of "new media." The media are "new" for us if they are recent additions to the electronic mass media system, such as cable broadcasting, satellite broadcasting, videocassette recorders, teletext, and viewdata. We also consider as "new" the addition of terrestrial radio and television stations or the significant expansion of broadcast time (such as the introduction of "breakfast television") when those additions produce radical departures from tradition. The introduction of *local* radio in Germany would be another such example. In other words, we focus on new developments in the *electronic* distribution of materials to a potentially unlimited audience. We do not deal with new *print* magazines, for instance, and we do not cover new means of individual communication, such as home computers, video telephones, and telefax.

## EARLIER PERIODS OF CHANGE
## IN THE MEDIA ENVIRONMENT

The 1980s were certainly dramatic in the amount of media change taking place. But they were not unique. In fact, the media environments of *Western* societies have never been static over long periods of time. Rather, they have experienced major changes on at least three separate occasions in the past. The first was the introduction of the printed press. The second occurred with the introduction of radio. The third resulted from the introduction of television.

In 1608-1609, the first organs of the printed press—two weekly newspapers in Germany—entered a system of social communication that had been defined mainly by three ways of message transportation: letters, books, and the spoken word (e.g., Groth, 1928). The earliest source of information about people and events outside one's own village or town were the oral reports of travellers—traders, soldiers, pilgrims, and troubadours.

But early on, since organized trade had become important, business people had written letters to their companies, families, and friends that had also served as newsletters. For example, the employees of the Augsburg Fugger Company, via their letters in the 1400s and the 1500s from all over the world, kept the people at home posted as to what was going on—particularly in terms of events restricting trade, such as wars or new customs regulations. Those letters often went through many hands and thus resembled handwritten newspapers. As soon as printing with flexible letters was invented in Europe, leaflets became another source of both information and opinion about the world. And books were spreading knowledge and ideas.

Both oral and handwritten reports, as well as printed leaflets, however, were fairly irregular and often not very timely sources of what was going on in other parts of one's country or the world. Books, in that respect, from the start were not supposed to be means of timely information. Their purposes were education, enlightenment, and entertainment.

For the audience, printed newspapers were superior to those older mass media both in terms of their timeliness and the regularity of their appearance. They began to take over from oral stories, letters, and leaflets the functions that they could better serve: providing a potentially large audience with more and more up-to-date and regular information. The potential audience consisted of those who could either pay for a newspaper or otherwise had access to it. The older mass media did not disappear because of the newspapers, but they were somewhat reduced in what tasks they had to fulfill. Oral stories could focus more on entertainment. Letters increasingly became a means of transmitting private messages from one person, group, or institution to another. Leaflets did not have to tell their readers about what had happened as much as to tell them what to do about a specific event.

Anxieties about how the new medium would harm both the individual reader and society arose almost immediately. There were books from the late 1600s warning their readers about the loss of eyesight from too much newspaper consumption and about the spreading of laziness if everybody merely read newspapers (Fritsch, 1676; von Stieler, 1695). These fears are very similar to those expressed when radio arrived about 300 years later.

Radio, as the newspaper did before, restructured the media systems all over the world. First of all, its information could be even more timely than any newspaper's. Also, it could transmit live impressions of events. As a consequence, newspapers could no longer rely on being the first source of information. A process started that was accelerated by TV in the 1940s and 1950s: Newspapers, more and more, were becoming sources of background information after the basic facts of an event had already been spread by the faster electronic media.

The second important audience function that radio, in part, took away from older media was entertainment: It made music accessible to everybody, even to those who could not afford to buy records. Also, plays were available that only theaters had carried earlier. Radio also invented its own entertainment forms, such as daytime serials and radio dramas.

When television started in the late 1940s, we could again observe changes in media behavior: Television could not only make events audible at the time that they happened, but it also could make them visible. And it added vision to the plays and shows that had made radio a success. It started to reduce the audience use of radio to that of a background medium, mostly carrying music and brief information. For many people, television made movie theaters superfluous. Newspapers as a source of background information, entertainment, and advice were also harmed.

What those earlier changes in the media system show is that, in the end, the functions that a new medium served for the *audience* made it successful and forced the older media to adapt themselves to the changed environment. Both legal measures and pressure by groups with vested interests could not secure the survival of the medium just as it was before. The use of new media necessarily took some time away from other activities. For instance, time spent with television resulted in reductions in time spent listening to radio, reading magazines and books, and at the movies (Comstock, 1982).

What also becomes clear, however, is that none of the earlier media really disappeared. They were increasingly reduced to the purposes they could best serve (Lerg, 1981). The German historian Riepl (1913) called this pattern of media change a "law" as early as 1913. In more recent work, Dimmick and Rothenbuhler (1984a,

1984b) have argued that each medium finds it own niche in which it can survive in the face of change. Similarly, McCombs (1972) and McCombs and Eyal (1980) have shown that although change takes place in expenditures for individual media, it is done within a general pattern of overall consistency in consumer support for media products.

What was also obvious from such a historical review is that the development of every new medium is accompanied by fears and anxieties. Wartella and Reeves (1983) even found a plausible sequence of those emotions. Fears, they argue, start in the field of physiology: the new medium is expected to harm people's ears, eyes, or whatever senses the medium requires. Then, in a second phase, psychological dangers are envisioned: the new medium makes people apathetic, restless, or dumb. In a third step, finally, threats to the order of the whole society play an important role: Society is expected either to break apart or to become overintegrated, de-individualized.

Not surprisingly, a large body of literature has developed in recent years dealing with various aspects of media change. Much of that literature has dealt with changes in the technologies themselves and the industries embracing these technologies. A great deal of attention has focused on policy implications, particularly in those countries where the technologies threatened media arrangements that protected and favored domestic organizations and domestic content. On an international, comparative level, the compilations of de Bens and Knoche (1987), Ferguson (1986), McQuail and Siune (1986), and Rogers and Balle (1985) dealing with technical and policy issues are particularly relevant. Dutton, Blumler, and Kraemer (1987) concentrated largely on cable developments in the United States, France, Germany, Britain, and Japan.

Although it is not the purpose of this book to report on technological change itself or the industries and organizations that employ them, the authors of the individual chapters provide relevant information on these matters. Specific policy issues of interest within the realm of our topic also are discussed in the individual chapters and again in the final chapter to the volume.

The primary issue of this volume is audience responses to changes in content brought about by changes in the media environment. This is a topic that has been rather unevenly explored. In the United States, on the one hand, much has already been written about this topic. In other countries, this quite clearly is not the case. The chapters that follow provide a window into the literature in the respective countries.

## THE NATURE OF CHANGE IN AUDIENCE BEHAVIOR

The existing literature and evidence from earlier periods of media change suggest that audience members can produce two major responses to new offerings. The first is rejection. The second is some type of adaptation and integration of the new offerings into the existing order.

Adaptation and integration are of three types. First, the new media can bring about change in the allocation of resources. The most important resources, it seems, are attention, time, money, and space. For a new medium to gain audience support, it must receive at least part of some of these resources. They can be taken from other media, nonmedia activities, or from both. It is important to keep in mind that all media compete for attention, time, money, and space with a wide range of services not media-delivered. In the area of entertainment, for example, the media compete with a growing number of recreational industries fiercely trying to win resources.

The second type of audience change is in behaviors combined with or following this reallocation of resources. Included are changes in the situations of media use or the social context of media use. For instance, individual rituals (such as time of day of watching) or behavior could be altered by introduction of a VCR because the materials watched on video may attract more attention than regular television. The actual time spent on television may remain the same. Or, the way families watch television, once cable is in the household, may change, although there might not necessarily be a change in the amount of time spent with television or even in the type of programs watched.

The third type of audience change is intrinsically bound to the content of the new media. For example, audience members could change their views of the world as a result of the introduction of new media content. Again, some adaptation or reallocation of resources is necessary for this to take place, although it may be that total attention, time, money, or space remain constant.

This discussion of change has been in terms of individual audience behaviors. Such changes in individual behaviors can have significant societal implications. Societies in which audience members allocate resources to one industry at the expense of another would be expected to be different from societies with other allocation formulas. For example, if too many individuals in a society allocate resources entirely to entertainment, the political system should suffer.

Even if there is no form of individual adaptation and integration of the new media by audience members, media organizations may continue to exist. Government subsidies in a variety of forms and for a variety of reasons can keep these organizations operating even when audiences have rejected them. The presence or absence of these industries can nonetheless have impact on other media industries.

Industry or organizational adaptation as a result of new media is an important issue, although not one of prime concern to us here.


## THEORETICAL PERSPECTIVES ON AUDIENCE BEHAVIORS

How do we explain, or how have others explained, audience behaviors? In other words, what kind of theoretical perspective helps us in our examination of audience rejection or adaptation and integration of the new media? How can we anticipate audience allocation of resources, modification of behaviors associated with these allocations, or changes in audience perspectives and attitudes as a result of the new media? How can we understand and ultimately predict societal implications of these shifts in audience behaviors?

Concern with audience behavior and its relationship to media offerings has been a dominant issue in the communications literature since at least the 1930s. Many have been the attempts to determine whether or how human activities either depend on or shape mass media contents. Several major lines of thought emerge in this literature. One is the "uses and gratifications" perspective on media audience behavior. Another is the perspective of leisure research. A third perspective can be assembled under the heading of "critical theory" and its approach to culture industries, including the mass media. Still another perspective on the relationships between the media and their audiences focuses on changes in the perceptions of reality and thinking brought about by the consumption of specific media content. In the following sections, we exploit these theoretical approaches for the purpose of studying audience responses to changes in media content. Our goal is to arrive at a theoretical framework that allows us to integrate and make sense of the evidence assembled in the individual reports that follow.


### Uses-and-Gratifications Research

One of the most popular theoretical perspectives in the study of audience behavior is fitted under the general label of "uses and gratifications" research. Its focus on audiences' uses of the media and the gratifications received from those uses has been viewed as particularly important in understanding selection among the media, new and old.

A defining characteristic of the uses-and-gratifications tradition is its concern with the motives of audience members, who are viewed as active seekers and selectors in the media environment. Consistent with the theoretical position is the idea that audience members must assess their options before making decisions about which media actually will be used. Such use is then expected to lead to a type of gratification, or satisfaction of the motivating need.

Of more than passing interest is the observation that the initial development of the uses-and-gratifications position took place at another time when the number of media choices was expanding greatly; namely, when broadcasting capabilities increased the choices given the media consumer. Early citations in the literature are to audience research conducted at Columbia in the 1930s and 1940s. Included is the work on audience uses of newspapers (Berelson, 1949), quiz shows (Herzog, 1940), soap operas (Herzog, 1944), and music (Suchman, 1941), as well as the more general work of Lazarsfeld (1940), Lazarsfeld and Kendall (1948), and Lazarsfeld and Stanton (1942, 1944).

The intellectual roots of this early uses-and-gratifications research are in the field of psychology. The terms "need," "drive," "motive," and "gratification" were all common in the psychological literature when the uses-and-gratifications research began to emerge in the mass communications area. As the reviews of Atkinson (1964), Berkowitz (1969), Cofer and Appley (1964), and others make clear, early motivational research defined human organisms as possessing certain innate needs, such as the need for food and water. These needs stimulate behavior designed to satisfy the needs. In other words, naturally occurring deprivation arouses a need that energizes behavior, the goal of which is to satisfy the need. The behavior was thus said to be motivated.

The basic model was expanded to account for socially derived needs, such as a need for achievement or a need for social interaction, which were thought to motivate behavior in much the same way as the basic needs motivated behavior. In the broadest sense, then, a motivation was viewed as any determinant of behavior. Applying the uses-and-gratifications perspective to the relationships between new media offerings and audience behavior, then, would mean asking the basic question: What do people do with these media? (see Waples, Berelson, & Bradshaw, 1940). New media behavior would then be a consequence not of what offering is available but of specific expectations that people have about it. Reviews of the relevant communications literature and the fundamental difficulties of the uses-and-gratifications perspective are found in Blumler and Katz (1974), Dimmick and McCain (1979), Kubey (1986), McQuail (1987), Rosengren, Wenner, and Palmgreen (1985), Rubin (1986), and Swanson (1987).

## Leisure and Media Behaviors

The concept of leisure is a very complex one as, Cheek (1971) and Kando (1975), among many others, have observed. Kelly (1983), in fact, argued that the concept exists in the literature at three different levels of theorizing: psychological, social-psychological, and sociological. At the psychological level, leisure is defined in terms of the perceived experiences of the individual engaging in the leisure activity. Leisure is the perceived experience, rather than the activity. Neulinger (1974), for example, said that leisure "is a state of mind; it is a way of being, of being at peace with oneself and what one is doing" (p.xv). Sociological theorists, on the other hand, see leisure as a cultural phenomenon (Dumazedier, 1967, pp. 3-4). As such, leisure activity is viewed as being determined by such things as social class, community associations, social role, and economic and family situation. Social-psychological definitions of leisure attempt to integrate these two approaches. Gunter and Gunter (1980), for example, conceived of leisure as "necessarily involving some interaction of both individual and situational factors, representing a convergence of sociological restrictions and freedoms and individual responses to them" (p.364).

As Kelly (1983) has noted, it is essential in understanding leisure to recognize that the same activity can have different meanings for different people, and different activities may have the same meaning for different individuals. In addition, one activity can serve both leisure and nonleisure ends for a single individual. Yet the same activity may have different meanings for the same individual at different times. Gunter and Gunter (1980) argued that leisure should be viewed as a continuum rather than a discrete phenomenon. There may be some leisure in virtually every activity an individual undertakes.

Typologies of leisure abound in the literature. Gunter and Gunter (1980) spoke of four types of leisure, based on a cross-classification of activities on the dimensions of involvement and amount of choice in selecting the activity. *Institutional leisure* is high in involvement but low in choice and is represented by the activities of professionals and others who carry into their leisure much of the nature of their work. Reading professional journals, for example, would be one form of leisure for a social scientist, whereas a lawyer might become involved in community service organizations. *Pure leisure*, on the other hand, is high in involvement and low in constraint. Here, there is a notion of "child's play," or separation from the restrictions of everyday life. There is a spontaneity and sense of adventure or exploration. *Alienated leisure* is constrained and uninvolved. Here, the individual is engaged in activity without much choice largely out of necessity or habit. Visits to sick relatives or similar family commitments are illustrative. Finally, there is *anomic leisure*, or leisure that is low in involvement but high in freedom of choice. Activities in this quadrant are those of persons with too much free time. They could be persons condemned by age or social position to a situation with almost no demands on their time. The activities engaged in are not involving.

Kelly (1983) differentiated between four types of leisure based on the social involvement they provide. They are *solitary leisure* (such as reading), *intimate leisure* (with family and close friends), *group leisure* (such as a party setting), and *mass leisure* (such as attendance at a sporting event or something similar providing for a degree of anonymity in a crowd). Elsewhere (Kelly, 1978), he has classified leisure as *unconditional* (chosen for intrinsic satisfaction related to accomplishment, learning, growth, excitement, health, or some other self-related benefit), *recuperative* (providing recovery from the constraints, tensions, or exhaustion of employment or other required activity), *relational* (offering primarily social consequences), and *role-determined* (providing social contact, but primary based on social obligation).

Leisure researchers integrate activities associated with the mass media into their perspective. For the leisure researcher, however, media use behaviors are not inherently distinctive. Berk and Berk (1979), for example, have examined media use in the home in the context of routine household activities. Hornik and Schlinger (1981) have examined the relationship of media use habits to lifestyle. Kelly (1983) argued that the two technolgical developments that have had the greatest impact on leisure in Western nations in this century are the automobile and television. For the leisure researcher, watching television, reading newspapers, books or magazines, going to movies, or listening to radio are simply leisure behaviors. Time spent with these activities is considered leisure time.

Media researchers, in contrast, have at least implicitly argued for the distinctiveness of a concept of *media time* from overall leisure time. The concept of media time is subdivided into such things as time spent watching television, listening to radio, attending movies, reading a newspaper, reading a book, and reading magazines. The relationship of *media time* to *leisure time* or other uses of time has been dealt with only infrequently. Exceptions are (a) the classic work of Bogart (1972), dealing with the introduction of television in America; (b) Samuelson, Carter, and Ruggels (1963), who showed that time allocated among the media differed by levels of formal education, presumably because of the different demands on time associated with occupations requiring large amounts of formal education; and (c) Kline (1971), who found that time spent around the home was associated with higher levels of time spent with the media. Bakke (1978) showed how media use is integrated into overall leisure orientation patterns.

The medium most often examined in the leisure-time context by both media and leisure researchers is television. In a review of this literature, Comstock (1982), and Comstock, Chaffee, Katzman, McCombs, and Roberts (1978) showed that television viewing dominates leisure activities both in terms of direct viewing and when viewing is combined with other activities, such as doing homework. Three fourths of the time that Americans spend using the mass media, in fact, is spent with television. As a consumer of time, television viewing ranks third behind sleep and work. Time spent with television results in reductions of time spent sleeping, at social gatherings away from home, listening to radio, reading magazines and books, at the movies, talking with friends, on household tasks, and with other leisure activities.

The very concept of time is problematic for many leisure researchers. Kelly (1983) said that viewing leisure only in terms of time allocation treats leisure as segmented from the rest of life and the time given over to leisure as time remaining after other demands on time are met. Yet leisure happens in work interactions and during lulls in other routine activities, such as traveling to work or doing chores around the home. It is both planned and unplanned. In addition, as Parker (1983) noted, many activities occur during the same time. A person can watch television while doing chores or listen to radio while commuting to work or even while working. And one's leisure activity, such as a hobby, can develop into a revenue source, perhaps supplementing the primary job or pension income.

This overlap of activities has been well documented in the time-use literature—a literature somewhat distinct from the leisure literature, but one that has given considerable attention to media use behaviors. Perhaps the most significant of the time-use studies was carried out under the auspices of UNESCO and involved diaries of 24-hour time allocations during 1965 in 11 countries (Szalai, 1972). Included were the United States and several European communities. The researchers concluded that the media rather uniformly absorb large portions of free time everywhere, dominating all other leisure activities (Robinson, Converse, & Szalai, 1972). There also was evidence that television, while replacing radio listening as a functional alternative, also brought about an increase in the amount of time being devoted to the mass media (Robinson & Converse, 1972). Television had taken some of that time from such nonleisure activities as sleep and household care (Robinson, 1972). Robinson (1977), drawing on the U.S. segment of this research, noted that much of the time devoted to the mass media is of a secondary nature, occurring at the same time as other activities, such as working, doing household chores, eating, and even participating in other types of leisure activity. The media, in this sense, "deepen" time, Robinson (1977, pp. 101-102) argued, and introduce more leisure into obligatory activities.

Robinson and Jeffres (1979), in a comparison of U.S. time diary data from 1965 to 1975, showed that people who devote time to one medium also are likely to devote time to another. Specifically, people who read newspapers also are likely to read books, magazines, and other printed matter and to watch television news programs. Over time, however, there was evidence that as time devoted to television in general and television news in particular increased, time devoted to newspapers declined. Audience members seemed to be trading off one behavior for the other. Robinson (1981, 1985), reporting on those same data, showed that the increase in time devoted to television during the 10-year period dwarfed increases in time devoted to other free-time activities. Television as a consumer of time seems to compete most with activities outside the home, such as shopping, traveling, visiting bars, and working.

Although the UNESCO study documented similarities in the ways in which persons in the various societies allocated time to the media, there were differences as well. In more recent research, McCain (1986) has documented that these changes have persisted into the 1980s. Evidence of a European/American difference in orientation toward television is shown by some recent poll results (Opinion Roundup, 1986). Americans are considerably more likely to consider a television set, for example, to be a necessary part of a household than are either Britains or residents of Denmark. Of U.S. respondents to a poll on the needs of recipients on public assistance, 79% said that such people should receive enough assistance to afford a television set. In Britain, 51% said a television was something that adults should be able to afford and not have to do without, whereas 55% gave that response in Denmark.

Explaining audience responses to new media offerings from the perspective of leisure-time theorists implies studying how individuals are able and willing to fit the consumption of these materials into the pre-existing patterns of their everyday lives. Similar to the uses-and-gratifications perspective, leisure-time theories also can be used to address questions like: What audience needs are fulfilled by new media offerings?

## Critical Theory Considerations

One of the basic notions of the so-called "critical theory," represented, for instance, in the work of the Frankfurt School (Max Horkheimer, Theodor W. Adorno, Juergen Habermas, among others), is that mass media in capitalistic societies are part of the "culture industry" (Negt & Kluge, 1972). The basic purpose of the media is not, as most Western social ideologies demand, to inform, educate, and enlighten their audiences, but rather simply to make profits. Even when the media are non-profit organizations, they serve the interests of the ruling class. Mass media are supposed to keep the populations quiet—even apathetic. For this purpose, media entertainment is a major vehicle. Entertainment has the task of maintaining the stability of the unjust social conditions and emphasizing their unalterable nature. Entertainment offers escape and distraction. It thus keeps people from becoming aware of their class interests. Social harmony is the picture that most mass media perpetuate for their audiences.

New media offerings are suspected of expanding the confirmatory functions of the mass media. Almost everywhere in the world, new media have meant a further erosion of the nonprofit media organizations, making it, according to this perspective, even more difficult for the audience to receive information and education. In addition, entertainment in the new market situation tends to be even more of the lowest-common-denominator type than before. It is simple, reactionary, and narcotizing.

## Mass Media and the Social Construction of Reality

In recent years, the perspective on mass media effects has widened considerably. The decades before saw mostly the investigation of restricted, highly specific, cognitive, attitudinal, and behavioral consequences of mass media use. Starting in the 1950s, researchers, theorists and educators such as Guenther Anders, George Gerbner, Neil Postman, Joshua Meyrowitz, Jerry Mander, and Marie Winn have made us aware of more secular changes brought about primarily by television. Television, they argue, not only affects knowledge about some public affairs or the images of specific prominent people, but it also changes our pictures of the world and of ourselves. It makes people scared (Gerbner & Gross, 1976; Gerbner, Gross, Morgan, & Signorielli, 1986), passive (Mander, 1978; Winn, 1977) and makes them lose their "sense of place" in society (Anders, 1956; Meyrowitz, 1985). It even changes changes people's ways of thinking (Postman, 1982, 1985). Postman suggests that causal thinking may be giving way to associative thinking because of the abundance of noncausally related pictures that television forces on its audience.

New media are mostly new television media. They make more television programs available. For some audience members, these programs are almost certainly even more appealing than those previously available. One would expect, then, that the new media would further strengthen the impact of television on society as the dominance of the visual images of television increases.

## Integration of the Models

That the uses and gratifications literature and the leisure literature have much in common has become increasingly obvious (Hirschman, 1985). There is between these two bodies of literature a shared functionalist underpinning, parallel conceptual difficulties, and common problems of measurement. Kelly's (1983) list of leisure needs of individuals is not so different from lists in work appearing in the communications literature, such as in Katz, Gurevitch, and Haas (1973) or Mc-

Guire (1974). The discussion of methodological problems in leisure by Kelly (1973) or Gunter (1987) raises similar issues to those of Becker (1979) in the media uses-and-gratifications literature. In both cases, questions about the abilities of individuals to articulate explanations for their behaviors are paramount. One can argue—and it is our argument here—that there really is no reason to maintain the distinctiveness of the two perspectives. Each, in some fashion, includes the other. What is more important, in our view, is the argument that for a model of media behavior to be most helpful in understanding changes in audience uses of the media and audience adaptations to new media, it must integrate these two approaches.

On the other hand, both the critical-theory and the social-construction-of-reality approaches assign to media organizations a more decisive role than do either uses-and-gratifications or leisure-time theorists. In the view of critical theorists and those concerned with the media's impact on the construction of reality, the audiences are in the firm grip of the media. The media determine the offerings. They also, to a great extent, define both what is perceived and how it is perceived. Only joint efforts of the deprived social classes or of the well-meaning people of society could counter the mass media's power.

For a full understanding of audience responses to new media diversification, it is certainly useful to take into consideration both major perspectives (audience-oriented on the one hand and media-dominated on the other).

The model that we offer is not unique. Its origins are well based in the uses and gratifications literature (Katz, et al., 1973; Katz, Blumler, & Gurevitch, 1973-1974; Blumler, 1979). It has been stated in a political context by McLeod and Becker (1981) and in the context of understanding use of new media in Becker, Dunwoody, and Rafaeli (1983). Parallel work has been presented by Williams (1987).

For our part, we wish to define social needs as states that are *analogous* to those of hunger and thirst. These social needs have their origins in the social situation, as the term implies, rather than from within the individual. The needs can be satisfied by behaviors, and something *paralleling* deprivation is thought to take place. Needs, once stimulated (i.e., not satisfied), direct behavior, leading to need satisfaction. In other words, these behaviors can be considered to be motivated.

We also draw from the motivational literature of psychology the notion that individuals actively consider various alternative behaviors that might lead to need satisfaction, or gratification. In other words, individuals have certain expectations about the abilities of behaviors to satisfy needs. These expectations are modified by past experiences with the behaviors, or others like them. Such a view has been labeled "expectancy theory" in the psychology literature (Atkinson, 1964; Feather & Davenport, 1981), and has received recent attention in the communications literature (Galloway & Meek, 1981; Palmgreen & Rayburn, 1985; Van Leuven, 1981).

Our model is presented diagrammatically in Fig. 1.1. In this model, needs of audience members (labeled social needs) have their origin in the social situation and the background of the respondent, as well as in the more basic needs. These social needs lead the individual to an assessment of the means of satisfying the needs. The availability of the behaviors has impact on the assessment, which would be expected to weigh costs of the behavior in terms of attention, finances, time, and space. The assessment would include some probabilistic notion of the likelihood that any given behavior would satisfy the existing need. Based on this assessment, audience members would select a behavior. Depending on the need, some of these behaviors might be linked to the media. Others clearly would not. The behavior might produce the desired effect, that is, satisfaction of the need. Such a consequence would then become information to be used in future assessments of the various needs and ways of their fulfillment. In addition to the satisfaction effect, the behavior might produce some other effect, of course, possibly related (or unrelated) to the need driving the behavior. An example of this secondary effect would be information gain. The former is called subjective effects (need satisfaction) in the model and the latter are called objective effects.

Note that the motives leading to the behavior are expected to determine, in

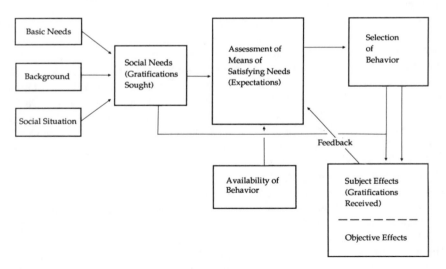

**FIG. 1.1.** Decisional models based on needs.

part, the nature of the effect by interacting with exposure. For example, a person watching television for rest and relaxation might learn something from unintended exposure to a newscast, but that learning would be less than that of a person turn-ing to the newscast to learn about the day's events. See Frueh and Schoenbach (1982), McLeod and Becker (1974), Schoenbach and Frueh (1984), and Schoen-bach and Weaver (1985) for a discussion of this transactional perspective.

This model focuses attention on the choices that audience members make to satisfy needs. Audience members, naturally enough, can only make choices among options actually available to them. The uses-and-gratifications research has often been insensitive to this issue, ignoring limitations on choice resulting from decisions made away from the individual. In other words, the individual decision is restricted to what is offered (Schoenbach & Weaver, 1985). It is here that the power of the mass media as suggested by critical theorists and scholars such as Gerbner and Postman becomes an important component of our model.

The decision-making process, of course, is the crucial issue in trying to un-derstand the relationship between the new media and audience behavior—the core question of this volume. Although much of the uses-and-gratifications and leisure-time literature has concerned itself with the nature of needs (and we share an inter-est in the topic), it is not essential to identify specific needs to map out the possible decisional outcomes of the introduction of new media. These outcomes are presented in Fig. 1.2.

Figure 1.2 begins with the proposition that a need either exists or does not exist. If no need whatsoever exists or comes into existence, introduction of a new medium will result in no adoption and no change. When a need exists, however, that need can be either currently satisfied or currently unsatisfied.

As Rosengren and Windahl (1972) in the uses-and-gratifications area and Veal (1987) in the leisure field have noted, there is almost always a variety of ways of meeting needs. That is to say, our needs may be basic, but we do not need specific goods or services to satisfy them. Which goods and services we select naturally depends on their availability (Weibull, 1985). Choice from the available options, then, is in part determined by market forces, particularly advertising. It is this promotion of new products, including those of the media, that leads to the assess-ment (represented on the left-hand side in Fig. 1.2) of the ability of a new medium to meet needs. The product or service is judged likely to be able to meet the needs or unlikely to be able to meet them.

The next issue is cost. Products and services have four different types of cost: attention, time, money, and space. Attention is often neglected as a cost factor. But it certainly makes a difference for audience members whether the consumption of a medium demands undivided attention or allows other simultaneous activities. Greater attention is demanded by a medium that offers exciting, appealing material, employs more than one sense, and/or demands high decoding efforts compared to a medium without these characteristics. Reading, for instance, normally is more

|                                                      |                             | need exists                 |                             | no need exists  |
| ---------------------------------------------------- | --------------------------- | --------------------------- | --------------------------- | --------------- |
|                                                      |                             | need now satisfied          | need not satisfied          |                 |
| new medium not judged able to meet need              | cost of new medium low      | very low adoption           | low adoption                | no adoption     |
|                                                      | cost high                   | extremely low adoption      | very low adoption           | no adoption     |
| new medium judged able to meet need                  | cost of new medium low      | moderate adoption           | high adoption               | no adoption     |
|                                                      | cost high                   | low adoption                | moderate adoption           | no adoption     |

**FIG. 1.2.** Model of audience decision-making in selecting new media.

demanding and requires more decoding (language) skills than other media (Schulz, 1971). Pornographic videocassettes, television (as opposed to radio), and foreign-language newspapers could be examples of media requiring more attention than others. Time and money are more commonly recognized costs. Space also is frequently ignored as a factor. Few homes, however, have unlimited space, and the media do not make equal demands in this regard. Over time, radios have become increasingly space-efficient. Although the same is true for televison, increasing the size of the visual images of televison has meant a receiver that is more demanding in terms of space. Viewdata terminals require a new space investment as well as investments of money, time, and attention.

When the new medium is judged unable to meet the needs, and the cost is low, we would expect some adoption of it on the part of those with unmet needs, depending largely on the certainty of the assessment of the inability of the medium to meet the need and the strength of the need. In other words, if there was even some chance that the medium could meet a deeply felt need, it might be tentatively adopted. If there was absolute certainty that it could not meet the need, such experimentation would be unlikely. In the case where the cost is quite high and the need is satisfied, adoption would be extremely low. The remaining two conditions in the top of Fig. 1.2 would be between these two conditions.

When the medium is judged capable of meeting the needs, we would expect high adoption where the cost is low and the need is not yet met, contrasted to the situation where the cost is high and the need is already met. The remaining two cells at the bottom of the figure would fall between these two conditions.

To put it simply, our model predictions about the impact of the new media on the potential audience are based on the best possible assessment of needs, projections of how the media will be assessed in terms of those needs, and estimations of perceived costs and resources available to cover those costs. Media content is of paramount importance. Is there a need for a specific type of content and is that need currently being satisfied? In terms of costs, we should judge the medium in terms of alternatives and the success of alternatives. In terms of perceptions of the ability of the media to meet the needs, we should look at promotional strategies of the industries in the first instance and audience reports on the product in the second. We should be sensitive to the idea that the characteristics of a given medium are not always inherent but rather are often built up as a result of promotion and sometimes as a result of the activities of early adopters. For example, the appeal of the music video channel MTV in the United States may not have been obvious or even as intended by the producers. But it appealed to teenagers, who apparently had a need for this type of program aimed at them. Watching MTV and knowing what was going on with it became important to teenagers, and this gave MTV a characteristic that it didn't have at the beginning. Costs were low and, unlike records or tapes, borne by the family rather than the children themselves.

At the very minimum, these considerations would suggest that the impact of cable television should be greater than the impact of viewdata, because cable is low in costs (in terms of attention, time, money, and space) whereas viewdata is high, and because there is a clear need for the diversion of television in contrast with only a vague need for the informational services of viewdata.

These models are mostly common sense, spelled out in some detail. They also are admittedly simple, suggesting that needs are turned on and off with great ease. In fact, the needs most important for understanding media behavior are not likely to be so simple. People need rest and relaxation almost every day. Many also feel a need to be informed not only today but again tomorrow, as the world changes. The point is that the models in Figs. 1.1 and 1.2 are only a glimpse of a set of processes that are ongoing. This means that when an individual evaluates television or any other medium, it is not only in terms of its ability to meet a present need but also its ability to meet anticipated ones. So one might say that the existing content is sufficient to meet a need at the present, perhaps because the wanted movie or sporting event was available. But will it satisfy the need for relaxation tomorrow, when the movie will not be present and the sporting event will not be telecast? It is this kind of constant projection and reassessment of a means of satisfying a need that makes the models in Fig. 1.1 and Fig. 1.2 only approximations for understanding why decisions about media are made.

These models nonetheless provide our best estimates of how audience members will respond to changing media environments. They are presented as a guide for looking at change in the context of this volume. As such, they direct us in our examination of audience behavior in the selected 11 Western media systems.

## REFERENCES

Anders, G. (1956). Die Welt als Phantom und Matrize [The world as phantom and matrix]. In G. Anders, *Die Antiquiertheit des Menschen* (pp. 97-211). Munich: Beck.

Atkinson, J. W. (1964). *An introduction to motivation.* New York: Van Nostrant.

Bakke, M. (1978, September). *Leisure time activities and mass media consumption.* Paper presented to the International Association for Mass Communication Research, Warsaw, Poland.

Becker, L. B. (1979). Measures of uses and gratifications. *Communication Research, 6,* 54-73.

Becker, L. B., Dunwoody, S., & Rafaeli, S. (1983). Cable's impact on use of other news media. *Journal of Broadcasting, 27,* 127-140.

Berelson, B. (1949). What "missing the newspaper" means. In P. Lazarsfeld & F. N. Stanton (Eds.), *Communication research, 1948-49* (pp.111-129). New York: Duell, Sloan, and Pearce.

Berk, R. A., & Berk, S. F. (1979). *Labor and leisure at home: Content and organization of the household day.* Beverly Hills: Sage.

Berkowitz, L. (1969). Social motivation. In G. Lindzey & E. Aronson (Eds.), *Handbook of social psychology: Vol. 3* (pp. 50-135). Reading, MA: Addison-Wesley.

Blumler, J.G. (1979). The role of theory in uses and gratifications studies. *Communication Research, 6,* 9-36.

Blumler, J. G., & Katz, E. (Eds.). (1974). *The uses of mass communications: Current perspectives on gratification research.* Beverly Hills: Sage.

Bogart, L. (1972). *The age of television* (3rd ed.). New York: Frederick Unger.

Cheek, N. H. (1971). Toward a sociology of not-work. In T. B. Johannis & C. N. Bull (Eds.), *Sociology of leisure* (pp. 7-20). Beverly Hills: Sage.

Cofer, C. N., & Appley, M. E. (1964). *Motivation: Theory and research.* New York: Wiley.

Comstock, G. (1982). Television and American social institutions. In D. Pearl, L. Bouthilet, & J. Lazar (Eds.), *Television and behavior: Ten years of scientific progress and implications for the eighties: Vol. II* (pp. 334-348). Washington, DC: U.S. Government Printing Office.

Comstock, G., Chaffee, S. H., Katzman, N., McCombs, M. E., & Roberts, D. (1978). *Television and human behavior.* New York: Columbia University Press.

de Bens, E., & Knoche, M. (Eds.). (1987). *Electronic mass media in Europe: Prospects and developments.* Dordrecht, The Netherlands: D. Reidel.

Dimmick, J., & McCain, T. (Eds.). (1979). Use of mass media: Patterns in the life cycle. *American Behavioral Scientist, 23* (1).

Dimmick, J., & Rothenbuhler, E. W. (1984a). Competitive displacement in the communication industries: New media in old environments. In R. E. Rice (Ed.), *The new media* (pp. 287-304). Beverly Hills: Sage.

Dimmick, J., & Rothenbuhler, E. W. (1984b). The theory of the niche: Quantifying competition among media industries. *Journal of Communication, 34* (1), 103-119.

Dumazedier, J. (1967). *Toward a society of leisure.* New York: The Free Press.

Dutton, W. H., Blumler, J. G., & Kraemer, K. L. (Eds.). (1987). *Wired cities: Shaping the future of communications.* Boston: G. K. Hall. & Co.

Feather, N. T., & Davenport, P. R. (1981). Unemployment and depressive effect: A motivational and attributional analysis. *Journal of Personality and Social Psychology, 41,* 422-436.

Ferguson, M. (Ed.). (1986). *New communication technologies and the public interest: Comparative perspectives on policy and research.* London: Sage.

Frueh, W., & Schoenbach, K. (1982). Der dynamisch-transaktionale Ansatz [The dynamic-transactional approach]. *Publizistik, 27,* 74-82.

Fritsch, A. (1676). *Discursus de novellarum, quas vocant neue zeitunge, hodierno usu et abusu* [Discourse about newspapers called "neue zeitunge," their present use and abuse]. Jena.

Galloway, J. J., & Meek, F. L. (1981). Audience uses and gratifications: An expectancy model. *Communication Research, 8,* 435-449.

Gerbner, G., & Gross, L. (1976). Living with television: The violence profile. *Journal of Communication, 26* (2), 173-199.

Gerbner, G., Gross, L., Morgan, M., & Signorielli, N. (1986) Living with television: The dynamics of the cultivation process. In J. Bryant & D. Zillmann (Eds.), *Perspectives on media effects* (pp. 17-40). Hillsdale, NJ: Lawrence Erlbaum Associates.

Groth, O. (1928). *Die Zeitung* [The newspaper]. Vol. I. Mannheim: Bensheimer.

Gunter, B. G. (1987). The leisure experience: Selected properties. *Journal of Leisure Research, 19*, 115-130.

Gunter, B. G., & Gunter, C. (1980). Leisure styles: A conceptual framework for modern leisure. *The Sociological Quarterly, 21*, 361-374.

Herzog, H. (1940). Professor Quiz. In P. R. Lazarsfeld (Ed.), *Radio and the printed page* (pp. 64-93). New York: Duell, Sloan, and Pearce.

Herzog, H. (1944). What do we really know about daytime serial listeners? In P. Lazarsfeld & F. N. Stanton (Eds.), *Radio research, 1942-43* (pp. 3-33). New York: Duell, Sloan, and Pearce.

Hirschman, E. C. (1985). A multidimensional analysis of content preferences for leisure-time media. *Journal of Leisure Research, 17*, 14-28.

Hornik, J., & Schlinger, M. J. (1981). Allocation of time to the mass media. *Journal of Consumer Research, 7*, 343-355.

Kando, T. M. (1975). *Leisure and popular culture in transition.* St. Louis: C.V. Mosby.

Katz, E., Blumler, J. G., & Gurevitch, M. (1973-1974). Uses and gratifications research. *Public Opinion Quarterly, 37*, 509-523.

Katz, E., Gurevitch, M., & Haas, H. (1973). On the use of mass media for important things. *American Sociological Review, 38*, 164-181.

Kelly, J. R. (1973). Three measures of leisure activity: A note on the continued incommensurability of oranges, apples and artichokes. *Journal of Leisure Research, 5*, 56-65.

Kelly, J. R. (1978). A revised paradigm of leisure choices. *Leisure Sciences, 1*, 345-363.

Kelly, J. R. (1983). *Leisure identities and interactions.* London: Allen & Unwin.

Kline, F. G. (1971). Media time budgeting as a function of demographics and life style. *Journalism Quarterly, 48*, 211-221.

Kubey, R. W. (1986). Television use in everyday life: Coping with unstructured time. *Journal of Communication, 36* (3), 108-123.

Lazarsfeld, P. (Ed.). (1940). *Radio and the printed page.* New York: Duell, Sloan, and Pearce.

Lazarsfeld, P., & Kendall, P. L. (1948). *Radio listening in America: The people look at radio again.* New York: Duell, Sloan, and Pearce.

Lazarsfeld, P., & Stanton, F. N. (Eds.). (1942). *Radio research, 1941.* New York: Duell, Sloan, and Pearce.

Lazarsfeld, P., & Stanton, F. N. (Eds.). (1944). *Radio research, 1942-43.* New York: Duell, Sloan, and Pearce.

Lerg, W. B. (1981). Verdraengen oder ergaenzen die Medien einander? *Publizistik, 26*, 193-201.

Maletzke, G. (1963). *Psychologie der Massenkommunikation*. [Psychology of mass communication]. Hamburg: Hans-Bredow-Institut.

Mander, J. (1978). *Four arguments for the elimination of television*. New York: Morrow.

McCain, T. (1986). Patterns of media use in Europe: Identifying country clusters. *European Journal of Communication, 1*, 231-250.

McCombs, M. E. (1972, August). Mass media in the marketplace. *Journalism Monographs, 24*.

McCombs, M. E., & Eyal, C. H. (1980). Spending on mass media. *Journal of Communication, 30*, 153-158.

McGuire, W. (1974). Psychological motives and communication gratification. In J. G. Blumler & E. Katz (Eds.), *The uses of mass communications: Current perspectives on gratifications research* (pp. 167-196). Beverly Hills: Sage.

McLeod, J. M., & Becker, L. B. (1974). Testing the validity of gratification measures through political effects analysis. In J. G. Blumler & E. Katz (Eds.), *The uses of mass communications: Current perspectives on gratifications research* (pp. 137-164). Beverly Hills: Sage.

McLeod, J. M., & Becker, L. B. (1981). The uses and gratifications approach. In D. Nimmo & K. Sanders (Eds.), *Handbook of political communication* (pp. 67-99). Beverly Hills: Sage.

McQuail, D. (1987). Functions of communication: A nonfunctionalist overview. In C. Berger & S. Chaffee (Eds.), *Handbook of communication science* (pp. 327-349). Beverly Hills: Sage.

McQuail, D., & Siune, K. (Eds.). (1986). *New media politics: Comparative perspectives in western Europe*. London: Sage.

Meyrowitz, J. (1985). *No sense of place: The impact of electronic media on social behavior*. New York: Oxford University Press.

Negt, O., & Kluge, A. (1972). *Oeffentlichkeit und Erfahrung*. Frankfurt: Suhrkamp.

Neulinger, J. (1974). *The psychology of leisure*. Springfield, IL: Charles C. Thomas.

Opinion Roundup (1986, January). All they need to get by...in Britain, Denmark and the United States. *Public Opinion*, p. 40.

Palmgreen, P., & Rayburn, J. (1985). An expectancy value approach to media gratifications. In K. E. Rosengren, L. A. Wenner, & P. Palmgreen (Eds.), *Media gratifications research* (pp. 61-72). Beverly Hills: Sage.

Parker, S. (1983). *Leisure and work*. London: Allen & Unwin.

Postman, N. (1982). *The disappearance of childhood*. New York: Delacorte Press.

Postman, N. (1985). *Amusing ourselves to death*. New York: Viking-Penguin.

Riepl, W. (1913). *Das Nachrichtenwesen des Altertums mit besonderer Ruecksicht auf die Roemer* [News organization in the old ages, with special consideration of the Romans]. Leipzig: Teubner.

Robinson, J. P. (1972). Television's impact on everyday life: Some cross-national evidence. In E. A. Rubinstein, G. A. Comstock & J. P. Murray (Eds.), *Television and social behavior: Vol. 4. Television in day-to-day life: Patterns of use.* Washington, DC: Government Printing Office.

Robinson, J. P. (1977). *How Americans use time.* New York: Praeger.

Robinson, J. P. (1981). Television and leisure time: A new scenario. *Journal of Communication, 31* (1), 120-130.

Robinson, J. P. (1985). Changes in time use: An historical overview. In F. T. Juster & F. P. Stafford (Eds.), *Time, goods, and well-being* (pp. 289-311). Ann Arbor, MI: Institute for Social Research, The University of Michigan.

Robinson, J. P., & Converse, P. E. (1972). The impact of television on mass media usage. In A. Szalai (Ed.), *The use of time: Daily activities of urban and suburban populations in twelve countries* (pp. 197-212). The Hague: Mouton.

Robinson, J. P., Converse, P. E., & Szalai, A. (1972). Everday life in twelve countries. In A. Szalai (Ed.), *The use of time: Daily activities of urban and suburban populations in twelve countries* (pp. 113-144). The Hague: Mouton.

Robinson, J. P., & Jeffres, L. W. (1979). The changing role of newspapers in the age of television. *Journalism Monographs, 63.*

Rogers, E. M., & Balle, F. (Eds.). (1985). *The media revolution in America and western Europe.* Norwood, NJ: Ablex.

Rosengren, K. E., Wenner., L., & Palmgreen, P. (Eds.). (1985). *Gratifications research.* Beverly Hills: Sage.

Rosengren, K. E., & Windahl, S. (1972). Mass media consumption as a functional alternative. In D. McQuail (Ed.), *Sociology of mass communications* (pp. 166-194). Harmondsworth: Penguin.

Rubin, A.M. (1986). Uses and gratifications and media effects research. In J. Bryant & D. Zillmann (Eds.), *Perspectives on media effects* (pp. 281-301). Hillsdale, NJ: Lawrence Erlbaum Associates.

Samuelson, M., Carter, R. F., & Ruggels, L. (1963). Education, available time and use of mass media. *Journalism Quarterly, 40,* 491-496, 617.

Schoenbach, K., & Frueh, W. (1984). Der dynamisch-transaktionale Ansatz II [The dynamic-transactional approach II]. *Rundfunk und Fernsehen, 32,* 314-329.

Schoenbach, K., & Weaver, D. (1985). Finding the unexpected: Cognitive bonding in a political campaign. In S. Kraus & R. M. Perloff (Eds.), *Mass media and political thought* (pp. 157-176). Beverly Hills: Sage.

Schulz, W. (1971). *Medienwirkung und Medienselektion* [Media impact and media selection]. Hamburg: Gruner + Jahr.

Suchman, E. (1941). An invitation to music. In P. Lazarsfeld & F. N. Stanton (Eds.), *Radio research* (pp. 140-188). New York: Duell, Sloan, and Pearce.

Swanson, D. (1987). Gratification seeking, media exposure and audience interpretations: Some directions for research. *Journal of Broadcasting and Electronic Media, 31,* 237-254.

Szalai, A. (Ed.). (1972). *The use of time: Daily activities of urban and suburban populations in twelve countries.* The Hague: Mouton.

Van Leuven, J. (1981). Expectancy theory and media message selection. *Communication Research, 8,* 425-434.

Veal, A. J. (1987). *Leisure and the future.* London: Allen & Unwin.

von Stieler, K. (1695). *Zeitungs Lust und Nutz* [Enjoyment and use of newspapers]. Hamburg.

Waples, D., Berelson, B., & Bradshaw, F. R. (1940). *What reading does to people.* Chicago: University of Chicago Press.

Wartella, E., & Reeves, B. (1983). Recurring issues in research on children and media. *Educational Technology, 23,* 5-9.

Weibull, L. (1985). Structural factors in gratifications research. In K. E. Rosengren, L. A. Wenner, & P. Palmgreen (Eds.), *Media gratifications research* (pp. 123-147). Beverly Hills: Sage.

Williams, F. (1987). *Technology and communication behavior.* Belmont, CA: Wadsworth.

Winn, M. (1977). *The plug-in drug.* New York: Viking.

# 2

# The Netherlands:The Cable Replaces the Antenna

**Frank Olderaan**
**Nick Jankowski**
*University of Nijmegen*

As is the case in most developed nations, considerable change has taken place in the Dutch media during the past 2 decades. It has been suggested that the Netherlands is in the forefront among European countries, and has been called the "cockpit of Europe" regarding media innovations.[1] This change has manifested itself in both the form and content of the media and has been frequently catalyzed by technological advances. Audience behavior also has been affected, although it has not always been clear to what degree and for how long.

This chapter charts Dutch media behavior, particularly that related to television, information services resulting from cable distribution, and satellite transmission facilities. To appreciate these changes, a brief overview is provided of media policy development in the Netherlands. After this overview, a sketch is given of recent changes in the electronic media, with emphasis on the introduction of cable television, satellite transmitted programming, video recorders, and cabletext services.

Thereafter, available data on audience responses to these media developments are presented. In the concluding section of the chapter some implications of these audience reactions to media change are discussed.

## MEDIA POLICY

Dutch broadcasting began in the 1920s and was molded along the societal divisions that were then prominent.[2] These divisions, referred to as "pillars," determined the character of institutional life in the country and were organized around religious and ideological world views. In 1930, when regulations were first formulated for radio, broadcasting time was made available to the societal sectors then prevalent: the Protestants and Catholics as the primary religious sectors, and the socialists and politically conservative liberals as the main ideological divisions.

Television, which was introduced on an experimental basis in 1951, was organized along the same lines as radio. The religious, social, and cultural sectors of Dutch society were allotted broadcasting time. The amount of air time was related to the number of organization members. The regulations exhibited a wide latitude of openness to organized life in the country. This aspect—access to the media by publicly recognized organizations—became the hallmark of the Dutch broadcasting system and has remained both a concern and a source of controversy with the introduction of new media, particularly commercial media. Broadcasting airspace was considered a scarce societal commodity that most political parties felt should remain free of commercial influence. This principled position resulted in the fall of the government coalition in 1965. Two years later when parliament ratified the first broadcasting law, proponents of advertising had secured a foothold within the system. Limited blocks of time were reserved for this commercial activity between programs.

Several other modifications, most displaying elements of political compromise, emerged when the broadcasting law took effect in 1969. An overarching organization—Nederlandse Omroep Stichting (NOS)—was created to provide technical facilities to the broadcasting organizations. The NOS was to coordinate the organizations and to produce programming that extended beyond the concerns of these broadcasting organizations—programming related to special national events, sports, and news. New broadcasting organizations were given access to the airwaves, provided that they exhibited at least basic characteristics of the pillar system. Candidates for air time were to be nonprofit organizations that were representative of ideological, cultural, or religious sections of the population intending to provide informational, educational and cultural programming.

By the time the broadcasting law went into effect, the traditional divisions of the society into ideological and religious pillars had become less prominent. The broadcasting organizations, following this general trend, also became less reflective of these pillars. During the 1970s, this characteristic came under increasing pressure through the competition between broadcasting organizations for new members and more favorable audience ratings. Competition manifested itself most clearly between the ideologically based organizations and those lacking a clear political or cultural position. The struggle resulted in a strengthened position of the nonideological broadcasting organizations in terms of membership and program attendance. It also resulted in a transformation of the ideologically based broadcasting organizations; aspects of commercial enterprise—publication of slick television guides, organization of disco shows, and similar activities—became prevalent within these organizations as well.

These developments and discussions regarding the future of Dutch media resulted in a government-requested report on proposals for media policy (Wetenschappelijke Raad voor het Regeringsbeleid, 1982). Several recommendations were made, having consequences for further development of the electronic media. In the 1980s business could for the first time participate in the development of videotext (viewdata) systems and pay television. In keeping with the traditional division between commercial press and public broadcasting, the latter was not allowed to participate in the development of pay television. These memos, reports, and discussions culminiated in a new media law that was approved by both houses of parliament in 1987.

A core theme in media policy discussions during the last two decades is whether, and to what degree, the traditional, protective status of broadcasting should be maintained (McQuail & Siune, 1986, pp. 8-9). This concern has raised several additional issues involving new media developments: whether broadcasting organizations should be involved in pay television, whether advertising should be allowed on local origination programming, and whether satellite transmitted programming and advertising should be allowed to be subtitled in Dutch.

## CHANGES IN DUTCH MEDIA LANDSCAPE

In this section, an overview is provided of communication and information services that have transpired in the Netherlands during the last 15 years. During this period, major developments with communication technologies have taken place. Given the central role of television and cable distribution systems in this development, these parts of the infrastructure are first sketched. Pay television and cabletext services are then introduced. Finally, currently available interactive services are reviewed.

## Television and Cable Distribution Systems

By 1986, 98% of the Dutch households had a television set. Whereas in 1977 there were more black-and-white than color receivers, by the following year this situation had been reversed. It is now estimated that color television sets have reached a saturation point. In 1985, 91% of the population had color television sets in their households. Remote channel control capacity increased by 20% during the 4-year period 1981-1985, from 18% to 38%. Penetration of video recorders had initially proceeded slowly after introduction in the late 1970s. Since 1984, however, rapid diffusion has been evident. As Table 2.1 shows, penetration stood at 30% by 1986. A major stimulus for the development of new information and communication services has been the increase in cable networks in the country. One reason for rapid cabling of Dutch communities was the need for clear reception of radio and television programming in heavily populated sections of the country. Increase in channel capacity and improvement of city appearance through removal of rooftop antennas were also factors that prompted investment in cable networks. In 1978, slightly more than half of the population was connected to a cable system; by 1985, this number had increased to 71% (Table 2.2).

The number of radios connected to cable systems is considerably lower than that of television. Most radios, especially portables, are equipped with built-in antennas, which makes connection to a cable system unnecessary for program reception. Since 1979, as Table 2.3 shows, the number of radios connected to a cable system also has increased, although not as quickly as for televisions.

Channel capacity of the cable systems varies. Most of the older systems are capable of distributing seven channels; recently constructed systems with mini-star switching systems have capacities of 24 and more channels. The new media law, effective from 1988, requires distribution of all Dutch language programs, that is, television signals from both Belgian (Flemish) and Dutch national stations and local cablecasting stations. Individual cable operators may determine what additional signals are distributed. Generally, three German television stations, the two Belgian (French language) stations and the two Dutch stations are relayed by Dutch cable companies. In 1985, the first satellite programs were made available on many cable systems, which led to a substantial increase in the number of Dutch homes able to receive these signals (see Table 2.4). In many parts of the country, of course, some foreign signals are available even without cable.

One of these satellite channels, Europa-TV, was an initiative of broadcasting institutions in five European countries, in which the Dutch NOS played a central role. The consortium was intended to promote exchange of European originated programming. The service began transmissions in 1985. The anticipated advertis-

TABLE 2.1

Video Recorders in Dutch Homes

| Year | Percentage Homes |
|------|------------------|
| 1978 | 1 |
| 1979 | 1 |
| 1980 | 3 |
| 1981 | 4 |
| 1982 | 6 |
| 1983 | 11 |
| 1984 | 17 |
| 1985 | 23 |
| 1986 | 30 |

Note: From Bekkers (1987); van Dammen (1986). N=7000.

TABLE 2.2

Percentage of Population With Cable TV and Individual Antennas

| Year | Cable Systems | Roof Antenna | In-House Antenna | No TV |
|------|---------------|--------------|------------------|-------|
| | % | % | % | % |
| 1978 | 53 | 42 | 2 | 3 |
| 1979 | 54 | 41 | 2 | 3 |
| 1980 | 63 | 32 | 2 | 3 |
| 1981 | 63 | 31 | 3 | 3 |
| 1982 | 67 | 28 | 3 | 2 |
| 1983 | 72 | 24 | 2 | 2 |
| 1984 | 71 | 24 | 2 | 2 |
| 1985 | 71 | 24 | 3 | 2 |

Note: From NOS (1986a). N=9500.

TABLE 2.3

Percentage of Radios Connected to Cable Systems

| Year | Not connected to Cable System | Connected to Cable System | Not Known | No Radio |
|------|-------------------------------|---------------------------|-----------|----------|
| | % | % | % | % |
| 1978 | 61 | 37 | 1 | 1 |
| 1979 | 61 | 37 | 1 | 1 |
| 1980 | 53 | 45 | 1 | 1 |
| 1981 | 53 | 44 | 1 | 1 |
| 1982 | 49 | 49 | 1 | 1 |
| 1983 | 49 | 49 | 1 | 1 |
| 1984 | 47 | 51 | 1 | 1 |
| 1985 | 47 | 50 | 2 | 1 |

Note: From NOS (1986a). N=9500.

TABLE 2.4

Households Able to Receive Foreign Television Signals

|                      | 1973 % | 1980 % | 1986 % |
|----------------------|--------|--------|--------|
| German 1             | 52     | 68     | 84     |
| German 2             | 49     | 68     | 83     |
| German 3             | 31     | 57     | 77     |
| Belgium 1 & 2        | 19     | 40     | 66     |
| Belgium (fr) 1 & 2   | -      | 36     | 44     |
| England 1 & 2        | -      | 4      | 16     |
| France 1 & 2 & 3     | -      | -      | 8      |
| ITV                  | -      | -      | 6      |
| SKY Channel          | -      | -      | 50     |
| Music Box            | -      | -      | 35     |
| TV-5                 | -      | -      | 24     |
| Europa-TV*           | -      | -      | 28     |

Note: From Bekkers (1987). N=9500.
* Europa-TV ceased transmission at the end of 1986.

ing revenue failed to materialize, however, and 11 months after the start, in late 1986, the transmissions ceased.

Table 2.5 provides a summary of the number of channels Dutch households can receive from cable systems and roof antennas. Since 1979 there has been a continual increase in households able to receive more than six television signals. The average number of channels receivable has increased from 3.2 in 1979 to 5.1 in 1984. The number of subscribers who are able to receive eight or more channels increased dramatically since 1980, in large part because of the rapid development of cable systems. In 1984, 14% of the population could receive this many channels.

One of the more prominent transformations in Dutch media has been the decentralization of broadcasting. Since the mid-1970s both regional ether radio stations and local origination cablecasting have been developing. By 1980, there were six regional radio stations. In 1987, after reorganization of regional broadcasting, 10 stations located around the country were providing supplementary informational and entertainment programming for their respective geographic regions.

Local origination cablecasting has experienced a more turbulent development than its regional counterpart. The national government was not inclined to permit this activity other than on a temporary experimental basis. As illegal radio and television pirates multiplied throughout the country in the early 1980s, however, regulations were formulated allowing for local cablecasting by authorized organizations. In 1980, there were only six experimental status permits for such

TABLE 2.5

Reception of Foreign Television Signals in Dutch Households

| Year | Number of Foreign TV Signals | | | | | | | | | Mean |
| | 0 % | 1 % | 2 % | 3 % | 4 % | 5 % | 6 % | 7 % | 8+ % | |
|---|---|---|---|---|---|---|---|---|---|---|
| 1979 | 27 | 1 | 6 | 29 | 4 | 11 | 6 | 17 | - | 3.2 |
| 1980 | 20 | - | 6 | 29 | 4 | 12 | 7 | 21 | 1 | 3.7 |
| 1981 | 18 | - | 6 | 27 | 4 | 12 | 5 | 22 | 6 | 4.0 |
| 1982 | 15 | - | 5 | 28 | 3 | 14 | 4 | 24 | 7 | 4.2 |
| 1983 | 12 | - | 5 | 26 | 3 | 13 | 4 | 25 | 12 | 4.7 |
| 1984 | 11 | - | 4 | 26 | 3 | 12 | 5 | 26 | 14 | 5.1 |

Note: From NOS (1985a). N=6704.

cablecasting—local stations that had participated in an experiment with community television in the mid-1970s. Once governmental regulations were formulated in 1984, this number had increased to 41; by 1987, some 127 permits had been issued for local cablecasting, and another 60 organizations were preparing local origination activity. Of the stations holding permits in 1987, 64 cablecast radio programming, 11 transmitted television, and 47 provided both radio and television programming.

An important distinction between regional and local broadcasting is the financial basis. Regional broadcasting stations are funded by national revenues; local stations are funded by locally allocated revenues. The national revenues are sufficient for the regional stations to maintain professional studios and hire staff. In the case of local stations, reliance on local financial support and the prohibition of advertising have led to considerable difficulty in developing stations with professional equipment and paid staff.

## Pay Television and Cabletext Services

In 1984, the Minister of Culture approved experimentation with pay television. Initially, there was considerable interest in this development; 17 companies requested and received governmental approval to initiate pay television services (Oosterwijk, 1986). It soon became evident, however, that the amount of investment required was prohibitive for most of the candidates; by 1986, only four companies had commenced actual transmissions.

Of these four, only one, Filmnet, is available in several regions of the country. This international concern is primarily owned by the Swedish firm Esselte and is the international representative for Universal, Paramount, and MGM/UA. Despite the fact that Filmnet is the only major provider of pay television programming, the company is still operating at a financial loss. The number of subscribers has not increased as anticipated; in 1986, there were approximately 60,000, located primarily in the metropolitan areas of Amsterdam, The Hague, and Rotterdam.

In the same governmental decree that allowed for pay television, two types of cabletext services were approved for experimentation: local origination teletext and cable newspapers. Local origination teletext uses a number of television signal lines for transmission of textual information that is appended to another television signal at the headend of a cable system. Unlike the teletext service provided nationally by the NOS, this teletext version is locally produced and inserted into individual cable systems. Growth of this service has been slow, largely because of the limited penetration of television sets with teletext reception capability. In 1987, about a dozen local institutions—governmental bodies, community cable television stations, and commercial publishers—were providing this service on cable systems in their respective localities.

Cable newspapers have been implemented at a slightly stronger rate than locally originated teletext services. These are textual services shown on television screens connected to cable. As of December 1986, there were 35 cable newspapers in operation around the country. One of the reasons for this modest growth was the limitations imposed by the government on these cable newspapers: Neither moving images nor newspaper-provided audio signals were permitted. The signal from the national radio stations could be used to supplement the visuals. In contrast to the prohibition of advertising on local origination cablecasting, there are no restrictions regarding advertising on cable newspapers. Few of the cable newspapers operating in 1987, however, reported financial earnings. Cable newspapers required no special converter for reception.

## Interactive Information Services

The Netherlands has been the site of some experimentation with interactive information services for the consumer market. For example, the town of Zaltbommel has been equipped with a two-way cable system connecting approximately 3,000 households. The development of this experiment has been monitored by social science research (Olderaan, 1985; Stappers, Hollander & Jankowski, 1984). As of 1987, however, only one interactive service had been implemented: an Arabic language course for Moroccan women (Jankowski & Mol, 1986).

A national viewdata or videotext system, Viditel, was put into operation in 1980 by the Post, Telegraph and Telephone (PTT). It utilizes large mainframe com-

TABLE 2.6

Number of Subscribers to Viditel

| Year | N |
|------|------|
| 1981 | 3,944 |
| 1982 | 5,665 |
| 1983 | 7,945 |
| 1984 | 11,380 |
| 1985 | 17,789 |
| 1986 | 21,390 |

Note: From Media Info (1986).

puters for information storage and retrieval. Consumers access the system via telephone lines.

Teletext also was introduced in the Netherlands in 1980. Information in this system is made available, as with Viditel, in the form of videotext pages. The information is transferred on four video lines in the conventional national television signal. The capacity of this system is limited to approximately 300 television screen pages. Unlike Viditel, Teletext is not interactive in the true sense of the word. Teletext users are only able to consult pages of text on a revolving carousel; they are not able to react to information provided, that is, to request further information, order products, make reservations, and so on, as is possible with fully interactive videotext systems.

Neither of these services has been adopted by large segments of the population. Business users are the primary beneficiaries of Viditel. Table 2.6 shows the increase of subscriptions to Viditel between 1981 and 1986. The reason for limited application of this service in the private sector is its relatively high user cost. Teletext, on the other hand, requires only initial investment in a specially equipped television set. Teletext use, it is estimated, will increase as more households become equipped with these sets. In 1986, about 18% of the households had television sets with Teletext capability (Bekkers, 1987).

## AUDIENCE RESPONSES

In this section, research findings related to audience responses to the availability of new electronic media are reviewed. First, the increase in the number of channels is presented. Thereafter, use of video recorders and Teletext are considered. The following section treats the impact of cable newspapers, and, in the last section, changes in the amount of time spent attending to other media is related to use of television.


## Increase in Channels

Although Table 2.5 shows that there was an increase in the number of channels that viewers were able to receive in the period 1980-1984, Table 2.7 shows that there was no substantial change in the amount of time spent watching television or in the proportion of time spent watching Dutch and foreign channels in that period. The average time spent watching television in 1980 was 105 minutes per day, and in 1984 110 minutes. In 1985 and 1986, however, the average time increased substantially—from 110 minutes in 1984 to 129 and 140 minutes respectively. Although some of this increase was the result of increased foreign channel viewing, the increase also results from increased viewing of Dutch channels.

Research conducted on the use of Sky Channel (NOS, 1984, 1985b) suggests that the introduction of this channel has contributed to an increase in the time spent viewing television. This trend is also evident in the town of Zaltbommel, which has been monitored by research activity since 1984. Subscribers to the cable system in Zaltbommel have been able to receive three satellite channels since 1985. A year later, 75% of the survey respondents indicated that they occassionally watched the channels, and of these persons 22% stated that they were spending more time viewing television than before the introduction of these channels. This was particularly true for respondents who watched the satellite programs 30 minutes or more per day (Table 2.8). Some 34% of the satellite television viewers stated that other persons in the household also spent more time with television because of the satellite programs.

As is evident from both national data and the Zaltbommel research project, persons younger than 40 years as well as those who generally spend much time watching television are the most heavy users of the satellite channels available in the Netherlands.

When the duration of viewing in Table 2.7 is closely examined, increase in attendance to foreign channel programming is seen to be largely a phenomenon since 1984—when the satellite services Sky Channel and Music Box were initiated. The amount of viewing time since 1985 seems to be declining.

The increase of viewing of Dutch channels can be largely attributed to the increase in transmission time by Dutch stations, particularly in the afternoon (Bekkers, 1987, p. 13). It appears that viewers have remained extremely loyal to Dutch channels, especially programs of native origin on these channels (Bekkers, 1987, p. 17). Table 2.7 shows that the ratio of viewing time for Dutch versus foreign chan-

TABLE 2.7

Time Spent Viewing Dutch and Foreign Channels

|  | Year | Dutch channels Minutes | Foreign channels * Minutes | Total Minutes |
|---|---|---|---|---|
| Time in minutes per day | 1980 | 93 | 12 | 105 |
|  | 1981 | 87 | 13 | 100 |
|  | 1982 | 88 | 11 | 99 |
|  | 1983 | 91 | 11 | 102 |
|  | 1984 | 98 | 12 | 110 |
|  | 1985 | 105 | 24 ** | 129 |
|  | 1986 | 119 | 21 ** | 140 |
|  | Year | % | % | % |
| Ratio of Dutch to foreign channels | 1980 | 89 | 11 | 100 |
|  | 1981 | 87 | 13 | 100 |
|  | 1982 | 89 | 11 | 100 |
|  | 1983 | 89 | 11 | 100 |
|  | 1984 | 89 | 11 | 100 |
|  | 1985 | 81 | 19 ** | 100 |
|  | 1986 | 85 | 15 ** | 100 |

Note: From Saarloos (1984); Bekkers (1987).
* This column constitutes total time spent on three German channels and two Belgian channels.
** For 1985 and 1986 this column also includes time spent viewing satellite channels.

TABLE 2.8

Average Time Spent per Day Viewing Satellite TV and Assessment Of Overall TV Viewing Time

| Assessment | Viewing Time Satellite Television per Day | | | |
|---|---|---|---|---|
|  | 0 Minutes | 1-30 Minutes | More Than 30 Minutes | Row Total |
| More Time Than Before Satellite Channels Available | 1 ( 3) | 19 ( 21) | 15 ( 44) | 35 (22) |
| Constant | 38 ( 97) | 70 ( 79) | 19 ( 56) | 127 (78) |
| Total | 39 (100) | 89 (100) | 34 (100) | 162 (100) |

Note: From Olderaan (1986). Chi-square = 18.5  p=0.05.

nels had altered only slightly from 1980 to 1986. This loyality is, however, to a degree involuntary because satellite programming, which is primarily English language, may not by subtitled in the Netherlands. This means that, for those Dutch viewers with limited command of English, satellite programs are less interesting than those on the Dutch stations. This language problem is also present with regard to non-satellite delivered foreign channel programming. The primary reason given for not watching foreign channels is difficulty with the language (Saarloos, 1984, p. 28). Given this, there is little reason to anticipate major change in channel preferences. But should the current prohibition of subtitling of programming be removed, viewing preferences could change dramatically.[3]

## Use of Video Recorders

In 1986, as Table 2.1 indicates, 30% of all Dutch households contained video recorders. Ownership of this equipment was relatively high among heavy television viewers and members of households with high income levels.[4] In that year, 70% of all households with video recorders occasionally rented prerecorded cassettes (vs. 50% in 1982), but of all cassettes viewed at home, 86% contained recordings of television programs. Use of video recorders is relatively high on weekends 50% of the total time in use—especially on Sundays (van Dammen, 1986, p. 23).

The video recorder has caused a shift in the time of day when television is watched. Table 2.9 indicates the time periods in which persons start to view VCR programs during 1983 and 1985. Almost 50% of video recorder viewing is done during the time that the Dutch channels are not broadcasting—before 4:00 p.m. and after 11:00 p.m. This remained constant in the 2 years, 1983 and 1985, for which data were available.

Research results suggest that video recorders in households contribute to an increase in general television viewing by members of those households. Among respondents queried in early 1986 regarding the influence of the video recorder on their viewing habits, 45% indicated that they watched more television, 11% watched less, and 45% noted no difference in the amount of viewing time (van Dammen, 1986). Data from the Zaltbommel research project duplicate this finding: Among those respondents owning video recorders, 33% said that they spent more time attending to television because of the VCR. Another third said that they would delay their television viewing sessions to more convenient time periods.

In all probability, increase in the number of channels and availability of video recorders have not only affected time budgeting, but also the kinds of programs watched. The primary reason that viewers attend to foreign programming, for example, is to see more movies, serials, and sports (Saarloos, 1984, p. 29). Moreover,

TABLE 2.9

VCR Program Viewing per Period of the Day

| Viewing Begins Between: | October 1983 | November 1985 |
|---|---|---|
| 7:00 - 13:00 | 17% | 22% |
| 13:00 - 16:00 | 19 | 19 |
| 16:00 - 19:00 | 19 | 19 |
| 19:00 - 23:00 | 36 | 32 |
| 23:00 - 1:00 | 6 | 6 |
| 1:00 - 7:00 | 2 | 1 |
| Unknown | 1 | 1 |
| Total | 100% | 100% |

Note: From van Dammen (1986). N=215.

TABLE 2.10

Broadcasting Time per Program Type and Viewership of Dutch Channels

| Program Type: | Broadcasting Time | | | Viewership | | |
|---|---|---|---|---|---|---|
| | 1978 % | 1980 % | 1986 % | 1978 % | 1980 % | 1986 % |
| Information | 38 | 43 | 41 | 24 | 25 | 31 |
| Art | 4 | 3 | 4 | 1 | 1 | 1 |
| Drama | 23 | 16 | 23 | 32 | 31 | 31 |
| Entertainment | 17 | 11 | 7 | 28 | 25 | 15 |
| Sports | 7 | 10 | 7 | 6 | 9 | 11 |
| Children's pgms. | 6 | 12 | 14 | 5 | 7 | 8 |
| Commercials | 6 | 4 | 4 | 4 | 2 | 3 |
| Total | 101 | 99 | 100 | 100 | 100 | 100 |

Note: From Bekkers (1987).

about 50% of all television recordings with VCRs are of drama productions—films, serials, and televised theater—and 18% of entertainment programs—quizzes, shows, and music programs—(NOS, 1986a, p. 6). These figures suggest that television viewing—especially regarding foreign channels and use of VCRs—is becoming more and more used for consumption of drama and entertainment programs. But when the viewership of Dutch stations only is examined in Table 2.10, independent of other stations, attention to informational programs appears to have increased in the past years.

TABLE 2.11

Teletext Use and Age of Viewer

| | Each day | 1 - 6 | Almost | Mean: | Mean: | |
|---|---|---|---|---|---|---|
| | | Days/Week | Never | Days/Week | Min./Day | |
| | % | % | % | | | |
| 12-18 years (n= 61) | 23 | 67 | 10 | 3.6 | 5.2 | (n= 55) |
| 19-34 years (n=192) | 35 | 48 | 17 | 3.9 | 6.3 | (n=160) |
| 35-49 years (n=141) | 25 | 43 | 32 | 2.9 | 4.5 | (n= 96) |
| 50-64 years (n=128) | 23 | 51 | 26 | 3.1 | 8.1 | (n= 95) |
| 65 and older (n=55) | 33 | 33 | 34 | 3.3 | 11.8 | (n= 36) |

Note: From NOS (1986b).

## Use of Teletext

In 1986, as noted previously, 18% of all Dutch households had television sets capable of receiving teletext services. Ownership of these sets is highest among persons 19-34 years of age. Among owners, it is senior citizens, however, who devote the most time to teletext services (NOS, 1986b, p. 10). See Table 2.11.

The information most frequently requested concerns news, weather, and sports reports. Between 86% and 93% of the teletext users stated that the use of this service had little or no effect on use of other information sources (NOS, 1986b, p. 36). Relatively limited time is spent using teletext each day and this, in all probability, contributes little to the total time that people spend watching television.

## Cable Newspapers

Limited research has been conducted on cable newspapers, and what has been done is primarily marketing research intended for publishers involved in developing this new cable service. Two research activities, however, extend beyond basic marketing concerns and have been publicized: a national survey (van Lieshout, 1986) and the results of a survey conducted in Amsterdam (Becker & Jankowski, 1986).

The national survey provides information on awareness and use of cable newspapers around the country. Slightly more than half of the respondents who subscribed to cable television systems that distribute cable newspapers were aware of the service. Men were more aware than women, and respondents in the age category 25-34 were more aware of the service than older persons. Readers of conventional regional newspapers were more aware of the cable papers than were nonreaders of regional newspapers.

TABLE 2.12

Use of Cable Newspapers in Amsterdam

| Time Reported | Average Day % | Yesterday % |
|---|---|---|
| No Time Reported | 43 | 84 |
| 1-9 Minutes | 23 | 4 |
| 10-19 Minutes | 21 | 7 |
| 20+ Minutes | 13 | 5 |
| | 100 | 100 |

Note: From Becker and Jankowski (1986). N=244.

Of those persons familiar with the service, three fourths indicated that they occassionally viewed the service. Again, men watched more than women. Approximately two thirds of the respondents indicated that they had viewed cable newspapers within the past week, and of these persons about half viewed the service the day prior to the interview.

Similar figures were reported from the Amsterdam survey. Half of these respondents had seen one or both cable newspapers operating in the city. Many of these viewers, however, did not report spending time watching a cable newspaper on an average day; even fewer reported watching on the day prior to the interview—indicated as "yesterday" in Table 2.12.

Among the users of the services, a number of characteristics seem to predominate. Persons who have lived longer in Amsterdam, reside with other adults, have less education, and are younger are more likely to have made use of cable newspapers than their counterparts. Cable newspaper users also attend more to other broadcast media, have more television sets in their households, in particular with teletext capability. They are also more often readers of the popular national newspapers than nonreaders, and are not readers of so-called quality newspapers. Cable newspaper users do not differ from nonusers in their evaluation of television programs generally. There is, however, some indication that, among users, the cable services are preferred over radio and television for local information. There is, however, no indication that the services are replacing newspapers.

## Television Use and Other Media

Table 2.13 indicates changes in time spent with electronic and printed media for the last 10 years. Considering all of the media, only time spent with television has increased, and, of the other media, only the amount of time devoted to newspapers

TABLE 2.13

Attendance to Electronic and Print Media in Hours/Week

|      | Television * | Radio ** | Play Back Equipment | Newspapers | Magazines | Books |
|------|------------|---------|---------------------|------------|-----------|-------|
| 1975 | 9.8        | 1.1     | 0.7                 | 2.3        | 1.9       | 1.6   |
| 1980 | 9.9        | 1.0     | 0.6                 | 2.2        | 1.8       | 1.6   |
| 1985 | 11.5       | 0.9     | 0.4                 | 2.2        | 1.6       | 1.4   |

Note: From Sociaal Cultureel Planburo (1986).
* Includes use of video and teletext.
** Includes use of both telvision and radio, but latter as major activity.

TABLE 2.14

Circulation and Sales of Print Media (in Millions)

|            | 1975   | 1980   | 1981   | 1982   | 1983   | 1984   | 1985   |
|------------|--------|--------|--------|--------|--------|--------|--------|
| Newspapers | 4,192  | 4,612  | 4,587  | 4,560  | 4,513  | 4,474  | 4,496  |
| Magazines  | 8,946  | 10,617 | 10,450 | 10,442 | 10,581 | 10,282 | 10,240 |
| Books      | 33,385 | 32,984 | 34,130 | 35,045 | 31,864 | 31,532 | 30,337 |

Note: From Sociaal Cultureel Planburo (1986).

has remained constant. The table also suggests that there is a slight shift from print toward electronic media. This is especially the case for the younger generation: The proportion of time spent with electronic media for people younger than 20 years has increased from 73% in 1975 to 82% in 1985. Another illustration of this trend is that the difference in time spent with print media by younger and older persons has increased: "heavy users" of newspapers and magazines have become older (Sociaal Cultureel Planburo, 1986, pp. 211-216).

The same trend is found in the circulation figures of the printed press. Table 2.14 suggests that the sale of books is gradually declining; newspapers and magazines seem to have reached a stable rate of sales. An interesting aspect of this development is that the circulation rates of news and opinion magazines have declined dramatically since 1981. This decline, however, has been compensated by a rise in circulation figures for women's magazines and television guides.

In the last few years, much concern has been expressed regarding the influence of the increase of television-related activities—viewership of satellite channels and use of video recorders—on the cinema. Attendance to the cinema has declined dramatically in the past 5 years, as shown in Table 2.15.

TABLE 2.15

Frequency of Cinema Visits per 100 Residents

| 1980 | 1981 | 1982 | 1983 | 1984 | 1985 |
|------|------|------|------|------|------|
| 183  | 173  | 143  | 141  | 115  | 106  |

Note: From Sociaal Cultureel Planburo (1986).

TABLE 2.16

Cinema Attendance and VCR Ownership

| Cinema Attendance | VCR Ownership | | Total |
|---|---|---|---|
| | Yes % | No % | % |
| In 1985 More Often than in 1982 | 10 | 12 | 11 |
| In 1985 as Often as in 1982 | 15 | 17 | 17 |
| On 1985 Less than in 1982 | 36 | 24 | 27 |
| No Attendance in 1985 nor in 1982 | 36 | 43 | 41 |
| Unknown | 3 | 4 | 4 |
| Total | 100 | 100 | 100 |
| (N) | (215) | (462) | (677) |

Note: From van Dammen (1986).

Research findings suggest that television use is an important factor related to a decline in cinema attendance, but not the only one. Table 2.16 indicates that 27% of the persons interviewed went to the cinema less in 1985 than 3 years earlier. When taking video recorder ownership into account, 36% who owned recorders said that they attended less, in comparison to 24% of the nonowners. When queried regarding the reason for less attendance, 50% of the VCR owners cited the presence of video recorders in their homes as the primary reason. Other reasons given by these respondents were: changes in private and family life (mentioned by 20%); less interest in movies (9%); and financial limitations (8%). Persons not owning

VCRs indicated changes in private and family life (39%) as the main motive for going to the cinema less (van Dammen, 1986, p. 54).

## CONCLUSIONS

In this chapter, three features of electronic media development in the Netherlands have been traced: policy transformation, alterations in the media landscape, and audience reactions to these alterations. Media policy development has been largely a reaction to technological advancements and transformations in society as a whole. Although an effort was made in the first half of the 1980s to create an integrated media policy, political compromises limited its success. Determination of broadcasting policy is still very much in the hands of the government, as is the power to provide or withhold access to these media. The private sector, however, is being increasingly encouraged to take part in these developments, in the hope that this may improve the economic position of the country. An example of this development is government stimulation and partial financing of a 5-year cable services experiment in South Limburg.

As for the media landscape, major changes in its contour have become visible since 1980. Cabling of the country has progressed rapidly. By 1985 some 71% of the population was connected to cable systems. These signal distribution systems have provided opportunity for a parallel growth in the number of television channels made available. In 1984, the average number of channels was 5. Cities, such as Amsterdam, were distributing programming for 12 channels in 1987, and new systems are capable of carrying between 20 and 30 channels. Services for those cable systems, however, have not progressed at a similar rate; pay television is still marginal and interactive informational services have yet to begin.

An exception is the growth of cable newspapers; in 1985, some 35 had been established on cable systems. But once cable-delivered teletext services become widespread, it is anticipated that these newspapers will decline in number. Newspaper publishers have nevertheless become involved in this development in order to gain experience with electronic media and to secure a foothold for commercial local television.

The central question examined in this chapter is how the Dutch audience has reacted to these changes in the media landscape. Although limited research has been conducted on this issue, several trends can be drawn from the evidence available. First, an increasing amount of the public's time is being devoted to the electronic media. This is to only some extent at the expense of other media. There is evidence of a net increase in the amount of time devoted to the media. This additional time is in all likelihood at the expense of other leisure activities. Data are unavailable, however, to substantiate this hypothesis.

Second, the total time that people watch television had been relatively constant until 1984. In 1985, however, the first satellite-relayed television programs were distributed on cable systems in the country, and, at the same time, Dutch television stations began broadcasting afternoon programming. In addition, video recorder ownership has increased substantially since 1985. These three aspects have contributed to an overall increase in attendance to television. Although the number of channels and variety of programs have increased, audience members still prefer the national channels above the foreign alternatives. It is especially during time periods when the two national channels are not transmitting programming that satellite programs and foreign broadcasts attract a sizeable portion of the Dutch audience. This aspect played a role in the recommendation proposed by both the Scientific Advisory Council of the government and the NOS to extend broadcasting time of the Dutch channels to the afternoons (Wetenschappelijke Raad vor het Regeringsbeleid, 1982, p. 220; Bekkers, 1987, p. 14). In this way, it was felt, Dutch television could more successfully compete against the foreign channels for viewers.

Third, research findings suggest that foreign channels are primarily viewed for the entertainment and drama programming they provide. An increasing number of these programs are being recorded at home for delayed viewing. As for programming on Dutch stations, there seems to be an increase in viewership of documentary and news programs.

Fourth, there may be a transformation in the degree and character of viewer attendance to television programming underway. Although the number of channels that can be received in the Netherlands is still small in comparison to channel availability in North America, considerably more channels are anticipated. And it appears as if the amount of time that the Dutch spend watching television has not yet reached a saturation point. Along with this, preliminary research (Olderaan, 1987) suggests that, for some viewers, television viewing is coming to resemble the way most listeners attend to radio: as a background medium. This is particularly evident in households with children interested in watching video clips transmitted by the satellite channels.

Finally, little can be said about the consequences related to pay television and the interactive tele-information services. These developments have not been implemented long enough for sufficient portions of the audience to consider them. The safest prognosis in this area is caution regarding anticipation of major changes in audience motivations and behaviors.

In summary, the Netherlands may be perhaps the "cockpit of Europe" in terms of cable penetration and initiation of one-way conventional television services, but it is far from being in the forefront regarding experimentation and implementation of interactive services. There is, furthermore, little evidence that audience members are predisposed to considering television more than what it, until now, primarily has been: a source of entertainment.

## NOTES

[1] Comment made by a member of the Board of Directors of the London-based research organization Communications & Information Technology (CIT) during a new media seminar held in Amsterdam in October 1984.

[2] Several English language texts outline the history and development of broadcasting in the Netherlands; for further information, see: Brants (1986), Brants and Jankowski (1985), van der Haak (1977).

[3] Since 1984, the Dutch government has prohibited the distribution of satellite-delivered programming accompanied by Dutch subtitles, or of programming accompanied by advertising directed at the Dutch market. Both regulations have been contested in the European High Court.

[4] Ownership among members of households with relatively low incomes has increased, however, in the past 2 years; see van Dammen (1986).

## REFERENCES

Becker, L., & Jankowski, N. (1986). Use and assessment of cabletext services. *Massacommunicatie, 14*, 245-258.

Bekkers, W. (1987). *De nederlandse omroep in het satelliet-tijdperk: Positie verzekerd of bedreigd?* [Dutch broadcasting in the satellite era: Position safe or threatened]. (Research Rep. No. B87-002). Hilversum: NOS Research Department.

Brants, K. (1986). Broadcasting and politics in the Netherlands: From pillar to post. In R. Kuhn (Ed.), *Broadcasting and politics in western Europe* (pp. 104-122). London: Frank Cass Ltd.

Brants, K., & Jankowski, N. (1985). Cable television in the Low Countries. In R. M. Negrine (Ed.), *Cable television and the future of broadcasting* (pp. 74-102). London: Croom Helm.

Dammen, R. van (1986). *Videorecorder-gebruik 1985/1986* [VCR use 1985/1986]. (Research Rep. No. R86-390). Hilversum: NOS Research Department.

Haak, C. van der (1977). *Broadcasting in The Netherlands*. London: International Institute of Communications.

Jankowski, N., & Mol, A.-L. (1986, August). *The electronic writing tablet and Arabic language instruction.* Paper presented to the International Association for Mass Communication Research, New Delhi.

Lieshout, J. van (1986). *De kabelkrant in Nederland: een overzicht van de experimentele kabelkranten in Nederland* [The cable newspaper in The Netherlands: A overview of the experimental newspapers in The Netherlands]. Amsterdam: Het Media Institute.

McQuail, D., & Siune, K. (Eds.). (1986). *New media politics: Comparative perspectives in Western Europe.* London: Sage.

Media Info. (1986). Viditel in cijfers [Some figures on Viditel]., *Media Info, 11,* 125.

NOS. (1984). *Onderzoek inzake het kijken naar Sky Channel-juni/juli 1984* [Research on viewership of Sky Channel, March 1985]. (Research Rep. No. B84-182). Hilversum: NOS Research Department.

NOS. (1985a). *Ontvangstmogelijkheden buitenlandse zenders, najaar 1984* [Receiving facilities of foreign stations, Fall 1984]. (Research Rep. No. B85-097). Hilversum: NOS Research Department.

NOS. (1985b). *De kijkdichtheid van Sky Channel, maart 1985* [Viewership of Sky Channel, March 1985]. (Research Rep. No. B85-143). Hilversum: NOS Research Department.

NOS. (1986a). *Bezit AV-apptuur en ontvangstmogelijkheden 1977-1985* [Penetration of audio-visual equipment and receiving facilities 1977-1985]. (Research Rep. No. R86-055). Hilversum: NOS Research Department.

NOS. (1986b). *Teletekst: het vijfde jaar* [Teletext: The fifth year]. (Research Rep. No. R86-386). Hilversum: NOS Research Department.

Olderaan, F. (1985). Kabelexperimenten in Zaltbommel [Cable experiments in Zaltbommel]. *Informatie en Informatiebeleid, 12,* 21-26.

Olderaan, F. (1986). *Tussenverslag van de Derde meting van het onder zoek naar het Kabelkommunikatieproject in Zaltbommel* [Intermediary report on the third survey of the research project on the cable communication project in Zaltbommel]. (Research Rep.). Institute of Mass Communication, Catholic University, Nijmegen, The Netherlands.

Olderaan, F. (1987). *Verslag van een gespreksronde over de recht streekse uitzendingen van de vergaderingen van de gemeenteraad en de uitbreiding van het televisieprogramma-aanbod in Zaltbommel.* [Report of interviews regarding live broadcasting of city council meetings and media diversification in Zaltbommel]. (Research Rep.). Nijmegan: Institute of Mass Communication, Catholic University.

Oosterwijk, F. (1986). Dossier abonee-tv: Zonder reclame begin je niets [Pay-tv: You cannot start without advertising]. *Adformatie, 47,* 20-24.

Saarloos, J. (1984). *De belangstelling voor buitenlandse tv-zenders* [Interest in foreign television stations]. (Research Rep. No. 84-358). Hilversum: NOS Research Department.

Sociaal Cultureel Planburo. (1986). *Sociaal en Cultureel Rapport 1986.* [Social and cultural report 1986]. The Hague: National Publishing House.

Stappers, J., Hollander, E., & Jankowski, N. (1984, August). *Researching cable television in Zaltbommel: A community study in changing communication patterns.* Paper presented to the International Association for Mass Communication Research, Prague.

Wetenschappelijke Raad voor het Regeringsbeleid. (1982). *Samenhangend Mediabeleid* [Toward a coherent media policy]. Scientific Advisory Commission for Government Policy. The Hague: National Publishing House.

# 3

# Belgium: Language Division Internationalized

**Roselyne Bouillin-Dartevelle**
*Free University of Brussels*

## THE AUDIO-VISUAL LANDSCAPE IN BELGIUM [1]

### Television and Cable

Twenty-five years ago, Belgium was said to be the pioneering country in terms of audio-visual media. In fact, the first cable television experiment was conducted there as early as 1961. From that date until 1969, the number of cable subscribers had increased slowly, followed by a very rapid expansion lasting until the beginning of the 1980s. Whereas there were 49,014 subscribers by the end of 1969 and 87,930 by the end of 1970, this number had climbed to an estimated 1,300,000 by the end of 1975 and to 2,259,718 by the end of 1980 (Thoveron & Huens, 1985, p. 19).

In 1986, 95% of the Belgian households had at least one television set. Nineteen percent of those households in the French-speaking part of Belgium had at least a second one. The figure was 22% in the Dutch-speaking part. More than two thirds of all the households with a TV set were equipped with a color TV. At present, cable subscription is still more widespread than owning a color TV set. In spite of the slowing down of subscription rates, 87% of the French-speaking households and 83% of the Dutch-speaking households were wired by the middle of the 1980s. (RTBF, 1986a; BRT, 1985). These average figures, however, veil strong differences between regions in Belgium. For instance, 88% of the households in Brussels are connected to cable, and 93% in Namur are. In some

51

communities in the province of Liege, 95% of the homes have cable. On the other hand, in the province of Luxembourg in the south of the country, cable reaches only about 20% of the households (RTBF, 1986b). This situation can be partly explained by the fact that this area, located close to the border, does not need cable to receive the French and Luxembourg channels.

In general, income and age play only a secondary role in explaining cable subscription. Geographic location, however, and ownership of a color TV set are more important discriminating factors. In the French-speaking section of the country, there are still more cable households than in the Dutch-speaking area, although there are more color TV sets in the latter (86% of the households as opposed to 78% in the French-speaking provinces).

In Belgium, cable households are able to receive additional TV channels from France, West Germany, Britain, the Netherlands, Italy, and Luxembourg. The cable households also can receive some European satellite channels, such as Sky Channel, Music Box, and TV5. TV5 is the joint product of several European, French-language stations offering French programs for all Europe and even North Africa. In principle, wired households can watch up to 17 different TV channels. In reality, however, only 50% get TV5, 28% BBC2 from Britain, 21% RAI from Italy, 9% Sky Channel, and only 4% Music Box.

The Belgian cable networks, installed by the state, by private companies, or by mixed enterprises, would allow a great number of experiments in principle. At present, however, those experiments are restricted to some local television channels. The Royal Decree of December 24, 1966, indeed, allows only channels to be distributed by cable that initially could have been received over the air and defines exceptions to that rule very rigidly.

The recommendations of an audio-visual media study group have led to the tentative installation of 11 local TV channels in the French-speaking part of Belgium. Depending on the local setting, the organizers of the channel are differently privileged. The local setting also determines the options of the local broadcasting council, the quantities of local information or of educational material, the organization of and the support by local interest groups, and the experiments with viewdata. The legal status, the perspectives for the future, and the functioning of those pilot projects are very different (van Apeldoorn, 1985). All of them are subsidized by the Ministry of the French Community according to the new regulations of the Council of the French Community of July 17, 1985. Some decided to cooperate with the French-speaking Belgian Broadcasting System (RTBF) and/or the community they serve. Their impact on the population is also fairly different.

According to a 1984 survey of cultural activities in French-speaking Belgium, involving 3,000 persons and conducted by the Catholic University of Louvain and the Free University of Brussels, about 10% of the population in that area could watch the local TV programs described heretofore. Some of the channels, though, are particularly popular—such as RTC-Liege or No Tele in Tournai. No Tele reaches up to 90% of those able to watch it, whereas others have a very weak impact. For example, in La Louviere, more than half of the cable subscribers claim to have never watched the local TV channel Antenne Centre (Klein, 1984). Unfortunately, there is no similar study in the Dutch-speaking part of the country.

## Teletext

In the beginning of the 1980s, both Belgian broadcast systems—the French-language RTBF and the Flemish BRT—started teletext services. RTBF, however, implemented its "Perceval" system following the French ANTIOPE norm, whereas BRT used the British "Ceefax." As a consequence, viewers equipped with decoders for one of the two systems are not able to watch the other. Also, the two systems were supposed to fulfill different purposes.

*The Teletext System "Perceval" of the RTBF*. In a first experimentation phase, both an analog teletext system (carrying a "carousel" of short messages) and a digitalized one were tried. For that purpose, a dozen terminals were placed at different locations in the city of Liege. This system was commercialized in 1984, but the number of terminals actually used is still fairly low. Initially, two types of services were offered: a national one geared toward the French community as a whole, and a regional one for the province of Liege. Both were distributed alternately at different times of the week.

The information provided by "Perceval" mainly consisted of news (produced in cooperation with the Belgian newspaper publishers' association), weather reports, program information by the RTBF, consumer tips, stock market reports, cultural and tourist events information, sports news, games, road conditions, and placement ads. In 1984, three new services were offered: "Telechamps" for farmers, "Courrier des marins" for sailors, and "Loisir-Tourisme," a service containing leisure time and tourist information. Agreements with governmental and semi-governmental institutions and with professional organizations secure regular information for "Perceval."

*The "Teletekst" of the BRT*. This service is a digital one. The necessary decoders are provided by commercial companies. A service of 150 pages is distributed all over the Flemish part of Belgium, without any further regionalization. The information offered was structured according to the results of a survey designed to identify the demands of the audience. Thus, the Flemish "Teletekst" succeeded in serving its audience more adequately than "Perceval" did. The BRT service, for instance, provides cooking advice, gardening tips, health tips, a service for language problems, and the addresses of service institutions. All those services are accessible daily between 9:00 a.m. and midnight.

## Viewdata

In the beginning of the 1980s, the "Regie des Telegraphes et des Telephones (RTT)", the state postal service responsible for installation and maintenance of communication lines, planned an experiment with an interactive viewdata system for the general public, similar to the French Teletel 3V. The objectives of that project were to gauge the potential demand by the audience, to master the technical difficulties, and to find out about legal problems involved. However, the start of the project was postponed several times. In 1987, the only viewdata services actually working were professional in nature (Pichault, 1985). An electronic phone directory service for the general public on viewdata was in the planning stages at that time.

## Videocassette Recorders

In 1982, according to a RTBF report, 4% of the households with a TV set also had a videocassette recorder (VCR)(RTBF, 1982a). In 1984, a survey of cultural activities in French-speaking Belgium suggested a household coverage of about 7% (Thoveron & Huens, 1985). In 1986, a video recorder could be found in 12% of households with a TV set, and in the summer of 1987, the estimated household coverage of VCRs was about 15% (RTBF, 1986b). This is still less than in most of Belgium's neighboring countries. In general, the owners of VCRs are younger, more educated, and better-equipped with communication devices than other people (Table 3.1).

TABLE 3.1

Audio-Visual Equipment of VCR Households

|  | VCR Households % | All Households % |
|---|---|---|
| Stereo | 72 | 35 |
| Color TV Set | 97 | 81 |
| Remote Control | 81 | 44 |
| Two TV Sets | 44 | 19 |
| Video Games | 29 | 15 |

## AUDIENCE BEHAVIOR

### The Impact of Cable Television

Since 1971, cable has enabled an increasing number of Belgians to receive more and more foreign TV channels. That quantitative enlargement of the TV offering obviously had an impact on the audience: In 1971, all channels considered, Belgians were offered 1,340 hours of TV programming during prime time, that is, between 7:00 and 11:00 p.m. In 1977, this number had risen to 2,304 hours. On the other hand, the larger the number of channels became, the more those services were competing with one another for prime time, thus reducing each one's chance to be watched. In other words, the more channels, the more the gap between the supply and the actual reception has threatened to widen. The question is important, however, whether this phenomenon is a general one or whether it concerns only specific types of programming. As it stands, the issue raised by the virtually total wiring of the country is twofold: (a) What is the relationship like between the existing supply and the one that is actually used by the individual audience member, depending on the complementarity, the redundancy, or the competition of the channels, and (b) What is the difference between those who are able to watch television at a given moment in time, and those who really watch, considering, for instance, the interest of the audience for a specific genre as well as the time devoted to TV in general?

Answers to these questions can be useful only if they are based on studies over a sufficiently long time to neutralize the ephemeral oscillations both of the supply and the reception. For this purpose, results from an investigation in the French-speaking part of Belgium are the only ones that can be used. The study was conducted jointly by the Free University of Brussels, the Continuous Survey Service and the Research Bureau of the RTBF. It looks at the relationships between the prime time TV offering (7:00-11:00 p.m.) and viewing behavior from November 15th to December 15th in 1971, 1973, 1975, and 1977, respectively. The study covers the phase in which cable subscribership experienced its greatest expansion. In each year, TV stations reaching at least 5% of the households were considered. In 1971, those were the French-language Belgian TV channel RTB, plus TF1 and Antenne 2, both from France; in 1973, RTL from Luxembourg was added for the first time; 1977 finally saw the foundation of RTBis, the second French-language Belgian channel, later called Tele 2.

In our study, the contents of those services were categorized in seven genres: information; movies and TV dramas; documentaries and artistic programs; entertainment (game shows, music shows); sports; youth programs; and philosophical, political, and religious programs. Similar studies were conducted in Quebec, Canada (Caron, 1977) and in France (Souchon, 1977).

All three studies revealed, among other results, that the Belgian, French, and Canadian audiences showed a fairly stable viewing behavior and did not consume programs proportionately to the amount offered. In general, viewers use more entertainment programs than high culture ones, more movies and TV plays than news and information. In all three countries, we found a virtually constant composition of the genres viewed, almost independent from what was offered: About 70% of the viewing time was devoted to entertainment of all sorts, about 22% to information, and about 5% to high culture programs (Les televisions francophones, 1980, p. 147).

This comparative study was expanded in 1978, supported by UNESCO, and then contained seven countries. Results were very similar to those found before (Caron, Souchon, & Thoveron, 1981):

> Everywhere, one might state, entertainment is over-consumed and information and high culture are under- consumed; and this is true independently of whether materials are over- or under-offered. It is as if the audience, whatever programs are broadcast, reestablished a universal equilibrium of consumption; as if it resisted the program planners, may they follow demagogical or paternalistic principles; as if it used a consumption model that (at least in industrialized countries) is fairly uniform. (p. 147) (See also UNESCO, 1981.)

A more profound analysis of the Belgian results also reveals evidence of some more short-term developments both of the supply and its reception.

*The Global Development of the Offer and the Accessibility of the Channels, 1971-1977.* The multiplication of the number of channels between 1971 and 1977 had led to an increase in programs offered, a fairly imbalanced one, though: The amount of movies and TV plays rose by 94%, that of information programs by 69%, high culture programs by 67%, and entertainment by 65%. This offering certainly implies an overlap, even a clash of similar programs, thus reducing the audience's capability to watch all of them. Whereas high culture programs do not compete with one another on the program schedules, the competition between movies and TV plays on the one hand, and information programs on the other started as early as in 1973, was even more accentuated in 1975, and stabilized in the following years. Competition among game shows, however, remained fairly weak.

*The Development of Viewing Behavior, 1971-1977.* How did the audience react to the increasing abundance of the supply and the growing number of program

TABLE 3.2

Changes in the Volume of Programs Broadcast, Programs Available,
And Programs Watched, by Genre

|  | Programs Broadcast % | Available % | Watched % |
|---|---|---|---|
| Information | +69 | +20 | +28 |
| High Culture | +67 | +49 | - 6 |
| Movies, TV Plays | +94 | +20 | + 4 |
| Entertainment | +65 | +40 | +112 |
| Sports | +32 | +44 | + 79 |

Note: From Les televisions francophones (1980).

clashes? A closer look at viewing behavior between 1971 and 1977 reveals that two types of programs show the most spectacular increases in viewership: entertainment programs (112%) and sports programs (79%).

Information programs, on the other hand, won 28% in additional viewers, movies and TV plays only 4%. High culture programs lost 6% of their viewers, although their share of the programming (about 15%) remained stable.

If one compares the 1971-1977 developments (a) of the amounts of programs broadcast, (b) of those that—given their simultaneous broadcasting—were actually accessible to a specific audience member, and (c) the actual reception by the audience, one can easily realize strong disparities of what happened to specific genres (Table 3.2).

Those different movements suggest a polarization of the audience's channel preferences, caused not only by the genres presented by those services, but also by some specific programs of those channels. For example, many people liked to turn to Antenne 2 from France for entertainment purposes, because there they found a selection of very popular game shows. On the other hand, many French-speaking Belgians preferred their national channel for programs dealing with their everyday lives, such as news and sports. Claude Geerts (1979) reported that, whereas the average reach of the Belgian TV channel RTB dropped considerably between 1973 and 1977, the proportion of those watching its newscasts remained a stable 80% of the total audience (Table 3.3).

The impact of some events during the period in question only supports those general tendencies. When, for instance, France introduced daylight-saving time in 1976, the RTB newscasts had to compete directly with those successful programs

TABLE 3.3

Use of Television, the Domestic Channel RTB
And of RTB's Nightly News

|      | TV use (in min. per day) | Use of RTB (in min. per day) | Reach of RTB News % |
|------|------|------|------|
| 1973 | 152 | 97 | 52 |
| 1974 | 141 | 88 | 50 |
| 1975 | 145 | 71 | 46 |
| 1976 | 147 | 71 | 43 |
| 1977 | 137 | 59 | 42 |

on the French TV channels. A sharp decline of the news audience—down from 41% to 27%—was the consequence. This loss was only in part compensated by watching news on other channels. Also, when the audience was dissatisfied with the considerably reduced RTB news coverage during a strike, the other services were never regarded as serious alternatives (Geerts, 1979, p. 177).

Again, these events point out (a) generally, how important entertainment for the audience is, compared to information; and (b) when it comes to information, how much the audience likes to know about events concerning its daily life. This latter preference contributes to the audience's switching between the domestic channel for news and the foreign ones for entertainment. This picture becomes very clear, if one compares entertainment and information actually broadcast by those channels accessible to the audience member and the percentages of the audience watching the two genres (Table 3.4).

The Belgian government's permit to install an airwave connection between Brussels and Luxembourg in 1983 allowed the Luxembourg channel RTL to improve its news program for Belgium. Since then, the audience of that program has increased without causing a drop in the audience of the RTBF newscast. Because the two programs are not scheduled at the same time, people obviously watch the RTL news first (at 7:00 p.m.) and then switch over to the RTBF news (at 7:30 p.m.) (Table 3.5).

After 8:00 p.m., however, the new game show on FR3 from France draws more viewers than the newscasts of the French channels TF1 and A2 together do. At 10:00 p.m., though, some of these viewers leave the entertainment programs and turn to the late evening newscasts of TF1 and A2 (RTBF, 1985).

In the Flemish part of Belgium, the situation is different. There, the audience seems to be more attached to the two national channels, BRT1 and TV2, that succeeded in increasing their audience in recent years. Whereas there is a 20-point gap between the percentage of TV viewers in general and that of the French-speaking

TABLE 3.4

A   Comparison of the Amounts of Programs Broadcast
And Watched, 1977, by Genre and Channel

|                          | RTB  | RTL  | TF1  | A2   | FR3  |
|--------------------------|------|------|------|------|------|
| **Information**          |      |      |      |      |      |
| - broadcast              |      |      |      |      |      |
| (in %)                   | 39.2 | 21.2 | 32.9 | 28.5 | 35.8 |
| - watched                |      |      |      |      |      |
| (in %)                   | 40.0 | 11.5 | 12.2 | 10.1 | 3.2  |
| **Movies, TV plays**     |      |      |      |      |      |
| - broadcast              |      |      |      |      |      |
| (in %)                   | 24.7 | 62.0 | 35.4 | 22.2 | 36.4 |
| - watched                |      |      |      |      |      |
| (in %)                   | 32.5 | 70.7 | 66.2 | 32.9 | 70.5 |

Note: From Geerts and Thoveron (1979, p. 39).

TABLE 3.5

Use of the RTBF and RTL Nightly News

|      |                  | Reach Among TV Owners in Brussels and Wallonia of | |
|------|------------------|-----------|-----------|
|      |                  | RTBF News % | RTL News % |
| 1982 | January-May      | 43.0 | 10.1 |
|      | October-December | 44.4 | 10.9 |
| 1983 | January-May      | 43.4 | 6.3  |
|      | October-December | 45.2 | 6.1  |
| 1984 | January-May      | 44.5 | 6.1  |
|      | October-December | 42.5 | 8.9  |
| 1985 | January-May      | 42.5 | 11.2 |
| 1986 | January-May      | 43.7 | 13.9 |

Note: From RTBF, Bureau d'etudes, research reports S.T.V. 74, 83, 92, 96, 99.

RTBF, there is almost none as far as the BRT channels are concerned, indicating that, in the Dutch-speaking area, watching TV means mainly watching BRT. But both in Wallonia and in Flanders, it is the news and sports that most strongly attract the audience to the national channels.

In general, the domestic channels are still ahead of the foreign ones, even in the French-speaking region, although there more people watch channels originating in France (68%) than the audience in Flanders watches services from the Netherlands (55.7%). All the stations, however, both domestic and foreign, increased their audiences between 1984 and 1986. This development was not due that much to more time spent on TV, but to a tendency toward fragmentation of the audience's interests and tastes (Table 3.6).

This fragmentation, however, stops at the language barriers. In the north of the country, French-language channels are rarely watched; in the south, people virtually ignore Dutch-language programs. But the greater number of French-language channels and the strong competition by RTL contributed to a greater segmentation of the French-speaking audience and to its turning away from RTBF (Table 3.7).

Like the French-speaking audience, however, the Flemish switch between the channels available to them in order to watch their favorite programs. For instance, sports programs and entertainnment shows are more frequently watched on the first channel from the Netherlands, and some TV series are more frequently viewed on the second one (BRT, 1986).

Within the general preference for entertainment, there are specific productions that certain groups of the society like better than others, depending on age, education, and where they live. The previously-mentioned study of cultural activities in the French-speaking area, for instance, reveals this intra-stratum isomorphism of TV behavior (Table 3.8).

Also, a high selectivity and the tendency to watch the same TV station all the time (9.2% of the respondents) is most widespread among the elderly and the less educated.


## The Use of Teletext

As mentioned heretofore, the technical norms and the functions of teletext differ considerably between the two language groups. This is also true for the behaviors of the audience. In Wallonia, for instance, the public terminals for teletext were increasingly removed because not very many people used them. Those who did were mostly interested in TV program information, games, sports, and placement ads.

TABLE 3.6

Reach of TV Channels in Belgium

| | 1980 % | 1982 % | 1984 % | 1986 % |
|---|---|---|---|---|
| Dutch-language Belgian channels | | | | |
| BRT1 | 30.4 | 34.2 | 33.2 | 34.7 |
| TV2 | - | - | 4.5 | 6.4 |
| French-language Belgian channels | | | | |
| RTBF1 | 19.2 | 21.7 | 22.5 | 24.9 |
| TELE 2 | - | - | 3.1 | 2.2 |
| French channels | | | | |
| TF1 | 8.5 | 7.9 | 6.7 | 10.4 |
| A 2 | 7.8 | 9.0 | 9.8 | 10.9 |
| FR3 | - | - | 4.6 | 5.5 |
| Dutch channels | | | | |
| Nederland 1 | 9.0 | 7.1 | 10.8 | 15.8 |
| Nederland 2 | 8.4 | 8.3 | 7.2 | 8.1 |
| RTL (Luxembourg) | 17.4 | 20.0 | 21.3 | 22.8 |
| West German channels | | | | |
| ARD | - | - | - | 3.2 |
| ZDF | - | - | - | 2.3 |
| WDR | - | - | - | .8 |
| British channels | | | | |
| BBC1 | - | - | - | 3.8 |
| BBC2 | - | - | - | 2.0 |
| RAI1 (Italy) | - | - | - | .9 |

Note: The base is persons more than 14 years old and watching at least one of the channels listed above.

TABLE 3.7

Reach   of Television Channels in the Dutch-Speaking and the
French-Speaking Areas of Belgium, 1984

|  | Dutch-speaking area % | French-speaking area % |
|---|---|---|
| Dutch-language Belgian channels |  |  |
| BRT1 | 52.6 |  |
| TV2 | 8.6 | 1 |
| French-language Belgian channels |  |  |
| RTBF1 | 2.4 | 40 |
| TELE 2 | .6 | 7 |
| French channels |  |  |
| TF1 | 1.3 |  |
| A 2 | 1.8 | 31 |
| FR3 | .7 |  |
| Dutch channels |  |  |
| Nederland 1 | 14.9 |  |
| Nederland 2 | 8.4 | - |
| RTL (Luxembourg) | 3.0 | 20 |
| West German channels |  |  |
| ARD | 1.4 |  |
| ZDF | 1.3 | 1 |
| WDR | .3 |  |

TABLE 3.8

Time Spent on Television in Wallonia and in Brussels
By Social Class

| | Blue-Collar Workers | Lower Middle Class | Upper Middle Class | Upper Class | Farmers |
|---|---|---|---|---|---|
| | % | % | % | % | % |
| Less than 10 hours/week | 28.3 | 39.7 | 41.4 | 52.3 | 45.3 |
| 10-19 hours/week | 37.8 | 38.7 | 43.7 | 34.2 | 37.7 |
| 20 hours/week and more | 34.0 | 21.6 | 14.8 | 13.5 | 17.0 |

Note: From Universite Libre (1986).

A 1983 survey conducted by the RTBF among 500 persons in the Liege area revealed that less than half of them had seen teletext at least once. Forty-four percent did not even know about its existence (RTBF, 1983). Even if teletext transmits news of local interest—for example, the results of local elections—very few TV viewers watch it instead of the traditional TV programs (RTBF, 1982b, p. 7). This reluctance is mainly due to reasons such as that teletext is regarded as too slow in providing its information and that this information is poor and often not up-to-date.

In Flanders, more people seem to use teletext. There, the conceptualization of this medium took both the specific features of its technology and the audience's needs more adequately into account. In addition, "Teletekst" allows the presentation of important news as subtitles of the TV program on air—a service highly appreciated by the audience. In a 1983 survey, more than half of the respondents claimed to use "Teletekst" at least 15 minutes per day. Eight to nine pages were said to be looked at on an average. It seems, however, as if people use "Teletekst" because they bought a new TV set that happened to have a built-in decoder. Only 6% had purchased their decoder independently and on purpose (de Meyer, Fauconnier, & Hendriks, 1984, p. 46). Almost all "Teletekst" users also consult the Dutch system, and more than half of them use the British and West German teletext services.

## The Use of the Videocassette Recorder

A 1984 survey showed that a VCR was used for about 7 hours per week on an average—mostly to tape television programs. So, buying a VCR obviously means an attempt to bridge the gap between the offering available thanks to cable and the actual reception. The Nielsen Company estimates that the number of blank cassettes in use for each VCR has been rapidly growing, from four in 1980 to nine in 1985. In 1984, less than half of all the VCR owners in Belgium had viewed prerecorded cassettes. The inhabitants of the French-speaking area, however, proved to have consumed considerably more of those cassettes than the ones in Flanders. A study conducted by the RTBF research bureau in April of 1986 shows that, in Wallonia, the renting and exchanging of cassettes (72% of the respondents) was catching up with the viewing of taped television material (87 %). The latter function of the VCR is still dominant in the Dutch-speaking part of the country, however.

In general, VCR owners rent movie cassettes and tape a little bit of everything on TV—entertainment shows as well as documentaries or sports programs. The genres preferred vary somewhat according to geographical regions, although everywhere adventure, detective, and science fiction movies are liked best, and documentaries are somewhat neglected. In Flanders, adventure, erotic, and pornographic films attract more viewers; in Wallonia and in Brussels, comedies and fantasy movies are liked better (Table 3.9).

So, both rental cassettes and taped TV programs are mostly used to get more of what has already been consumed heavily on TV and in movie theaters, that is, above all, fiction. The movies most asked for remain the ones that have already

TABLE 3.9

Proportion of Rental Cassette Genres by Area

|  | Flanders % | Brussels % | Wallonia % | Total % |
|---|---|---|---|---|
| Adventure, detective movies | 21.1 | 20.8 | 15.1 | 18.9 |
| Comedies | 8.9 | 12.3 | 12.9 | 11.6 |
| Documentaries | 2.9 | 1.2 | 4.6 | 2.8 |
| Erotic movies | 14.9 | 7.6 | 7.2 | 10.0 |
| Fantasy, horror, science fiction | 13.1 | 18.6 | 19.3 | 17.3 |
| Children's movies | 5.9 | 6.9 | 6.4 | 6.4 |
| Pornography | 13.4 | 13.3 | 10.1 | 11.6 |

Note: From Mediatheque de la Communaute francaise (1985).

filled movie theaters. Outside the realm of education, documentary and education-al series, as well as artistic movies, are rarely rented or bought. Also, the produc-tion and distribution companies, mistrusting the small Belgian market, do not take chances. Some companies, however, such as Belga Films Video, or institutions with some educational goals, at least started to develop an alternative production. For example, since 1983, the "Mediatheque de la Communaute Francaise de Bel-gique" has tried to bridge the gap between creators and works outside the commer-cial circle and the audience that is mostly attracted by the big international produc-tions. Except for those initiatives, one has to admit that both production and dis-tribution of video films is dominated by the big multinational companies, such as Warner Home Video, RCA, CBS Fox, Cinema, and Thorn-EMI Video.

The linguistic and cultural separation of Belgium renders this country par-ticularly attractive for foreign companies: Brussels and Wallonia are very depend-ent on French companies, whereas Flanders is more inclined toward Anglo-Saxon programs. Plus, in the south of the country, people ask for movies dubbed in French, whereas the audience in the north readily accepts the less costly subtitled version of movies.

As was already mentioned, the expansion of the video market allows the audience to get more of what it got already. It also allows the audience to consume in a different way. In many cases, the purchase of video equipment is caused by the desire to be freed from the impositions of the programming and the schedule. Cable conditions people to avoid less attractive programs, to watch programs they missed because of the competition on cable, at otherwise "empty" times (the use of TV5 is quite revealing in that respect), and to organize the evening according to individual tastes.

The increasing use of VCRs is related to the increasing desire to determine one's own leisure time according to increasingly individualized norms. As a con-sequence of this development, the mere expansion of time spent in front of the TV screen has stopped: in 1973, the average time spent watching TV was 2.5 hours; in 1977, however, it had decreased to 2.25 hours and seems to have remained stable ever since.

These averages do not mirror the total reality, however. They mask profound disparities. The previously mentioned survey of cultural activities in French-speak-ing Belgium, for instance, shows that 36.9% of the respondents watched television for less than 10 hours a week, 37.9% spent between 10 and 19 hours in front of the screen, and 24.3% even watched for 20 hours or more—three levels of TV con-sumption that are related to very different backgrounds and needs.

One of the three groups, the *heavy TV viewers*, shows little selective behavior and concentrates on one channel mainly (in many cases, on RTL). Their use of other media is fairly weak: They rarely read newspapers and magazines, they do not like to listen to the radio. These are mostly the elderly and the less educated. More often they are blue-collar workers. For this social group, television seems to fill a cultural and social gap almost completely. Now that cable is available, they are not even forced to select anymore.

The *medium viewers*, spending 10-19 hours a week in front of the TV screen, are more selective, trying to balance their viewing in terms of both the channels and the contents available. But although they are quite willing to watch more sophisticated programs, they still consume much more entertainment than information. This group uses cable and VCRs (if in the household) more extensively than the "heavy viewers" group. In its selection behavior, however, fictional materials are still favored.

The *light viewers*, watching less than 10 hours per week, differ from others by their fairly negative attitude toward television. Some regard TV as an instrument of stultification, some see it as not very interesting or enlightening—in any case, TV does not seem to fulfill their needs. This very selective part of the audience spends more leisure time outside the home and wants to be integrated in a broader social network.

These are attitudes mainly to be found among younger and better-educated people wishing to structure their leisure time activities considering all the possibilities available to them and their wider range of interests. They even try to work out a sort of "ecology" of their leisure time. Openness toward high culture, exercise of the body, and social contacts have much higher priorities for them than for the two other groups. Time spent listening to music, on sports activities, on meeting friends, and on dining out makes much more sense to them than the absorption of TV programs imposed on them. Among this group, we find the listeners of those local radio stations broadcasting mostly uninterrupted music, and the fans of video.

Video use is not uniform in this group, however. Some increase their movie consumption through video, others use video for further integration into social groups. This latter aspect is particularly important among adolescents. They have tended to replace group listening to rock music records with "video nights." Their preference for violent and erotic videocassettes indicates attempts both to break norms and to mature socially.

## CONCLUSIONS

Does the accelerating expansion of the video market endanger the balanced system of media use? The almost total supply of Belgian homes with cable in the 1970s had led to a repartitioning of the audience between the channels. Also, the selective behavior of the audience had changed according to the enlarged offering, particularly to more entertainment. Simultaneously, the consumption of high culture and information programs had decreased. The policy of the national public broadcasting systems, to secure educational programs an important role, has not shown remarkable effects.

The abundance of the TV offering has also led to a reallocation of temporal and financial resources. Between 1984 and 1986, for instance, the Belgian newspapers lost 200,000 readers. Also, the proportion of Belgian households' expenses on entertainment outside their homes dropped dramatically, from .86% in 1960 to .26% in 1975 and .18% in 1984 (Institut National des Statistiques, 1960 ff.).

The most noticeable decrease doubtlessly concerns movie attendance. Statistics show a drop of more than 25 percentage points in the number of moviegoers between 1974 and 1984, hardly explainable by a decrease in household income or by the repercussions of the economic crisis. As Michel Jaumain and Guy Vandenbulcke (1986) in their analysis of cinema use in Belgium have demonstrated, the three waves of an eroding movie audience coincide with important expansions of the audio-visual equipment:

- 1957-64: the number of black and white TV sets multiplies by 7.
- 1964-67: the number of black and white TV sets is raised by another 35.4%.
- 1972-79: the increase in the number of color TV sets accelerates and reaches 54.9% of the total ownership of TV sets.

Finally, the last strong decrease of movie attendance has developed parallel to the rapid expansion of the video market.

The increased use of VCRs will certainly contribute to a broadening gap between a program scheme trying to provide viewers with information, and an "a la carte," fragmentized one serving the audience's need for fictional material. In this process TV risks to lose some of its entertainment functions the same way radio did by the end of the 1950s.

Whatever the growth of video will be like in the next years, it seems to have little chance to fundamentally endanger the balance that the most dynamic groups of society have established between their indoor activities based on a diversified and complementary use of the media and their activities outside their homes based on a need for social contacts—a need that has seemingly grown stronger in the recent years of crises and insecurities.

## NOTES

[1] This chapter was translated from the original French by Marianne and Klaus Schoenbach.

## REFERENCES

Apeldoorn, R. van (1985). Les televisions locales et communautaires [Local and community TV stations]. *Courrier Hebdomadaire du CRISP*, 1075-1076.

BRT Studiedienst (1985). *Quelques aspects des sondages en 1984* [Some aspects of the surveys in 1984].

BRT Studiedienst (1986). *Enkele facetten van het kijk- en luisteronderzoek in 1985* [Some aspects of the viewer and listener survey in 1985].

Caron, A. (1977). Les frontieres culturelles de l'imagerie televisuelle [The cultural boundaries of TV pictures]. In *Violence in Television Films and News: Report of the Royal Commission on Violence in the Communication Industry*. Toronto, Canada.

Caron, A., Souchon, M., & Thoveron, G. (1981). Trois semaines—sept pays— vingt-six chaines de television [Three weeks—seven countries—26 TV channels]. *Les Cahiers de la Communication, 1*, 37-50.

Geerts, C. (1979). Heures et malheurs du journal televise [Hours and accidents of the "journal televise"]. *Cahiers JEB, 1*, 177-185.

Geerts, C., & Thoveron, J. (1979). *Television offerte au public, television regardee par les publics ou les effets du cable* [Television offered to the audience, television watched by the audience, or: The impact of cable]. (Enquete permanente sur les programmes, S.T.V. 48). Brussels: RTBF.

Institut National de Statistiques. (1960 ff.) *Comptes nationaux, Consommation privee* [National surveys: Private consumption].

Jaumain, M., & Vandenbulcke, G. (1986). L'exploitation cinematographique en Belgique: Audience et mutation de l'offre [The exploitation of the Belgian cinema: Audience and changes in offerings]. *Courrier Hebdomadaire du CRISP*, 1129-1130.

Klein, L. (1984). *Approche d'une television communautaire dans la region de Charleroi: Analyse de son impact sur la population, de son observation a l'action dans les emissions* [Test of a community television in the area of Charleroi: An analysis of its impact on the population and of a participant observation during the programs]. Mons: Universite de Mons.

Les televisions francophones. (1980). Etude comparee: France, Belgique, Quebec [Francophone TV. A comparative study: France, Belgium, Quebec] *Cahiers JEB, 2*, 147.

Mediatheque de la Communaute francaise. (1985). *Rapport sur la distribution des videocassettes dans la Communaute francaise de Belgique* [A report about the distribution of video cassettes in the French region of Belgium]. Brussels.

Meyer, G. de, Fauconnier, G., & Hendriks, A. (1984). *Het gebruik van teletekst in Vlaanderen* [The use of teletext in Flanders]. Leuven: Katholieke Universiteit, Centrum voor Communicatiewetenschapen.

Pichault, F. (1985). La telematique dans le cadre reglementaire et institutionel de la Belgique [Telematics within the legal and institutional framework of Belgium]. *Courrier Hebdomadaire du CRISP*, 1101-1102.

RTBF, bureau d'etudes. (1982a). *Enquete permanente* [Continuous survey] (S.T.V. 65).

RTBF, bureau d'etudes. (1982b). *Les elections communales du 10 octobre 1982* [The local elections of October 10, 1982]. (Enquete permanente sur les programmes, S.T.V. 62).

RTBF, bureau d'etudes. (1983). *Teletexte: Enquete menee durant la semaine de 7 au 13 mars 1983* [Teletext: A survey during the week of March 7-13, 1983] (Enquete permanente sur les programmes, S.T.V. 70).

RTBF, bureau d'etudes. (1985). *TV5: Resultats des sondages effectues en Belgique francophone du 2 au 29 septembre 1985 par panel postal* [TV5: Results of mail surveys conducted in French-speaking Belgium, September 2-29, 1985].

RTBF, bureau d'etudes. (1986a). *Enquete permanente* [Continuous survey] (S.T.V. 98).

RTBF bureau d'etudes. (1986b). *L'equipement en radio television dans la partie francophone du pays* [Equipment with radio and television in the French-speaking part of the country]. (Enquete permanente, S.T.V. 97).

Souchon, M. (1977). *La television et son public* [Television and its audience] Paris: INA.

Thoveron, G., & Huens, M. (1985). *La Radio et la television* [Radio and Television].

United Nations Education and Science Organization. (1981). *Trois semaines de television. Une comparaison internationale: Belgique, Bulgarie, Canada, France, Hongrie, Italie et Japon* [Three weeks of television. An international comparison: Belgium, Bulgaria, Canada, France, Hungary, Italy and Japan].

Universite Libre. (1986). *Les pratiques culturelles dans la communaute francaise* [Cultural practices in the French region]. Brussels: Universite Libre.

# 4

# The U.K.: Measured Expansion on a Variety of Fronts

**Barrie Gunter**
*Independent Broadcasting Authority*

The 1980s have been a decade of unprecedented media expansion in the United Kingdom, marked by technological developments that have brought a wide range of new media channels and equipment within the grasp of the ordinary consumer. The most significant developments have occurred in broadcast and electronic media. Increasingly, homes have come to possess not just one, but two, three, or even more television sets. Furthermore, the set has acquired a range of accessories and attachments such as videocassette recorders (VCRs), personal computers, and remote controls, which have significantly modified the way it is used (Independent Broadcasting Authority, 1986, 1987).

This same period has witnessed the expansion of broadcast television services with the introduction of a new fourth channel in November 1982 and two early morning news and talk shows on both major channels (BBC1 and ITV) in January 1983. The further extension of broadcasting hours during the day and throughout the night has also begun. Teletext information services appeared in 1980 on the two main channels and have since become available on the two minority channels (BBC2 and Channel Four). In addition to these *broadcasting* developments, the 1980s saw the inception of the concept of *narrowcasting* in the U.K., with the emergence mid-decade of the first localized cable television services.

As well as being a decade of increased variety and choice of home media, the 1980s have also seen viewers gain greater control over entertainment in the home. Perhaps the most significant new electronic media phenomenon during this period has been the emergence of the VCR, or, as it is called in the U.K., home video.

Video recorders now give viewers, who were once totally at the mercy of the broadcasters' television schedules, the capacity to control for themselves when to watch the programs they most like to watch.

The 1980s have not been a period of growth for all mass media, however. As television, the VCR, and various other appendages have acquired increasing prominence and popularity, certain other traditionally popular sources of information and entertainment have, in the face of this extra competition for people's leisure time, either suffered loss of custom (e.g., cinema) or have had to change the nature of the service they provide, their styles, and their emphases, in order to survive. At this time, we appear to be on the verge of a new era in mass communications, heralding radical changes to traditional patterns of media use and promising new modes of amusement and edification.

This chapter examines the growth of electronic media in the U.K. during the 1980s. Its focus is on developments in broadcast television, cable television, and home video, all of which have had some impact on the way people use their television sets. As the range of media and media accessories grows, so too does the complexity of decision-making by media consumers in choosing how to divide their time between the various media options that are available. The technological developments that have given rise to this media diversification have progressed rapidly and left behind research into their impact on users' behavior. Although reliable growth trend statistics are available for various electronic media services, research that deals with the ways in which the uses of different media complement, supplant, or interact with each other is less advanced. This chapter examines available data for the U.K. and points the way to where more work needs to be done.

## TELEVISION IN THE HOME

Nearly every household in the U.K. contains at least one television set. The latest estimates indicate a nationwide penetration of around 98% of homes (Independent Broadcasting Authority, 1987). Since 1980, however, there has been a steady trend towards multiple set ownership; by 1985 over half of the population claimed to have more than one television set at home. As this trend continues, the old norm of one set per household is rapidly being left behind (Table 4.1).

The locations of television sets within the home have also changed (Fig. 4.1). Virtually everyone has a set in the main living room; the next most popular location is a bedroom (41%). Fewer than one in 10 has a set in the kitchen, or a dining room, or in any other room (Independent Broadcasting Authority, 1985).

TABLE 4.1

Number of TV Sets in U.K. Households: 1980-1986

|              | 1980 % | 1981 % | 1982 % | 1983 % | 1984 % | 1985 % | 1986 % |
|--------------|--------|--------|--------|--------|--------|--------|--------|
| Only one TV  | 67     | 66     | 61     | 54     | 51     | 45     | 44     |
| More than one| 33     | 34     | 39     | 46     | 49     | 54     | 56     |

Note: From Independent Broadcasting Authority (1986).

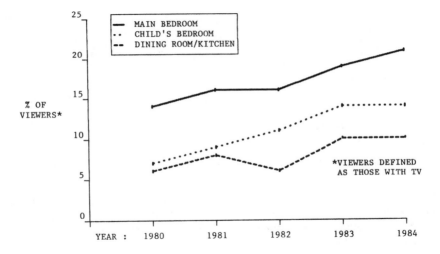

**FIG. 4.1.** Location of the sets outside main living room (IBA, 1985).

## ENHANCEMENT TO THE TV SETS

As a device used simply to receive off-air broadcasts, a television set is used for about 5 hours per day on average in the U.K. (Independent Broadcasting Authority, 1986). Nowadays though, there exists a range of accessories and enhancements that can be used in conjunction with a basic television set, which include video recorders, video disc players, teletext and viewdata services, video games, and home computers.

By 1985, half of the U.K. population was found to have at least one extra feature among a range of alternatives given (see Table 4.2). Most widespread was the

TABLE 4.2

TV-Related Equipment in the Home: 1985

|  | All Adults % | Adults With Children % |
|---|---|---|
| Have: |  |  |
| VCR | 38 | 51 |
| Home computer | 18 | 33 |
| Teletext | 17 | 17 |
| Video games | 9 | 15 |
| Cable TV | 1 | 2 |
| Video computer | 1 | 1 |
| Video disc player | * | * |
| Prestel/ Viewdata | * | * |
| Have one or more of these | 50 | 68 |
| Have none of these | 50 | 32 |

Note: From Independent Broadcasting Authority (1986).

VCR, with almost 4 in 10 having one. Just under one in five (17%) had a teletext receiver, a small increase on the previous year when it was at 14%. The growth of teletext penetration has been much steadier than the dramatic rise in VCR owner-ship. The ownership of home computers was found to be at around the same level as teletext, although nearly twice as extensive among homes with children. As with multiple-set ownership, the households most likely to have any television-based accessory equipment were those with children (Independent Broadcasting Authority, 1986).

Despite these important enhancements and, as we see in later sections of this chapter, despite the introduction of new television services bringing additional off-air broadcasts, the amount of television-watching done by the average viewer has not radically changed. The recent period of media development in the U.K. has not produced substantially increased volumes of viewing.

In making statements about television-use trends during this period of change, however, an important caveat must be kept in mind. The validity of trend viewing figures depends on the accuracy and consistency and comparability of measure-ment definitions and techniques over time. In the U.K., there have been significant changes in the way television audiences and viewing behavior are defined and measured that preclude uncontaminated trend analysis before and after these developments.

Until recently, television viewing was measured via set meters attached to the sets of some 3000 households that constitute a national viewing panel. The meter recorded information about when the television was switched on and the channel to which it was tuned at the time. In addition, householders of the panel filled in a viewing diary to indicate the times when they were present in front of the television when it was turned on. Recently, the diary component was replaced with a remote control device that has come to be known as a "Peoplemeter," through which householders can indicate electronically when they are present and watching television. In addition, some 2 years prior to the introduction of the "Peoplemeters," the definition of a program viewer had been changed. Prior to this change, an individual was categorized as being a viewer within any quarter-hour segment if he or she watched television for at least 8 minutes out of the 15. Subsequently a person was classifed as a viewer if he or she watched for at least 3 continuous minutes within a quarter-hour.

## THE CHANGING SHAPE OF BROADCAST TELEVISION: CHANNEL FOUR

Broadcast television in the United Kingdom is controlled by two bodies, the British Broadcasting Corporation (BBC) and the Independent Broadcasting Authority (IBA). The BBC runs two national television channels, BBC1 and BBC2. The former caters to the mass audience with a variety of popular drama, entertainment, educationally oriented and news programs, whereas the latter, although not exclusively devoted to, has specialized in programs of a more serious nature, with a minority appeal. The BBC is funded by money received from the government, which is raised through an annual tax or license fee that all television set owners are legally obliged to pay.

The IBA controls Independent Television (and Independent Local Radio). This system is financed by the sale of advertising time between and within television programs. At the present, the IBA is responsible for two television channels (ITV and Channel Four). ITV, however, is not a single entity, but a network of 15 separate companies selected and appointed under a fixed-term contract with the IBA to provide the ITV program service in 14 areas. (London is served by two companies; one for weekdays, one for weekends.)

In addition to the licensing of the regional ITV contractors, the IBA has additional responsibilities that include the supervision of program planning, control of advertising and the transmission of programs. Although not itself a maker of programs, the IBA is required through the Broadcasting Act of 1981 to ensure that programs provide a proper balance of information, education, and entertainment, a high general standard in all respects, accuracy in news, due impartiality in matters of political and industrial controversy, and the avoidance of offence to good taste and decency.

The 1980s brought an end to the three-channel television system in the U.K.. The publication and eventual enactment of the Broadcasting Bill in 1980 marked the end of nearly 2 decades of debate and uncertainty about a fourth television channel. The new service, which was placed under the responsibility of the IBA, was seen as having its own distinctive character. It would complement the ITV service and provide a choice of programs appealing to different minority interests. Special arrangements were also made for the service to be provided in Wales. Sianel Pedwar Cymru (S4C), the Welsh Fourth Channel, was created to carry all Welsh language programs on the fourth channel. Because there was a wish among Welsh-speaking people in the province to have programs in their own language, this special provision enabled all programs in Welsh to be concentrated on one channel. In addition, S4C relays most of Channel Four's programs each week, either simultaneously or rescheduled.

Channel Four marked a new departure in British broadcasting structures. It is advertising-financed, but is not solely dependent on the income it generates for itself. The IBA has overall responsibility for the channel, but the subsidiary—the Channel Four Television Company—has the task of providing the program service.

The new channel is statutorily obliged to encourage experimentation and innovation in the form and content of programs. It took a while, however, for the audience to become familiar with its new programs and scheduling. During its first year, the channel had a rough ride from the press, as its audiences failed to reach

TABLE 4.3

Average Daily Hours of TV Viewing (Individuals)*

|  | 1978 | 1979 | 1980 | 1981 | 1982 | 1983 | 1984 | 1985 |
|---|---|---|---|---|---|---|---|---|
| Total TV | 3.4 | 3.4 | 3.4 | 3.4 | 3.0 | 3.0 | 3.2 | 3.6 |
| BBC1 | 1.3 | 1.5 | 1.3 | 1.3 | 1.1 | 1.1 | 1.1 | 1.3 |
| BBC2 | 0.3 | 0.4 | 0.4 | 0.4 | 0.4 | 0.3 | 0.3 | 0.4 |
| ITV | 1.8 | 1.8 | 1.7 | 1.7 | 1.5 | 1.4 | 1.5 | 1.7 |
| Channel 4 |  |  |  |  |  | 0.1 | 0.2 | 0.3 |

Note: From AGB/BARB (1986).
* Excluding breakfast television.

target levels straight away. Nevertheless, as time went by, more and more people came to dip into it. After 2 years, it regularly reached 33% of all viewers each day and nearly 80% across an average week. These levels have been sustained ever since.

The average amount of time viewers spent watching Channel Four increased threefold from around 50 minutes per week in 1983 to more than 2 hours in 1985 (Table 4.3). At the same time, the Channel's weekly share of television audience increased from 4% to 7%, occasionally achieving 10%. Meanwhile, the share for the other minority channel, BBC2, remained constant, and it was those of the major channels, BBC1 and ITV, that suffered losses.

## TELEVISION IN THE EARLY MORNING

Traditionally, the U.K. is a country of radio listeners at the beginning of the day. Indeed, apart from special occasions, Open University course programs, and a limited experiment in the late 1970s, there were no television transmissions at breakfast time. This state of affairs suddenly changed in the early 1980s.

Television at breakfast time, as a regular service in the U.K., began on January 17, 1983, with the launch of BBC1's "Breakfast Time" program. Two weeks later, TV-am, the independent television contractor, took to the air with a program that, like the BBC's, offered an informal mixture of news, views, weather forecasts, gardening hints, and medical and consumer advice. Initially it had stars as presenters. TV-am is an independent company with the IBA contract to broadcast early morning programs between 6:15 a.m. and 9:25 a.m. on weekdays, and between 6:55 a.m. and 9:25 a.m. on Saturdays and Sundays on a nationwide basis. As with other ITV companies, its financial support derives from the sale of advertising time during its programs.

Whereas the BBC's program was to be a 5-day-a-week operation, TV-am offered broadcasts on weekends, too. Apart from a limited, 9-week experiment run by two ITV regional companies nearly 6 years earlier, and occasional broadcasts of special events (e.g., Olympics, World Cup), British viewers had no prior experience of watching television before 9:00 a.m. Breakfast viewing was therefore a new experience, requiring a change to customary early morning media habits.

In the space of 4 years, however, habits did change. This happened slowly at first. As Figs. 4.2 and 4.3 show, however, both the average numbers of viewers watching either program at any time and the numbers who tuned in at all across the week (reach) have grown steadily since the first year. The fortunes of TV-am in particular improved during this period (Gunter, 1986).

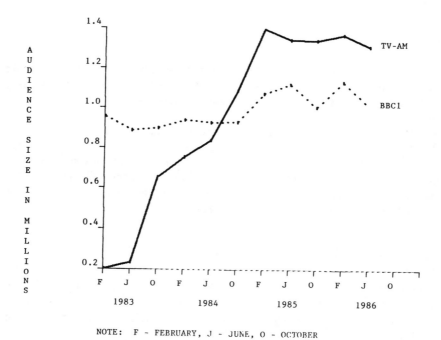

NOTE:   F - FEBRUARY,   J - JUNE,   O - OCTOBER

**FIG.4.2.** Average all quarter-hour audience for TV-AM and BBC1 1983-1986 (Gunter, 1986).

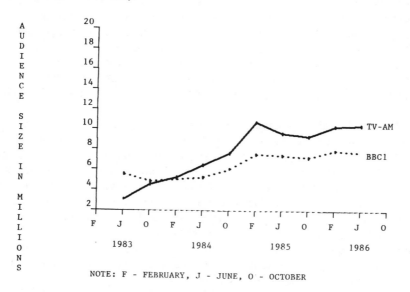

NOTE:   F - FEBRUARY,   J - JUNE,   O - OCTOBER

**FIG. 4.3.** Weekly reach (Monday-Friday) for TV-AM and BBC1 (Gunter, 1986).

Following an uncertain start in 1983, when the BBC's "Breakfast Time" dominated, TV-am's "Good Morning Britain" has experienced a steady audience growth. Since 1984, TV-am has consistently been the more watched breakfast program. Across the duration of its weekday editions, an average of more than 1.3 million people tuned in, with audiences routinely peaking at well over the 2 million mark. As Fig. 4.2 indicates, the latest viewing figures show the ITV station holding a commanding lead over the BBC.

Audience ratings indicate how many or what proportion of people in homes with TV sets watch the two breakfast television services. Another interesting question is how long, on average, viewers spend watching breakfast television. Both TV-am's "Good Morning Britain" and BBC's "Breakfast Time" present brief items, some of which (e.g., the news and weather bulletins) are repeated. It was understood even before transmissions began that most people watching at this time of the day would view only for brief spells of maybe 15-20 minutes at a stretch.

Figure 4.4 shows average viewing durations for both breakfast television services' Monday to Friday broadcasts from their beginning in 1983 to August 1986. During the first 3 years of breakfast television, total minutes viewed has more than doubled. This change is almost totally accounted for by the increase in amount

**FIG. 4.4.** Duration of watching breakfast television (total minutes viewed: Monday-Friday).

of viewing of TV-am, whose minutes viewed showed a fivefold increase. During its early days, viewers watched TV-am on average for about 5 minutes per day. During 1985, this figure had jumped to 25 minutes. During the first half of 1986, viewing duration for TV-am had averaged 26 minutes, about 10 minutes more than the average for the BBC.

The early mornings are a traditional time for peak radio usage in the U.K.. The question arises as to whether the new early morning television services have driven audiences away from listening to radio at this time of day. It is reasonable to assume that as the popularity and acceptability of watching television over breakfast grows, radio listening will become displaced. In 1985, one in five radio listeners said their listening had been reduced because they now watched some breakfast television, a proportion unaltered from that found in 1984 and 1983 (Independent Broadcasting Authority, 1986). Most of these people said that their early morning radio listening had been reduced either by a little or a lot (89% of those acknowledging a reduction). Few, however, said that they no longer listened to radio at all at this time. Only 15% of those who said that breakfast television had changed their listening said they had stopped listening altogether, and they represented less than 1 in 20 of all radio listeners. This latter figure was unchanged from that found in 1984, suggesting that although radio listening in the mornings had declined to some extent since the onset of early morning television, the decline had ended. Most radio listeners still claimed to be unaffected in their listening patterns as a direct result of the introduction of breakfast television services.


**TELETEXT**


In addition to traditional broadcast services, the television networks in the U.K. offer other information services via teletext. On the two major channels, these services are called Ceefax (BBC1) and Oracle (ITV). Teletext services are also provided on BBC2 (by Ceefax) and Channel Four (by 4-Tel). Oracle and 4-Tel are independent contractors with a fixed-term franchise with the IBA to provide these services. All offer a range of information, in page form, covering news (headlines and background), travel information, retail prices and availability, financial reporting, weather, cooking advice, gardening, and so on. Each page of information is accessed by the viewer calling up the page number (given in an index page) and can be held and read at leisure.

A more complex, interactive system (viewdata) also is available. This is not a broadcast system as such, because information is displayed on an adapted television set using a telephone line to gain access to a computer "library." Viewdata or videotext, known in the U.K. as Prestel, offers a range of information services similar to teletext but also incorporating advertising and other material to give a wider range than teletext. The British Telecom operates Prestel. From a negligible penetration in 1980, by 1986 some 17% of householders claimed to have a teletext receiver (Independent Broadcasting Authority, 1986). Svennevig (1981/2) reported that towards the end of 1981, 76% of the U.K. population had heard of teletext. Greenberg (1986) found that teletext users in Britain were more likely to be from higher social classes proportionately than were the television audience members in general. The main reasons for acquiring a teletext set were because a friend had such a set (35%) and because of advertisements for teletext (31%). A friend's influence was distinctly stronger in terms of the degree of its influence; 12% said it was of "much" influence, compared to 4% for advertisements.

Two thirds of teletext households had more than one television set; 16% had three sets. The teletext set was most often located in the lounge, as the main set of the house. Remote control is a constant factor for teletext sets, because the remote hand unit is needed to operate the set. Greenberg also found that teletext is used more often during peak viewing hours between 7:00 and 10:00 p.m. than at any other time. Nearly two thirds of all users use it at that time. A near majority also access it between 4:00 and 7:00 p.m. Far fewer use it earlier in the day. Therefore, patterns of teletext use run parallel to the use of other broadcast television services. Most of teletext use is goal-directed. Two thirds of the time, individuals are seeking some specific information, and about a quarter of the time they are just browsing.

Daily use of teletext was commonplace. Sixty-eight percent of Oracle fans were daily users compared with 53% of Ceefax fans. Typically, teletext was examined once (32%) or twice (25%) each day that it was accessed, and this was done equivalently by preferrers of Oracle and Ceefax. Viewing sessions averaged 9-10 minutes; 79% of all sessions with teletext were 10 minutes or less.

During the typical viewing session with teletext, users looked at two or three different topical sections. Within these sessions, the number of pages examined was irregularly distributed; 23% looked at 1 or 2 pages, and 23% looked at more than 10 pages each session. Heavier users (i.e., those who use teletext daily) tend also to access more pages.

Which topics do teletext users use most? Among Oracle users, the sections mentioned most often were TV guide (61%), weather/travel (55%), news (47%), and sport (45%). Among users of Ceefax, these sections featured once again as the ones accessed most often: weather/travel (64%), TV/radio guide (62%), news (53%), and sport (50%). Mostly, users went to specific pages and knew what they wanted.

Although no special analyses on other media use were done with teletext users, they were asked to make some comparisons. Because teletext competes with other media that provide parallel services, for example, news, sports, weather, television program information, and so on, it was of interest to assess the preferences expressed by teletext users across these media. This was done by asking "whether you think the newspaper, television, teletext, or radio is best for each of these things?" Teletext was most often preferred over television, newspapers or radio for travel information (61%) and as a TV guide (50%). Teletext users thought that television was best for entertainment (77%), children's use (55%), and weather (46%).

Thirty-seven percent of teletext users had a home computer, as compared with general estimates of 18% (Independent Broadcasting Authority, 1986). Four out of five used their television receiver as the computer video display unit, although heavy teletext users were more likely to have a separate monitor.

## DEVELOPMENTS IN HOME VIEWING

The 1980s have seen significant changes in the character of use of the television set at home. Although viewing levels have remained fairly constant over the first half of the decade, with individuals in the U.K. watching television on average for 3.5 hours a day, the nature of the behaviors has altered in certain important respects. We have already seen that there has been a steady but continuous increase in homes with more than one television set (Independent Broadcasting Authority, 1987). An even more significant factor, perhaps, has been the rapid penetration of home video recorders between 1980 and 1985.

In 1979, only a tiny percentage of homes in the U.K. had a VCR. But within the next 6 years, VCRs had been acquired by around 40% of all homes—and more than half of the homes with children (Independent Broadcasting Authority, 1986).

TABLE 4.4

Frequency and Type of Video Use

|  | For Viewing Self-Recorded Programs % | For Viewing Rented Films % |
|---|---|---|
| More than once a week | 73 | 15 |
| About once a week | 12 | 14 |
| Less than once a week | 7 | 35 |
| Hardly ever/never | 9 | 36 |

Note: Base = 962 VCR users. From Independent Broadcasting Authority (1987).

Home video provides an alternative to viewing off-air broadcasts. The most popular use of VCRs by far is to record programs off-air for viewing at a more convenient time. Recent data indicate that whereas one in three individuals with a VCR said they "never" or "hardly ever" rent prerecorded material, less than 1 in 10 said this in the case of recording programs themselves (Table 4.4).

What types of programs do video users record? By far the most commonly reported use is to record films, followed by soap operas. Further down the list come documentaries, sports, and single plays or dramas (Table 4.5). There are also differences found between demographic groups' claimed tastes in recording. Soap operas are particularly popular for recording among younger adults, women, and people with children. The latter demographic groups are also more likely to record children's programs. Films are most popular among young adults, whereas sports are best liked by men (Independent Broadcasting Authority, 1987).

Further U.K. research has revealed that VCR users generally intend to view off-air recordings fairly quickly so that tapes can be re-cycled and used for further recordings. Some VCR households have been found to build their own tape libraries, however. The significance of video for most people seems to be that it

TABLE 4.5

Types of Programs Recorded

|  | All with VCR % | Age: 16-34 % | 35-55 % | 55+ % | Sex: Men % | Women % | Adults with Children % |
|---|---|---|---|---|---|---|---|
| Films | 68 | 71 | 68 | 56 | 67 | 68 | 70 |
| Soap Operas | 46 | 56 | 40 | 34 | 34 | 56 | 51 |
| Documentaries | 27 | 18 | 35 | 32 | 29 | 25 | 25 |
| Sports | 22 | 18 | 25 | 24 | 29 | 16 | 20 |
| Plays/Drama | 18 | 16 | 19 | 22 | 15 | 20 | 18 |
| Adventure/Police | 9 | 10 | 7 | 10 | 11 | 8 | 10 |
| Children's programs | 11 | 16 | 9 | 3 | 8 | 14 | 17 |
| Comedy | 8 | 8 | 9 | 6 | 10 | 6 | 8 |
| Cartoons | 5 | 8 | 4 | 1 | 5 | 6 | 8 |
| Current Affairs | 2 | 1 | 4 | 3 | 4 | 1 | 2 |
| News | 2 | 1 | 3 | 1 | 2 | 1 | 2 |
| Other types/not classifiable | 16 | 10 | 8 | 13 | 10 | 10 | 10 |
| "It depends" | 2 | 3 | 4 | 8 | 6 | 3 | 3 |

Note: From Independent Broadcasting Authority (1987).

gives them greater control over when to watch television programs and films. Watching video is seen as providing an enjoyable way for the family to spend time together, and saves the trouble and expense of going to the cinema. The most serious problem people had with their home videos was lacking the time to view all of the programs that they had taped (Gunter & Levy, 1986).

## IMPACT OF VCR ON CONVENTIONAL TV VIEWING

Descriptive statistics concerning the penetration and use of video recorders paint a remarkable picture of a rapidly changing media environment. However, what is perhaps an even more interesting issue, and one of considerable importance to broadcasters, concerns the impact the VCR has had on conventional television viewing.

In Britain, this became an especially sensitive issue when the Broadcasters Audience Research Board (BARB) reported a big reduction in viewing in the autumn of 1982 compared to 1981. Was this caused by VCR usage? At the time, BARB did not have the technical facility to measure VCR impact on television viewing. In particular, it became known that people were widely using their VCRs as tuners during live TV viewing. People with remote controls for their VCRs who did not have one for their TV sets could and often did choose to view using the VCR as the receiver, giving them a remote channel-switching facility while watching material off-air. Because the eletronic viewing meters ceased to function when the VCRs were used in this way, these live viewers were lost to the system and were recorded as nonviewers.

A BARB special analysis, issued in 1982, attempted to explain the extent to which viewing losses could be attributed to VCR use. This assessment concluded that up to half of the "loss" in live viewing was probably due to video usage. Of the 7% decline in hours of viewing per home, BARB estimated that 2% could be accounted for in terms of live viewing via the VCR tuner, 1.5% in terms of time-shift viewing of self-recorded programs, and 0.5% in terms of watching prerecorded tapes.

## CABLE TELEVISION

In some parts of the country, during 1985, a number of further television services became available via cable. By December 1985, over 976,000 homes were within reach of cable. Of these, just over 126,000 actually subscribed to cable TV channels—12.9% of potential cable homes. Surveys in March and November of that year conducted by the medium's audience research body, Joint Industry Committee for Cable Audience Research (JICCAR), showed that although cable uptake in penetrated areas was rather disappointing, cable homes were watching more of cable-only channels at the expense of BBC and ITV services. There was also a growth in the share of viewing time devoted to cable TV in cabled households—21% of all viewing in November compared with 18% in March (Joint Industry Committee for Cable Audience Research, 1985). The predominant cable programming is movies, popular music, news, sports, and children's programming, with movies being the most popular.

Although cable uptake has not so far been as extensive as cable operators would like to see, research undertaken in cable homes has indicated that cable services have a substantial impact on patterns of viewing among subscribers. Comparisons were made between cable and non-cable homes in the same areas (AGB Cable and Viewdata, 1986). Altogether, respondents in the sample watched an average of 4.50 hours of television daily. The average amount of daily viewing was greater in cable homes (5.46 hours) than in noncable homes (4.32 hours). Viewing is heaviest of all in cable homes with VCRs (5.55 hours). The presence of both VCRs and cable television added to the amount of television that people watched. VCR usage was slightly greater in noncable homes (0.55 hours daily) than in cable homes (0.51 hours), however. As Table 4.6 shows, in cable homes, cable television services occupy easily the greatest percentage share of total viewing time (40%).

For each daypart, at least one quarter of all viewing is to cable specialist services rather than to the broadcast services also carried by cable. During the mornings, young children's viewing accounts for much of the cable use, but the rest of day it is adults' viewing. After 10:00 p.m. is found the most dramatic impact—largely accounted for by cable film channels. But even during prime time (7:00 to 10:00 p.m.), cable makes a large dent in the broadcasters' share of overall viewing. The brunt of cable seems to be borne by the BBC rather than by ITV. However, the ITV/Channel Four share is also reduced substantially (Table 4.6).

VCR usage data in cable households indicate that a great deal of video use is devoted to time-shift recording of cable television programs, particularly from film channels. Television viewing in family households with cable and video was greater when there were young children around. Cable subscribing households with children (aged up to 9 years) and that had VCRs watched 5.58 hours of television daily, compared with an average of 5.35 hours for all cable-plus-video homes. Cable channels attained a greater share of total television viewing time in households with children aged up to 9 years (50%), compared with cable households generally (40%). The presence of video in cable homes with young children, however, reduced cable's share (43%) with 10% of viewing time being taken up by video playback.

TABLE 4.6

Percentage Share of Viewing at Different Times of Day
In Cable-Using Households

|  | ITV/ C4 | BBC1 BBC2 | All Cable Services | Types of Cable Service Most Used |
|---|---|---|---|---|
| 7:00-9:00 am | 38 | 11 | 51 | Children's Channel |
| 9:00 am-1:00 pm | 27 | 13 | 60 | Children's Channel |
| 1:00 pm-3:00 pm | 44 | 28 | 28 | Children's/Music Box |
| 3:00 pm-5:00 pm | 47 | 27 | 26 | Premiere (Films) |
| 5:00 pm-7:00 pm | 48 | 26 | 26 | Premiere (Films) |
| 7:00 pm-10:00 pm | 39 | 26 | 35 | Premiere (Films) |
| 10:00 pm-Mid. | 30 | 20 | 51 | Premiere (Films) |
| Midnight-3 am | 17 | 10 | 74 | Premiere (Films) |
| All hours share in cable households | 38 | 22 | 40 |  |
| All hours share in noncable households | 49 | 51 | - |  |

Note: From AGB Cable and Viewdata (1986).

## THE FUTURE

The 1980s have been a period of continuing development and growth in both the availability and the use of mass media. This chapter has indicated a few of the more significant areas of media diversification and expansion in the U.K. and how audiences have responded. The near future heralds further media growth. British broadcasters have plans to extend transmissions on all four television networks so that by 1990 round-the-clock television will be available. A new daytime service has begun on BBC1, and experiments with late-night and 'through the night' broadcasts have been conducted by parts of the ITV system. Home ownership of teletext receivers, VCRs, and personal computers continues to increase. And if all this were not already enough, the prospect of further multiples of television channels broadcast direct by satellite by both domestic and foreign services looms large.

The main goal of this chapter has been not simply to assess the extent and ways in which new media services and associated accessory equipment have been used, but also to say something, where data are available, about the impact they

TABLE 4.7

Distribution of TV Use

| | Watching Live Broadcasts | | | Watching Recorded Broadcasts | | | Watching Hired Video Material | | | Using Teletext | | | Using Video Games/Home Computers | | |
|---|---|---|---|---|---|---|---|---|---|---|---|---|---|---|---|
| | '83 % | '84 % | '85 % | '83 % | '84 % | '85 % | '83 % | '84 % | '85 % | '83 % | '84 % | '85 % | '83 % | '84 % | '85 % |
| **Hours spent per average day:** | | | | | | | | | | | | | | | |
| 4 or more | 41 | 49 | 42 | 42 | 1 | 1 | 2 | 1 | 1 | 0 | 0 | 0 | 0 | 0 | 0 |
| 2-4 | 40 | 37 | 41 | 5 | 7 | 2 | 4 | 5 | 4 | 1 | 1 | 1 | 3 | 0 | 1 |
| 1-2 | 5 | 3 | 4 | 8 | 11 | 12 | 10 | 16 | 13 | 6 | 9 | 8 | 2 | 3 | 4 |
| Less than 1 Never use/ don't know | 1 | 0 | 0 | 78 | 69 | 66 | 81 | 73 | 77 | 91 | 89 | 88 | 95 | 95 | 94 |

Note: Video games and home computers refer specifically to those which require the use of a television set as a monitor. From Independent Broadcasting Authority (1986).

have had on the use of existing broadcast television services. As the media menu grows and offers a wider range of choices, so consumers need to give more thought to how they will allocate their available time to different media.

The relative impact of television-based activities on actual viewing of broadcasts can be judged from analysis of viewers' estimates of the amounts of time spent on a range of these activities. Over 4 in 10 claimed to spend at least 4 hours a day watching television broadcasts "live," far more than claimed similar amounts of time devoted to the remaining possibilities. However, almost one in four of all viewers claim to watch recordings of programs for at least 1 hour a day on average (Table 4.7).

Over the years, the amounts of time spent using video have increased, because more people have acquired VCRs for themselves. Most of those who claim to use video (or teletext, games, or home computers) estimated relatively small amounts of time—up to 2 hours a day on average or less—whereas the majority of broadcast viewing claims were greater than 2 or more hours per day (Independent Broadcasting Authority, 1986).

What is not yet clear is whether the time devoted to nonbroadcast uses of the television set is taken from a fixed "viewing budget" or whether further free time is being gleaned from other daily activities such as housework, hobbies, chores, and so on. Speculating about possible effects of one medium on another, recent attitudinal data suggest that VCR use may be negatively related to an inclination to go the cinema. Increased use of the VCR to play prerecorded tapes was found to be associated with the opinion that having a VCR saves one the trouble and expense of going out to the cinema. This perceived advantage of having a VCR was reflected in the reported behavior of the sample of video householders investigated in this survey. More than 80% had not gone out to the cinema even once in the 3 months prior to the interview, and most of the remainder had seen only one or two movies outside their homes (Levy & Gunter, 1987).

If, from a practical point of view, the decisions facing consumers with regard to how to spread their time between the ever-increasing array of media is complicated, the problems facing mass communications researchers in devising ways effectively to measure this behavior are even more complex. Many of the findings reported in this chapter have derived from studies or data bases where the use of perhaps two or three media sources were explored. Often, the impact of levels of use of one source on the extent of use of another has been the limit to which comparisons were made. But media consumers' behaviors in a multi-media environment need to be examined in a multi-dimensional fashion. To what extent do different media sources cluster together in the way they are used? It is clear that a great deal more thought will have to be given to this problem by researchers in academic and commercial sectors if we are to begin to understand how different media interact with, complement, or supplant each other.

A recent study of media use among children in the U.K. has revealed that there are those who are media-rich and those (far fewer in number) who are media-poor. The media-poor tend to make do with fewer sources of amusement. Among media-rich children, however, the new media are not totally replacing the old. Children who played with new electronic media such as video, personal computers, or teletext, for example, still read newspapers and magazines. Although some displacement of the old by the new was indicated, it was believed to happen when a new medium provides the same gratification as an old one, but in a more attractive package. For example, total amount of television viewing appeared to make no difference to reading books, comics, magazines, or newspapers, but children who watched more television drama read fewer comics (Gunter & Greenberg, 1986). In today's multi-media era, therefore, people may be learning to identify certain special benefits and gratifications that can be derived from different media, and choose which one, out of the many that are available, to go to according to their needs at a particular time.

## REFERENCES

AGB/BARB. (1986). *Trends in television.* London: Audits of Great Britain/Broadcasters Audience Research Board.

AGB Cable and Viewdata. (1986). *The 1986 cable monitor.* London: AGB Cable and Viewdata Ltd.

Greenberg, B. S. (1986). *Patterns of teletext use.* London: Independent Broadcasting Authority Special Report.

Gunter, B. (1986). *The audience for TV-am.* London: Independent Broadcasting Authority Special Report.

Gunter, B., and Greenberg, B. (1986, October 10). Media-wise. *Times Educational Supplement.*

Gunter, B., & Levy, M. R. (1986, April 28). Transmission control. *The Times Educational Supplement.*

Independent Broadcasting Authority. (1985). *Attitudes to broadcasting in 1984.* London: IBA.

Independent Broadcasting Authority. (1986). *Attitudes to broadcasting in 1985.* London: IBA.

Independent Broadcasting Authority. (1987). *Attitudes to broadcasting in 1986.* London: IBA.

Joint Industry Committee for Cable Audience Research. (1985). London: JICCAR.

Levy, M. R., & Gunter, B. (1987). *Home video and the changing nature of the television audience.* London: IBA and John Libbey and Company, Ltd.

Svennevig, M. (1981/2). Ceefax, public awareness and knowledge: The effects of publicity. In *Annual Review of BBC Broadcasting Research Findings No. 8* (pp. 107-114). London: British Broadcasting Corporation.

# 5

# The U.K.: The Constancy of Audience Behavior

**Joseph Mallory Wober**
*Independent Broadcasting Authority*

Change is a metaphor for optimism in most Western societies, as it is felt to be synonymous with growth, the process of establishment, and enhancement of life, and is therefore unquestionably good. However, not all change corresponds to growth; in many non-Western cultures, there is an equally acute awareness that change can also correspond to decay, and it is quite possible to greet the prospect of change with some circumspection. Examination of a major field of cultural expression, such as Western classical music, is instructive in putting the concept of change as an unquestionably positive phenomenon into doubt. In the history of orchestral composition, the ninth symphony by Beethoven is seen as the culmination of several decades of development, growth, and thus change in the form and standard of achievement. After this work, much subsequent effort was constrained by comparisons explicitly or implicitly made with this pinnacle; and, although few musical scholars would want to assert that change after the choral symphony constituted decay, nevertheless the equivalence of change and improvement, so easily in parallel before the event, was no longer so convincingly evident after it.

In the field of communication to the mass, many might consider television to be an example of change (over the cinema that preceded it as the vehicle of popular visual entertainment) that is positive and evidence that the civilization that produced it had grown and improved. True, there have been strenuous denials that television is of benefit, but the public at large clearly takes little heed of such prophecies, and people have continued to buy and use screen equipment.

The year 1946 can be taken as a convenient milestone of the arrival of television in the United States and the U.K., and over the next 30 years ownership of sets became nearly universal. Apart from this, sets were made larger, in color, and with better definition. In all of these changes, the public eagerly patronized "progress." Not only were these innovations widely purchased, but people also bought more than one ordinary set for use in different rooms of the home.

In biblical terms, the number 40 signifies a unit of plenty (thus, years or days in the wilderness, rain and flood, and so on), and, as a modern equivalent, 40 years of television's development brought us to 1986, when the arrival of new forms of hardware began to pose serious problems to the institutions that had grown up and established themselves in the first age of television. These new forms are often said to be myriad in number, although they really only have four or five basically different manifestations.

Videocassette recorders can be counted as one form, and cable as another. The first enables the user to reschedule material (often referred to as time-shifting, although no unit of time has ever been known actually to have shifted) and to store the material physically as well as to carry it about, to use it as an item of exchange, and by all these means to extend one's freedom of choice. The second system, cable, offers users a range of choice at any one time, but without the facilities of storage and exchange offered by cassettes. It may disappoint the enthusiasts of technical innovation, but satellite channels are not essentially different, as far as the user is concerned, from cable. Satellite offers multiplicity of channels, and the user has an increased choice, again without the retentiveness of cassette. The economics of satellite are undoubtedly quite different from those of cable, and these will have implications for the range of commodities that the purveyors want and are able to provide. For the user, it is still a matter of choice from an array.

To add to videocassette and to the pair of cable and satellite distribution options, there are the computerized devices that enable the user to encode on the screen. These are the three "families" of new devices that constitute the main arena of present change in the world of the domestic screen.

## METHODS OF STUDY

The question now is: What will the users want and be able to make of these changes? There are at least four ways in which bearings can be developed on the directions that users will be likely to take. One way is to ask people what they may do with new commodities if they became available (with the drawback that they may not fully anticipate their benefits and costs). A second strategy is to set up or to examine field experiments where new devices become available and to see how people use them. A third method is to monitor occasions when the screen services have become absent (by strike, or by special project), again to see how people develop substitute activities or yearn for the return of what they have been used to. Finally, one may study patterns of use of or preferences for the existing commodity; from any generalizations that emerge can be deduced the existence of needs, and these needs are essential pointers to bear in mind when considering how to predict (or explain) evolving patterns of use of new hardware facilities.

Although something of value can be derived from each of these approaches, the main substance of this chapter is derived from studies based on the last strategy. The essence of this method is to deduce the nature of viewing needs (enduring personal characteristics) that determine how people will behave in altered external circumstances. This chapter, therefore, examines studies of viewers' personal characteristics, turning only at the end to dynamic study of audience responses to variation in program provision of the sort that the new firms of hardware might produce

## PERSONAL VIEWER CHARACTERISTICS

In an early study relevant here (Wober, 1981a), I attempted to explore the extent of welcome for three communications innovations listed within a context of four non-communications developments. Although the cost disadvantage of any single innovation was not fully spelled out, its appearance on a list of alternative items did do something to create an environment of comparison. During a week in September of that year, 373 viewing appreciation diaries and supplementary questionnaires were obtained from members of a panel then maintained in the London region. The diaries provided measures of amounts of viewing to each of several program types, and the questionnaire carried items on viewers' own personal characteristics and on attitudes of welcome towards various technical novelties.

At the top of the list of welcomeness came "reliable birth control." Next after this came videocassette recorders—even though the questionnaire had gone some way to explain an offsetting cost of the innovation. (Respondents were told that the VCR would allow them to buy or borrow programs like books and see them when they want to. But the VCR may make cinemas close and harm the quality of existing TV.) After the VCR came pay TV meters in every home. (Respondents were told that these meters would be used to replace license fees. Users would pay less if they viewed less but pay more if they viewed more than now. This would keep up choice and quality of programs.) A satellite with five more TV channels, described as carrying the same drawback as had been listed for VCR, earned itself a net result lying between unsureness and unwelcome. Two unwanted innovations were a new large airport near the city and more nuclear power stations. These results not only throw those concerning the broadcasting innovations into a useful perspective, they also show that, with help, the public is able to be discriminating in thinking about technical innovation. It by no means accepts all progress simply because it is new.

The importance of this study here, however, is that it introduced a personality measure to help identify which people welcome innovation. The variable chosen for this potential explanatory function was the sensation-seeking construct of Zuckerman (Zuckerman, Bone, Neary, Mangelsdorff, & Brustman, 1972). Zuckerman's starting point had been with a theory that individuals differ in the extent to which they seek arousal (see also Eysenck, 1973). This arousal might be relevant to a desire to have more TV channels or a VCR (though not necessarily to a welcome for other developments such as reliable birth control). He and his colleagues measured sensation-seeking without paying particular attention to whether gratification might be sought for one sense system rather than another, or all of them. Having enunciated a theory of sensotypes, which organized evidence that psychomotor skills and sensibilities made use of particular groups of senses, reflecting particular cultural structures, I (Wober, 1975) then found it opportune to investigate whether the sensation-seeking construct was a unitary one or whether it might function differently with regard to each of the senses and thus provide a more complex key to any gratifications sought from new technical equipment. The scale was therefore expanded so as to include items measuring a desire to have each of the major senses of vision, hearing, and smell excited by intense stimuli.

The outcome was that there was no marked propensity for people with a general desire for new sensations to be the ones who favored technical innovations. Unexpectedly, a desire to explore new foods' taste sensations was linked with a more marked welcome for the VCR. People who were more ready to welcome nuclear power were those who expressed a welcome for noise and bustle or acoustic sensation seeking. These links between features of personality and the pattern of welcome for various technical innovations suggested it might be fruitful to use personality measures as potential indicators of readiness or welcome for technical innovations of various kinds. Personality characteristics of actual audiences were the subject of another study (Wober, 1980b) in which responses were obtained from 322 members of a routine, 1-week appreciation diary sample. The series of personality items were factored, producing four groups corresponding to recognizable dimensions. One consisted of items taken from Gerbner's "scary world" concept (Gerbner & Gross, 1976), and a second was the locus of control dimension developed by Rotter (1965). The third construct measured "selfish aggression," and the fourth dealt with satisfaction with the material quality of life. The Gerbner items included "we live in a frightening world" and two others. Rotter's included "I feel that I have little influence over the things that happen to me" and four others. Selfish aggression included "you've got to be pretty selfish these days" and one other item. The material satisfaction scale consisted of "I am perfectly satisfied with my present standard of living" and one other item.

A first step was to relate the scary-world measure with amounts of viewing of television, with locus of control partialled out. This showed immediately that viewing was not related to feelings about a scary world in an independent manner. Controlling in the other direction for feelings about a "scary world" still left significant relationships between locus of control and amounts of viewing. The direction of the results showed that it was those with greater feelings of external control over one's fate who tended to view more fiction and also more informational material—though not any more or less comedy than was seen by people with greater internal feelings of control.

The two other measures, of selfish aggression and of lifestyle satisfaction, had their small correlations with amounts of viewing effectively nullified when age, class, and position on the locus of control measure were partialled out. This study indicated that, among the personality measures, only one—locus of control—was robust in its links with some pattern of viewing. The interpretation deduced for the overall pattern of results relied on an aspect of psychological theory that holds that personality is a feature of structure established early in life and situated at a deep level. This is in contrast to the kinds of attributes that lie closer to the surface, attitudes and perceptions that are more amenable to change and could be more readily influenced by experiences at the screen. If there is no robust link between viewing and an attitude construct, then television experience is unlikely to be influencing that attitude. If there is no influence at the level of attitude, then it is even less likely that there would be influence at the level of personality. Thus, if there is a link between a personality measure and a viewing behavior one, then it is much more likely that the former is influencing the latter than the other way around.

These findings and conjectures invite a coherent account of why certain personality attributes may be linked with viewing behavior and recall that one such line of reasoning was advanced by Eiser, Sutton, and Wober (1978) in the course of research on smoking and an attendant health campaign on the screen. Using theory put forward by Eysenck (1973), it was hypothesized that extroversion, which requires greater external stimulus to maintain optimum levels of cortical arousal, would link with higher reported incidence of smoking and also with heavier television viewing; consequently, viewing amounts of television should correlate with extroversion. This was found to be the case, although the possible root of the finding in a secure basis of theory was not at that stage underpinned by having measured levels of extroversion. This omission was later rectified in a study that focused on alcohol but also included a measure of smoking frequency as well as a short extroversion scale (Wober, 1986). In this study, it was found that, having controlled age, sex, and class, more viewing of news, general informational programming, and even sports was linked with introversion; heavier viewing of adventure action was linked with extroversion. These results pointed to what had been clear with the diary studies for a long time—that television viewing is not a homogeneous experience in terms of its functions. That is to say, program types link in different ways with personality attributes or with attitude and perceptual measurements.

At least two further sets of data help to underline the importance of viewer characteristics. In one study done in connection with broadcasting of the Falklands war (Wober, 1982), authoritarianism was measured, together with perception of the broadcasters' efforts and the patterns of viewing behavior. As before, the relevant questions on attitudes and other personal attributes were sent to members of the London panel from whom, in this case, 624 usable replies were received. More authoritarian people were found to have viewed less news and current affairs programs on the commercial channel, although in general more authoritarian people were heavier viewers of this channel.

In a separate set of studies (Wober & Gunter, 1985), perceptions of the likelihood of various hazards were measured and related to amounts of viewing. It was found in one survey based on a sample of 414 panelists in London that people who considered there to be a higher level of risk from lightning and flooding were heavier viewers overall. A later study fielded in two television regions in 1983, namely London and Scotland (N=640 and 615, respectively) pinpointed this use to a greater level of viewing of soap operas. Soap operas in Britain do not contain stories of such major natural calamities, so it cannot be the viewing that produces such perceptions. It is likely that such perceptions are signs of an underlying attribute of personality that becomes manifest both in the risk estimates and in the recourse to soap opera viewing.

Precisely the same mechanism was observed in Wober (1986), based on 425 completed diaries and associated questionnaires, returned from the London panel for a week in March 1985. Here, heavier viewing of soap operas was linked with higher levels of perception of risk from diseases associated with alcohol, with exposure to asbestos, and with sexual contact (AIDS). Because it was established that the soap operas then available had no characters or even story lines involving AIDS, it followed that influence did not flow from viewing experience to inform perceptions, but that the kind of person who felt there to be higher levels of risk from actuarially rare disease (compared, say, with the common cold) sought higher amounts of soap operas.

The alcohol study also carried a measure of extroversion, and this showed that less viewing of news, of general informational material, and sports was recorded by more extraverted people (controlling for age, sex, and class). Extroverts also viewed more adventure action programs than did introverts. These results clearly point to the importance of distinguishing between program types rather than treating television as a homogeneous entity.

## PATTERNS OF VIEWING BEHAVIOR: PROGRAM LOYALTY

One of the possible ways in which viewing behavior may be found to show regular patterns is the choice of patronage of program serials. To examine patterns of viewing of serials, I (Wober, 1983) assembled a list of 30 episodes of "Coronation Street," spanning 15 consecutive weeks. A schedule of 30 other programs shown at the same time on different days, on the same channel, also was assembled. The same was done for 30 episodes of "Crossroads." "Coronation Street" is a soap opera set in Salford, which by 1983 had been networked on the Independent channel for over 20 years, two evenings a week at 7:30. "Crossroads" was a similar soap opera set in a midlands motel, shown three nights a week at 6:30. Both had a traditional working class ambience and featured strong female characters. The purpose was to note the "reach" or percentage of the sample of individuals belonging to a nationwide panel of over 3,000 homes who had seen any number out of each of the three lists of 30 episodes.

The outcome of these observations was plotted on a graph and resulted in two sets of two curves. Each pair of curves resembled a banana or a crescent moon. At one end of the graph the two curves met, at a point where about 70% of the viewers had seen at least one program in the schedule, whether it was of the soap opera list or of the comparison non-soap opera list; the curves then diverged, the lower one representing the control schedule and the upper one the array of soap opera items. At the midpoint of the curve it was found that 38% among women had seen 16 of the "Coronation Street" episodes, against 17% who had seen 16 of the control array of programs. The "banana" for male viewers was slimmer, as 12% had seen 16 of the control list, but only 26% had seen 16 of the "Coronation Street" episodes. At the lower end of the curves they met again, where 5% or fewer of the sample had seen 28 of the 30 episodes in any of the lists, and the numbers seeing 30 out of 30 are negligible or not significantly different from zero. Figure 5.1 illustrates the curves for "Coronation Street." Those for "Crossroads" reveal less of a distinction between the pattern for the soap opera and that for the same time slot but on different days.

These "banana" curves are one way of demonstrating that there is some loyalty of viewing to a particular serial. But based on findings from these two serials, at least, it does not appear to be inconsistent with the stereotypes commonly found among cultural studies analysts of the genre (e.g., Hobson, 1982). We see presently, however, that although it is more difficult to show strong segmentation or loyal-

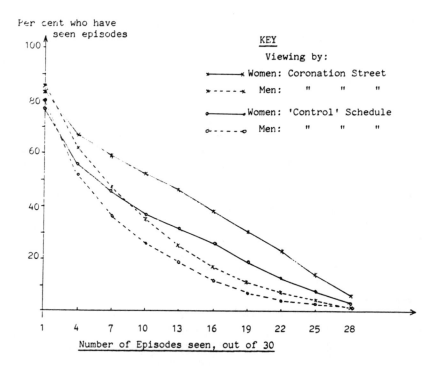

**FIG.5.1.** Cumulative viewing of soap opera and "control" schedule.

ty to a particular series, it is a different matter to demonstrate consistency of behavior with regard to genres.

Aside from the just-mentioned 3,000-strong panel of homes equipped with
set meters, used essentially for audience size measurement, the Independent Broadcasting Authority until 1985 had run a program appreciation measurement system
based on diaries. Members of viewing panels endorsed a mark within a 6-point
scale to show the extent of their appreciation for each item they viewed. It was the
practice to assign programs to each of seven categories on the basis of viewer perceptions of program likeness. It was possible therefore to count the number of
programs each respondent had endorsed (viewed) within a program type for that
week as well as to calculate the appreciation experienced by the same respondent
for the programs that had been viewed. The data in Table 5.1 derive from an average
of 17 diary weeks recorded in 1983 and 1984 and 3 additional weeks fielded in
1985. What is shown are correlations within a single week (averaged across a set

of separate weeks); there were not less than 264 individuals in each of the "ingredient" correlations, but as many as 598 in others (Table 5.1).

The results in each of the two periods are equal in ranking and similar in size. They show that for serial material of the most familiar format (soap operas, news), there is some concordance between amount that is viewed and appreciation. In genres whose contents are less predictable (films, general information), there is no significant link between viewing and appreciation. These results go some way towards establishing that program types are separable entities in terms of actual behavior.

Further evidence of segmentation of behavior with regard to program types is shown in a form of analysis that makes comparison across weeks. This has been carried out with an adult sample in London spanning a 4-week gap in 1984 and with a children's sample across a 6-week gap in 1986. The adult core sample consisted of 268 people. Whereas this adult sample was located in the London region only, the children's sample was nationwide. For the 6-week children's panel, 399 diaries were found in which records were available from the same child for both weeks. For each individual, the number of items viewed within a program type in the first week is noted as part of a pair with the number of items viewed in the same type in the second week. The same is done for the amount of viewing to each of the program types. The correlations for amounts of viewing either within the same type or across types are then worked out across the sample as a whole (Table 5.2).

The indications here are that habits or tendencies of patterns of viewing reflecting adherence to particular program types are very well marked. This is seen not only in the average correlation of .74 within program types, but in the contrast between this and the relationship of .28 across types. This latter figure is the index of an individual tendency to heavy or to light viewing in general. Thus, there is no doubt that heavy viewers of news are also heavy viewers of general information programming, which is not surprising, but they are also to some extent heavier viewers of adventure action or sports. Likewise, heavy viewers of soap operas are likely to be heavier viewers of comedy and light entertainment, and so on. These correlations of amounts of viewing are referred to as being "across types." The point is that the values of the coefficients, on average (.28), are substantially lower than the average of the coefficients within any one type (the lowest of which is .14 for sports, among children aged 4-6 and highest of which is .92, among adults for adventure action).

## RESPONSE TO VARIATIONS IN AVAILABILITY

Swedish researcher Olof Hulten (1979) was one of the first systematic observers of change in viewing patterns over the effects of a second TV channel. Across the

TABLE 5.1

Appreciation and Amount of Viewing, Within Program Type

Sample:     17 Weeks 1983/4     3 Weeks 1985

Averaged Correlations* Linking
the Score of Appreciation
(Ranging from 1 to 6) and
Number Seen for:

| | | |
|---|---|---|
| Soap opera | .21 | .23 |
| News | .15 | .21 |
| Adventure/action | .10 | .17 |
| Sport | .10 | .17 |
| Comedy/light entertainment | .03 | .05 |
| Films, non-serial drama | -.01 | .01 |
| General information | -.04 | -.00 |

* Pearson product moment correlation coefficients.

TABLE 5.2

Viewing Within Program Types, Correlated Across Weeks

| | Correlations* Across Weeks Among: | | | |
|---|---|---|---|---|
| | | | Children | |
| | Adults 16+ | 4-6 | 7-9 | 10-12 |
| N | 268 | 118 | 191 | 90 |
| Soap opera | .74 | .68 | .74 | .79 |
| Adventure/action | .92 | .62 | .66 | .45 |
| Comedy/light entertainment | .76 | .58 | .48 | .45 |
| Films, non-serial drama | .56 | .45 | .49 | .43 |
| General interest, information | .72 | .47 | .43 | .44 |
| News | .79 | .28 | .41 | .54 |
| Sport | .68 | .14 | .24 | .18 |
| Average correlations: | | | | |
| within type | .74 | .46 | .49 | .48 |
| across types | .28 | .17 | .15 | .14 |

* Pearson product moment correlation coefficients.

decade ending 1975, Hulten noted that although amounts of material available had increased, the overall composition of programming offered remained relatively unaltered. Viewers' choices, however, shifted significantly toward a higher proportion of weekly series, films, and other fiction, Hulten found. Following Hulten, Belgian Claude Geerts (1979) reported patterns of adaptive response to a major diversification in available broadcasting. Geerts noted that, in 1977, a third national channel was opened in Belgium. The greatest proportionate increase in availability was of religious programming, but the consumption of this as a fraction of the total viewing actually fell. In the opposite direction, the availability of sports and quizzes increased somewhat, but the proportion of these types in the actual viewing diet was greatly increased.

In Britain an 11-week strike in 1979 hit Independent Television (ITV), the major channel out of the three then available. ITV went completely off the air, leaving the two BBC channels running. A study (Wober, 1980a) took measures of use for 3 weeks each before, during, and after the strike. Availability was measured by simple numbers of titles broadcast within program types, disregarding the question of clashes (two items of the same type on competing channels—a low likelihood event, given that the two surviving channels were the BBC's complementary pair).

Into the strike (with a net reduction in the available number of programs), there was also a small reduction in the proportion of comedy and of general informational material available. The proportion of material viewed within these types actually rose. This "production" of scarcity within the general information type is one of the rare occasions, or even the only one, in which a measure of the use of this type has shown an increase. Coming out of the strike, the third (and major) channel was restored. Availability of news and general informational material (as of all types of programming) was increased, but consumption of news and general information, both in absolute numbers of programs endorsed, as well as in terms of proportion of an individual's viewing (compared with that during the strike), decreased. Comparisons across the strike show that the whole episode appears to have resulted in a noticeable, if temporary, setback for news viewing, both in terms of amount of newscasts endorsed and of their proportion out of total viewing, with a minor reduction of general interest viewing (even though distinctly more of this type was offered than before the strike). (See Table 5.3.)

The next step (Wober, 1981b) was to use the existing changes in availability from week to week in 1980 across a year to explore any concomitant changes in viewing. Twenty-three diary weeks were available from independent samples in regions outside London. Twenty-five alternate weeks' data from a panel in London also were studied. In all, over 15,000 program titles were listed, yielding nearly 900,000 opinions, from over 2,400 diarists, all at a rate of 36.5 items per person, per week. The method was to correlate the amounts available and viewed, within program types, across these sets of weeks (Table 5.4).

With the limited number of cases (weeks) in each of the aforementioned correlations, a value of .65 is only just enough to be significantly different from zero. The meaning of this is that for the first four types listed it should be true to say that in weeks when more is available more also is seen. For soap operas, general information, and news, it is not the case that greater (or less) provision influences the

TABLE 5.3

Changes in Program Availability and Viewing Across a Strike

| Program Type | Into the Strike | | Out of the Strike | |
|---|---|---|---|---|
| | % Avail- ability* | % View- ing** | % Avail- ability* | % View- ing** |
| Adventure Action | -70 | -37 | +280 | +65 |
| Soap Opera | -78 | -67 | +410 | +195 |
| Sport | -30 | +3 | +25 | -29 |
| Comedy, Light Entertainment | -19 | +27 | +95 | +10 |
| News | -44 | +5 | +72 | -15 |
| General Interest, Information | -16 | +25 | +54 | -19 |
| Feature Films, Plays | -39 | -8 | +35 | -18 |

* Change in hours of programming available per week.
** Change in numbers of programs endorsed for appreciation per week.

TABLE 5.4

Viewing and Availability Correlated Over Time

| N (weeks) | London Panel 25 | Other Regions 23 |
|---|---|---|
| Correlations* for: | | |
| Films, plays | .91 | .89 |
| Sport | .86 | .90 |
| Adventure/action | .90 | .75 |
| Comedy/light entertainment | .84 | .80 |
| Soap Opera | .62 | .74 |
| General information | .67 | .49 |
| News | .09 | .21 |
| (Across types) | -.06 | -.08 |

* Pearson product moment correlation coefficients.

amount of consumption accordingly. The final pair of correlations effectively on zero indicate that where more is made available for one type, there is no systematically greater or less consumption of material on average across each of the other types listed.

A more recent analysis was based on 3 weeks' diaries fielded in the first half of 1985. What has been done is to count the number of programs available (that is, listed in the diary—a nearly 100% inventory, barring some problems of definition and last-minute changes) in each category and the number of programs seen, per viewer, across the week within that category. This time, the analysis was carried

TABLE 5.5

Program Type "Efficiency" Levels and Channels

|  | Soap Opera | Film, Drama | Advent. Action | Comedy, Lt. Ent. | News | Sport | General Information |
|---|---|---|---|---|---|---|---|
| No. shown in 3-week period | 66 | 138 | 38 | 198 | 253 | 116 | 334 |
| No. seen, per person, per week | 4.4 | 7.4 | 1.9 | 9.5 | 9.6 | 3.3 | 4.5 |
| "Efficiency" Index* | | | | | | | |
| All channels | 5.0 | 6.2 | 6.7 | 6.9 | 8.8 | 11.7 | 24.7 |
| ITV | 4.1 | 2.8 | 5.1 | 5.0 | 6.4 | 11.7 | 17.5 |
| C4 | 13.5 | 25.8 | 15.6 | 21.0 | 115.5 | 28.5 | 81.1 |
| BBC1 | 6.9 | 5.1 | 6.9 | 4.8 | 9.7 | 10.0 | 15.3 |
| BBC2 | - | 14.3 | 7.5 | 14.0 | 43.0 | 11.0 | 25.0 |

* The efficiency index is computed by dividing the number of programs shown by 3 and then dividing this figure by the number seen per person per week.

out separately for each of the four channels available, yielding differences that are instructive.

In Table 5.5 we see that not only are some program types more "efficient" than others, but also some channels are distinctly more efficient than others. Undoubtedly, the reasons for interchannel differences are complex. They involve historical trends in the establishment of identity and scheduling formulas in the consideration of program types. Clearly, if a channel provides larger proportions of material from less efficient program types, then that will be a less efficient channel overall. But what Table 5.5 also shows is that if a channel is "less efficient" this tends to hold true across the board. The "laws" of inheritance of audiences (Goodhardt, Ehrenberg, & Collins, 1975) suggest that running more demanding programs will not only affect the audience sizes for those programs but for adjacent areas as well, so that the so-called "minority" channels receive smaller audiences for programs that would "earn" much larger audiences if and when they were shown on the more "popular" channels. What this means is that "dedicated" channels on cable or satellite are likely to do better than general-purpose ones that "dilute" their schedule sufficiently with items from more demanding—and hence less "efficient"—program types.

## IMPLICATIONS FOR THE NEW MEDIA FORMS

The evidence from numerous British studies is that some particular programs, and certain program types, are not just cited as more desirable to watch prospectively, but they also are more widely used when they become available. It does not follow, however, that what is more extensively viewed is the same as what is more highly appreciated. In predicting what kinds of uses are likely to be made of new screened commodities in the future, the behavioral patterns just demonstrated are more likely to be effective than are the patterns of appreciation.

Several different methods of analysis have shown that news and general informational material are neither as heavily patronized as their availability would make possible nor "demand flexible." That is, aside from "inheritance" effects, they produce small audiences and, when more of them is made available, they are not likely to be used more in similar proportion. In contrast, comedy and light entertainment are most widely used, and, when more are made available, more are used. Serial drama (in the two separate types of adventure action and soap opera), quite apart from journalistic stereotype, is not so heavily viewed in the average person's daily diet as are comedy and even news; but these two serial types, the structure of which—if not the day-to-day events—are relatively well known, are used particularly heavily in proportion to the limited extent to which they are actually available. They are also "demand elastic" so that when more is available, more is used. Films and nonserial drama (but including short-run miniseries) are an intermediate program type in that they are not particularly heavily viewed per person, but they do respond to greater availability with more extensive use—although not thereby delivering greater satisfaction.

Where studies of viewing behavior have included personality measures, the evidence has begun to accumulate that the two constructs may be related. Thus, in the study of perceived risks of alcohol (Wober, 1986) and in previous studies of other risk perceptions (Wober & Gunter, 1985), the most likely explanation is that it is people with a higher propensity to estimate risks (which are not depicted in the programming, such as of lightning, flooding, and AIDS) who choose to watch this genre. They do not have systematically higher viewing of adventure action or other genres. Among children (Wober, Reardon, & Fazal, 1987) there is similar evidence of links between personality attributes and viewing patterns. Not enough is yet known about how various personality attributes link with patterns of viewing each of the program types or genres. Several personality attributes have been tried out, such as locus of control, sensation seeking, extroversion, neuroticism, need for privacy, and authoritarianism, some of which have been alluded to in some detail in this chapter. Enough is known to establish that personality cannot be ignored as

TABLE 5.6

Availability and Use of Program Types in Britain

| Program Type | Current Availability* | Use-Patronage** | Demand Flexibility*** |
|---|---|---|---|
| News | medium-high | medium-high (6.0) | low |
| General Interest, Information | very high | medium (3.5) | low-medium |
| Comedy-Light Entertainment | medium-high | high (8.5) | high |
| Serial Drama (Soap Opera and Action Adventure) | low | medium-low (3.3, 2.5) | high |
| Film, Nonserial Drama | moderate | medium-high (6.5) | high |
| Sport | moderate | low (1.5) | high |

\* Labels refer to conditions in 1981 and, generally, for remainder of the 1980s.

\*\* Figures refer to measurements taken in 1981-1983 of average number of items seen per person per week.

\*\*\* Based on a 1980 study of 28 weeks of viewing diaries (Wober, 1981b).

one principle that, among other social determinants, helps to construct the shape and pattern of the viewing diet.

What has been quantified more systematically in some of the studies discussed here are aspects of program availability, use (or patronage, as some call it), and demand flexibility, which relates to availability to use. These features are outlined in Table 5.6.

The inference is that material of greater informational content and difficulty will be sought after by fewer viewers or to a lesser extent by an average viewer. More predictable material, such as soap operas and adventure action serials, whose characters and plot structures are well known, will be more extensively patronized by a wider array of users. This means that satellite channels carrying news or even sports are not likely to have such large shares of viewing time as are channels purveying serial drama, situation comedy, and light entertainment. The film channels so high in the limelight may turn out to be less viable than would be the more traditional type of network contents—namely soap operas, recurrent formula adventure series, and long-running situation comedies. The film channels are in the limelight at present partly because videocassette material has to this point neglected the serial form for the one-off blockbuster.

Screen forms where the user is more heavily involved, as in word processors or more cognitively complex games as chess or Dungeons and Dragons, are less likely to develop truly mass markets of the kind in "traditional" television, where many series may have monthly reach figures of up to or over half of the population. A multiplicity of channels certainly makes it more difficult for series to achieve the kind of pre-eminence of the past. Such a status is aided by the greater visibility afforded when there are but a few channels from which to choose. This indicates that in the new environment of cable and satellite, initial attempts will be to provide multitype packages in the hope that something in each package will appeal to everyone. These are likely to jostle each other relatively unprofitably until certain channels, carrying more attractive serial dramas and comedies, emerge, aided by their own merits and energetic off-screen promotion. The videocassette market, already experimenting with the conjoined movie form exemplified in the *Rambo* and *Porky's* "serials," would perhaps do well to follow the example of print since Dickens' day and of radio and television soap operas. It should develop its own weekly take-away packages of cassetted serials.

What this analysis implies is that underlying change, in outward form, is continuity. This continuity is a result of unchanging human needs that, linked with the structure of personality, point to the materials that satisfy these needs. The needs most widely found are for a modicum of arousal that is best developed by the serial form. In this, a relatively constant (and therefore reassuring) outer structure displays a limited amount of inner change. These changes are dramatized by the press as cataclysmic, but this is an illusion. *Plus ca change, plus c'est la meme chose.*

**REFERENCES**

Eiser, J. R., Sutton, S., & Wober, J. M. (1978). Can television influence smoking? Further evidence. *British Journal of Addiction, 73,* 281-298.
Eysenck, H. J. (1973). *Eysenck on extraversion.* London: Crosby Lockwood Staples.
Geerts, C. (1979, June). *Une enquete internationale: Television offerte au public, television regardee par le public* [An international survey: Television offered

to the public, television watched by the public]. Paper presented at Group of European Audience Researchers, Paris.

Gerbner, G., & Gross, L. (1976). Living with television: The violence profile. *Journal of Communication, 26* (2), 173-199.

Goodhardt, G. J., Ehrenberg, A. S. C., & Collins, M. A. (1975). *The television audience: Patterns of viewing.* Lexington, MA: Lexington Books.

Hobson, D. (1982). *Crossroads: The drama of a soap opera.* London: Methuen.

Hulten, O. (1979). *Mass media and state support in Sweden.* Stockholm: The Swedish Institute.

Rotter, J. B. (1965). Generalized expectancies for internal versus external control of reinforcement. *Psychological Monographs, 80* (1), No. 609.

Wober, J. M. (1975). *Psychology in Africa.* London: International African Institute.

Wober, J. M. (1980a). *Chance and choice: Changes in the distribution of viewing across program types, when the availability is altered.* London: Independent Broadcasting Authority Research Report.

Wober, J. M. (1980b). *Patterns of personality and of television viewing.* London: Independent Broadcasting Authority, Special Report.

Wober, J. M. (1981a). *Pyramids or chariots: The satellite question.* London: Independent Broadcasting Authority, Special Report.

Wober, J. M. (1981b). *A box for all seasons: The ebb and flow of television viewing and appreciation over a whole year, 1980.* London: Independent Broadcasting Authority, Special Report.

Wober, J. M. (1982). *The Falklands conflict: Further analysis of viewers' behavior and attitudes.* London: Independent Broadcasting Authority, Special Report.

Wober, J. M. (1983, May). *A twisted yarn: Some psychological aspects of viewing soap operas.* Paper presented at the meeting of the International Communication Association Conference, Dallas, TX.

Wober, J. M. (1986). *Alcohol on television and in viewers' experience.* London: Independent Broadcasting Authority, Reference Paper.

Wober, J. M., & Gunter, B. (1985). Patterns of television viewing and of perceptions of hazards to life. *Journal of Environmental Psychology, 5,* 99-108.

Wober, J. M., Reardon, G., & Fazal, S. (1987). *Personality, character aspirations and patterns of viewing among children.* London: Independent Broadcasting Authority, Research Report.

Zuckerman, M., Bone, R. N., Neary, R., Mangelsdorff, D., & Brustman, B. (1972). What is the sensation seeker: Personality and experience correlates of the sensation-seeking scales. *Journal of Consulting and Clinical Psychology, 39,* 308-321.

# 6

# Sweden: Opening the Doors—Cautiously

**Ulla Johnsson-Smaragdi**
*University of Lund*

The structure of the mass media in a country is never a static phenomenon, something to be taken for granted. It is constantly subject to change. These changes are faster and more thorough during specific historical periods. A few years ago, like many other industrialized countries, Sweden entered into such a period of fast and radical change of its media structure. A series of both powerful and attractive mass media are now available to the public at large. These include videocassette recorders (VCRs), cable television, satellite television, and different computer-aided combinations such as teletext and viewdata. Sweden's national media network is now being incorporated into an international media network with all of its implications. These changes began in the 1980s and will certainly continue throughout the coming decade.

Changes in the existing media structure not only affect the individual use of the mass media but also the surrounding society. The most important new media technologies are methods of storing and distributing mainly traditional media fare on the TV screen. This has already caused substantial changes in the prevalent media scene as well as in the posture of the audience to the media. The entire range of the media fare and subsequent audience choice will be radically enlarged.

The ongoing structural changes within the mass media and their consequences have been subject to an animated public debate. The potential effects caused by the new media and modes of distribution will probably be very marked in Sweden and the Nordic countries, with their relatively isolated geographical position. For a long time, Sweden has been able to preserve its media broadcasting monopoly with relatively few radio and TV channels. Traditionally, these are of a public service type and have a media ideology best characterized in terms of social responsibility.

The purpose of this review is to give a brief description of the present media situation in Sweden, the changes that are occurring, the reactions of the audience, and the possible consequences of these changes. At issue is the way in which the reshaping of the media structure has or can be expected to affect mass media use and the way of life in Sweden.

## THE SWEDISH MEDIA SCENE

In order to grasp the meaning of the newly inaugurated changes in the Swedish media structure, a short description is provided of the previously prevailing media scene and the audience's media use. The changes occurring in the media environment during the 1980s are described thereafter, along with the ways in which they have already affected media use. Finally, some of the possible consequences of these changes are discussed.

### The Media Situation to the Present

Swedish households are among the most well equipped in the world in terms of mass media and home electronics. Ninety-six percent of the entire population has at least one television set (92% has a color set). Almost a quarter of the households have more than one TV, usually one color and one black-and-white. There are very few households completely without radio; on an average each household possesses three radio receivers. About 80% of the population has different kinds and combinations of sound cassette recorders or stereo systems (Monten, 1985; SOU, 1984).

The Swedish Broadcasting Corporation (Sveriges Radio AB) enjoys a monopoly status, although it is not state-controlled. It is funded mainly by audience license fees. Advertising is not permitted on radio and TV broadcasting. The question of whether advertising should be permitted or not is continually being reconsidered within the forum of public debate, because many of the foreign satellite-transmitted TV channels that can now be received in Sweden contain advertising.

Swedish television is transmitted on two national channels, mainly during the late afternoon and in the evening. Each channel has a broadcast time of approximately 50 hours per week. During the autumn of 1987 there was a minor reorganization of the company and of program scheduling with some increase in broadcast time. Programs produced in Sweden, both nationally and regionally, account for about half of the output. The other half is filled by programs of foreign origin, about 75% of which were originally produced in the United States and Western Europe. Besides the two national channels, the television corporation transmits separate programs for 10 regional districts, which together are on the air for approximately 6 hours of regional broadcasting each week.

On an ordinary day, TV and radio each reach about 75% of the population (aged 9-79), with an average individual viewing time of nearly 2 hours of TV a day. Listening to the radio amounts to around 2.5 hours (Fig. 6.1). There are substantial variations in viewing time among different groups of the population. Men tend to view more than women, less educated persons more than those who are highly educated, children and the elderly more than teenagers and young adults. Over the last 15 years there has been a continual decline in the time spent watching TV among children under 15 years of age (Filipson & Rydin, 1987; Mediebarometern, 1986).

The kind of TV programs preferred are to some extent dependent on the age of the viewer. Children and adolescents appreciate fiction and entertainment (especially foreign entertainment programs), and they avoid news and informative programs. Sports programs are preferred mostly by men. The elderly usually avoid foreign programs, probably due to the deficient language training of this generation.

There are three national radio channels, each of which specializes in a different kind of content. The first channel provides general news, information, and high culture. The second specializes in classical and avant-garde music, whereas the third provides popular music, light entertainment, sports, and local programs. The total weekly transmission time amounts to 400 hours, rather evenly distributed over the three channels. However, the public prefers listening to the third channel. It reaches about 70% of the daily listeners. This is to be compared to the first channel with 18%, and the second with only 1 to 2%.

The third national radio channel is also used for 24 regional radio stations, each on the air for 3.5 hours per day. This type of programming is now rapidly expanding. It draws many listeners with its mixture of local news, music, entertainment and topical programs produced specificially for a local public (Nordstroem, 1987; Strid & Weibull, 1986).

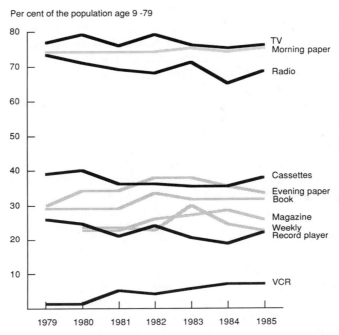

**FIG.6.1.** Proportion of the population using mass media on an average day 1979-1985 (Mediebarometern, 1985; Nordstroem, 1987).

## Changes During the 1980s

In the 1980s, profound changes occurred in the Swedish mass media. The new media and modes of distribution had already been available in Sweden in the 1970s, but it was not until the 1980s that there was a substantial increase in their dissemination or development. With the availability of satellite and cable technology has come a great expansion in broadcasting. Therefore, it is important to distinguish between the first and the second generation of what is commonly called the new media (Burgelman, 1986). The first generation refers to old media distributed in new ways (e.g., satellite TV, cable TV, VCRs). The second generation is generally designated telematics (e.g., teletext, viewdata, personal computers) (Roe & Johnsson-Smaragdi, 1987). Empirical research has traditionally been almost exclusively concerned with the first type of new media. This overview is confined mainly to this area as well. Some data concerning teletext are briefly mentioned.

*Videocassette Recorders.* Of the new media, VCRs are the most widely disseminated. In the last few years, the penetration of the VCR into the marketplace has increased rapidly. At the beginning of 1987, 32% of the Swedish population had access to a VCR at home. This expansion has entirely taken place during the last 10 years. Although VCRs had been available for household use since the early 1970s, the larger public was very indifferent during the main part of that decade. At the end of the 1970s, only 1% of the households had a VCR. Not more than 60,000 VCRs had been sold at that time. The real breakthrough came at the end of 1981. Since then, the expansion has proceeded almost continuously, and as yet there are no signs of its diminishing (Gahlin & Nordstroem, 1987; Mediebarometern, 1986).

Access to mass media equipment, however, is not evenly distributed throughout the population. As a rule, new technology is accepted and tried out at different rates by different groups in a society. The inclination to procure new media is dependent on several disparate but partly concurrent factors, such as age and family structure, place of residence, education, and gender. Very often, those who first acquire new media devices are male urban dwellers who are younger, well educated, and have higher incomes. From there, diffusion proceeds to other groups in the society. This pattern was very evident with the spread of VCRs in Sweden. Access to VCRs is still greatest in the larger urban centers, but other areas are now steadily closing the gap as the growth rate shows a tendency to be somewhat reduced in the urban centers (Johnsson-Smaragdi & Roe, 1986).

Once VCR sales had taken off, ownership rapidly spread from the early innovators to other groups in society. Many families with children soon discovered that VCRs were well suited to their needs. These families often lead those acquiring new media equipment. So it is that more than half of the children under 15 years of age have home access to a VCR. The proportion of VCR owners among adults is slightly above a quarter. For the elderly, this is no more than 6%. This proportion is even higher for families with children in larger urban centers, where it is now approaching two thirds. Family circumstances, place of residence, and social background together play an important role in determining access to a VCR.

VCRs are reaching far more people than only those possessing the equipment. This is particularly the case with children and adolescents. To a great extent being a peer medium, the VCR has been made accessible for a majority of the young. Most youth have used a VCR at least a few times, although far from all can be said to be regular viewers (Hoejerback, 1986; Johnsson-Smaragdi & Roe, 1986). The fact that in most specialized VCR shops it is now possible to rent a VCR in order to play one's own or rented cassettes helps to explain the availability of the VCRs. There exist about 3,500 places where one can rent prerecorded cassettes, ranging from specialized shops to kiosks and gasoline stations. The number of different titles that can be rented is about 7,000, with almost 1,000 titles being added each year (DsU, 1987).

*Cable Television.* In Sweden, the interest in cable TV has long been fairly limited. The reception of national broadcasting was good and the possibilities for tuning in stations from neighboring countries were restricted. A general interest was not developed until the start of broadcasting by international satellites.

Cable TV networks came into operation during the autumn of 1983, when the first real cable TV system was started in Lund in southern Sweden. During 1985-86, cable TV experiments were begun in more than 40 areas, an activity continued on a regular basis since 1986. Cable TV networks operate in about 70 of the 272 local districts in Sweden. Three different types of productions are transmitted. These are locally produced programs, channels from neighboring Denmark, Norway, and Finland, and satellite stations.

The national parliament has responded to these developments by passing a cable TV law. It went into effect on January 1, 1986, and was very liberal, both when it came to the installation of cable TV networks and the transmission of foreign satellite channels. No special permits were required in order to construct a cable network. Permits were required, however, for the distribution of satellite TV via the cable network, as well as for the distribution of locally produced programs, if the system connects more than 50 households. All systems must carry Swedish television. Scenes portraying pornography, explicit violence and racial discrimination are banned. This is true as well for advertising and commercial sponsorship of programs originating from within Sweden (Djerf 1986; Gustafsson, 1986; Hedman & Holmloev, 1986; and Hulten, 1986).

The growth of cable TV in Sweden has been slower than anticipated, due primarily to economic factors. The proportion of the population with access to satellite TV over cable is still small and increasing only slowly. In the spring of 1985, about 80,000 households had access to cable TV. Two years later, about 240,000 households, or almost 7% of the total population, were connected (Mediebrev, 1987a). Other figures indicate that this may be an overestimation of the actual situation. According to some studies, only about 5% of the Swedish population state that they can receive satellite TV channels over cable. The difference is probably due to the fact that not all of the dwellings passed by cable are connected, and not all of these households are able to receive satellite channels because their TV set is out-of-date (Gahlin & Nordstroem, 1987). As with VCRs, families with children have greater access to cable TV than do other groups.

TABLE 6.1

Home Access to Mass Media in Sweden
Winter 1987 (% of the Population, Ages 9-79)

|  | Total % | Gender | | Age | | | | |
|---|---|---|---|---|---|---|---|---|
|  |  | M % | W % | 9-14 % | 15-24 % | 25-44 % | 45-64 % | 65-79 % |
| Access to.. |  |  |  |  |  |  |  |  |
| Swedish TV | 96 | 96 | 96 | 100 | 91 | 96 | 98 | 95 |
| VCR | 32 | 34 | 30 | 51 | 42 | 41 | 22 | 6 |
| Neighboring country TV | 15 | 16 | 15 | 16 | 15 | 15 | 16 | 14 |
| Satellite TV | 5 | 5 | 5 | 7 | 6 | 6 | 4 | 3 |
| Local TV | 2 | 2 | 2 | 2 | 2 | 2 | 1 | 1 |

Note: From Gahlin and Nordstroem (1987).

As Table 6.1 indicates, the availability of cable TV is still fairly modest. Predictions concerning its future expansion vary considerably. The most optimistic forecast is that 30 to 50% of Swedish households will be connected to a cable TV network in 1990 and a further 10% will be able to receive satellite TV directly from receiving dishes. Somewhat more realistic estimates predict that, at most, 25% of the households will be able to take in satellite TV over cable by this time. The Cable TV Board reports that the rate of new connections of households per month now has stabilized at around 14,000. This means that only about 20% of the population will have cable TV in the beginning of the 1990s (Mediebrev, 1987a). On the whole, the forecasts have been moderated with time. Not more than 60 to 70% of the Swedish households are predicted to eventually be connected to a cable network. Less densely populated areas will not be connected (Hedman & Holmloev, 1986; von Feilitzen, 1986).

There are large variations by region and locality in the access to cable services. This includes access to both networks as well as satellite channels, ranging from cities with more extensive networks to large areas completely without cable. Thus, nearly half of all households with cable TV are to be found in the 10 most densely populated local areas, whereas only 2% are to be found in scarcely populated ones (Hellerstroem, 1987). In all, about a dozen satellite TV channels may be received in different parts of the country, although few systems carry the whole range. Sky Channel is the most widely available, followed by Music Box, French TV5, World Net and Russian Ghorizont. In general the output of the foreign satellite channels is characterized by an emphasis on popular music, general entertainment, fiction, and sports (Roe, 1985c).

*Radio*. The broadening of the supply and the increase in choices for the audience due to new media and models of distribution is not restricted to television, however. In the 1980s, national and regional radio has been complemented by public access radio, begun on a trial basis in 1979. It is a private, local radio reserved for non-commercial organizations. By 1987, there were about 80 such stations in operation throughout the country, with almost 1,500 organizations and associations having been given permission to transmit programs. Advertising is not permitted. There are large local variations in the level of activity of the different stations. At first, the transmissions were dominated by churches and religious groups. Their proportion of the total transmission time has been falling, however, as local political organizations have become more active. Public access radio is reaching only a minor segment of the population, its daily audience varying from 2% to 10%. An interesting exception is public access radio in the far southwest of the country where, in some areas, the daily audience amounts to 15 to 25%. Through its strictly local emphasis and its connection with groups that are active locally in these areas, public access radio has actually become a competitor with national and regional radio. It is an important complement to the general media fare (Hulten, 1986; Strid & Weibull, 1986).

*Teletext*. The discussion up to here has dealt with the first generation of the new media. The second generation, including diverse computer-aided media such as teletext, viewdata, and personal computers, has attracted less attention. Of these, teletext is the most widely diffused. In the spring of 1987, about 20% of the adults had access to teletext. Among children and adolescents, this figure was even higher, being 25% and 32%, respectively. Teletext was started on a regular basis in 1980 by the Swedish Television Corporation. By the middle of the 1980s, teletext was producing three kinds of services: namely, subtitling Swedish programs in Swedish for the hearing-impaired; providing general information such as news and sports events; and subtitled comments to live, televised programs, primarily sports. By 1987, teletext was in a period of rapid expansion, with 250 pages of information being transmitted, half of them renewed daily. News, sports, and information about the weather, exchange rates, and TV programs are the main contents (Schyller, 1986; Strid & Weibull, 1986).

There exist very few studies in Sweden concerning personal computers (PCs). Figures regarding their diffusion do show, however, that in 1985, 4% of the total population had access to a PC of their own (ranging from very small to advanced PCs) in the home. The majority of them was to be found in the younger segment of the population. At that time, 10% of children (aged 9-14) and 6% of adolescents (aged 15-24) had home access to a PC. As with the diffusion of the VCR, the access to computers was related to age, place of residence, and social background. In the spring of 1986, 21% of the adolescents aged 15 to 16 years living in the city of Malmoe in southern Sweden had a PC in their home (Johnsson-Smaragdi & Roe, 1986; Monten, 1985).

## Changes in the Options Available

The changes in the structure of the mass media in Sweden in the 1980s imply that, in the long run, the options available to the audience will increase considerably. This holds true for both the choice of media as well as for the choice of programming; but the process has only begun. In practice, the real options are as yet unevenly distributed throughout the population. They are limited not only by place of residence, but also by social background and economic characteristics.

Present developments in the media arena have taken place mainly within the old media. The new satellite and cable-distributed TV channels, however, will broaden the media fare of traditional television. What it will mean to the users when it comes to more choice in viewing content is ultimately dependent on how diversified the contents in and between the different TV channels will be. Should the media fare appear to be too homogeneous, the options for the audience will in practice be limited. The contents already available arouse certain apprehensions in this regard, being dominated by entertainment and fictional programs. Locally produced programs, distributed through cable, with their connection to the local environment and local culture, may counterbalance this general tendency. The same may also be true to some extent for public access radio over which local organizations and associations may be heard. With VCRs, the options for the audience to sort out, to store, and to decide when to replay a program are considerably increased. Through the use of VCRs, traditional cinema films will largely become accessible for viewing in the homes. The audience's options as well as its controlling power are increased in terms of choice of medium and content.

## AUDIENCE USE OF NEW MEDIA

Despite the fact that cable TV in Sweden did not start until 1983-84, there exists an accumulated body of research on the use of cable and satellite television. The results stem mainly from relatively limited cross-sectional studies made in close proximity to the start of cable TV at diverse locations around the country. Reference is also made to the results from two separate panel studies, carried out in Gothenburg and in Lund. Data on the use of VCRs come in great part from work undertaken at the Research Department of the Swedish Broadcasting Corporation (PUB) and from the Department of Sociology at the University of Lund. The results of the research summarized here are based upon overviews and studies reported by Djerf (1986), von Feilitzen (1986), Gahlin and Nordstroem (1987), Hedman and Holmloev (1986), Hellerstroem (1987), Hoejerback (1986), Hulten (1986), Johnsson-Smaragdi and Roe (1986), Roe (1985a, 1985b, 1987b), Severinsson (1985), and Sonesson (1987).

During the 1980s, the use of mass media in Sweden reached an average of almost 6 hours per day (for those aged 9-79). TV and radio occupy about two thirds of this total, compared to printed media together sharing only 20% of the time (Fig. 6.2). For small children (aged 3-8) the average is considerably lower, about 2.5 hours per day. Older children (aged 9-14) spend 4 hours each day on media use, whereas for adolescents (aged 15-24) this time amounts to nearly 7 hours. These differences are mainly due to the fact that children are not very avid radio listeners, whereas adolescents are great consumers of music (Filipson & Rydin, 1987; Mediebrev, 1987b).

## Use of VCRs

The use made of VCRs on an average day in Sweden is considerably lower than is indicated by their diffusion. Despite the rapid increase in VCR ownership, the proportion of users in the population has long been stable. During 1987 the number of users had increased slightly and averaged 10% of the population, or about 700,000 persons per day. Not surprisingly, among VCR owners this figure is substantially higher. A quarter of this group is watching on an average day, and for children with a VCR in their home the figure is as high as 40% (Table 6.2).

The viewing is not distributed evenly over the week. The VCRs are more frequently used during weekends than during weekdays. Viewing normally takes place for all age groups in the afternoons as well as in the evenings. This means that the VCR is used during regular television time, probably causing a reduction in or partly replacing TV viewing. On the other hand, VCR viewing in the afternoons is an addition to the time devoted to television.

In general it is slightly more common to view recorded TV programs than rented cassettes, with the exception being the adolescent group. There are also considerable differences in this respect due to gender. Among women, taped TV programs predominate over rented cassettes. Twice as many men as women view rented cassettes. In general, the longer a household has had a VCR, the less likely it is to rent such cassettes and the greater is the proportion of recorded TV programs viewed. During weekends, 300,000 to 350,000 persons rent cassettes each day,

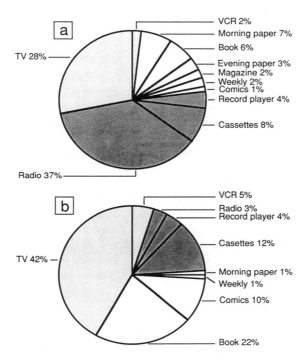

**FIG.6.2.** Proportion of total time spent on different media (a) Among the population aged 9-79; (b) Among the children aged 3-8 (Mediabarometern, 1986).

TABLE 6.2

Last Time of VCR Viewing
(% of the Swedish Population, Ages 9-79, Cumulative Distribution)

|  |  | Gender |  | 9-14 | 15-24 | 25-44 | 45-64 | 65-79 | VCR Access |  |
|---|---|---|---|---|---|---|---|---|---|---|
|  | TOT | M | W | | | | | | Yes | No |
| Viewed... | % | % | % | % | % | % | % | % | % | % |
| ...yesterday | 10 | 11 | 8 | 23 | 18 | 10 | 4 | 1 | 24 | 3 |
| ...with VCR | 24 | 25 | 23 | 39 | 29 | 20 | 16 | 15 | | |
| ...no VCR | 3 | 3 | 2 | 7 | 9 | 3 | 1 | 0 | | |
| ...last week | 32 | 34 | 28 | 60 | 54 | 34 | 18 | 6 | 67 | 15 |
| ...last month | 52 | 56 | 46 | 82 | 82 | 59 | 36 | 10 | 91 | 34 |
| ...last year | 90 | 91 | 88 | 99 | 99 | 98 | 88 | 60 | 100 | 85 |

Note: From Gahlin and Nordstroem (1987).

whereas on weekdays the figure amounts to half of this. The majority of those renting cassettes are young.

It is not surprising that children and teenagers, having better access to VCRs, watch more videos than their elders. Teenagers with home access to a VCR use it for an average of more than 7 hours per week. This is to be compared to users of the same age without home access, who average 2.5 hours per week. The difference is substantial and well worth taking into consideration when discussing the extent of VCR use.

Boys generally spend more time in VCR viewing than girls, and men spend more time than women. Among adolescents, the average difference is about a couple of hours per week. Socioeconomic status has also been found to be a significant factor in determining the time spent with VCR viewing. Those adolescents watching video most frequently come from homes with unskilled working-class fathers. The children of academics watch the least. The difference between the group viewing the most (lower-working-class boys) and that viewing the least (girls from academic backgrounds) is over 4 hours per week. The heaviest VCR consumers of all the adolescents are lower-working-class urban boys with access to a VCR in their homes. They view approximately 10 hours per week.

School achievement has also been found to be a significant factor behind adolescent VCR use. Below-average achievers tend to have better home access to VCRs and to have had it for a longer time. They use them more frequently, view in larger groups, and more often view pre-recorded cassettes with violent, horrific, and pornographic material. Even if the influence of social background is controlled for, there is an independent, negative relationship between school achievement and VCR use (Roe, 1987a).

The films most viewed among adolescents belong to the categories of police/detective stories, horror films, and adventure films, followed by violence and comedy. Least often viewed is pornography, a fact that at first may seem surprising. Studies have shown, however, that for boys, viewing pornographic films is a temporary phase that they go through and quickly leave behind. These films are regarded as extremely dull and repetitive by many, whereas others find that they are more of an adult pastime. There are significant variations in content preference according to gender and social background. Most popular among the boys are violence and adventure films, whereas the girls seem to prefer detective stories and horror films. The lower the socioeconomic status of the adolescents, the more they tend to view violent, karate, and detective films. Furthermore, social background and gender interact to produce wide variations in the content viewed, the greatest differences existing between lower-working-class boys and upper-middle-class girls. These results provide convincing support for the thesis that huge sociocultural and gender differences exist in VCR viewing among Swedish adolescents (Johnsson-Smaragdi & Roe, 1986; Roe, 1987a).

There are a number of explanations for why the VCR quickly gained popularity among children and adolescents after its market breakthrough. One of the most obvious is the considerably greater control that can be exercised over both content and time of viewing. Furthermore, VCR use provides an opportunity to demonstrate independence from parents as well as from society with its culture and values. It also provides a gratifying object around which the peer group may organize its activities. Particularly, boys are able to demonstrate their "toughness" to their peers. For the teenagers, the VCR thus becomes a medium to be used foremost in company with peers, not with parents. The relatively restricted access during the initial years reinforced this tendency even further. As VCRs have become more accessible, this pressure toward joint viewing has been reduced. At first, the most common group size was 5 to 6 persons, then it dropped to 3 to 4. By the middle of the 1980s, it was most common to watch with 1or 2 other persons (Gahlin & Nordstroem, 1987; Roe, 1981, 1983; Roe & Salomonsson, 1983).

The increase in VCR ownership has been followed by an animated debate over the pros and cons of the VCR. Usually the drawbacks, in particular for children and teenagers, have been dominating the discussion (Roe, 1985a). From the very beginning, the term "VCR" has initiated emotionally charged negative associations for many people. The main reason for this impression was that the rental market for prerecorded cassettes was dominated by violent and pornographic material. The VCR enabled the youth to bypass the cinema censorship and rent such prerecorded cassettes. In recent years, the range and quality of the rental market has increased considerably. By 1987, there were a relatively large number of quality films to be rented. Certain restrictions for selling and renting cassettes were introduced in an attempt to clean up the market. The VCRs were used by many, especially by the highly educated, as a device to free oneself from the time schedule of television. In this connection, the VCR functions as a complement to television, giving greater control over both time and content.

There is evidence that the VCR has harmed movie theater attendance. Visits to the cinema decreased by 28% between 1980 and 1984. That year, consumers for the first time spent more money on VCR cassette rentals than on cinema tickets (Hulten, 1986; Strid & Weibull, 1986).

## Satellite and Cable TV

Most studies show that people think cable TV is a good idea, but willingness to pay for it is low. As many as 50 to 70% want to pay only 25 SKR per month ($4.50). This may be compared to the license fee for regular Swedish TV, amounting to 75 SKR a month. In areas where cable has been introduced, however, interest and willingness to pay for it has increased. This interest differs between different areas and groups in society depending on sociodemographic characteristics, language abilities, and the number of TV channels in the area. The young are more enthusiastic than the old, men more than women, those with higher incomes more than those from lower-income categories. Likewise, families with children, heavy consumers of television, and those who already possess several media devices are more enthusiastic than other families.

One finding of most studies is that the time devoted to TV viewing increases after the introduction of cable. The average overall increase in total viewing time ranges from 10 to 30% in the different areas with cable, with considerably higher figures for children and adolescents. The time used for satellite TV viewing is taken in part from the Swedish channels and in part from other activities (Fig. 6.3). About a third of the total viewing time is devoted to foreign satellite channels. The use of domestic television consequently declines to some extent, but still dominates the total viewing time. As a rule, viewing consists primarily of Swedish television, whereupon different groups choose their specific patterns of additional viewing from Swedish as well as from foreign television.

This result is based predominantly on cross-sectional studies. One longitudinal study conducted in southern Sweden (Roe, 1987b) points to a somewhat different pattern. Three different groups were compared. First were the noncable households. The second group was made up of cable households without a decoder, thus having access only to basic fare consisting of five channels, including the two Swedish channels and Danish TV. The third group consisted of households with a signal decoder, which is required to tune in satellite channels in addition to the basic fare. Roe found that the average daily viewing time increased in all three groups between 1983 and 1985, but the increase in time spent viewing was actually *less* among decoder subscribers than that for the other two groups. This may be a result of the fact that viewers with a decoder were already watching more TV than the others before obtaining cable TV. Decoder subscribers still remain the most avid TV viewers, although they increased their viewing least of all. Those completely without cable increased their viewing the most.

Despite the fact that with cable TV it is possible to watch television almost around the clock, most of the viewing on cable TV takes place during the same hours as Swedish TV is broadcasting. One reason for this is that TV viewing usual-

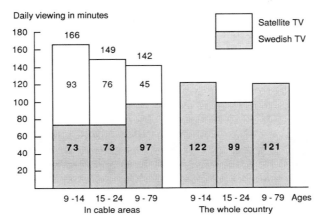

**FIG.6.3**. TV viewing in different age groups, Oct./Nov. 1985 (Westrell, 1986a, 1986b; Filipson & Rydin, 1987).

ly has its firm place in people's everyday life and is a leisure-time activity. Programs broadcast during prime time automatically have a large audience. Consequently, the competition is intensified.

Age is, in fact, by far the strongest determinant of the viewing of cable and satellite TV. Chiefly it is children, teenagers, and young adults up to the age of 30 who watch cable TV. Beyond this age, viewing of cable steadily decreases. Up to the age of 30, half or even more of the total viewing time is devoted to satellite TV. A consequence of this is that adolescents, who in relation to other age groups had previously not watched much television, have increased their total TV consumption. At the same time, they have decreased their viewing of Swedish television more than other groups. The older age groups in the audience remain more loyal to Swedish television.

The percentage of the people that watch TV at all has not been dramatically affected by the introduction of cable. Even in areas with access to cable TV, only 75% of the population watch TV daily. On an average day, less than half of the cable households watch foreign satellite channels. Based on total population, the viewing of satellite channels is very slight indeed. Only about 2% view satellite TV over cable on an average day (Table 6.3).

Of all the satellite channels available, Sky Channel is by far the most popular. Some studies indicate that as many as 70% of all cable owners tune in to Sky Channel at least a few times per week, with as many as 30% watching it more often. The audience of French TV5 and Soviet Ghorizon is substantially smaller. Normally, language ability is found to be of great importance for use of foreign television. An

TABLE 6.3

Last Time of Satellite TV viewing
(% of the Swedish Population, Ages 9-79; Cumulative Distribution)

|  | Gender | | | Age | | | | | VCR Access | |
|---|---|---|---|---|---|---|---|---|---|---|
|  | TOT | M | W | 9-<br>14 | 15-<br>24 | 25-<br>44 | 45-<br>64 | 65-<br>79 | Yes | No |
| Viewed... | % | % | % | % | % | % | % | % | % | % |
| ...yesterday | 2 | 3 | 2 | 5 | 5 | 2 | 2 | 1 | 46 | 0 |
| ...last week | 6 | 8 | 6 | 11 | 14 | 7 | 5 | 2 | 80 | 3 |
| ...last month | 12 | 15 | 11 | 17 | 26 | 13 | 9 | 5 | 91 | 9 |
| ...last year | 32 | 37 | 27 | 38 | 58 | 38 | 21 | 9 | 99 | 29 |

Note: From Gahlin and Nordstroem (1987).

exception is made in the case of adolescents, who appear to use foreign TV a lot regardless of their language ability (Fig. 6.4). This is probably explained by the fact that viewers in this age group are to a considerable extent attracted by the music video output of Music Box and Sky Channel (Elg & Roe, 1986).

The audience tends to use relatively few of the channels available to it. The data indicate that more channels do not necessarily mean increased time spent on TV. Generally, the audience's knowledge about the full range of channels available via cable seems to be surprisingly low, particularly in the more extensive cable systems. VCR owners are those who utilize the most channels. This is also the case for men and younger persons in comparison to other viewers. But even if the number of channels used by a specific individual is limited, total audience viewing is scattered over most of the channels. Each channel captures only a limited part of the audience, however. Many persons in the cable audience are only scanning the different channels in order to find the best-liked program. This behavior is more common among the younger viewers.

To summarize, the audience use of cable and satellite TV is, above all, determined by age. To a great extent, foreign TV is young people's television. Children and adolescents with access to cable TV devote considerably more time to watching TV than children and adolescents without cable. On the whole, foreign programming, particularly the Anglo-American, has a strong appeal for the young. Cultural orientation and language ability are of central importance for cable viewing. Foreign TV is used only for recreational viewing. It provides entertainment, relaxation, and is regarded as a suitable pastime. None of the foreign satellite channels can be compared to Swedish television in terms of the magnitude and regularity of the audience.

## Teletext

Most studies undertaken on the new media in Sweden have only touched incidentally on teletext and personal or home computers. Schyller (1986) in a study of

TABLE 6.4

Percent of the Swedish Population, Age 9-79
Yesterday Viewed Mass Media

| Yesterday viewed . . . | TOT % | Gender | | Age | | | | | With Access To Medium % |
|---|---|---|---|---|---|---|---|---|---|
| | | M % | W % | 9- 14 % | 15- 24 % | 25- 44 % | 45- 64 % | 65- 79 % | |
| Swedish TV | 79 | 80 | 79 | 85 | 70 | 74 | 83 | 92 | 82 |
| VCR | 10 | 11 | 8 | 23 | 18 | 10 | 4 | 1 | 24 |
| Neighboring countries TV | 2 | 2 | 2 | 0 | 4 | 2 | 2 | 1 | 11 |
| Satellite TV | 2 | 3 | 2 | 5 | 5 | 2 | 2 | 1 | 46 |
| Local TV | 0 | 0 | 0 | 0 | 0 | 0 | 0 | 0 | - |

Note: From Gahlin and Nordstroem (1987).

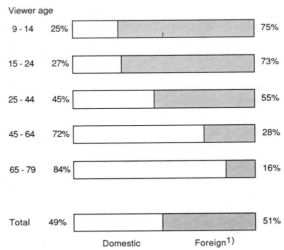

**FIG.6.4.** The proportion of foreign and domestic programs viewed by different age groups in a cable area (Westrell, 1987).
[1] This category includes both foreign programs on the Swedish channels as well as satellite channels.

teletext, found that of the 250 pages available, the most used were those that displayed information about the TV programs. About 80% use such a page regularly. Other popular pages are those with news, sports, the weather, and mixed information, used by some 70 to 75% of those with access to teletext. There has been a continuous increase in the use of most of the different types of teletext information. Teletext is used predominately in the evening hours. The news pages appeal mostly to adults over 25. There are no noticeable gender differences, except that men are more interested in the sports coverage. Children and adolescents are over-represented among those seeking information about TV programs.

In 1984, 37% of the users stated that they had acquired certain information only through teletext. Two years later, this figure had dropped to 29%. On the other hand, use had intensified. There is no difference in use dependent on the time of acquisition of a teletext TV set. This indicates that its use cannot be explained by novelty appeal, but rather that the advantages of the medium are discovered and continually used.

## Media Combinations

Several studies have provided support for the media accumulation hypothesis, that those who acquire and use one new medium also acquire others (Johnsson-Smaragdi & Roe, 1986; Monten, 1985; Roe, 1987b; Severinsson, 1987). The frequencies of use of the media also tend to correlate positively. Several studies have found that VCR access is related to the use of both TV and cable TV. The VCR so far has not proved to be a serious competitor to TV viewing. Among adults it has tended rather to complement TV by facilitating the shifting of programs (von Feilitzen, 1986; Johnsson-Smaragdi, 1986a, 1986b; Johnsson-Smaragdi & Roe, 1986). In his panel study, Roe (1987b) found that cable households with a decoder were substantially more likely to use VCRs and to use them more frequently than were cable households without a decoder or noncable households. This pattern, however, had been established prior to the advent of cable TV. The decoder households reported no change in the amount of time spent with the VCR on each viewing occasion between 1983 and 1985, whereas the other two groups reported an increase and, in 1985, even recorded higher levels of use than decoder households. There was no evidence that decoder households increased the frequency with which they used VCRs to record TV programs.

In general, however, positive correlations have been found between the use of different electronic media. Furthermore, in the Swedish experience, there are no indications that time devoted to TV, cable TV, or VCRs is taken from newspaper reading. On the contrary, TV viewers tend also to be the most loyal newspaper readers, presumably because, at present, these media fulfill different functions (Weibull, 1986). Even for adolescents, a positive correlation between TV viewing and the reading of newspapers and magazines was found. In general, there was no relation at all between amount of TV viewing and the propensity to read books. Here, however, an exception to this can be found among adolescents: There is a negative correlation between use of VCRs and book reading (Johnsson-Smaragdi, 1986a, 1986b). There even exists a group of adolescents who are relatively heavy VCR consumers but who never read a book. It is very likely, however, that these adolescents would not even read without the VCR. In other words, it is not the VCR that is the primary cause of nonreading. The main cause is probably to be found in the factors determining overall media choices made by the viewer.

## SUMMARY

Swedish media consumption has remained quite stable in the 1980s. Despite the growing access to a range of new media, the total consumption of media has increased only slightly. Thus, though the VCR has obtained a fairly high degree of diffusion, with over a third of the population and half of the families with children having access, its daily use by the population has not grown to the same extent. So far, the VCR has not proved to be a serious competitor to TV viewing. At least among adults, it has instead tended to complement TV by facilitating the shifting of programs.

Children and adolescents are far more avid users of the new media than adults are. They use the VCR more frequently and spend more time with it, usually viewing prerecorded cassettes with their peers. Depending on several background factors, such as gender, social background, age, place of residence, and school achievement, there is considerable variability in the time devoted to viewing as well as in the content viewed. This is true even within the adolescent group.

Additional evidence shows that foreign television is, above all, young people's television. For those young people living in cable areas, national TV has a serious competitor. But even if viewing of Swedish TV is reduced in those areas with cable, it still dominates the viewing time of most groups. Furthermore, viewers in the cable areas tend to ascribe other functions to Swedish TV, giving it more of an informational role than the average viewer does. Cable TV seems to be viewed mainly for entertainment and pastime purposes.

In general, relatively few of the available channels are actually used by the average cable viewer; each channel does have its own portion of the total audience. In fact, the more channels available, the fewer are used in proportion. There is also a great deal of scanning of the channels in order to find the best program for the moment. This is particularly so for the younger viewers. This combination may lead to rather fragmented viewing by a similarly fragmented audience.

From the aforementioned, it is readily apparent that in the near future, Sweden will increase its consumption of foreign television distributed through satellite, cable, and VCRs. Swedish national television will diminish in relative importance. It is also likely that the overall content will shift toward more entertainment, fiction, and light music, containing less information and high cultural programming

The eventual impact of the new media is difficult to assess at present. It is feared by some observers that cable TV will fragment the audience, will lead to declining cultural standards, and will overwhelm the national culture with foreign material. Others regard the same development as exciting and liberating. Different kinds of effects may arise. On the one hand may be those that can be traced to the actual amount of time devoted to the media; on the other may be those that emanate from its content. At present, it is hard to tell if the additional time spent on the new media has had any great impact on other activities. The effect of traditional TV on other activities had generally been negligible and, at least for children and adolescents, the chain of events has been reversed. In other words, it is the children who are already the most passive who are drawn to TV to a greater extent (Johnsson-Smaragdi, 1983, 1986a, 1986b). Overall, the time devoted to TV by viewers in general has been taken from previously empty time or from other media. Secondary viewing and listening also has increased with consumption. The time for the viewing of new media need not come primarily from other activities. It may instead be taken from free time or time freed up by more efficiency in its use.

Swedish longitudinal studies have shown that children and adolescents may be negatively affected by the content viewed on TV and VCRs. Certain mutual relationships have been established. These studies show both that adolescents are negatively affected by heavy consumption of violence and horror and that emotionally disturbed adolescents prefer this type of content (DsU, 1987; Sonesson, 1987). There are also other effects to be taken into account. The viewing of VCRs and cable, often late at night, causes children to be tired and restless in school. This has consequences for their school work, grades, and ultimately for their future as well.

The sometimes-heated debates over VCR use have now decreased in intensity, but the discussions surrounding cable and satellite TV are very much alive. The future relationship between cable TV and VCRs is uncertain. The increased number of available channels may correspond to an increase in the number of program collisions. This would make the VCR's program-shifting capability indispensable. But it is also possible that the easy availability of large amounts of TV around the clock may enable viewers to find something to view directly, making the VCR superfluous.

At the national level there exists an uneasiness about the possible consequences of the developments in the media and information technologies field. At the same time, there is a general consensus that this should not deter development. Whatever the eventual extent of media adoption and use, the developments in media technology are forcing changes in the structure and role of Sweden's broadcasting institutions. Which direction the Swedish media will take is uncertain. They may become more national and local and more informational; or they may seek to compete with VCRs and cable TV by offering fiction and entertainment with a more international flavor.

## REFERENCES

Burgelman, J.-C. (1986). The future of public service broadcasting: A case study for a "new" communications policy. *European Journal of Communication, 1*, 173-201.

Djerf, M. (1986). *Funktioner hos kabel-TV* [Functions of cable TV]. (Rapporter fran Avdelningen foer masskommunikation 11). Goeteborg: Statsvetenskapliga Institutionen.

DsU (1987). *Videovald: En rapport fran valdsskildringsutredningen* [Video violence: A report about an analysis of violent contents]. Stockholm: Utbildningsdepartementet.

Elg, P.E., & Roe, K. (1986). The music of the spheres: Satellites and music video content. *The NORDICOM Review Of Nordic Mass Communication Research, 2*, 15-20.

Feilitzen, C. von (1986). *Nordiska satellitsaendningar och publiken* [Nordic satellite channels and their audiences]. (Sveriges Radio/PUB, nr 14). Stockholm.

Filipson, L., & Rydin, I. (1987). *Barn och medier--da, nu och i framtiden* [Children and media: Then, now and in the future]. (PUB 87--forskning om radio och television). Stockholm: Sveriges Radio/PUB.

Gahlin, A., & Nordstroem, B. (1987). *Video och utlandsk tv i Sverige varen 1987* [Video and foreign TV in Sweden, 1987]. (PUB informerar, 1987: III). Stockholm: Sveriges radio/PUB.

Gustafsson, K. E. (1986). Media structure and media development. In U. Carlsson (Ed.), *Media in transition.* Goeteborg: NORDICOM-Sweden

Hedman, L., & Holmloev, P.G. (1986). *Kabel-TV i Sverige* [Cable TV in Sweden]. Stockholm: Raben & Sjoegren.

Hellerstroem, A.-M. (1987). *Fran tvekamp till triangeldrama* [From due to triangle drama]. Specialarbete i masskommunikation, Avd. for masskommunikation, Goeteborgs Universitet.

Hoejerback, I. (1986). *Video i Malmo*e [Video in Malmoe]. (Forskningsrapporter i kommunikationssociologi, 3). Lund.

Hulten, O. (1986). Current development in the electronic media in Sweden. In U. Carlsson (Ed.), *Media in transition*. Goeteborg: NORDICOM-Sweden.

Johnsson-Smaragdi, U. (1983). *TV use and social interaction in adolescence: A longitudinal study*. Stockholm: Almqvist & Wiksell International.

Johnsson-Smaragdi, U. (1986a). Familjen, kamraterna och TV-tittandet [Family, friends and watching TV]. In K. E. Rosengren (Ed.), *Pa gott och ont: Barn och ungdom, TV och video*. Helsingborg: Allmaenna Barnhuset och Liber Utbildningsforlaget.

Johnsson-Smaragdi, U. (1986b). *Tryckta kontra audiovisuella medier---konkurrens eller samexistens?* [Print vs. audio-visual media: Competition or coexistence?] (Wahlgrenska stiftelsens rapportserie, 3). Malmoe: SDS.

Johnsson-Smaragdi, U., & Roe, K. (1986). *Teenagers in the new media world: Video recorders, video games and home computers*. (Lund Research Papers in the Sociology of Communication, 2). Lund.

*Mediebarometern*. (1985). Stockholm: Sveriges Radio.

*Mediebarometern*. (1986). Stockholm: Sveriges Radio.

Mediebrev, (1987a). *Tema: Kabellaeget i Sverige* [Topic: The cable situation in Sweden]. (Planeringsgruppen). Stockholm: Sveriges Radio.

Mediebrev. (1987b). *Tema: Barn, ungdom och medier* [Topic: Children, adolescents and the media]. (Planeringsgruppen). Stockholm: Sveriges Radio.

Monten, R. (1985). *Hemelektronik i Sverige* [Home electronics in Sweden]. Stockholm: Sveriges Radio/PUB.

Nordstroem, B. (1987). *Vad haender med radiolyssnandet?* [What is happing to radio listening?]. (PUB 87--forskning om radio och television). Stockholm: Sveriges Radio/PUB.

Roe, K. (1981). *Video and youth: New patterns of media use*. (Media Panel Report, No. 18). University of Lund: Department of Sociology.

Roe, K. (1983). *The influence of video technology in adolescence*. (Media Panel Report, No. 27). University of Lund: Department of Sociology.

Roe, K. (1985a). The Swedish moral panic over video 1980-1984. *The NORDICOM Review Of Nordic Mass Communication Research*.

Roe, K. (1985b). *Media and social life in Lund before the start of cable transmissions*. (Research project: The advent of cable systems in Sweden. Report No. 4.) Uppsala/Lund.

Roe, K. (1985c). *The programme output of seven cable-TV channels*. (Research project: The advent of cable-TV systems in Sweden. Report No. 5.) Uppsala/Lund.

Roe, K. (1987a). Adolescents' video use: A structural-cultural approach. *American Behavioral Scientist, 30*, 522-532.

Roe, K. (1987b). *Media and social life in Lund two years after the start of cable transmissions* (Research Project: The advent of cable-TV systems in Sweden. Report No. 9.) Uppsala/Goeteborg.

Roe, K., & Johnsson-Smaragdi, U. (1987). The Swedish "mediascape" in the 1980s. *European Journal of Communication, 2*, 357-370.

Roe, K., & Salomonsson, K. (1983). *The uses and effects of video viewing among Swedish adolescents.* (Media Panel Report, No. 31). University of Lund: Department of Sociology.

Schyller, I. (1986). *Text-TV och dess public* [Teletext and its audience]. (Sveriges Radio/PUB, Nr 15.) Stockholm.

Severinsson, R. (1985). *Publiken moter kabel-TV: En panelundersokning om tittande pa kabel-TV i Goeteborg* [Audience for cable tv: A panel investigation on the watching of cable tv in Goeteborg]. (Rapporter fran Avd. foer masskommunikation 4). Goeteborgs Universitet.

Severinsson, R. (1987). *Den nya medieframtiden--TV via satellit och kabel* [The new media future: TV via satellite and cable]. (Rapporter fran avdelningen foer masskommunikation 9). Goeteborgs Universitet.

Sonesson, I. (1987). *Fran forskola till hogstadium, fran TV till video* [From preschool to university, from TV to video]. Unpublished manuscript.

SOU. (1984). *Via satellit och kabel* [Via satellite and cable]. Stockholm: Utbildningsdepartementet.

Strid, I. & Weibull, L. (1986). *Mediesverige 1986* [Media Sweden]. (Rapporter fran avdelningen foer masskommunikation 8). Goeteborgs Universitet.

Weibull, L., (1986). *Massmediernas framtida utveckling: Tre korta inlaegg* [The future development of the mass media: Three short contributions]. (Arbetsrapport Nr 7, avdelningen foer masskommunikation). Goeteborgs Universitet.

Westrell, C. (1986a). *Satellit-TV's publik: Publikrakning i Borlaenge kabel-TV omrade* [The audience of satellite TV: A survey in the Borlaenge cable TV area]. Stockholm: Sveriges Radio/PUB.

Westrell, C. (1986b). *Satellit-TV's publik: Publikraekning i Kalmar kabel-TV omrade* [The audience of satellite TV: A survey in the Kalmar cable TV area]. Stockholm: Sveriges Radio/PUB.

Westrell, C. (1987). *Den svenska "mediepuffen"* [The Swedish "media puff"]. PUB 87, forskning om radio och television. Stockholm: Sveriges radio/PUB.

# 7

# Switzerland: A Multilingual Culture Tries to Keep Its Identity

**Heinz Bonfadelli**
**Walter Haettenschwiler**
*University of Zurich*

Switzerland is a small, multicultural state in the center of Europe. The population by the end of 1985 was 6.5 million, 930,000 of them being foreign workers. The country is culturally segmented by four different language groups: German, 73.5%; French, 20.1%; Italian, 4.5%; and Romansch, 0.9%. This population is, however, unevenly distributed geographically due to the partly alpine nature of the country. Therefore, 23% of the inhabitants are living in the 16 cities with a population of more than 30,000 (Bundesamt fuer Statistik, 1986).

Switzerland's political system is a confederation of 26 regional states (Cantons) and functions as a very stable direct democracy based on highly developed mechanisms of consensual politics with opportunities for political participation by the Swiss citizens. Besides voting, they have to decide several times a year on almost all important political issues in plebiscites on the local, state, and national level (Saxer, 1986).

## MEDIA SYSTEM

The order of the Swiss press rests upon market mechanisms and, politically, on the rights of freedom of commerce and trade, as well as freedom of the press (Articles

31 and 55 of the Swiss constitution). Radio and television have been structured as a public monopoly.

The number of Swiss newspaper titles in relation to the size of population is very high as a result of the culturally and politically segmented country. It is a fact, however, that geographical segmentation and the small size of the three main language markets cut down newspaper circulation to minimal figures. Thus, the number of newspaper titles has been reduced since 1939 from 406 to 310 in 1971, and to 292 in 1983. Most of them (192) have circulations smaller than 10,000. Only five sell over 100,000 copies, 199 newspapers are produced in the German-, 73 in the French-, 14 in the Italian- and only 6 in the Romansch-speaking parts of Switzerland. It is not surprising then that media imports—magazines, books, films, television programs, records—from next-door neighbors Germany, France, and Italy play an important part in the media system.

Broadcasting is institutionalized as a "public service monopoly," as it is in most European countries. Radio and television freedom, for decades without a proper constitutional foundation, is now based on Article 55 of the Swiss constitution, which was accepted by the citizens in the plebiscite of December 2, 1984. It states that legislation on broadcast media is an obligation of the confederation. It names information, education, and entertainment as the main functions that radio and television are supposed to fulfill. It secures their independence and demands consideration for other media, especially the press. Finally, it creates an independent board for complaints.

Radio and television in Switzerland have been run since 1931 by the Swiss Broadcasting Corporation, a nonprofit company characterized by a dual structure. This includes the politically autonomous professional organization with 3,500 employees who produce the programs, and the nonprofessional organization with about 20,000 members. The latter represents the different regions and organized interests of the country, acting as a mediator to the public and exerting control and election functions. The cultural and linguistic diversity of Switzerland is mirrored in the federalistic structure of the Swiss Broadcasting Corporation, which produces three television programs (one in German, one in French, and one in Italian) and three German, three French, and two Italian radio programs. All of the television programs are distributed in each of the three main language regions of Switzerland. The small fourth language group (50,000 people), speaking Romansch and living in the mountain region of the German part of Switzerland, is served with special programs in Romansch included in the German radio and television channels of the Swiss Broadcasting Corporation.

The Swiss Broadcasting Corporation and its program production are financed by a combination of license fees and advertising. But advertising on television is very restricted in time. It is confined to five blocks of 4 minutes per day, and forbidden for certain products like alcohol, tobacco, and pharmaceuticals. At present, there is no radio advertising. Radio is thus financed partly by television advertising.

In 1984, 60,034 hours of radio programs and 12,594 hours of television programs were broadcast by the Swiss Broadcasting Corporation. The television programming consists of news and information (26%), films and shows (20%), sports (16%), culture and education (14%), and light entertainment (8%). Fifty-five percent of the radio and 36% of the television programming originate in foreign countries.

## THE CHANGING MEDIA ENVIRONMENT: NEW OPTIONS AVAILABLE TO THE AUDIENCE

Technological innovations, market forces and changes in media policy have altered the media landscape in Switzerland since the 1970s (Table 7.1). The installation of cable systems has increased the number of television programs available to the audience from foreign countries and via satellites. As a result, there is more commercialization and internationalization. The diffusion of videocassette recorders has stimulated the personalization of time and the individualization of program choice. Plus, the "old" electronic media—television and radio—have penetrated new areas through experiments with local radio and television. Decentralization, local focus, and more participation are products of this transformation. New information and entertainment services, such as teletext, videotex, and pay television, have been created for the public, which thus is becoming more specialized and fragmented (Jakubowicz, 1985; McCain, 1986).

## CABLE AND SATELLITE TELEVISION: COMMERCIALIZATION AND INTERNATIONALIZATION

Geographically determined factors, such as poor television reception in the alpine regions, have accelerated the installation of cable systems in Switzerland since the early 1960s. As a result, 31% of the households with television were wired in 1980, and between 50% and 60% in 1985 (Tables 7.1 and 7.2). Most of these cable systems are privately owned. "Rediffusion," a multinational corporation, is the market leader and owns the biggest cable system with more than 100,000 subscribers in the region of Zurich. These systems have been used as a means for delivering over-the-air signals of the three national, foreign, and satellite TV programs to otherwise hard-to-reach areas (Bigman, 1986). The penetration of cable is especially high in medium and small towns (70% of the households are wired there), whereas the diffusion rate is only about 50% in the countryside due to high construction costs, and zero in several of the big cities like Basel that still have no cable system.

The number of opportunities to watch television has increased steadily (Table 7.1) as a result of the cable system expansion. In 1986, 90% of the households in the German-speaking part of Switzerland owned at least one television set and were able to watch the three different TV programs of the Swiss Broadcasting Corporation. In addition to that, over two thirds of the households could receive the three channels of the German system (ARD, ZDF, "Third" Channels) and the two of the Austrian Broadcasting Corporation (ORF 1 and 2). In the bigger cable systems in the German part of Switzerland, several satellite programs and television programs of private stations can be received, too: 3SAT (a German speaking program, jointly produced by the public broadcasting corporations of Germany, Austria, and Switzerland), Sky Channel, Super Channel (formerly Music Box), RTL-PLUS (German Program of Radio-Television Luxemburg), and SAT1 (a private television program produced by German publishing houses). As a consequence the mean number of channels that television viewers were able to receive doubled from four to over eight in the 10-year period of 1976 to 1986. But this increase in the number of channels that television viewers are able to receive had no significant impact until now on the overall quantitative amount of television use, as Table 7.1 shows.

Table 7.2 shows the distribution of different technical possibilities of receiving television programs, based on data of the Univox-Survey. In 1987, 44% of the households in the German and French parts of Switzerland had television sets with antennas on the TV set itself or on top of the roof, 25% were connected to a local cable and 31% to a regional CATV company. Connection to a local or regional CATV system increases the mean number of television channels available from 4 to 12 and the frequently used channels from two to four. A further analysis of the frequently used television channels shows a significant increase of foreign stations in comparison to Swiss television if one has access to cable television. Seventy percent of the generally watched television stations in CATV households are foreign and 4% are satellite. In households that have antennas on the set, 60% of the regularly used channels are Swiss and only 38% are foreign. Introduction of cable television in Switzerland thus increased television options for the viewer and caused a stronger internationalization for the programs available.

TABLE 7.1

Access to Television Options
In the German Part of Switzerland, 1976-1986

| Options Available (%) | 1976 | 1980 | 1982 | 1984 | 1986 |
|---|---|---|---|---|---|
| Number of TV sets: more than one | 2 | 4 | 7 | 7 | 10 |
| one | 87 | 88 | 86 | 83 | 80 |
| none | 11 | 8 | 7 | 10 | 10 |
| TV remote control | * | * | * | 72 | 83 |
| TV reception: connection to cable sys. | * | 31 | 31 | 41 | 50 |
| joint antenna | * | 34 | 37 | 28 | 25 |
| rooftop antenna | * | 35 | 32 | 32 | 25 |
| Television channels available: | | | | | |
| Swiss TV: German Channel | * | 99 | 99 | 99 | 100 |
| French Channel | * | 85 | 88 | 90 | 92 |
| Italian Channel | * | 84 | 87 | 90 | 91 |
| German TV: ARD | * | 87 | 88 | 90 | 93 |
| ZDF | * | 77 | 81 | 86 | 88 |
| "Third" Channels | * | 56 | 62 | 68 | 72 |
| Austrian TV: 1. Channel | * | 45 | 54 | 80 | 73 |
| 2. Channel | * | 36 | 45 | 54 | 65 |
| French TV: 1. Channel | * | 12 | 15 | 25 | 34 |
| 2. Channel | * | 12 | 15 | 19 | 32 |
| 3. Channel | * | 6 | 9 | 11 | 23 |
| Other (Satellite TV) | * | 3 | 9 | 11 | 30 |
| Number of TV channels available (mean) | 4.4 | 6.0 | 6.5 | 7.2 | 8.8 |
| TV set with teletext decoder | * | * | * | * | 10 |
| Subscription to Pay Television | * | * | * | * | 4 |
| Video recorder | * | 3 | 4 | 12 | 21 |
| TV: People reached per weekday in % | 62 | 66 | 65 | 63 | 61 |
| Use in minutes per weekday (Mon.-Fri.) | 76 | 88 | 89 | 89 | 84 |
| Sample Size | 5625 | 1406 | 1406 | 1019 | 4771 |

Note: *No data available. Base of remote control, reception,
availability, and number of TV channels, teletext decoder
and pay television are those people with television at
home; base of TV sets, VCR, penetration, and use of TV is
the total population. From Audience Research Department of
Swiss Broadcasting Corporation.

TABLE 7.2

Access to Television Channels and Use of Television Channels
In German and French Switzerland, 1987

| | | Technical Reception of Television by: | | | |
| | Total | Antenna on TV set | Antenna on roof | Local CATV | Regional CATV |
|---|---|---|---|---|---|
| Owners of TV sets (%) | 100 | 9 | 35 | 25 | 31 |
| Total number of re- ceived channels (means) | 9 | 4 | 6 | 11 | 12 |
| Frequently used TV channels (means) | 3 | 2 | 3 | 4 | 4 |
| Frequently used chan- nels (%)    Swiss | 31 | 60 | 34 | 27 | 26 |
| foreign | 67 | 40 | 66 | 70 | 70 |
| satellite | 2 | 0 | 0 | 3 | 4 |

Note: Table is based on ownership of TV (90% of the sample, N=622).
From Saxer and Bonfadelli (1987), N=689 persons aged 20-85 years old.

## VIDEO RECORDER AND PAY TV: PERSONALIZATION AND FLEXIBILITY

The diffusion of videocassette recorders (VCRs) steadily increased from 3% in 1980 to 21% in 1986 and about 25% in 1987 (Tables 7.1 and 7.3). In contrast to the diffusion of television, adoption of the video recorder occurred earlier in the higher educated and younger age segments (Table 7.3). This pattern is in sharp contrast to the result that there is still a culturally based rejection of television by the young and well-educated people in Switzerland, as Table 7.4 displays: 14% of the 20-34 age group and 22% of those who have a university education have no television set. On the other hand, penetration of the various new electronic media—cable, satellite, VCRs, and pay television—is especially high in the 30-39 age group, the upper class and the segment with secondary school education (Table 7.3). For each group, Table 7.4 shows, 35% of the people have a television set with at least two of the new electronic services. Ownership of a television set without access to cable is still widespread in rural areas.

In 1982, the first continental test with pay television started in Switzerland. It was licensed by the government to determine if there was a demand. "Teleclub," as it is called in Switzerland, was offered as an additional service to the cable subscribers of "Rediffusion". The service provides 20 films, 10 of which are replaced every month. In 1986, 600,000 households could receive this service; but there

TABLE 7.3

Access to New Media in German and French Switzerland, 1987

| Owners/Users in % | Total N | Cable TV | Video Recorder | Tele- text | Pay TV | Homecom- puter/PC |
|---|---|---|---|---|---|---|
| Total population | 689 | 51 | 24 | 21 | 5 | 11 |
| Owners of a TV set | 622 | 56 | 27 | 23 | 6 | 11 |
| 20-34 years | 193 | 58 | 38 | 24 | 7 | 13 |
| 35-49 years | 208 | 55 | 29 | 24 | 9 | 12 |
| 50-85 years | 221 | 55 | 14 | 20 | 1 | 7 |
| Men | 314 | 54 | 29 | 22 | 6 | 14 |
| Women | 308 | 58 | 24 | 24 | 5 | 7 |
| High SES | 206 | 53 | 30 | 23 | 6 | 16 |
| Middle SES | 327 | 58 | 25 | 22 | 6 | 8 |
| Low SES | 85 | 57 | 28 | 26 | 5 | 9 |
| High school | 161 | 45 | 19 | 18 | 4 | 7 |
| Trade school | 336 | 61 | 29 | 25 | 7 | 9 |
| University | 125 | 57 | 30 | 22 | 5 | 17 |
| Big city | 237 | 58 | 35 | 24 | 7 | 10 |
| Medium town | 149 | 58 | 20 | 24 | 7 | 9 |
| Countryside | 235 | 52 | 23 | 21 | 3 | 12 |
| German Switzerland | 455 | 65 | 27 | 25 | 6 | 10 |
| French Switzerland | 165 | 31 | 25 | 16 | 3 | 13 |

Note: Penetration of Home/Personal Computers is based on total
population; access to CATV, VCR, Teletext and Pay TV is
based on owners of a television set, who are 90% (N=622)
of the total sample. From Saxer and Bonfadelli (1987), N=689 persons
aged 20-85 years old.

were only about 40,000 subscribers in 1987, 7% of the households in the German-
and French-speaking parts of Switzerland, who paid a monthly fee of Sfr. 28 (about
$17).

## LOCAL RADIO AND TELEVISION: DECENTRALIZATION, LOCAL FOCUS, AND PARTICIPATION

Since 1972, the federal government has allowed, from time to time, short-term experiments with local television channels. In 1977, the government generally per-

TABLE 7.4

Amount of Television Options Available to Social Segments
In German and French Switzerland, 1987

| Owners or Users in % | Total N | No TV | TV only | TV with CATV only | More TV Options |
|---|---|---|---|---|---|
| Total population | 689 | 10 | 29 | 33 | 28 |
| 20-34 years | 224 | 14 | 22 | 26 | 38 |
| 35-49 years | 225 | 8 | 30 | 30 | 32 |
| 50-85 years | 240 | 8 | 34 | 43 | 15 |
| Men | 343 | 9 | 31 | 31 | 29 |
| Women | 346 | 11 | 27 | 36 | 26 |
| High SES | 225 | 8 | 29 | 33 | 30 |
| Medium SES | 354 | 8 | 29 | 37 | 26 |
| Low SES | 105 | 19 | 30 | 26 | 25 |
| University | 159 | 22 | 25 | 27 | 26 |
| Trade school | 358 | 6 | 26 | 37 | 31 |
| High school | 172 | 6 | 41 | 31 | 22 |
| Big city | 269 | 12 | 24 | 30 | 34 |
| Medium town | 170 | 13 | 27 | 38 | 22 |
| Countryside | 249 | 6 | 36 | 33 | 25 |
| German Switzerland | 511 | 11 | 23 | 38 | 28 |
| French Switzerland | 176 | 6 | 48 | 19 | 27 |

Note: "More TV-Options" means connection to at least two of the
following new media: CATV, VCR, satellite programs, or pay
television. From Saxer and Bonfadelli (1987), N=689 persons
aged 20-85 years old.

mitted experiments in local television without any advertising. Only a few attempts
were made in the cities of Renes (1977-78), Fribourg (1973, 1975, and 1978),
Lucerne (1978), Solothurn (1981), and Wil and Zug (1980-81). Although these
limited experiments were received positively by the audience in most cases, they
have been terminated as a result of a lack of financial support (Haettenschwiler &
Jedele, 1987).

In 1982, the experimental phase with local television was replaced by a
government decree (RVO) that made commercial local radio and television possible until 1988. It limits local FM radio stations to a broadcasting radius of 10
kilometers (6.21 miles) and allows advertising for 15 minutes per day. In 1984, this
advertising quota was increased to 20 minutes per day. Furthermore, the private

radio stations were obliged to obey fairness rules, to cover local issues, and to organize evaluative research. The goal of this test-phase was to find out: (a) if there was an interest in producing for and using local radio; (b) what the effects of local radio are on other media (e.g., on local newspapers) and on society; (c) if there are possibilities for audience participation, and (d) what the optimal communication policy regulations should look like.

Over 250 individuals and organizations applied for licenses in 1982. Of these, 36 received one, and, by 1987, 30 radio stations provided programs for their local audiences in German, French, and Italian Switzerland. In 1985, these stations sold advertising of 30 million Swiss francs.

## INFORMATION SERVICES: TELETEXT AND VIDEOTEXT

Tests with over-the-air teletext began in Switzerland in 1981; in 1984, it was publicly introduced on the basis of a license given to the Swiss Broadcasting Corporation (SRG) and the Swiss Newspapers and Magazines Publishers' Association (SZV). The service is produced by a joint corporation, the Teletext AG in Biel. It is financed partly by fees from the Swiss Broadcasting Corporation and by advertising, which is not to exceed 20% of the TV pages offered to the audience. In the same governmental decree (RVO) that allowed local television and local radio, several experiments with local teletext or cable newspapers also were approved.

As in other European countries, the introduction of telephone-based videotext in Switzerland has proved to be more difficult than originally expected. At the end of 1979, the Swiss postal service (PTT) started a technical pilot project on a small scale basis, which was transformed at the end of 1983 into a 2-year-long test phase. Only 220 organizations delivering information and 2,700 subscribers to the videotext service (700-800 of them in private households) had been connected to this computerized public data source by the end of 1985. As a consequence, the PTT started an advertising campaign in 1987 to increase public awareness and interest for this new electronic information service. The service started its full operation in January 1987. An evaluative study, required by the federal government and paid for by the PTT, analyzed the diffusion and acceptance of the service by the public; the potential beneficial and/or harmful effects on the other media, especially the press, on the economy and on private households, were also studied (Meier & Bonfadelli, 1987).

## AUDIENCE RESPONSES TO CHANGING MEDIA ENVIRONMENT

What are the audience responses in Switzerland to these new developments in technology, which provide media users with a variety of options concerning what program material to use and when to use it? The following analyses and interpretation are preliminary steps toward a better understanding of how such changes in the whole media environment of the people affect the uses, functions, and integration of these new media options in the everyday life of media users. Evidence is so far tentative because until now there has been no empirical study in Switzerland to tackle these questions in a systematic manner. The following observations and case studies, then, are based mainly on two sources: data of annual media surveys and the electronic audience-meter panel of the Department for Audience Research at the Swiss Broadcasting Corporation (SRG), and two representative media studies—Univox-Surveys 1986 (N=704) and 1987 (N=689)—done by the Institute for Communication Research at the University of Zurich (Saxer & Bonfadelli, 1986, 1987). They analyzed the use, preferences, and evaluation of the old and new media in the German and French regions of Switzerland.

## TELEVISION CHANNEL CHOICE: COMPETITION
## VERSUS COMPLEMENTARITY

High cable penetration of more than 50% (see Tables 7.1 and 7.2) in Switzerland makes access to a multitude of foreign television programs possible for the majority of the audience in the three different language parts of Switzerland. As a result, there is a strong competition between the different television channels, and the stance of the Swiss Broadcasting Corporation is relatively weak due to a lack of financial and personal resources in comparison to the public and private television stations in Germany, France, and Italy.

As Table 7.5 shows, the television programs produced by the Swiss Broadcasting Corporation still reach the largest numbers of viewers in their language region compared to the competing foreign television stations (Steinmann, 1978, 1986): 56% in the German, 50% in the French, and 52% in the Italian part of Switzerland. But a look at the daily viewing time devoted to the different national and foreign TV programs in Table 7.6 shows something different. Only 40% of the viewing time in the German- and the French-language regions is spent on programs of the Swiss Broadcasting Corporation. The remaining 60% goes to foreign stations.

The position of the Swiss TV programs is even weaker in the Italian part of Switzerland. Here, the Swiss Italian viewer devotes only 32% of his or her total

TABLE 7.5

Audience per Day of Swiss and Foreign Television Stations
In the Three Language Parts of Switzerland, 1985

|  | People Reached per Weekday (%) in | | |
|  | German Switzerland | French Switzerland | Italian Switzerland |
|---|---|---|---|
| Swiss/foreign TV channels | (N=1224) | (N=896) | (N=536) |
| Swiss German language channel | 56 | 17 | 22 |
| Germany:    ARD | 41 | - | - |
|             ZDF | 39 | - | - |
| Austria:    FS1 | 25 | - | - |
|             FS2 | 18 | - | - |
| Swiss French language channel | 17 | 50 | 22 |
| France:  1st Channel | - | 40 | - |
|          2nd Channel | - | 41 | - |
|          3rd Channel | - | 30 | - |
| Swiss Italian language channel | 15 | 16 | 52 |
| Italy:   RAI1 | - | - | 37 |
|          RAI2 | - | - | 34 |
| Other TV channels: | 37 | 22 | 52 |
| Total audience per day | 70 | 68 | 73 |

Notes: Entries are the percentages of people reached daily
(Mon.-Fri.) by television (at least 30 seconds of TV use)
based on audience-meter data. Other TV programs include
the third public or private foreign channels and
satellite programs. From SRG-Forschungsdienst (1986).

daily viewing time (44 minutes) to the Swiss television programs, but the average viewer consumes 93 minutes (68% of his or her total television time) with foreign television programs from public or private stations in Italy. The Italian region viewer, in sum, watches nearly as much Swiss television as the viewers in the German and French regions. But the Italian-region viewers watch more non-Swiss programming, and, consequently, more television overall.

As Table 7.7 shows, there has been a steady loss of audience by the Swiss television channel in the Italian language region since 1976. There always has been

TABLE 7.6

Viewing Time per Day of Swiss and Foreign Television Stations
In the Three Language Parts of Switzerland, 1985

| Swiss/foreign TV programs | Viewing Time by Individuals per Day (in Minutes) German French Italian Switzerland | | | (in Percent) German French Italian Switzerland | | |
|---|---|---|---|---|---|---|
| Swiss German language channel | 39 | 4 | 5 | 37 | 3 | 3 |
| Germany: ARD | 16 | - | - | 16 | - | - |
| ZDF | 16 | - | - | 15 | - | - |
| Austria: FS1 | 8 | - | - | 8 | - | - |
| FS2 | 4 | - | - | 4 | - | - |
| Swiss French language channel | 3 | 41 | 5 | 3 | 36 | 4 |
| France: 1st channel | - | 20 | - | - | 18 | - |
| 2nd channel | - | 22 | - | - | 19 | - |
| 3rd channel | - | 11 | - | - | 10 | - |
| Swiss Italian language channel | 2 | 2 | 34 | 2 | 2 | 25 |
| Italy: RAI1 | - | - | 16 | - | - | 12 |
| RAI2 | - | - | 14 | - | - | 10 |
| Other TV channels | 16 | 14 | 63 | 15 | 12 | 46 |
| Total------ | | | | | | |
| Swiss TV channels | 44 | 47 | 44 | 42 | 41 | 32 |
| Foreign TV channels | 60 | 67 | 93 | 58 | 59 | 68 |
| Total viewing per day | 104 | 114 | 138 | 100 | 100 | 100 |

Note: Average number of minutes that television is viewed by an
individual per weekday (based on audience-meter data). Other TV
programs include the third public and private foreign channels
and satellite programs. From SRG-Forschungsdienst (1986).

TABLE 7.7

Shifts in the Use of Swiss versus Foreign Television Programs
In the Italian Part of Switzerland, 1985

Use of Television by Adults in Minutes per Day
(Monday through Friday)

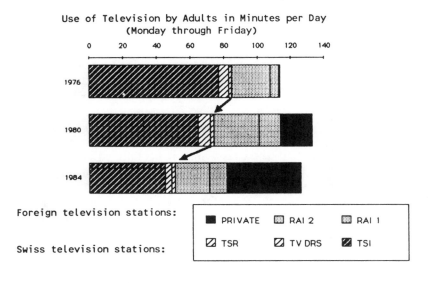

Foreign television stations:

Swiss television stations:

■ PRIVATE   ▨ RAI 2   ▨ RAI 1
▨ TSR       ▨ TV DRS   ▨ TSI

Shares of Audiences During Main News Show (20:00-20:15)

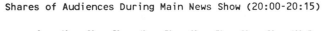
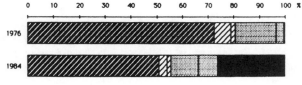

Note: RAI1, RAI2, Private: Italian TV stations. TSI, TSR, TV
DRS: Swiss television programs in Italian, French and German language.
From Audience Research Department of SRG; Steinmann and Weibel (1985).

strong competition between the Swiss Italian television channel and the public
television channels of Italy (RAI1 and RAI2), which reach especially the densely
populated Italian-speaking areas of southern Switzerland. This competition got
even stronger by the end of the 1970s, when a lot of small private Italian television
stations started transmitting their entertainment-based television programs as a
result of the liberalization of broadcasting in Italy. But, at that time, more than 50%
of the viewing time of the Swiss audience was still spent on the Swiss channel, and

the penetration of the Swiss channel during the main news show was still about 75%. This situation changed after 1980. Only a few very big private television networks remained after processes of radical concentration. Now they are strong competitors of the Italian public broadcasting system RAI because of their professionally made and audience-tailored shows and movies. In the southern part of Switzerland, there is now a multiple competition between the Swiss television, the few big private channels, the remaining small private channels, and the two public channels from Italy. As a result, even during the Swiss news show—the former stronghold of Swiss TV—half of the audience watches the quiz and movie programs on the foreign private television channels (Table 7.7).

An analysis of ratings for the German-speaking region in Table 7.8 shows that foreign television programs are used selectively. The Swiss viewers use the foreign TV channels mostly to gratify those needs that are not fulfilled sufficiently by the programs of the Swiss Broadcasting Corporation. These are primarily entertainment needs, which are satisfied by quiz, comedy, adventure, and crime shows or movies on the foreign channels. But information needs are, in most cases, still gratified by using the Swiss programs. Swiss viewers traditionally start their television evening by watching the news show at 7:30 p.m. on the Swiss channel. The other political magazine shows on Swiss TV too have much higher ratings than the comparable foreign programs.

The previously-stated general tendencies are illustrated in Table 7.8 by analyzing the program choice of the television audience on Tuesdays in the fourth quarter of 1986 as they are registered by the Swiss Broadcasting Corporation audience-meter system TELECONTROL, using a 450-member household panel in the German-speaking part of Switzerland.

Between 7:30 and 8:00 p.m., when the daily main news show is presented, almost three-quarters of the 60% of the television sets that are switched on are tuned to the Swiss channel (SRG). Only 25% of the households are watching one of the foreign channels at 7:30 p.m., when the ARD broadcasts crime show series and the Second German Television Station ZDF offers family shows and features.

After 8:00 p.m., the Swiss channel is still able to attract two thirds of the television audience for the next hour by showing every Tuesday its highly valued weekly crime show ("Der Alte," "Derrick," "Der Fahnder," "Ein Fall fuer Zwei"—by the way, all West German productions). The share of ARD is about 10% with alternately a popular quiz show (Robert Lembke's "Was bin ich?"), a game show ("Die Montagsmaler") or cultural and nature programs. ZDF, the second German channel, starts its prime time each Tuesday with a movie, getting a share of 15%.

The Swiss television evening continues with the only weekly political magazine (Rundschau) until 10:00 p.m. Due to the fact that at the same time the weekly political magazine (Report) is transmitted by the first German channel

TABLE 7.8

Determination of Program Choice by Program Content of Different
Television Channels in the German Part of Switzerland, 1986

| Time: | Household Ratings in % | | | | Household Shares in % | | | |
|---|---|---|---|---|---|---|---|---|
| | SRG | ARD | ZDF | TV Total | SRG | ARD | ZDF | Other |
| 19.30 | 40 | 13 | 2 | 60 | 67 | 22 | 3 | 8 |
| 19.45 | 46 | 5 | 3 | 61 | 75 | 8 | 5 | 12 |
| 20.00 | 42 | 6 | 5 | 62 | 69 | 10 | 8 | 13 |
| 20.15 | 43 | 7 | 9 | 65 | 66 | 11 | 14 | 9 |
| 20.30 | 43 | 7 | 10 | 67 | 64 | 10 | 15 | 11 |
| 20.45 | 41 | 8 | 11 | 68 | 60 | 12 | 16 | 12 |
| 21.00 | 25 | 4 | 18 | 61 | 41 | 7 | 30 | 22 |
| 21.15 | 17 | 3 | 20 | 57 | 30 | 5 | 35 | 30 |
| 21.30 | 16 | 5 | 18 | 56 | 29 | 9 | 32 | 30 |
| 21.45 | 13 | 24 | 2 | 54 | 24 | 44 | 4 | 28 |
| 22.00 | 10 | 30 | 1 | 51 | 20 | 59 | 2 | 19 |
| 22.15 | 7 | 29 | 2 | 47 | 15 | 62 | 4 | 19 |
| 22.30 | 11 | 6 | 3 | 34 | 32 | 18 | 9 | 41 |
| 22.45 | 10 | 3 | 3 | 28 | 35 | 11 | 11 | 43 |
| 23.00 | 9 | 1 | 3 | 24 | 37 | 4 | 13 | 46 |

Notes: Audience data are based on 13 Tuesdays of the 4th quarter of 1986
in the German Part of Switzerland (N=450 households). Brackets are explained
in the text.

ARD, between 10% and 20% of the households stay on the Swiss channel. But a
significant part of the Swiss crime show audience, probably the politically
uninterested viewers, switch the channel and watch the second half of the movie
on ZDF. So the share of the ZDF Tuesday movie starts with a modest 15% at 8:00
p.m. but increases to 30% after 9:00 p.m.

At the end of the ZDF movie at 9:45 p.m., a big shift to the ARD can be observed, from the ZDF on the one hand and also from the Swiss channel (SRG).
"Dallas," the very successful U.S. series, scheduled every Tuesday evening between 9:45 and 10:30 on the ARD, attracts about 30% of the households. As a
result, the share of the first German television program jumps up to about 60%.

The end of Dallas coincides with the beginning of the Tuesday live sports
magazine by the Swiss channel, which presents the hockey games of the national
league in the winter. Both factors together effect significant channel-switching at
that particular time.

These few comments should have made it clear that the differences in the
program grids of the three most popular television channels in the German-speaking part of Switzerland (SRG, ARD, ZDF) and their interplay in time are the main
factors in audience shifts during prime time. The success of the Swiss channel is
mainly a result of its attractive program planning (indigenous information, game

TABLE 7.9

Frequency of Television Use and Viewing Time per Day
in Different Audiovisual Environments, 1987

| Frequency of Television Use in % | Total | No TV | TV Only | TV with CATV Only | More TV Options |
|---|---|---|---|---|---|
| Daily, almost daily | 61 | 1 | 63 | 70 | 67 |
| Several times a week | 21 | 5 | 25 | 20 | 26 |
| Once a week | 5 | 14 | 5 | 4 | 2 |
| Less than once a week | 7 | 20 | 6 | 6 | 5 |
| Never | 6 | 60 | 1 | 0 | 0 |
| TV viewing (minutes/day) | 89 | 5 | 89 | 100 | 105 |
| Total   N | 676 | 64 | 198 | 226 | 188 |
| Sample % | 100 | 10 | 29 | 33 | 28 |

Note: "More TV-Options" means connection to at least two of the following
new media: CATV, VCR, satellite programs, or pay-television. From Bonfadelli
(1987), N=698 persons aged 20-85 years old.

shows, sportscasts, and competitive international entertainment) on the one hand,
and of the programs on the competitive foreign channels.

To sum up, one can say that the availability of more TV channels has not
strongly fragmented the mass audience until now. Evidence so far suggests that although some splintering occurs, it appears to be only marginal because most
television channels tend to offer broad-based and mass-appeal programming. As
people follow programs, not services, their viewing is spread over several channels, and switching channels is a prevalent practice (Bigman, 1986).

## TV ENVIRONMENT AND STIMULATION OF TV USE

Access to a television set is a prerequisite for television use. But today, it is not
only the question of yes or no to television; there are now different options available that increase the number of programs that the viewer can select (CATV and
satellite) and that weaken the dependence of the audience on the fixed program
schedule (video recorder, pay TV). These new viewing options prompt the following question: Do they cause an increase in television viewing?

Table 7.4 shows that 10% of the adult population in the German- and French-
speaking parts of Switzerland owned no television set at all in 1987. Another 29%
had a television set, but no further viewing options, and 33% owned a television
set with one more option, in most cases, access to a cable system. The remaining

TABLE 7.10

Relationship Between Frequency of Television Use and
Different Audiovisual Environment in Different Social Segments, 1987

| Daily Television Use in % | N | Total | No TV | TV Only | TV with CATV Only | More TV Options |
|---|---|---|---|---|---|---|
| Total audience | 698 | 61 | 1 | 63 | 70 | 67 |
| Men | 343 | 61 | 4 | 66 | 67 | 66 |
| Women | 346 | 60 | 0 | 61 | 73 | 67 |
| 20-34 years | 225 | 48 | 0 | 50 | 58 | 57 |
| 35-49 years | 354 | 58 | 0 | 62 | 60 | 68 |
| 50-85 years | 105 | 75 | 6 | 73 | 83 | 86 |
| High   SES | 225 | 60 | 5 | 53 | 72 | 68 |
| Middle SES | 354 | 61 | 0 | 65 | 67 | 65 |
| Low    SES | 105 | 61 | 0 | 77 | 78 | 69 |
| University | 159 | 45 | 0 | 50 | 62 | 63 |
| Trade school | 358 | 61 | 5 | 64 | 66 | 62 |
| High school | 172 | 75 | 0 | 71 | 85 | 85 |
| German Switzerland | 511 | 59 | 2 | 61 | 70 | 64 |
| French Switzerland | 176 | 64 | 0 | 67 | 67 | 72 |

Note: "More TV-Options" means connection to at least two of the
following new media: CATV, VCR, satellite programs, or pay-television.
From Saxer and Bonfadelli (1986), N=689 persons aged 20-85 years old.

28% had even more possibilities, such as video recorders, access to satellite television programs, or a subscription to Teleclub/Telecine, the Swiss pay television.

Table 7.9 shows that the audiovisual environment that someone lives in is correlated with the frequency of television use. It is the best predictor of the variance in television viewing time, if one performs a multiple regression analysis with the following dimensions: age, gender, education, SES, audiovisual environment, number of TV channels available, and interest in politics. The standardized beta coefficients are the following: audiovisual environment +0.27, age +0.20 (sig. at 0.00), education -0.16 (sig. at 0.00), and interest in politics -0.09 (sig. at 0.04).

Table 7.10 illustrates that although television use depends on the richness of the audiovisual environment, it is mediated by different social settings. Seventy-five percent of the 50-years-and-older audience with a TV set at home watches television daily. Access to cable or other television options increases daily viewing a bit more than 10%. About the same holds for the young age group, 20 to 34 years old, but on a deeper level because only 48% of them watch TV daily. The picture is different if one looks at viewing time: access to more viewing options increases viewing time for 50% (from 70 minutes to 106 minutes per day) in the young age group but only for 20% (104 to 127 minutes) in the oldest age group. Access to new media seems to have an especially strong homogenizing influence across the different SES segments too. Viewing frequency of low and high SES groups differs significantly if one analyzes the "TV-only" subgroup: 53% engage in daily TV use in the high SES group, in comparison to 77% in the low SES group. Interestingly, the viewing behavior of the three SES groups is much more homogeneous if they live in an environment with more AV-options such as CATV and a VCR.

About two thirds of the television viewers in the German and French part of Switzerland seem to be content with the amount and variety of television programs that are available to them. This is a result of the Univox-Survey, conducted in 1987 (Saxer & Bonfadelli, 1987). One fifth in general, 28% of the 15-29 age group and a third of those who receive not more than five television channels expressed a desire to get more than that. Viewers who were interested in more television services would like to get them from the Swiss Broadcasting Corporation (67%), from foreign public television stations (59%) or from satellite television stations (44%). Only 31% seemed to be interested in television programs from future private Swiss television stations. Viewers were interested primarily in more television news (55%) and entertainment, such as movies (55%). Only 39% asked for more local television.

## VCR: INDIVIDUALIZATION AND PERSONALIZATION
## OF TV VIEWING

In 1986, 29% of the households in the audience-meter panel of the Swiss German Broadcasting Corporation had VCRs. These data show that half of these households use the VCR on a typical weekday. The time spent with video is 90 minutes per day per household, as Table 7.11 shows. This means that about four video films are seen in the average video household per week (Aeschenbacher & Steinmann, 1987).

Playback of TV material is still the dominant use of the VCR. Three quarters of the households with a VCR watch material they have recorded themselves from television. Rented (25%) or bought (3%) cassettes play only a minor role. The younger video recorder owners buy or lease videocassettes more often than other owners. Analysis of the content preferences shows that crime/action films and entertainment, followed by comedies and sports, are dominant (Saxer & Bonfadelli, 1986; Steinmann, 1986).

TABLE 7.11

Use of Video Recorder in Households and by People
In German, French and Italian Switzerland, 1986

| Use of Video Recorder | Use in Percent | | | Use in Min. per viewer | | |
|---|---|---|---|---|---|---|
| | German | French | Italian | German | French | Italian |
| | | Switzerland | | | Switzerland | |
| **Weekdays** | | | | | | |
| Households | 11 | 14 | 8 | 90 | 93 | 113 |
| Adults | 5 | 8 | 4 | 66 | 73 | 85 |
| Children | 6 | 8 | 3 | 50 | 64 | 91 |
| **Saturday** | | | | | | |
| Households | 12 | 16 | 8 | 118 | 122 | 143 |
| Adults | 7 | 10 | 5 | 83 | 85 | 78 |
| Children | 7 | 12 | 4 | 73 | 79 | 114 |
| **Sunday** | | | | | | |
| Households | 14 | 18 | 9 | 148 | 126 | 156 |
| Adults | 9 | 12 | 6 | 113 | 100 | 83 |
| Children | 10 | 13 | 3 | 101 | 80 | 91 |
| **Households with VCR (%)** | 29 | 37 | 22 | 29 | 37 | 22 |

Note: Audience-meter data, time period was November 1986, N=450/350/200
households in German, French and Italian Switzerland. Children: 3-14 years old.
Adults: 15 years and older. From Aeschenbacher and Steinmann (1987).

Table 7.12 shows that there is a correlation between ownership of video recorders and frequency of television use. People who own a VCR show an increase of 8% in daily television use, from 51% to 59%, in comparison to those who use only a television set. However, this increase is not stable in the different social segments. Generally, access to a video recorder has the strongest influence in those segments that are low in television use: 20 to 29-year-olds, women, and the segment with low education. In this last group, 42% of the television audience with no access to a video recorder watches television every day compared to 75% with the same education but with a VCR. In the youngest age group, 20 to 29 years, access to a VCR increases daily television use from 27% to 53%.

## RADIO LISTENING: AUDIENCE FRAGMENTATION

After their introduction in November 1983, the Swiss private local radio stations gained quick acceptance from the young audience in the German-speaking part of

TABLE 7.12

Relationship Between Frequency of Television Use and
Ownership of Video Recorders in Different Social Segments, 1986

| Daily Tele- vision Use in % | N | Total | Video Recorder: No | Yes | Increase in TV Viewing (%) |
|---|---|---|---|---|---|
| Total Audience | 627 | 53 | 51 | 59 | +8 |
| Men | 307 | 55 | 54 | 59 | +5 |
| Women | 320 | 51 | 48 | 60 | +12 |
| 20-29 years | 131 | 37 | 27 | 53 | +26 |
| 30-49 years | 263 | 47 | 41 | 57 | +16 |
| 50-85 years | 232 | 70 | 68 | 79 | +11 |
| High   SES | 183 | 47 | 44 | 53 | + 9 |
| Middle SES | 326 | 54 | 51 | 61 | +10 |
| Low    SES | 101 | 62 | 60 | 71 | +11 |
| University | 107 | 66 | 64 | 71 | + 7 |
| Trade school | 328 | 47 | 46 | 49 | + 3 |
| High school | 191 | 51 | 42 | 75 | +33 |
| German Switzerland | 449 | 49 | 47 | 54 | + 7 |
| French Switzerland | 178 | 64 | 62 | 68 | + 6 |

Note: Data are based on owners of a television set (N=627)
From Saxer and Bonfadelli (1986), N=704.

Switzerland, whereas the French foreign private radios, due to technical and financial reasons, are still leading Swiss local radio in the French-speaking part of Switzerland. Table 7.13 shows the trends in the German-speaking part of Switzerland.

The introduction of the local radios stimulated an overall increase in time spent with audio media per weekday from 151 minutes in 1983 to 176 minutes in 1984. The time spent with foreign radio stations, such as SWF1/3 from Germany, decreased from 37 minutes in 1983 to 12 minutes per day in 1985. Due to the start of the new third public radio program DRS3 in November of 1983, which was designed for the young audience, the overall use of the Swiss Broadcasting Corporation channels was stable from 1982 to 1983 and increased from 1983 to 1984, before dropping in 1985. Radio listeners spent 31 minutes per day on the private Swiss local radio stations in 1984.

The introduction of the private local radios, on the one hand, and DRS3 by the Swiss Broadcasting on the other hand, caused a strong audience fragmentation, particularly along the age dimension. The young age segment, 15 to 29 years old, strongly prefers the new radio programs: Time per day spent on the local radios

TABLE 7.13

Shifts in Radio Use Between 1980 and 1985
In the German Part of Switzerland

| | | | Minutes per Weekday | | | |
|---|---|---|---|---|---|---|
| | 1980 | 1982 | 1983 | 1984 | 1985 | 1986 |
| Sample size | 2000 | 3483 | 1500 | 1500 | 1500 | 6748 |
| Swiss channels | | | | | | |
| DRS1 | 96 | 90 | 84 | 83 | 74 | 80 |
| DRS2 | 8 | 7 | 12 | 8 | 4 | 6 |
| DRS3 | - | - | 9 | 24 | 25 | 27 |
| other | 8 | 6 | 0 | 11 | 8 | 12 |
| Swiss public channels | 112 | 103 | 104 | 122 | 108 | 120 |
| Swiss local radios | - | - | - | 31 | 39 | 35 |
| German radio SWF1-3 | 25 | 23 | 25 | 12 | 10 | 13 |
| Swiss pirate radio 24 | 5 | 3 | 7 | - | - | - |
| Other foreign stations | 4 | 5 | 6 | 4 | 3 | 5 |
| Foreign radios | 34 | 31 | 37 | 16 | 12 | 18 |
| Records/cassettes | 12 | 13 | 10 | 8 | 12 | 9 |
| Total use of audio media | 152 | 146 | 151 | 176 | 171 | 181 |

Notes: Swiss local radio stations began in Nov. 1983. DRS3 began
in Nov. 1983. Radio 24 operated from Dec. 1979 until 1983. Data
based on weekdays, 15 years and older. From SRG-Forschungsdienst (1986).

is 47 minutes and on DRS3 57 minutes, whereas DRS1, the traditionally oriented main program, decreased in this age group from 67 minutes per day in 1983 to 42 minutes in 1984.

Introduction of private local radio stations on the one hand, and the third public radio program on the other, transformed radio listening in a qualitative way, too. Elderly listeners still use radio selectively as a medium for federal information and especially for local information. For the young listeners, radio today is a medium that mainly provides a music environment for the stimulation and control of their moods and feelings.

## TELETEXT VERSUS VIDEOTEXT: DIFFERENT SUCCESS
## OF INFORMATION SERVICES

In 1985, teletext was available to 11% of the television viewers in the German-speaking part of Switzerland. That translates to roughly 400,000 users age 15 and over. Since the introduction of teletext in 1981, its diffusion has increased slowly but steadily. The main factor of its acceptance is not as much its functional value or the perceived need of the audience for news and service-information as it is the purchase of a new television set. Almost all television sets available today have a built-in teletext decoder. The Swiss Teletext Corporation predicted a penetration of 20% for 1987, which is expected to double by 1990.

A first survey of teletext users shows above-average use in the 25 to 44 age group and in the high and medium SES groups. Television viewers with teletext decoders use teletext about four times a week on the average; its daily coverage is 59%. Teletext is used mainly in the evening. Typical usage occurs during commercial breaks in the television program, when the television program is not interesting enough, and before bedtime. Content preferences are weather forecasts, sports results, and political news (Haettenschwiler & Jedele, 1987).

Videotext, which makes possible access to computerized data bases by telephone, had a very slow start in Switzerland. Only 700 private users subscribed to the service during the pilot project (from September 1984 to October 1985), with about 1,500 additional offices connected. Of these early adopters, 95% were men, 73% between 30 and 49 years old, and 63% with college or university education (IBFG, 1985).

Videotext is used mainly for telebanking (45%), but other uses include teleshopping (9%), entertainment (7%), and travel/tourist information (5%). The evaluative research shows that presently only 40% of the users are satisfied with this electronic information service and videotext has not met the expectations of 51% of its subscribers. The main reasons for rejection of this new medium at the moment are technical deficiency (search process too complicated, delay of response), lack of useful content, and expense (lack of cheap videotext decoders). The initial euphoria after the introduction of videotext in Switzerland by the PTT and the information providers vanished, and a pragmatic and skeptical estimation of the future development of videotext dominated (IBFG, 1985).

## SUMMARY AND CONCLUSIONS

The last 10 to 15 years have seen fundamental transformations in the media options available to audiences in Switzerland. The restrictions of terrestrial broadcasting through a lack of available frequencies and geographical obstacles have been reduced by technical innovations. More foreign television programs have become accessible to most viewers through cable systems, and penetration will probably reach 70% to 80% by the 1990s, together with international program services distributed via satellites. The spread of video recorders has reduced the dependence on fixed time schedules of television. New information services are trying to attract the public, and different private local radio stations have started to produce and transmit programs for target audiences. This supply of old and new programs has had various and not yet fully conceivable effects on demand and uses of media by the more and more fragmented audiences.

## Television

The position of the Swiss Broadcasting Corporation has been weakened due to the very attractive and competitive foreign television programs, which profit from their much bigger financial and creative resources. Because viewing time hasn't increased in the last years and the television audience has the tendency to get even more of the same if possible—more entertainment, especially—this tends to erode channel loyalty with a loss of viewers by the Swiss television in general and particularly by its political and cultural programs. The specialized satellite programs—Music Box and Sky Channel—have become attractive, above all, to the younger television audience. Increasing numbers of targeted programs—especially transmission of sports events on the fourth channel—by the Swiss Broadcasting Corporation will increase audience fragmentation in the future.

## Radio

Installation of private radio in Switzerland has caused public service radio to improve program quality by competition and to provide new services (e.g., DRS3). As a result, public service radio hasn't lost much of the share it had in the early 1980s, partly due to an overall increase in listening time. At the same time, the audience of foreign radio stations has decreased since the introduction of the private local radios and the third youth-oriented radio channel of the Swiss Broadcasting Corporation. In general, the different radio programs today are much more tuned to the specific music tastes of the various age groups.

## Information Services

Diffusion of teletext depends strongly on the acquisition of a new television set. Due to this, its acceptance is increasing slowly but steadily. The diffusion of videotext is quite different from this pattern. It is not yet clear if a substantial segment of the population has or will develop information needs active and strong enough to stimulate subscription to the service and the necessary acquisition of a videotext.

Leo Schuermann, director-general of the Swiss Broadcasting Corporation, is aware of the limited scope that public service broadcasters must expect in the future as a result of limited resources, both personal and financial, together with market saturation. Schuermann (1986) has noted that one answer lies in program differentiation. Schuermann has observed, however, that public broadcasters are aware that program differentiation is only a partial solution if they wish to maintain their role as social integrators. Regardless, Schuermann argues, the public service broadcasters, as long as they continue to strive to improve program quality and range and better meet the viewers' and listeners' needs, will find reserves of strength in the present program service.

This seems to be quite an optimistic view, considering the just-beginning process of privatization in the field of electronic media in Switzerland and the introduction of even more private TV channels in the neighboring countries of Switzerland. Nevertheless, the steadily growing dependence on television and mass-mediated culture in general (cinema, book publishing, record production, electronic data sources, etc.) in Switzerland from foreign multinational media companies has increased the sensibility of the politicians. The question of rising cultural dependence and eroding national identity will be explored in research projects in the future.

## REFERENCES

Aeschenbacher, C., & Steinmann, M. (1987). *Video in der Schweiz: Analyse zur quantitativen und qualitativen Nutzung von Video in Privathaushalten der Schweiz* [Video in Switzerland: An analysis of the quantitative and qualitative use of video in Swiss private households]. SRG-Forschungsdienst. Bern: SRG.
Bigman, S. (1986). Changing media, evolving markets: New developments in electronic media from a worldwide perspective. In ESOMAR (Ed.), *Seminar on new developments in media research* (pp. 1-14). Helsinki: ESOMAR.
Bundesamt fuer Statistik. (1986). *Statistisches Jahrbuch der Schweiz* [Statistical yearbook of Switzerland]. Basel: Birkhaeuser.

Haettenschwiler, W., & Jedele, M. (1987). Akzeptanz von Lokalfernsehen und Bildschirmtexten in der Schweiz [Acceptance of local television and viewdata in Switzerland]. In F. Fleck, U. Saxer, & M. Steinmann (Eds.), *SGKM-Jubilaeumsband* (pp. 231-240). Zurich: Schulthess.

Interdisziplinaere Berater- und Forschungsgruppe AG Basel (IBFG). (1985). *Schlussbericht der Begleituntersuchung zum Videotext-Betriebsversuch* [Final report of the videotext pilot study]. Bern: PTT.

Jakubowicz, K. (1985). Mass and communication revisited. *InterMedia, 13* (1), 37-41.

McCain, T. (1986). Patterns of media use in Europe. *European Journal of Communication, 1*, 231-250.

Meier, W., & Bonfadelli, H. (1987). Comparative analysis of videotex pilot project studies in three European countries. *Telematics and Informatics, 4*, 144-152.

Saxer, U. (1986). Switzerland. In H. J. Kleinsteuber, D. McQuail, & K. Siune (Eds.), *Electronic media and politics in Western Europe* (pp. 296-315). Frankfurt: Campus.

Saxer, U., & Bonfadelli, H. (1986). *Univox-Studie Kommunikation* [Univox communications study]. Zurich: Schweizerische Gesellschaft fuer Praktische Sozialforschung.

Saxer, U., & Bonfadelli, H. (1987). *Univox-Studie Kommunikation* [Univox communications study]. Zurich: Schweizerische Gesellschaft fuer Praktische Sozialforschung.

Schuermann, L. (1986). Switzerland and developments in the field of electronic media and communications. *EBU-Review, 37* (1), 10-14.

SRG-Forschungsdienst. (1981). *Jahresbericht des Forschungsdienstes 1980, Band I: Allgemeine Daten* [Yearly report of the research service, 1980, vol. 1: General data]. Bern: SRG.

SRG-Forschungsdienst. (1986). *Jahresbericht des Forschungsdienstes 1985, Band I: Allgemeine Daten* [Yearly report of the research service, 1980, vol. 1: General data]. Bern: SRG.

Steinmann, M. F. (1978). Nutzung und Resonanz deutscher Rundfunkprogramme in der Schweiz [Use and acceptance of German broadcasting in Switzerland]. *Media Perspektiven*, (10), 709-716.

Steinmann, M. F. (1986). Elektronische Zuschauerforschung in der Schweiz: Das SRG TELECONTROL-System nach einem Jahr Praxis [Electronic viewer research in Switzerland: The SRG Telecontrol system after one year of practice]. *Rundfunk und Fernsehen, 34*, 709-716.

Steinmann, M. F., & Weibel, E. (1985). Reaktionen des Publikums auf private Rundfunk-Anbieter in der Schweiz [Reactions of the audience to commercial broadcasting stations in Switzerland]. *Rundfunk und Fernsehen, 33*, 480-493.

# 8

# France: Experimenting With Pay TV and Viewdata

**Isabelle Pailliart**
*The Stendhal University, Grenoble*

## INTRODUCTION [1]

Just recently, France has experienced some major changes in the amount and quality of audiovisual offerings. Besides the introduction of the videocassette recorder (VCR), several new and commercial TV stations have been added to what could be called a fairly restricted TV variety until the mid-1980s. The development of the new media technologies in France is somewhat paradoxical, however. On the one hand, cable and VCRs are not as widespread as in almost all other Western industrialized countries. On the other hand, France successfully introduced viewdata as a veritable "mass" medium and has played an innovative role in terms of establishing pay TV. Both "Minitel," France's viewdata system, and "Canal Plus," the first pay TV channel, are examples for how the audience is able to redefine the nature of a mass medium. This chapter attempts to describe the changes both in the French media landscape and—although based on regrettably scarce figures—in the behavior of the audience.

## TELEVISION

Between 1960 and 1970, the percentage of French households with a TV set had risen from 13.6 to 69.5. In 1984, 93% of all households had at least one TV set. The 1970s also saw the rapid penetration of color TV sets. But these sets can still be found more often among professionals, skilled workers, in medium and large provincial cities, and among persons between 40 and 59 years of age.

Slowly, the number of households with more than one TV set has been rising, too. In 1986, for instance, 15.7% of the households in France had at least two sets. Here again, France ranges behind other Western European countries such as Britain, the Netherlands, West Germany, and Italy. This lag may be one reason for what is regarded as a slow adaptation of both new and commercial TV channels and other new media in France. Households with more than one child between 8 and 14 years of age, and those in the upper class, more frequently belong to the multi-TV-set group.

On an average, the French spend a third of their leisure time watching television. Until 1985, the time devoted to TV had virtually remained stable—about 130 minutes per day, 16 hours per week. Since 1986, however, this time has slowly increased. In general, older people and those low in formal education watch more television than their counterparts (Souchon, 1985).

In March 1987, TF1, the first French television channel, formerly a non-commercial, publicly controlled institution, was changed into a commercial station. By the end of the 1980s, the following were available in France:

- Two publicly controlled channels, Antenne 2 (A2), with an audience of 36% per day in May 1987, and France-Regions 3 (FR3), reaching 15% of the French population.
- Canal Plus, a pay-TV channel, founded in 1984. After a difficult start, it had one million subscribers by May 1986 and was expected to double that figure by September 1987. That means it would reach about 10% of all households. Its daily reach was an estimated 4%.
- The commercial broadcast stations TF1, with a daily reach of about 40% in May 1987, "La 5," and M6. The latter two, not receivable everywhere in France, were watched by only about 6% of the French on an average.

TF1, A2, and FR3 were more family-oriented and somewhat more traditional, and thus had a slightly older and more rural audience than Canal Plus, "La 5," and M6.

One of the greatest difficulties that "La 5" and M6 had in 1985 when they first started broadcasting was their small technical reach. They could be watched only by a small percentage of the French population. By September of 1987, for instance, an estimated 15 million people could receive M6. That figure was expected to rise to 18 million by the end of 1987, that is, 45% of French households. About 15% of those able to receive it watch it regularly. In principle, 60% of the population could get "La 5," but only 21% had their TV sets tuned in a way that they could actually watch this channel. Twelve to 14% of the French population turn it on regularly.

The present strategy of "La 5" is to adopt the profiles of the two nationwide, general-audience channels, TF1 and A2. Its ambition is to become a channel that will reach a majority of the French audience. In doing so, "La 5" is fighting at several fronts. For instance, it has to increase the territory where people can get it, and it has to convince its present viewers not to return to the old services.

Canal Plus and M6, on the other hand, offer more specific services: Canal Plus focuses on sports and movies, and M6 primarily broadcasts series, movies, and music shows, hoping to win over 5 to 10% of the national audience. Also, on September 14, 1987, it started some local TV experiments.

### Canal Plus: A Unique Channel

Canal Plus probably is the TV station with the biggest success. What else could one call it if, 3 years after this pay TV channel was introduced in 1984, it already had 2 million subscribers, 10% of all the French households, and 92% of the subscribers renew their subscription? And that is in spite of a subscription fee of as much as 150 francs (about $28 U.S.) per month and in spite the fact that not all French households (only 80%) are able to receive it. Canal Plus is broadcast over the air, but subscribers need a decoder to unscramble the signals.

Those responsible for the programming of Canal Plus think that their success is mainly due to the audience's preference for movies and its feeling that Canal Plus serves specific program interests better than the big national channels do. Canal Plus' advertising campaigns obviously meet the feelings of its audience. Slogans like "Canal Plus, the bold one" or "Canal Plus, the one with punch" hit home with its generally younger and more urban viewers. Although the Canal Plus audience is nearing the national average, those two groups still prevail, along with more workers, employees, and high-ranking civil servants. Also, more housholds with an above-average number of audio-visual devices subscribe to Canal Plus. The same applies to households with children. Canal Plus subscribers watch more TV (3 hours per day) than the average viewers (about 2 hours and 10 minutes). They watch more selectively, however: 57% of them, as compared to 38% nationwide, claim to consciously select programs before they turn their TV sets on.

What are the reasons to subscribe to Canal Plus? Sixty percent of the subscribers say they did it mainly because of the movies on that channel. Another 30% mention sports as the primary reason, and 4.5% cite the convenient program schedule. These responses underline the peculiarities of Canal Plus: it is the first specialized TV service in France. Each year it broadcasts up to 365 movies, which are 50% of its programming. In contrast to the publicly controlled channels, Canal Plus is able to show movies that are only 1 year old. Other services have to wait at least 3 years.

Similar to pay-TV channels in other parts of the world, Canal Plus shows the same movie up to 5 times at different times of the day. This allows the viewers to watch programs on other TV channels without missing a movie on Canal Plus. So, Canal Plus supplements other services rather than actually competes with them.

But the success of Canal Plus cannot only be explained by the fact that its audience can—similar to households with a VCR—structure its TV programming more freely. Canal Plus viewers regard themselves as members of a club, a brotherhood, a group with special bonds to the station. The channel itself, for instance, started to supply its viewers in October 1987 with a free subscriber magazine. It provides games, offers cruises only for subscribers and tells its readers about audience research results. All of this is supposed to make the subscribers feel special, not like the viewers of the ordinary TV channels.

So far, Canal Plus has been a special interest-channel, concentrating on movies and sports. In order to reach more groups of society that want their interests more heavily represented on TV, Canal Plus in 1987 started a service for young people who have felt neglected by the other channels. More than other TV services, Canal Plus does both extensive and continuous audience research in order to gauge even slight changes in the interests of its viewers. French researcher Jean-Michel Salaun (1987) calls the possibilities offered by Canal Plus the third generation of audio-visual media after those of movie theaters and of traditional television. In his words, it allows television a la carte.

## Cable Television

As opposed to the development in other Western European countries, cable networks in France by 1987 were not very widespread, although in 1982 the socialist government had initiated an ambitious project called "Plan Cable." Its major goal was to make France one of the leading nations in glass fiber technology. The fiber networks were to be used for integrated information distribution. By late 1987, however, broadcast TV still dominated cable.

For a monthly subscription fee exactly the same as the one for Canal Plus (150 francs), viewers received 15 TV stations via cable. Included were the domestic channels, some from adjacent countries, plus some of the satellite services, such as TV5 and Superchannel. In addition, a local TV channel was added that broadcast some programs of local importance. Whereas, in 1985, only 20,000 households were passed by cable (with 3,000 subscribers, i.e., 15%), this figure was 467,000

TABLE 8.1

1984 Intentions to Subscribe to Cable Channels
By Ability to Receive More Than the Three TV Channels
Broadcasting in 1984

| Intention to Subscribe If They Could Receive | Respondents Able to Receive More than the 3 Channels % | Respondents Able to Receive Only the 3 Channels % | Total % |
|---|---|---|---|
| - the 3 channels with a better picture | 10.9 | 24.2 | 21.6 |
| - RTL Luxembourg and Tele Monte Carlo | 27.6 | 32.2 | 30.7 |
| - Swiss and Belgian television | 19.0 | 24.1 | 22.8 |
| - foreign channels, dubbed in French | 22.6 | 22.9 | 22.2 |
| - a channel devoted to the town or the county | 26.0 | 29.7 | 28.8 |
| - an educational channel | 28.8 | 33.6 | 32.0 |
| - a movie channel | 46.7 | 51.2 | 49.2 |
| - a sports channel | 18.6 | 20.6 | 19.8 |
| - a news channel | 24.0 | 22.5 | 22.5 |
| - a channel offering 20 video games | 14.7 | 13.6 | 13.3 |
| - a pop music channel | 18.9 | 15.7 | 15.7 |
| - a music and game show channel | 33.6 | 29.8 | 29.7 |

in 1987. In that year, 86,375 people had subscribed to cable, almost 20% of those who could get cable. For 1989, projections are 2,096,700 households passed by cable with 485,535 subscribers. These figures show that France does not have to reckon with a dramatic increase in cable's importance in the near future.

The stimulus for subscription to cable is, as Table 8.1 shows, the prospects of receiving local news and information on TV. Also, as in other countries, the pos-

TABLE 8.2

Sales of Video Cassette Recorders Per Year

| 1982 | 665,000 |
|------|---------|
| 1983 | 514,000 |
| 1984 | 651,000 |
| 1985 | 725,000 |

sibility to watch special-interest programs is an important reason to at least think of subscribing to cable.

## VIDEOCASSETTE RECORDERS

By the end of 1987, according to most recent estimates, about 4 million households in France had a videocassette recorder (VCR). Although this figure meant an increase of almost one third compared to 1986, the situation in France was still characterized by a relatively low distribution of VCRs. In 1983, for instance, only 3% of the French population had access to a VCR; in 1987, this figure may have risen to about 20%. But the percentage of households with a VCR still ranged behind that in Britain, West Germany, the Netherlands, and Denmark. In May 1986, for example, only 13% of the French even intended to buy a VCR soon. In general, owners of VCRs were young, had an above-average income and lived in larger cities. Table 8.2 gives a sense of the growth in VCR sales in France during the 1980s.

VCRs in France generally are a media technology that primarily accompanies traditional use of the television set. In fact, most French video owners use their VCRs for taping TV programs that they watch whenever the regular TV schedule does not offer interesting material. In other words, the VCR is in some ways a substitute for television. In 1987, on an average, households with a VCR had 12.7 blank cassettes as opposed to 0.5 prerecorded ones. A May 1986 survey showed that 29% of the video owners used their VCRs primarily for taping movies on TV. Fifteen percent claimed to use it mostly for recording other TV programs. Nineteen percent seemed mainly to watch prerecorded cassettes. Without particular preference for one of the three purposes just mentioned, the VCR was used by 37% of the French video owners.

In 1986, curiosity was an important factor for viewing prerecorded cassettes. A new owner of a VCR rented approximately 11 cassettes per month. After a while, the number of cassettes rented stabilized at about 2 per month. In general, there has been an increasing gap between the growing number of households with a VCR and the rather slow increase of cassette rentals.


## VIEWDATA

In the 1970s, France experienced a strong increase in the number of households equipped with a telephone. In 1971, there were only 5 million lines. That figure rose to 10 million in 1977, and in 1982, that number had doubled again. With about 30 telephone lines per 100 inhabitants, France in the late 1980s ranked 16th in the world. In order to counter the threatening stagnation of the telephone market and the increasing international competition in new communication technologies, the French Postal Administration (PTT) decided to offer a video display terminal with a small television screen to every telephone owner in the country. This so-called Minitel terminal, connected to the phone, is a simple and fairly inexpensive viewdata or videotext device. The keyboard and screen allow the user to send and receive messages and to retrieve centrally stored information through keywords. At the end of 1986, 2,237,000 "Minitels" had already been installed, up from 530,000 in 1984. By the end of the century, an estimated 14.5 million terminals will be in service in France.

One of the major services offered by Minitel is a national "phone book." Minitel users can find the phone number of anybody, anywhere in France. The first 3 minutes of this service are free. In 1987, about 20 million calls per month to find out phone numbers were counted by the Postal Administration. This very popular service and the flexibility of the French viewdata system were important factors in making it more successful than other viewdata systems. Although Minitel is run by the state, it is open to everybody who wants to offer services in it. Also, some of the money that users have to pay for Minitel services as part of their phone bill is used to subsidize those who furnish the services.

In December 1986, for instance, 4,125 persons, institutions, and companies provided viewdata services. During that same year, they were called roughly 287 million times, up from about 103 million times in 1985. The average user called Minitel 16 times in the month of December 1986 and spent about 97 minutes with this device. A year before, in December of 1985, the average number of calls had been 11.5, and the time spent on them had been 77 minutes.

The success of viewdata in France, however, should not mask some differences in the frequency of its use. In December 1986, for instance, only 3% of all the users made 24% of all the calls, and 23% of the users made 68% of the calls. So, it is still a very active minority that heavily uses Minitel.

Although, at first, viewdata was expected to be an instrument of person-machine communication, it has actually become the vehicle of a mediated person-to-person communication (Charon, 1987). In May 1985, the use of communication services—games and personal messaging—surpassed that of information services for the first time and has surpassed it ever since. What we are obviously observing is a redefinition of the purposes of that new medium.

## CONCLUSIONS

The introduction of new television channels, pay TV, VCRs, and viewdata has not only changed the media landscape in France dramatically; it has also demonstrated the important role of the audience. As far as our still unsatisfactory knowledge about the new media in France suggests, the audience defines both the use and the gratifications of a new medium as part of its environment. This environment consists of many other devices and cultural practices. In fact, the audience lives in its own time, and that is not necessarily the time of technology, economy, and politics.

## NOTES

[1] This chapter was translated from the original French by Marianne and Klaus Schoenbach.

## REFERENCES

Charon, J. M. (1987). *Les paradis informationels* [The information paradise]. Paris: Masson.
Salaun, J.-M. (1987). *La production de la television* [Television production]. These d'etat, Universite de Grenoble 3, Grenoble.
Souchon, M. (1985, March). *Petit ecran, grand public: Des nouvelles recentes* [Small screen, large audience: On recent news]. (Research Rep.). Issy les Moulineaux: Centre National d'Etudes des Telecommunications.

# 9

# Federal Republic of Germany: Social Experimentation With Cable and Commercial Television

**Elisabeth Noelle-Neumann**
**Ruediger Schulz**
*Institut fuer Demoskopie Allensbach*

Research on the effects of the mass media or on the effects of competition between public and commercial television or of competition between television and the print media still runs into enormous problems. The funds required are simply not allocated to such projects in communications research.

In this situation, German communications research was presented with an unusual opportunity when the advisory commission established by the Brandt administration to investigate new developments in the telecommunications system (the KtK—Kommission fuer den Ausbau des technischen Kommunikationssytems) under Dr. Eberhard Witte presented a report in 1976 recommending a kind of "social experimentation" (Bundesministerium fuer das Post- und Fernmeldewesen, 1976). The commission recommended conducting four "pilot projects" in order to determine the need for and effect of cable television in various areas of the Federal Republic of Germany under various conditions. Social experimentation based on representative samples is a practical political measure used in the United States in a great variety of areas, for example, education (tuition vouchers, busing), transportation (speed limits), tax policy (negative income tax), or criminal justice (paying unemployment benefits to released prisoners), but it had been almost unknown in the Federal Republic of Germany. The recommendation of the Witte Commission thus opened the door for social experimentation based on sample surveys in West Germany.

The pilot projects recommended by the Commission were introduced in four states: the Ludwigshafen region in Rhineland-Palatinate, an urban area of Munich in Bavaria, Dortmund in North Rhine-Westphalia, and West Berlin. This initiative provided a great opportunity for broadly based media effects research. It was possible to begin research before broadcasting of cable TV began and to follow developments over a period of several years with a quasi-experimental "pretest-posttest" design under natural conditions and with a broad sample. Unfortunately, this opportunity was not fully exploited. In only one of the four pilot project regions—Ludwigshafen—was a study of this kind conducted. There, a survey of a representative cross section of 2,470 persons in 1,295 households was used to ascertain the situation before cable television was introduced. Developments in attitudes and behavior were observed over a period of almost 3 years in a panel investigation comparing households that subscribed to cable TV with those that did not.

In 1978, approximately 2 years after the publication of the Witte Commission recommendation, work began in Rhineland-Palatinate on a state law that would provide a legal base for the pilot project in Ludwigshafen. Advice from the field of communication research was provided from the beginning by Dr. Elisabeth Noelle-Neumann in her capacity as Professor of Communications Research at the University of Mainz (Rhineland-Palatinate) and also as director of the Institut fuer Demoskopie Allensbach.

The Rhineland-Palatinate state law governing the cable pilot test took effect in December 1980. It is very likely the first German law that expressly takes the requirements of communications research into consideration. It states that before broadcasting of cable TV is begun, a representative survey is to be conducted, to be followed by additional surveys. Households desiring to receive the cable programming must also agree to be interviewed beforehand and repeatedly in the course of the test period without recompense. The law outlines the goals of the pilot project as follows:

> It is the purpose of the project to test the application of new communication techniques, as exemplified in more extensive programming, new kinds of programs, program structures and program contents, local television and participation by commercial broadcasters. Specifically, 1. the subscribers' behavior in using the medium and 2. the effect on the individual and society, especially on the family and the local community . . . are to be studied. (Landesgesetz ueber einen Versuch mit Breitbandkabel, 1980, paragraph 2)

Cable TV began broadcasting in Rhineland-Palatinate on January 1, 1984, almost 8 years after the Witte Commission's recommendation to conduct pilot projects with cable television. The other three pilot projects began on April 1, 1984 (Munich), June 1, 1985 (Dortmund), and August 28, 1985 (Berlin).

Almost another 3 years passed—while the cable pilot projects were in progress—and a total of 16 conferences of the governors of the states were necessary to come to an agreement, providing the legal base required for a general introduction of cable TV on a nationwide basis, that is, the 1986 interstate media contract (Medien-Staatsvertrag der Laender). This was preceded by a change in government in the Federal Republic from a Social Democrat/Liberal coalition to a Christian Democrat/Liberal coalition in October 1982 with a corresponding change in policy by the new Federal Minister of Post and Telecommunications, Christian Schwarz-Schilling, who moved with great speed to expand the cable network in Germany.

These historical developments testify to the existence of significant political barriers to the introduction of cable television in Germany. These barriers were not directly related to the new cable technology, but rather were products of the efforts of the two public broadcasting networks, ARD (with two channels) and ZDF (with one channel), to defend their monopoly and of the Social Democrats' policy of protecting that monopoly. Of the four pilot projects, only one—the Ludwigshafen project, under a Christian Democratic state government—expressly permitted "commercially sponsored" cable television services by private operators.

The report that follows is based on research accompanying the cable pilot project in Ludwigshafen. The political background just described is not insignificant in this regard, as it explains a series of controversies that subsequently developed about the design and findings of the investigation. The political standpoint and power of the established public television networks (ARD since 1950 and ZDF since 1961) had an effect on the research, due, among other things, to the publication policy of the public networks and their professional journal *Media Perspektiven*, as is shown later in interpreting the Ludwigshafen pilot project findings.

The Ludwigshafen research project also was caught up in another conflict not typical of scholarly work. In line with the state law governing the pilot project, a 14-member commission was drawn up by the state government to direct the research; it was made up of scholars from various disciplines, public officials, and politicians. As director of the institute that had been commissioned to conduct the study, Dr. Noelle-Neumann did not want to belong to this commission as a full member, although she was granted the right to participate in the sessions. As a result, situations arose in which the commission was of a different opinion on points of empirical procedure than the Allensbach Institute. This resulted in various compromises in the design of the study, its implementation, and the reporting. [1]

In order to realize the most important elements of the panel investigation and to provide a broad statistical base, the Allensbach Institute had to contribute approximately 23% of the funding on its own. Part of the plans for the study had to be dropped as a result of lack of financial means. [2]

The study got off to an atypical start for a research project. The official commission did not meet until September 21, 1983, and the Allensbach Institute was not officially assigned the study until the beginning of October. In order to meet the goal of conducting a study before the broadcasting of cable television began, only 6 weeks remained for sampling in the test region and development and testing of the questionnaire, with field work starting on November 26, 1983.

Ironically, although the quasi-experimental "pretest-posttest" design was only used in one of four test regions, two studies were in fact conducted in this region. The readers of this book will find two reports on the Ludwigshafen pilot project: this chapter and chapter 10. Chapter 10 is based in part on a study in the Ludwigshafen test region that was begun about 2 years later than ours, in autumn 1985. At that time, the Allensbach project had already been reported on in public (Noelle-Neumann, 1984, 1985b), and documentation of the findings of the first two surveys of 1983/84 and 1984/85 appeared in Noelle-Neumann (1985a). The final report of the Ludwigshafen pilot project commission was published in July 1987, based on the final report by Allensbach presented to the commission in January 1987.

The presence of both reports on the Ludwigshafen pilot project in this book obviates the need for details on the contents of the cable programs, which are reported at length in chapter 10 of this volume. The two reports agree on the most important findings about the development of attitudes and behavior after the introduction of cable television in Ludwigshafen. In order to provide an overview, the following section will present the design of the Allensbach study and its methods, followed by a comparative synopsis of the two Ludwigshafen research projects.

## METHODS

The study designed and conducted by the Institut fuer Demoskopie Allensbach was a combination of a quasi-experiment and panel surveys. Subscribers to cable TV constituted the test group and nonsubscribers made up the control group. An attempt was made to match the test and control groups as well as possible. Field experiments, however, often achieve only limited success in this respect as a result of natural conditions. This is particularly so when membership in the test or control group is not randomized (i.e., when it is influenced by self-selection) and does not remain constant throughout the period of the investigation, so that adjustments to actual developments have to be made. When nonsubscribers from the control group opted for cable during the 3-year period of the investigation, they by definition became members of the test group the moment that they were connected to the cable network. Membership in the test and control groups was thus self-selected and subject to change. We thus speak of the quasi-test group and the quasi-control group, in order to indicate that as a result of necessary adjustments to changes in reality, the test and control groups are not strictly comparable for all characteristics.

A similar situation had already occurred in an earlier quasi-experimental panel study conducted by the Allensbach Institute in the mid-1960s. The subject of that investigation was the effect of the introduction of television. A survey was conducted with the test group prior to purchase of their first television set and approximately 1 year later, and also with a quasi-control group consisting of households that did not have a television set and did not plan to purchase one. The households in the control group and in the test group were approximated as well as possible according to the statistical twin method, that is, as a matched pair sample. In spite of this, the quasi-control group differed from the test group, especially regarding attitudes. Logically, the *changes* within the test group and the control group between time zero and time one were compared and not the actual percentages for the two groups (Institut fuer Demoskopie Allensbach, 1968; Noelle-Neumann, 1979; Noelle-Neumann, 1982).

In the study of the impact of cable TV the analysis also focused on the direction and extent of *changes* between the various points in time of the surveys and not on the differences in percentages between the quasi-test group and quasi-control group. In line with the design of the study and the requirements of the state law (discussed previously), a representative sample of both groups was interviewed *before* broadcasting of cable TV began in a presurvey in December 1983 and January 1984. The representative sample of the population was set up as a multistage, clustered random sample. The regional clusters were selected at random from that part of the test region that, according to the Postal Ministry's plans, would have cable available by the end of the first test year ("homes passed by cable"). A total of 1,868 persons in 965 households were interviewed in this representative sample.

It would not have been possible to follow the reactions of the "innovators" and "early adopters" to cable TV with the presurvey of a representative cross section of 1,868 persons alone, because "innovators" and "early adopters" are by definition a very small group within the representative sample.[3] In order to have a sufficient statistical base to be able to make observations over the full 3-year period of the cable trial, a second sample was formed consisting of "innovators" only, that is, persons from households that had already applied for cable TV before broadcasting began. For this purpose, addresses from the files of the Cable Communications Administration were drawn at random; these consisted of households that were about to be connected to the cable network. In the sample of cable applicants, 602 persons in 330 households were interviewed.

As a result, the test group of persons who had opted for cable was recruited from two sources: a representative subsample of the population as well as a representative sample of cable applicants, that is, a combination of "innovators" and "early adopters." The control group of non-participants was drawn from the representative sample of the population and consisted of households that had not been connected to the cable network (internal control group). It proved impossible to finance the plan for a supplementary control group with matching characteristics outside of the test region (external control group). At intervals of approximately 1 year, three repeat surveys with the same persons were conducted using essentially identical questions. These consisted of a first repeat-survey/panel wave in December 1984 and January 1985, a second panel wave in late fall 1985, and a third panel wave in fall 1986, a few weeks before the project ended.

Approximately halfway through the project, a second panel was put together to supplement panel I, the "innovators and early adopters." This second panel consisted of persons who were not included in the initial group of cable innovators because they had not subscribed to the cable network until early autumn 1985. At that time, 20,000 households were connected to the cable network. The members of the second panel belonged to the "early majority." For panel II, we also have panel responses to a presurvey conducted before the respondents had subscribed to cable TV. Panel II members were interviewed a second time shortly before the project ended, in the late autumn of 1986, about a year after they first had received cable TV. The findings from panel I (innovators and early adopters), which was conducted over a period of 3 years, and from the 1-year panel II (early majority) complement each other.

There were a variety of problems with the abstract model for the experimental study. As noted earlier, membership in the test and control groups was self-selected. This resulted in continual changes in the composition of the test and the control group. It was also impossible to prevent the experimental factor, cable TV, from having both a direct and an indirect effect on the members of the control group. Cable television has an impact on the entire project area and on everyone who lives there if we consider how many conversational topics originate with cable TV programs. In addition, the members of the control groups watch cable programs at the homes of friends.[4] Finally, there was also an impact on public television, which, confronted with competition from cable, adapted some of its programming in order to make it more attractive to a broad group of viewers.

This experimental design has been described by Campbell and Stanley (1966) as a quasi-experimental pretest-posttest with a nonequivalent control group.

Campbell and Stanley argued decisively against dismissing such a quasi-experimental design. The presurvey ascertains the situation before the experimental factor takes effect. Repeating the interviewing determines the extent to which persons in the test group and persons in the control group are affected by such influences as cultural trends, maturation, and reactions to repeated interviewing. Differences in the composition of the quasi-test group and quasi-control group in terms of their attitudes, however, limit the ability of the quasi-control group to serve as a yardstick for changes that come about in the test group as a result of the experimental factor.

In addition to the design of the study as a field experiment with panel surveys, there was an additional special methodological feature. Because one of the main concerns in the lengthy public debate prior to the introduction of cable TV and the expanded programming offered by commercial operators was that cable TV might be detrimental to the family, the surveys were designed as a cell analysis, that is, a relational analysis of the family as well, with all persons in the household 14 years old and older interviewed.[5] This created the opportunity to analyze the findings by household or family collective, rather than just by individual, combining the responses of different members of the family and testing them for agreement or contradictions. It was thus possible to observe reactions to cable TV in a variety of family situations as well as the perspectives of the various members of the family.

The findings from panel I are based on 620 respondents in the test group (374 households) and 283 respondents in the control group (181 households). All panel members were interviewed before cable broadcasting was introduced and again 3 years later. Panel II consisted of 583 persons interviewed before receiving cable TV and approximately 1 year afterwards. For detailed information on methods, see the comprehensive report on the investigation (Noelle-Neumann & Schulz, 1987b).

The cable study described in chapter 10 began with an initial survey conducted in November, 1985, almost 2 years after cable broadcasting had been initiated in Ludwigshafen. By that time, the majority of innovators and early adopters already had cable. The maximum period of observation in that study was 1 year. Figure 9.1 details the methodologies of the two studies.

## MEASURING MEDIA EFFECTS: A METHODOLOGICAL DISCUSSION

A detailed discussion of the methodological problems of media effects research cannot be presented here, nor is it required. It is clear that two extreme positions sometimes taken with regards to such research cannot be maintained: (a) the claim that it is impossible to measure media effects at all because the changes observed

| Noelle-Neumann and Schulz | Kutteroff, Pfetsch, and Schoenbach |
|---|---|
| (Chap. 9 in this volume) | (Chap. 10 in this volume) |

### Design of the Study

| | |
|---|---|
| Pretest-posttest design (Presurvey before cable broadcasting was introduced Nov. 83/Feb. 84. A portion of the interviews continued until late February. At that time, cable had been available for two months, but the audience was very small.) | Pretest-posttest design (Presurvey before households were connected to the cable network but about 2 years after broadcasting began in Nov. 85) |
| Panel study | Panel study |
| -1st panel: mainly cable innovators and early adopters | -Cable subscribers at the stage of the "early majority" |
| -2nd panel: cable subscribers at the stage of the "early majority" | -Convinced opponents of cable TV who were determined not to subscribe to cable TV |
| Both of the above in the test region | Both of the above in the test region |
| | A parallel study of a panel outside the test region with a similar composition, including persons interested in subscribing to cable and determined opponents |
| Field experiment | Field experiment |
| Quasi-test group: Households subscribing to cable (self-selected) | Quasi-test group (self-selected) in the test area: Cable subscribers |
| Quasi-control group in the test area (self-selected): Nonsubscriber households | Quasi-control group in the test area: Nonsubscriber households |
| | Quasi-test group outside the test region (self-selected): would subscribe to cable TV if they could |
| Nonsubscribers who in the course of the 3-year trial period opted for cable TV and became part of the quasi-test group | Persons originally not wanting to subscribe, who changed their minds during the 1-year period of observation were removed from the universe |

(continued)

<u>Number of panel waves</u>

1st panel:                          2 repeat surveys after the ini-
3 repeat surveys after the          tial survey at intervals of
presurvey (Dec. 83/Jan. 84)         about half a year (April 86
at intervals of about one year      and Nov. 86)
(Dec. 84/Jan. 85, fall 85,
fall 86

2nd panel:
1 repeat survey one year
after the presurvey
(late summer 85) in fall 86

<u>Maximum period observed</u>

Almost 3 years after con-           One year after connection to the
nection to the cable network        cable network (Nov. 1985 to
(Dec. 83/Jan. 84 to fall 1986)      Nov. 1986)

<u>Mode of interview</u>

Face-to-face interviews with        Face-to-face interviews with
all members of the household        one member of the household and
14 and over                         a written survey of all members
                                    of the household 14 and over; a
                                    diary for all members of the
                                    household 10 and over

<u>Sample</u>

1st panel:                          (See also Fig. 10.1)
 Presurvey n=2470                    Presurvey  n=1655 persons
          in 1295 households                    in 749 households
 Persons interviewed at least
 twice in presurvey and final
 (3rd) wave:
 quasi-test    n=620 persons
 group         in 374 households  1st repeat survey  n=1470 persons
 quasi-control n=283 persons       panel wave          in 670 households
 group         in 181 households

2nd panel:
 presurvey     n=1006 persons
               in 511 households
 repeat survey n=583 persons in  2nd repeat survey   n=1313 persons
               326 households     panel wave          in 599 households

(continued)

```
                          Units of analysis

  1. Households represented by      1. Households represented by one
     one person                        person
  2. Persons 14 and over in the     2. Persons in the households
     households                        (14 and over, 10 and over)
  3. The households as a col-
     lective according to demo-
     graphic and psychological
     characteristics and accord-
     ing to interpersonal relations

                          Methods of analysis

  1. Direct comparisons within a    1. Direct comparisons within a wave
     wave
  2. Trend comparisons from wave    2. Trend comparisons from wave to wave
     to wave
  3. Analyses of panel shifts       3. Analyses of panel shifts
  4. Relational analyses
     (so-called cell analyses)
```

**FIG.9.1.** Overview of the most important features of the two studies of the cable pilot project Ludwigshafen.

might be attributable to so many other factors and, (b) the assertion that it is possible to prove media effects under natural conditions as clearly as effects can be proved in the natural sciences. The goal can only be to design studies that will determine that media effects are responsible for stability or change with as much probability as possible. In addition, it can be the goal to heighten conclusiveness by continuing to improve the design of a study—in the present case, for example, by introducing a second panel with a presurvey and a postsurvey.

Anyone who contends that effects cannot be measured under natural conditions in social research because there are too many intervening factors will necessarily reject media pilot projects on principle. The Munich pilot project (Infratest, 1985; Witte, 1987) represents the opposite point of view. The study was, for the most part, based on self reports of change. The participants in the project—persons who had cable TV in their households—were asked whether they had devoted more time to television than before since they had been able to receive more channels. They also were asked whether they watched certain kinds of programs, for example, feature films or in-depth educational programs or television news more or less frequently. They were asked whether they had read less, attended fewer cultural events, gone out fewer evenings, talked less in the family about personal matters, and changed in general their behaviors and attitudes.

Although these subjective perceptions are of great interest, the task faced by the pilot projects cannot be dealt with adequately on this basis alone. In part, people's powers of observation are not up to determining such changes in attitudes and behavior in themselves. Also, some perceptions fade to a certain extent over time and therefore cannot be reported. Finally, some changes in attitudes and behavior are considered undesirable and are therefore not registered or at least not reported.

It also is a mistake to suggest, based on simple comparisons of persons who receive cable TV and those who do not, that differences between these groups represent the effects of cable TV. Publications about the varying amounts of daily television viewing are an example of this error (Kiefer, 1987a). Because households that had viewed more television already are more prone to opt for cable TV, differences in the amount of daily television viewing should not be interpreted as an effect until a presurvey/postsurvey has been conducted among households with cable TV and until these households show changes that were not found in the same period in households without cable TV.

A final comment on methodology relates to the role of tests of significance for changes found. It seems appropriate to comment here on the role of significance tests in social research. Does a particular research project involve testing hypotheses that are important in theoretical and practical terms, the validity of which must be assured? If so, tests of significance are of decisive importance. If the goal of a research project is exploration, however, the important thing is to develop search strategies. In this context, nonsignificant findings may be very important. They may indicate connections that had not been anticipated, which then could be observed in more detail in subsequent research projects. The instruments may then also become more sophisticated, and the analysis may focus on special groups. The observed effect, which was not significant initially, may now turn out to be highly significant. If such search strategies are nipped in the bud by premature significance tests, this unnecessarily reduces the potential of scholarly work. Because our main goal in this study is exploration, tests of significance were made and documented only for key statements.

## ACCEPTANCE OF CABLE TV

Right at the beginning of the cable TV trial period in Ludwigshafen, it was possible to discern a positive response to cable. Figure 9.2, showing the number of cable subscribers and households that had applied for cable for the period from early 1984 to late 1986, indicates steady growth in diffusion of the service. The extent of interest in cable is better shown by the number of households that were *connected* to the cable network and the number of households that had submitted applications than the former alone, because the actual connection of households

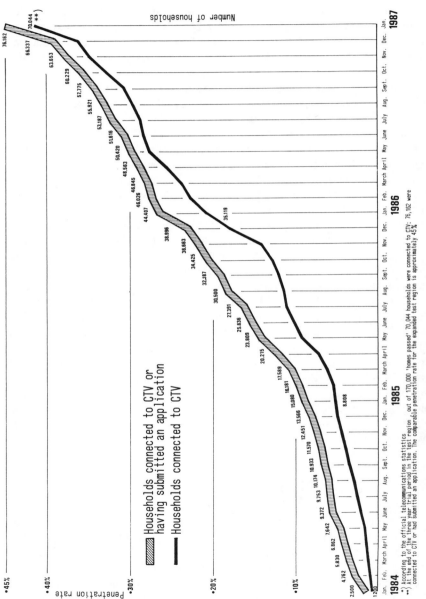

**FIG.9.2.** Diffusion of cable television in the test region Ludwigshafen/Vorderpfalz during the 3-year trial period*.

*) according to the official telecommunications statistics
**) At the end of the three year trial period in the test region, out of 170,000 'homes passed' 70,044 households were connected to CTV; 76,162 were connected to CTV or had submitted an application. The comparable penetration rate for the expanded test region is approximately 45%

TABLE 9.1

Development of Attitudes Toward Cable TV 1984-1986

QUESTION: "Do you approve of cable TV being available here now or don't you approve?"

|  | Representative Cross-Section* | | Nonsubscribers in the Cross-Section* | |
|---|---|---|---|---|
|  | Before Cable Began % | 3 Years Later % | Before Cable Began % | 3 Years Later % |
| Approve of cable | 38 | 65 | 26 | 38 |
| Do not approve | 24 | 8 | 33 | 14 |
| Don't care | 25 | 23 | 26 | 42 |
| Undecided, no answer | 13 | 4 | 15 | 6 |
| Total | 100 | 100 | 100 | 100 |
|  | (n=657) | | (n=283) | |

* Subscribers and nonsubscribers who were interviewed twice. The respondents chosen from the list of cable applicants were not included here.

depended on technical factors and at times proceeded very slowly. Figure 9.2 shows the curve for households with a connection alone as well as the combined curve for households connected and households having submitted an application. The latter is the total number of households that had been won over to cable TV in psychological terms. According to the official telecommunications statistics, at the end of the 3-year trial period, 76,162 households in the test region were connected to cable or had submitted an application out of 170,000 homes passed by cable, for a penetration rate of 45%. The penetration rate in the areas of the test region that our sample was drawn from (that is, homes passed by the end of the first test year) was 57%.

Prior to the introduction of cable TV in the Ludwigshafen area, as Table 9.1 shows, 38% of the population aged 14 and over welcomed the introduction, and 24% rejected it. At the end of the test period 3 years later, 65% welcomed it, whereas 8% rejected it. This means that only a small minority remained strongly opposed to cable. Even among the nonsubscribers there was an increase in approval during this period.

Table 9.2 shows that the majority of cable subscribers believed that the new competition between television operators would improve the quality of television programming. And although the cable subscribers' high expectations with regard to programming have not been completely satisfied, only a small minority (7%)

TABLE 9.2

TV Competition, Program Interest

QUESTION: "There are different opinions about the effect of many programs
being in competition with one another on cable TV. Some say: The programs
will improve and the quality will increase. Others say: The programs will
get worse and the quality will deteriorate. Which of these views do you
agree with, the first or the second?"

|  | Panel I | |
| --- | --- | --- |
|  | Before Cable Began % | 3 Years Later % |
| The quality of the programs will improve | 63 | 60 |
| The quality of the programs will deteriorate | 8 | 6 |
| Neither | 15 | 21 |
| Undecided | 14 | 13 |
| Total | 100 | 100 |
|  | (n=620) | |

QUESTION: "If you compare the new cable channels with the other channels,
i.e., ARD and ZDF, would you say that the new programs put out by these
channels tend to be more interesting, or more boring, or would you say
there is no difference?"*

|  | Panel I | | Panel II | |
| --- | --- | --- | --- | --- |
|  | Before Cable Began % | 3 Years Later % | Before Receiving Cable % | 1 Year Later % |
| More interesting | 70 | 46 | 76 | 44 |
| More boring | 3 | 7 | 2 | 6 |
| No difference | 27 | 47 | 22 | 50 |
| Total | 100 | 100 | 100 | 100 |
|  | (n=620) | | (n=583) | |

* In Dec. 83/Jan. 84 and late summer 85 the wording was "In comparison to
the current television channels, do you think cable television will be more
interesting or more boring, or would you say no difference?"

TABLE 9.3

Choosing a Role for Television

QUESTION: "Cable television now also includes channels from private commercial operators. Here are two people talking about this. Which of the two says what you also think? The first: Commercial television channels will show entertainment programs most of the time since they expect these to attract the largest audiences. Television's task of informing people will be neglected by commercial television. The second: I think it's good if commercial television channels show the things people really want to see and not always try to educate and inform people."

| | Panel I | | Panel II | | Quasi-control group | |
|---|---|---|---|---|---|---|
| | Before Cable Began | 3 Years Later | Before Receiving Cable | 1 Year Later | Before Cable Began | 3 Years Later |
| | % | % | % | % | % | % |
| First answer | 17 | 19 | 19 | 22 | 26 | 26 |
| Second answer | 61 | 58 | 61 | 57 | 41 | 43 |
| Unde-cided | 22 | 23 | 20 | 21 | 33 | 31 |
| Total | 100 | 100 | 100 | 100 | 100 | 100 |
| | (n=620) | | (n=583) | | (n=283) | |

Note: In late summer 1985 the first alternative was put in the present tense.

thought that the new programs on cable television were more boring than traditional programs on the public broadcasting networks (Table 9.2). One out of two did not see much difference between them.

In the course of the extended debate about cable television, one of the opponents' main arguments was that cable TV offers too much entertainment and neglects the task of providing information. But the population generally took the opposite view. An aversion to the German *Erziehungsfernsehen*—for decades the German public broadcasting systems emphasized political and educational programs—proved to be favorable for the growth of cable television. In the pretest-posttest surveys, this subject was approached directly in a dialogue question. There is definite evidence of a rejection of television's educational mission by all population groups, especially by cable subscribers (Table 9.3).

A high fluctuation rate expressed by frequent cancellations of cable subscriptions, which Sparkes (1983) reports from the United States, was not found in the cable project in Ludwigshafen. As a rule, those who had subscribed remained loyal. The cancellation rate was probably about 1%. This certainly shows the high level of satisfaction felt by cable subscribers after an average of 2 years of experience with cable TV. Table 9.4 shows that in the last interview conducted before the project ended, 84% of the subscribers said that the money for the cable subscription was well spent, with only 6% stating it was "not really well spent." In addition, the table shows that 84% would like to continue receiving the additional cable programs, 83% would advise others to subscribe to cable television, and only 2% would advise against this.

The positive climate of opinion also had an effect on non-subscribers. At the end of the trial period, as Table 9.1 shows, 38% of the non-subscribers definitely approved of cable TV, and 14% were opposed to cable. Only about 8% of the population in the test region could be categorized as definite opponents of cable TV (Table 9.1). They were essentially young people with a higher level of education as well as persons in the upper social strata. Many were supporters of the Social Democrats or the Greens. They watched relatively little television and often stated that radio was their most important source of information. Generally being unfamiliar with cable television programming, their attitude was very negative: 76% suspected that cable TV would have a negative effect on children. Many of them feared that commercial television would be so entertainment-oriented that it would fail to do its job of providing information. They expected the quality of television programs to deteriorate in this new competitive situation, but they recognized the fact that most people liked cable TV. These determined opponents of cable continued to employ all of the arguments against cable that had been used since the mid-1970s.

The extent to which the different population groups in the Ludwigshafen test region were interested in cable at the beginning and at the end of the 3-year trial period is shown by Tables 9.5 and 9.6. We can discern constant interest with certain slight variations, such as slightly more interest among people who watched a lot of television and among blue-collar workers. Tables 9.5 and 9.6 include an index showing the penetration of cable TV. All characteristics for which the index deviates clearly from 100, which indicates the average population, are of special interest.

The composition of cable subscribers roughly corresponds to a representative sample of the population 3 years after the introduction of cable TV. Single persons and supporters of the Greens—two characteristics that overlap very much—were underrepresented. Here again, we encounter indications of the politicized nature of the debate about cable TV in West Germany. This represented a very different constellation from the situation in the United States, where the debate between supporters and opponents of cable TV essentially focused on the influence of cable TV on the future quality of television programs, as Noam (1987) has shown.

TABLE 9.4

Final Evaluation of Cable TV

QUESTION: "The cable connection costs money and, in addition, you have to pay monthly fees. Has the money been well spent for cable TV or was it not really worth it?"

|  | Panel I:<br>Approximately 2 Years of<br>Experience with Cable<br>% | Panel II:<br>Approximately 1 Year of<br>Experience with Cable<br>% |
|---|---|---|
| Well spent | 84 | 76 |
| Not really worth it | 6 | 11 |
| Impossible to say | 10 | 13 |
| Total | 100 | 100 |

QUESTION: "Thinking now of yourself and your family---would you like to be able to continue seeing these additional programs or doesn't it matter to you whether you can see these programs or not?"

|  | Panel I:<br>Approximately 2 Years of<br>Experience with Cable<br>% | Panel II:<br>Approximately 1 Year of<br>Experience with Cable<br>% |
|---|---|---|
| Would like to continue | 84 | 85 |
| Doesn't matter | 10 | 10 |
| Undecided | 6 | 5 |
| Total | 100 | 100 |

QUESTION: "Assuming one of your friends asks your advice as to whether he or she should subscribe to cable TV---would you advise them to subscribe to cable TV or would you advise them against it?"

|  | Panel I:<br>Approximately 2 Years of<br>Experience with Cable<br>% | Panel II:<br>Approximately 1 Year of<br>Experience with Cable<br>% |
|---|---|---|
| Advise to subscribe | 83 | 81 |
| Advise against it | 2 | 1 |
| Undecided | 15 | 18 |
| Total | 100 | 100 |
|  | (n=620) | (n=583) |

TABLE 9.5

The Diffusion in the Areas First to Receive Cable TV by Background

| | Before Broadcasting of Cable Began | 3 Years Later | Index |
|---|---|---|---|
| | Already Subscribe to Cable, Have Submitted an Application, or Definitely Plan to Submit An Application % | % | Subscriber to Cable in Fall 1986 (60% of Total Population 14 & Over=100) |
| Population 14 & over | 19* | 60** | 100 |
| Gender | | | |
| Men | 20 | 59 | 98 |
| Women | 19 | 60 | 100 |
| Age groups | | | |
| 14-29 | 22 | 62 | 103 |
| 30-44 | 16 | 60 | 100 |
| 45-59 | 22 | 57 | 95 |
| 60 & over | 17 | 59 | 98 |
| Education | | | |
| Elementary | 2 | 62 | 103 |
| Intermediate | 17 | 58 | 97 |
| Secondary (Abitur), university | 25 | 52 | 87 |
| Occupation | | | |
| Semi- or unskilled blue-collar workers | 19 | 69 | 115 |
| Skilled blue-collar workers | 22 | 64 | 107 |
| Lower-level white-collar workers/civil servants | 17 | 55 | 92 |
| Upper-level white-collar workers/civil servants | 19 | 57 | 95 |
| Self-employed, free professions | 25 | 62 | 103 |
| Socioeconomic status | | | |
| Upper class | 16 | 62 | 103 |
| Upper-middle class | 21 | 57 | 95 |
| Middle class | 18 | 61 | 102 |
| Composition of household | | | |
| Live alone | 11 | 40 | 67 |
| Household with several persons & children under 14 | 20 | 64 | 107 |
| Household with several persons, no children under 14 | 21 | 61 | 102 |

(continued)

| | | | |
|---|---|---|---|
| Interest in politics | | | |
| Yes | 21 | 58 | 97 |
| Little, none | 17 | 60 | 100 |
| Voters of the: | | | |
| Christian Democrats | 22 | 62 | 103 |
| Social Democrats | 18 | 61 | 102 |
| Free Democrats | 28 | 73 | 122 |
| Greens | 5 | 31 | 52 |
| | (n=657) | | |

* 4% were already connected to cable TV, 6% had submitted an application, and another 9% definitely planned to do so.

** 54% of them were already connected to cable TV, 3% had submitted an application, and another 3% definitely planned to do so.

TABLE 9.6

The Diffusion in the Areas First to Receive Cable TV By Various
Behavior and Attitude Dimensions

| | Before Broadcasting of Cable Began | 3 Years Later | Index |
|---|---|---|---|
| | Already Subscribe to Cable, Have Submitted an Application, or Definitely Plan to Submit An Application % | % | Subscriber to Cable in Fall 1986 (60% of Total Population 14 & Over=100) |
| Average amount of time spent watching television weekdays | | | |
| Less than 2 hours | 18 | 55 | 92 |
| 2 to 3 hours | 16 | 63 | 105 |
| 3 hours or more | 26 | 68 | 113 |
| Persons who in Dec. 83/Jan. 84... | | | |
| approved of cable TV being available* | 41 | 77 | 128 |
| did not approve of cable TV | 3 | 39 | 65 |
| were undecided, did not care | 7 | 56 | 93 |
| Expected cable TV to show more programs in line with own tastes* | 28 | 65 | 108 |
| Did not expect this | 5 | 47 | 78 |
| Don't know, no reply | 12 | 55 | 92 |

(continued)

| | | | |
|---|---|---|---|
| Expected increased competition would... | | | |
| improve the quality of the programs | 31 | 69 | 115 |
| make it worse | 4 | 42 | 70 |
| neither, nor, undecided | 11 | 55 | 92 |
| | | | |
| Expected that children... | | | |
| would be promoted in their development | 32 | 73 | 122 |
| would become nervous and irritable, and be hindered in their development | 10 | 49 | 82 |
| undecided, no reply | 21 | 59 | 98 |
| | | | |
| Satisfaction with the German TV programs that had been available | | | |
| "Very satisfied" or "satisfied" | 16 | 58 | 97 |
| "So-so" or "somewhat satisfied, somewhat dissatisfied" | 22 | 62 | 103 |
| "Not so satisfied" or "pretty dissatisfied" | 17 | 58 | 97 |
| | (n=657) | | |

\* Asked of only half the sample.

According to public opinion theory, (Noelle-Neumann, 1980) people's attitudes and behavior are not only determined by their own judgments and experiences or by the influence of a person's primary environment, that is, family and friends, but also by the anonymous climate of opinion perceived by the individual. What do most people think? Is a specific opinion increasing or decreasing?

Questions about the climate of opinion were included in our survey in order to gain an impression of the acceptance of cable TV and its chances in the future. One question asked was whether most people approve of cable TV or do not approve, as well as whether in the next 10 years cable TV will have spread and become common or not. The climate of opinion changed considerably in favor of cable television between the beginning and the end of the pilot project, as Table 9.7 shows.

TABLE 9.7

The Climate of Opinion

QUESTION: "Aside from your own opinion, how do you think most people in this area feel about this: Do most of them approve of cable TV or do most of them not approve of it?"

| Most people in this area... | Representative Cross-Section* | |
| --- | --- | --- |
| | Before Cable Began % | 3 Years Later % |
| approve of it | 34 | 64 |
| do not approve of it | 30 | 8 |
| don't care | 14 | 9 |
| don't know, no concrete answer | 22 | 19 |
| Total | 100 | 100 |

QUESTION: "Do you think that in 10 years most people in the Federal Republic will subscribe to cable television or do you not think so?"

| Think that in 10 years most people will | Representative Cross-Section* | |
| --- | --- | --- |
| | Before Cable Began % | 3 Years Later % |
| subscribe to cable TV | 33 | 67 |
| Don't think so | 50 | 17 |
| Impossible to say | 17 | 16 |
| Total | 100 | 100 |
| | (n=657) | |

* Persons who were interviewed twice

In the German public debate about cable television, cost also played a major role. It was assumed that subscription costs would have a negative influence on the spread of cable (Kutteroff & Pfetsch, 1987). The findings from the Allensbach study, however, suggest that the regular monthly fees play a minor role as an impediment to subscribing to cable TV. As Table 9.8 shows, the majority considers the cost appropriate or even low. At the end of the 3-year trial period, the regular monthly cost of cable TV was considered just right by 54% of the population and rather low by 7%; 27% said that the fees were too high.

The design of the Allensbach project involved observing the "innovators" and "early adopters" of cable TV in the first panel and the subsequent "early majority," which did not opt for cable until after September 1985, in the second panel. These subscribers, who entered the market in certain phases of the diffusion of cable, are also described by Kutteroff, Pfetsch and Schoenbach in chapter 10 of this volume. Their observations essentially are in agreement with ours. We thus focus more on "the effects of cable TV," because our project enabled us to observe 1-year and 3-

TABLE 9.8

View of the Cost of Cable TV

QUESTION: "With cable TV you can get approximately 20 television channels and 24 radio stations with particularly good quality of picture and sound. A household has to pay DM 11 more for cable per month, in addition to the regular public broadcasting fees of DM 16.50. Do you think that this is pretty inexpensive for cable TV, or is it too much, or is it just right?"*

|  | Representative Cross-Section** | |
| --- | --- | --- |
|  | Before Cable Began | 3 years Later |
|  | % | % |
| State that the cost of cable TV is... | | |
| rather low | 5 | 7 |
| just right | 41 | 54 |
| too high | 38 | 27 |
| undecided, no response | 16 | 12 |
| Total | 100 | 100 |
|  | (n=657) | |

\* In the initial survey (Dec. 83/Jan. 84) the question read: "...DM 13.50 more per month..."

\*\* Persons who were interviewed twice.

year periods. In addition, the quasi-experimental panel project design and the "cell analysis" (relational analysis based on interviews with all members of the household 14 and older) was especially focused on observing change under conditions enabling us to determine with reasonable probability whether effects of cable TV were involved.

## CHANGES IN VIEWING HABITS RESULTING FROM COMPETITION WITHIN TELEVISION

Neither the expansion of programming from the four or five television channels previously in the area to 22 on cable television (Faul, 1987) nor the extension of the time available for all television programs to three to four times the previous amount did much to increase overall television consumption. Table 9.9 shows that cable subscribers watched an average of 2 hours and 13 minutes of television from Monday through Friday before cable was introduced and only about 10 minutes more after that. Whereas job holders and young people did not increase their television consumption at all, housewives increased it slightly (+ 19 minutes) and retired people even more (+ 30 minutes). Evidently, the extent of television consumption is determined far more by the leisure time available than by the breadth

TABLE 9.9

Changes in Amount of Time Spent Watching Television
By Sociodemographic Characteristics

QUESTION: "Could you estimate how much time you spend watching television
on average on a normal weekday---that is, Monday through Friday?"

| | Quasi-Test Group of Cable Innovators and Early Adopters | | | |
| | Before Receiving Cable | 2 Years Later | 3 Years Later | Change Over 3 Years |
|---|---|---|---|---|
| Total* | 2:13 | 2:24 | 2:22 | + 9 min. |
| Gender | | | | |
| Men | 2:17 | 2:26 | 2:22 | + 5 min. |
| Women | 2:08 | 2:23 | 2:21 | +13 min. |
| Age groups | | | | |
| 14-29 | 2:13 | 2:02 | 2:03 | -10 min. |
| 30-49 | 1:59 | 2:08 | 2:02 | + 3 min. |
| 50-64 | 2:16 | 2:28 | 2:37 | +21 min. |
| 65 and over | 2:38 | 3:18 | 3:01 | +23 min. |
| Education | | | | |
| Elementary | 2:27 | 2:41 | 2:41 | +14 min. |
| Intermediate (Mittlere Reife) | 2:11 | 2:14 | 2:11 | + 0 min. |
| Secondary (Abitur), university | 1:36 | 1:52 | 1:42 | + 6 min. |
| Employment status | | | | |
| Jobholders | 2:04 | 2:06 | 2:02 | - 2 min. |
| Housewives | 2:07 | 2:31 | 2:26 | +19 min. |
| Retirees | 2:35 | 3:10 | 3:05 | +30 min. |
| Most important source of information | | | | |
| Television | 2:25 | 2:32 | 2:35 | +10 min. |
| Newspaper | 2:01 | 2:22 | 2:08 | + 7 min. |
| Radio | 2:05 | 2:14 | 2:11 | + 6 min. |
| Interest in region | | | | |
| Strong | 2:13 | 2:41 | 2:41 | +28 min. |
| Limited | 2:08 | 2:07 | 2:13 | + 5 min. |
| Leisure time per day | | | | |
| Less than 4 hrs. | 1:56 | 2:03 | 1:54 | - 2 min. |
| 4 to 5 hrs. | 2:14 | 2:25 | 2:24 | +10 min. |
| More than 5 hrs. | 2:55 | 3:20 | 3:24 | +29 min. |

* Entries are the average amount of time spent watching per weekday (Hrs:Min)

and variety of programming generated by the new competition between public and commercial operators. Persons with less than 4 hours of leisure time per day did not increase their limited television consumption even after subscribing to cable television; in contrast, cable subscribers with more than 5 hours of leisure time per day increased their already extensive viewing time from an average of almost 3 hours by an additional half hour to almost 3.5 hours weekdays. Persons who did not have cable also increased their television consumption during the 3-year period. This is presumably because of especially attractive programming by the public television networks when competition with commercial operators began.

The new programs on cable television have essentially, albeit not completely, fulfilled the viewers' expectations. Hopes for more programs in line with one's own taste have evidently not been disappointed. Before subscribing to cable, 80% of cable subscribers had such hopes. After almost 3 years, more than three-fourths (76%) confirmed that they were able to find more programs to their taste.

Prior to being connected to the cable network and again just under 1 year later, members of panel II, that is, the early majority, were asked to name the programs for which it was worth subscribing to cable TV. Evidently, cable TV met people's expectations as far as movies, national and regional sports events and documentaries (programs on "nature, plants, animals, and foreign countries" or on "countries, people, and adventure") were concerned. But more people had expected to find worthwhile programs on cable TV in the areas of "public service, health care, environmental protection," "local information," "ways to spend leisure time," and "the most recent news." We may conclude that the need for local and regional reporting on television is not yet being adequately met.

In fact, fulfilling the need for local and regional information via television represents a very great change in West German television. Since the introduction of television in West Germany, and up until the introduction of cable television (i.e., over a period of several decades), the public broadcasting stations essentially had not fulfilled the need for local information at all. In part, this may have been in order not to intrude on the local newspapers' terrain in return for the newspapers respecting public television's monopoly and not provoking an expansion of competition. The self-restraint practiced by television over a period of decades in the area of local events will be slow to cede to routine programming of local information on television.

The EPF (Erstes Privates Fernsehen or First Private Television) channel, run by the main local newspaper in Ludwigshafen, the *Rheinpfalz*, and with a strong local orientation, attained surprisingly high levels of usage. It presented a mixture of light entertainment (some of it in dialect), local sports events, and local information. But the *Rheinpfalz* was not strong enough financially to absorb the losses of the initial period, and the EPF cable program was discontinued in late 1987.

Among the new nationwide commercial operators, SAT1 and RTL-PLUS—both of which have an above-average share of light entertainment—had already acquired a high percentage of viewers by late 1986 [6]. Although they had not displaced the traditional public programming, they took away about 25% of its share of the market. [7] Foreign programs, such as the British Sky Channel or the three French-language programs, TF1, FR3, and Antenne 2, rarely were used even by cable subscribers who state that they "speak or understand the language quite well." The language barriers are evidently too high. In order to follow a television program in a foreign language, a better knowledge of the language is required than is possessed by many people whose knowledge is limited to what they learned in school.

The public essentially did not watch the programs offered by the public service channel, the mixed channel, and the public access channel, which showed programs designed by the citizens themselves. It has proven more difficult and more expensive than initially anticipated by many operators to produce attractive programs that appeal to the public. The lead that the established public television networks have in terms of experience, personnel, and finances, their better program announcements, the public's long-standing familiarity with their programming, as well as established viewer habits, all make it difficult for new operators to compete successfully with the established programs on the public broadcasting networks.

Allensbach surveys do not confirm the image that the public broadcasting networks project of the public doing an "entertainment zigzag" through the variety of entertainment programs offered by the different channels at the price of neglecting information and public affairs programs (Frank & Klingler, 1987). There is no doubt that movies and other entertainment programs are especially appealing to cable subscribers; but panel surveys show that viewers who watch a lot of commercial television do not shun the educational programs on public television. They very often watch the main news programs as well as the business and economic news programs. Thus, it cannot be stated that the intensive users of commercial television are strictly entertainment-oriented. Instead, the available findings suggest that the "viewers who watch all types of programs but have a preference for information" dominate numerically over the "selective viewers of entertainment." Schulz (1986), in his viewer analysis, says that these are people for whom television represents *ritual consumption* and who watch a lot of programs, but most of all television news and other information programs. Our finding is essentially confirmed also by the major longitudinal study by Kiefer (1987b) that suggests that viewers who watch all types of programs but have a strong interest in information are comparatively strongly represented among heavy viewers.

The greater competition within the medium due to the new commercial operators thus far has not resulted in the traditional television programs being supplanted, aside from specific instances of politically controversial current affairs programs (such as ZDF Magazin, Kennzeichen D, Monitor, Report); here the audience has been reduced to about half, a finding that is discussed in more detail hereafter. Instead, the situation appears to be characterized by coexistence, with public programming continuing to dominate for the time being, albeit at a much lower level of usage. The battle between the public television contenders and their private challengers for a share of the market is likely to continue to be a tough one in the future, for the Allensbach study indicates that there are limits to how much television consumption can be expanded. The time devoted to television obviously cannot be extended indefinitely. It is true that the amount of leisure time is likely to increase in the future. However, television must compete with other attractive choices made available by the leisure industry; in addition, there seem to be psychological inhibitions that prevent people from watching more television.

Our panel investigations included a picture-association test adopted from Steiner (1963). Here, the respondents had to associate preformulated statements with illustrations showing the various media or other leisure-time activities, such as reading the newspaper, reading a book, listening to the radio, watching television, talking with friends, and playing tennis. The findings in Table 9.10 show that almost nobody associates the statement "I should do this more often" with "television" (1%). The response "Another evening shot" is frequently linked to television (40%), as is "Am I lazy!" (31%). Subscribing to cable TV does not do anything about a "bad conscience," tending to increase rather than reduce guilt feelings. Only one negative statement shows a significant reduction: "Another letdown," from 28% to 22%. Evidently the greater variety of programs on cable television reduces the likelihood of disappointment, which ultimately explains the high level of approval of cable that many cable viewers feel (Table 9.1).

## CHANGES IN THE COMPETITION BETWEEN MEDIA

Just before the introduction of cable TV, the specter of competition between media was conjured up, especially the competition cable represented to the daily papers and to books. Ever since television was introduced, the "decline of the culture of books" (Schmidtchen, 1974) has been debated in Germany, so there was great interest in how the expanded cable TV programming would affect use of other media.

Table 9.11 shows that cable subscribers were not only more oriented toward television than nonsubscribers, but they also read daily papers and magazines more, listened to the radio slightly more, listened to more than the average amount of music on records or cassettes, and made more than average use of video recorders, in line with the "more-and-more rule." In contrast to this, the more television they

TABLE 9.10

Associations with Television

QUESTION: "Would you please take a look at these pictures? They show a woman/a man involved in various activities. I'm now going to read you some things this woman/this man might be thinking and I'd like you to tell me for each one the letter of the picture which best fits the statement. Some pictures will apply to several statements. You can name any picture as many times as you want to. If a statement doesn't seem to fit any picture, just say so." (Presentation of an illustration)

| | Panel I | | Quasi-Control Group | |
| | Before Cable Began | 3 Years Later | Before Cable Began | 3 Years Later |
| Statements Assigned | % | % | % | % |
| **Positive statements** | | | | |
| "This fascinates me" | 30 | 28 | 25 | 25 |
| "A perfect way to relax" | 18 | 18 | 17 | 15 |
| "This really does you good" | 18 | 11 | 13 | 7 |
| "Boy, this is fun!" | 5 | 6 | 7 | 5 |
| "I should do this more often" | 1 | 1 | 2 | 2 |
| **Negative statements** | | | | |
| "Another evening shot" | 42 | 40 | 42 | 42 |
| "Am I lazy!" | 27 | 31 | 25 | 28 |
| "I really should be doing something else" | 25 | 25 | 23 | 27 |
| "I'm a little ashamed of myself for spending my time like this" | 21 | 25 | 25 | 28 |
| "Another let-down" | 28 | 22* | 23 | 21 |
| "I'll really regret this later" | 12 | 12 | 13 | 12 |
| | (n=620) | | (n=283) | |

* significant (5%).

TABLE 9.11

Media Use by Cable Subscribers and Nonsubscribers

| | | Television Viewed Weekdays | | |
| | Total | Less than 2 Hours | 2 to 3 Hours | 3 or More Hours |
|---|---|---|---|---|
| **Cable Subscribers** | | | | |
| Average amount of time spent watching television on a weekday (hrs:min) | 2:23 | 1:17 | 2:30 | 4:25 |
| Average amount of time spent listening to the radio on a weekday (hrs:min) | 2:14 | 2:07 | 2:19 | 2:23 |
| Read a daily newspaper | 79% | 77% | 78% | 82% |
| Average time spent reading a newspaper (in minutes) | 42 | 38 | 44 | 49 |
| Frequently read magazines | 60% | 58% | 62% | 63% |
| Have read a book in the last 12 months | 65% | 74% | 62% | 49% |
| Of these, readers who read a book daily or several times a week | 35% | 40% | 31% | 28% |
| Have not read a book in the last 12 months | 35% | 26% | 38% | 51% |
| Go to the movies at least once a month | 11% | 14% | 8% | 10% |
| Have not been to the movies in years | 61% | 53% | 65% | 72% |
| Often do videotaping | 13% | 10% | 17% | 17% |
| Often listen to music (records, cassettes, tapes) at home | 39% | 39% | 39% | 40% |
| | (n=1203) | (n=571) | (n=345) | (n=287) |
| **Nonsubscribers** | | | | |
| Average amount of time spent watching television on a weekday (hrs:min) | 2:02 | 1:09 | 2:30 | 4:06 |
| Average amount of time spent listening to the radio on a weekday (hrs:min) | 2:10 | 1:55 | 2:41 | 2:07 |
| Read a daily newspaper | 75% | 76% | 73% | 72% |
| Average time spent reading a newspaper (in minutes) | 42 | 37 | 43 | 60 |
| Frequently read magazines | 51% | 43% | 65% | 57% |
| Have read a book in the last 12 months of these | 72% | 75% | 72% | 62% |
| Of these, readers who read a book daily or several times a week | 43% | 46% | 40% | 38% |

(continued)

| | | | | |
|---|---|---|---|---|
| Have not read a book in the last 12 months | 28% | 25% | 28% | 38% |
| Go to the movies at least once a month | 13% | 17% | 12% | 4% |
| Have not been to the movies in years | 59% | 51% | 63% | 74% |
| Often do videotaping | 9% | 6% | 9% | 21% |
| Often listen to music (records, cassettes, tapes) at home | 35% | 37% | 33% | 32% |
| | (n=278 | (n=153) | (n=78) | (n=47) |

viewed, the less frequently they went to the movies. Another exception to the "more-and-more rule" does not become apparent until the general category of reading is divided into reading newspapers and magazines, on the one hand, and reading books, on the other. It then emerges that the more television was viewed, the less books were read. This applied equally to cable subscribers and nonsubscribers.

Table 9.12 shows the net changes in the use of competing media among persons who had cable for an average of 2 years (panel I) as well as in the control group of persons without cable. The changes are minimal in total. Use of the daily newspaper remained high even after subscription to cable. Books showed somewhat more change. Again, an important finding only becomes apparent by examining the reading of books separately. Whereas regular readers of books did not reduce their reading of books after subscribing to cable, irregular readers of books both in the test and control groups read fewer books, and the percentage of non-readers rose slightly. Although subscribing to cable TV also meant that a few additional radio programs were available, use of the radio both in the test group and in the control group decreased slightly. Up to now, the introduction of cable TV does not appear to have resulted in important changes in the use of the most important competing media.

It seems ironic that television, as represented by the public broadcasting networks, fought the introduction of commercial programs on cable TV with such determination only to gain in reputation in the end from an improved image of the medium after the introduction of cable. There are two indications of this. Viewing time increased among cable subscribers and nonsubscribers alike, the latter evidently resulting from the efforts of the public television networks to compete with the private operators by presenting more attractive programs (for example, their own family series, such as the very successful "Schwarzwaldklinik," "Ich heirate eine Familie," or "Die Drombuschs"). The second indication that television was strengthened due to competition is that even though there as yet have been no serious changes in use of the media, important subjective changes showed up when

TABLE 9.12

Changes in Media Use

|  | Panel I | | Quasi-Control Group | |
|  | Before Cable Began % | 3 Years Later % | Before Cable Began % | 3 Years Later % |
| --- | --- | --- | --- | --- |
| Television | | | | |
| Watch on a weekday... | | | | |
| more than 3 hours | 20 | 24 | 15 | 17 |
| 2 to 3 hours | 26 | 27 | 22 | 28 |
| less than 2 hours | 54 | 49 | 60 | 53 |
| Never watch television | 0 | 0 | 3 | 2 |
| Average (hrs:min) | 2:10 | 2:20 | 1:54 | 2:03 |
| | | | | |
| Radio | | | | |
| Listen on a weekday... | | | | |
| more than 3 hours | 28 | 22 | 25 | 23 |
| 2 to 3 hours | 12 | 14 | 16 | 13 |
| 1 to 2 hours | 30 | 30 | 26 | 28 |
| less than 1 hour | 24 | 29 | 29 | 29 |
| Never listen to the radio | 6 | 5 | 4 | 7 |
| Average (hrs:min) | 2:20 | 2:08 | 2:14 | 2:11 |
| | | | | |
| Daily Newspaper | | | | |
| Read... | | | | |
| every day | 73 | 80 | 74 | 75 |
| almost every day | 11 | 7 | 7 | 10 |
| less than that | 6 | 4 | 6 | 5 |
| Never read a newspaper | 10 | 9 | 13 | 10 |
| | | | | |
| Magazines | | | | |
| Frequently read magazines | 60 | 60 | 57 | 51 |
| | | | | |
| Books | | | | |
| Read... | | | | |
| every day or several | | | | |
| times a week | 33 | 38 | 43 | 43 |
| less than that | 38 | 28 | 36 | 29 |
| Have not read a book in | | | | |
| the last 12 months | 29 | 34 | 21 | 28 |
| | | | | |
| Movies | | | | |
| Go at least once a month | 11 | 12 | 11 | 14 |
| | (n=620) | | (n=283) | |

TABLE 9.13

Most Important Source of Information

QUESTION: "How do you find out about the news and what is going on in the world? Listed on these four cards are some of the ways you can find out about the news. Could you please put the cards in order according to what is most important to you, that is, from which you get the most information, and then what is second most important, etc."

| | Panel I | | Panel II | | Quasi-control group | |
|---|---|---|---|---|---|---|
| | Before Cable Began | 3 Years Later | Before Receiving Cable | 1 Year Later | Before Cable Began | 3 Years Later |
| | % | % | % | % | % | % |
| Ranked first: | | | | | | |
| Television | 33 | 44 | 39 | 43 | 26 | 35 |
| Newspaper | 41 | 28 | 38 | 31 | 40 | 34 |
| Radio | 20 | 24 | 20 | 23 | 27 | 26 |
| Conversations | 6 | 4 | 3 | 2 | 7 | 3 |
| Undecided, no reply | * | * | * | 1 | * | 2 |
| Total | 100 | 100 | 100 | 100 | 100 | 100 |
| | (n=620) | | (n=583) | | (n=283) | |

* less than 0.5 percent.

people were asked to rank the sources of information. These changes may well turn out to be relevant to behavior.

In response to the question, "How do you find out about the news and what is going on in the world?", persons who subscribe to cable, and to a somewhat lesser extent those who do not, significantly more often named television as their most important source of information (Table 9.13). Newspapers clearly suffered as a result. Before subscription to cable, newspapers had been named by 41% as the most important source of information, but 3 years later only 28% named newspapers. The developments in the Ludwigshafen test area represent a small-scale version of a pattern that has shown up in nationwide representative studies by the Allensbach Institute. Between September 1980 and December 1986, the newspaper's position as the most important source of information dropped by 5%, from 37% to 32%, with television showing slight gains (Noelle-Neumann & Schulz, 1987b).

In this connection, a key finding from the longitudinal investigations by the ARD and ZDF (Kiefer, 1987a) takes on added importance. Whereas there had only been a slight decrease in the usage of daily newspapers, there was a significant decrease in the intensity of use, as measured by the average time spent with the newspaper on the day before the interview from 51 minutes (1980) to 45 minutes (1985). This was the lowest figure since this trend investigation was initiated in

1964. The same longitudinal study shows that the subjective feeling that the daily paper is essential also was decreasing. In 1980, 60% said that they would miss the daily paper very much or quite a bit; by 1985, this figure had dropped to 57%. "While the most important section of the newspaper for most people continues to be the section with local news, loyalty to it as well as to the political section decreased in 1985 compared with 1980," according to Kiefer (1987a, p. 144).

Next, we take the analysis a step further and examine cable subscribers according to the amount of time spent viewing the three new commercial television channels: RTL-PLUS, SAT1, and EPF. (EPF was, as previously mentioned, discontinued at the end of 1987.)

So far, the most pronounced changes in media consumption are found among the intensive users of the new programs from private commercial operators. This group contained an above-average number of blue-collar workers, persons with a grade school education, and persons in the middle and older age groups. They did not focus their attention exclusively on commercial television but also made more than average use of public television (Noelle-Neumann & Schulz, 1987a). Even before they had cable TV, as Table 9.14 shows, a large percentage were heavy viewers, and they increased their television consumption by another 24 minutes. They watched an average of approximately 3 hours daily and also listened to an above-average amount of radio programs. They read a daily paper regularly, in fact more frequently "every day" than before they had subscribed to cable TV. A large percentage owned a video recorder and made more than average use of it. The "more-and-more rule" thus also applies to them, with the typical exception of reading books.

The intensive users of the new cable programming seldom were regular readers of books. Since subscribing to cable, the percentage of non-readers of books ("have not read a book in the last 12 months") rose from 36 to 52 in this group. A fluctuation analysis (Table 9.15) shows that almost one out of two (49%) of the occasional ("seldom") readers of books became non-readers ("never") of books in the heavy ("daily") viewing of the new television programming category. By contrast, 9% of occasional ("seldom") readers of books, who only "seldom" or "never" used the new programs, became non-readers. It seems likely that readers whose commitment to books is limited stop reading books if they are in a position to satisfy their needs for entertainment more effortlessly by using the diversified programs on television. Indications of a decline in reading along the fringes, that is, among occasional readers, are beginning to show in response to the growing competition between television and books. Intensive readers of books, however, did not use the new programming as much, remaining loyal to books.

Intensive users of the new programming by commercial television, who were generally also heavy users of public television, showed the most pronounced chan-

TABLE 9.14

Use of Competing Media
By Commercial Television Viewers

Persons in Households with Cable TV Who Watch
Commercial Television (SAT 1, RTL plus, EPF)...

| | Daily | | Several Times a Week | | Seldom, Never | |
|---|---|---|---|---|---|---|
| | Before Receiving Cable | 3 Years Later | Before Receiving Cable | 3 Years Later | Before Receiving Cable | 3 Years Later |
| Average amount of time spent watching TV on a weekday (hrs/min) | 2:33 | 2:57 | 2:01 | 2:10 | 1:54 | 1:53 |
| Difference | +24 min. | | +9 min. | | -1 min. | |
| Average amount of time spent listening to radio on a weekday (hrs/min) | 2:34 | 2:27 | 2:26 | 2:08 | 1:58 | 1:46 |
| Difference | -7 min. | | -18 min. | | -12 min. | |
| Never listen to radio | 4% | 5% | 6% | 3% | 7% | 6% |
| Read a newspaper every day | 75% | 80% | 73% | 80% | 71% | 82% |
| Have not read a book in the last 12 months | 36% | 52%* | 24% | 25% | 26% | 24% |
| Have a video recorder in household | 31% | 43% | 26% | 42% | 12% | 19% |
| Use video recorder every day or several times a week | -- | 59% | -- | 47% | -- | 34% |
| | (n=206) | | (n=222) | | (n=192) | |

* significant (1%).

TABLE 9.15

Stability of Reading Books with Varying Use of the
New Commercially-Operated Cable Programming (SAT 1, RTL plus, EPF)

|  | Autumn 1986 | | | |
|---|---|---|---|---|
|  | In the Last 12 Months, Have Read a Book/Books... | | | |
|  | "Daily or Several Times a Week"<br>% | "Seldom"<br>% | "Never"<br>% | Total<br>% |
| **1. Persons in households with cable TV who watch commercial television programs "daily"\*** | | | | |
| Dec. 83/Jan. 84<br>In the last 12 months, have read a book/books... | | | | |
| "daily or several times a week" | 57 | 18 | 25 | 100 (n=51) |
| "seldom" | 20 | 31 | 49 | 100 (n=80) |
| "never" | 5 | 20 | 75 | 100 (n=75) |
| **2. Persons in households with cable TV who watch commercial television programs "several times a week"\*\*** | | | | |
| Dec. 83/Jan 84<br>In the last 12 months, have read a book/books... | | | | |
| "daily or several times a week" | 71 | 16 | 13 | 100 (n=80) |
| "seldom" | 39 | 44 | 17 | 100 (n=89) |
| "never" | 17 | 26 | 57 | 100 (n=53) |
| **3. Persons in households with cable TV who watch commercial television programs "seldom, never"\*\*\*** | | | | |
| Dec. 83/Jan. 84<br>In the last 12 months, have read a book/books... | | | | |
| "daily or several times a week" | 70 | 20 | 10 | 100 (n=76) |
| "seldom" | 39 | 52 | 9 | 100 (n=66) |
| "never" | 10 | 26 | 64 | 100 (n=50) |

\* The diagonal cells contain 110 persons, the fluctuating cells, 96 persons. Turnover rate: 47%. Stuart Maxwell test: 16.40, i.e., a highly significant change (a is less than or equal to 1%). McNemar test for the characteristic "seldom": 3.45, i.e., a highly significant change (a is less than or equal to 1%).

\*\* The diagonal cells contain 126 persons, the fluctuating cells, 96 persons. Turnover rate: 43%. Stuart Maxwell test: 8.13, i.e., a significant change (a < 5%). McNemar test for the characteristic "seldom": 2.62, i.e., a highly significant change (a < 1%).

\*\*\* The diagonal cells contain 118 persons, the fluctuating cells, 73 persons. Turnover rate: 38%. Stuart Maxwell test: 1.4, i.e., no significant change. McNemar test for the characteristic "seldom": 0.52, i.e., no significant change.

TABLE 9.16

Most Important Sources of Information

QUESTION: "How do you find out about the news and what is going on in the world? Listed on these four cards are some of ways you can find out about the news. Could you please put the cards in the order according to what is most important to you, that is, from which you get the most information, and then what is second most important, etc."

| | Persons in Households with Cable TV Who Watch Television (SAT 1, RTL plus, EPF)... | | | | | |
|---|---|---|---|---|---|---|
| | Daily | | Several Times a Week | | Seldom, Never | |
| | Before Receiving Cable % | 3 Years Later % | Before Receiving Cable % | 3 Years Later % | Before Receiving Cable % | 3 Years Later % |
| Rank as their most important source of information (1st place) | | | | | | |
| Television | 34 | 53 | 33 | 44 | 33 | 35 |
| Newspaper | 36 | 25 | 43 | 28 | 45 | 31 |
| Radio | 24 | 18 | 19 | 24 | 14 | 28 |
| Conversation | 6 | 4 | 5 | 4 | 8 | 6 |
| Total | 100 | 100 | 100 | 100 | 100 | 100 |
| | (n=206) | | (n=222) | | (n=192) | |

ges in the ranking of the medium that is their most important source of information (Table 9.16). Television had definitely become more important to them, whereas newspapers and the radio had become less important. In the contrasting group of cable subscribers who did not use the new programming on SAT1, RTL-PLUS, and EPF, or only rarely did so, the radio rather than television had become more important as a source of information, and the paper had suffered as a result.

## MORE INTEREST IN LOCAL AND REGIONAL NEWS

The Rhineland-Palatinate state law concerning the cable TV pilot project explicitly set forth the task of studying changes in the level of interest in local information following the introduction of cable television. As has already been noted, prior to the introduction of cable television, local information had been neglected on television due to the special media situation in Germany. In analyzing changes in television consumption, we already reported that cable subscribers with a strong

Table 9.17

Effects of Watching Local Programming (Panel I)

| | Total | | Watch EPF Every Day or Several Times a Week | | Do not Watch EPF | |
|---|---|---|---|---|---|---|
| | Before Receiving Cable % | 3 Years Later % | Before Receiving Cable % | 3 Years Later % | Before Receiving Cable % | 3 Years Later % |
| **Rank as their most important source of information (1st place)** | | | | | | |
| Television | 33 | 44 | 32 | 50 | 35 | 38 |
| Newspaper | 41 | 28 | 40 | 26 | 42 | 32 |
| Radio | 20 | 24 | 24 | 22 | 17 | 23 |
| Conversation | 6 | 4 | 4 | 2 | 6 | 7 |
| **Read a daily newspaper...** | | | | | | |
| everyday | 73 | 81 | 82 | 83 | 69 | 79 |
| almost every day | 11 | 7 | 6 | 7 | 14 | 10 |
| now and then | 5 | 2 | 5 | 1 | 4 | 2 |
| seldom, almost never | 1 | 1 | * | 2 | * | 1 |
| never | 10 | 9 | 7 | 7 | 13 | 8 |
| **Average time spent reading a daily newspaper per day (minutes)** | -- | 43 | -- | 44 | -- | 44 |
| **If the local section of the newspaper were missing, would try to get hold of it elsewhere** | 39 | 44 | 49 | 53 | 40 | 45 |
| **Cable subscribers are...** | | | | | | |
| "better informed" | 53 | 56 | 59 | 68 | 45 | 42 |
| "not better informed" | 32 | 28 | 27 | 19 | 41 | 40 |
| undecided, no reply | 15 | 16 | 14 | 13 | 14 | 18 |
| **"It pays to have cable" because of following programs:** | | | | | | |
| sports events from the area | 43 | 44 | 49 | 54 | 35 | 35 |
| hobby or leisure time ideas | 45 | 34 | 54 | 44 | 36 | 28 |
| current events calendar | 32 | 17 | 36 | 17 | 27 | 16 |
| consumer hints | 53 | 39 | 58 | 47 | 52 | 35 |
| local news | -- | 62 | -- | 74 | -- | 58 |
| | (n=620) | | (n=227) | | (n=157) | |

* less than 0.5%.

TABLE 9.18

Interest in the Area

QUESTION: "How interested are you in what goes on in this area--could you tell me with the help of this ladder? Zero would mean you are not at all interested and 10 that you are extremely interested. Which step would you choose?"

|  | Panel I | | Panel II | | Quasi-Control Group | |
| | Before Cable Began | 3 Years Later | Before Receiving Cable | 1 Year Later | Before Cable Began | 3 Years Later |
| | % | % | % | % | % | % |
| Score: | | | | | | |
| 8-10 | 46 | 56** | 50 | 57* | 51 | 53 |
| 7 or lower | 54 | 44 | 50 | 43 | 49 | 47 |
| | (n=620) | | (n=583) | | (n=283) | |

* significant (5%).
** significant (1%).

interest in regional events increased their television consumption to an above-average extent (Table 9.9). In this connection, the effects of viewing local and regional information presented on cable TV (particularly in the EPF programs) on the use and evaluation of the local newspaper are of special interest.

Table 9.17 shows that the intensive users of the new regional television reporting did not reduce their newspaper reading. They evidently used the daily newspaper to complement TV. In psychological terms, however, loyalty to the newspaper medium definitely declined. Television was termed the most important source of information by 50% of subscribers who watched the new cable programming "daily" or "several" times per week, compared with 32% previously. Daily readership of the papers or time reading did not change. After subscribing to cable, however, 68% of intensive users of local and regional television felt more well-informed, whereas only 19% did not feel better informed. As far as they are concerned, the primary benefit of subscribing to cable TV has been local news and the reporting on local and regional sports events.

The introduction of cable television definitely stimulated interest in local and regional events. This is evidenced among cable subscribers in panel I (innovators) and also in panel II. The interest of nonsubscribers did not show a significant change in the comparable time period (Table 9.18).

## EFFECTS ON THE USE OF LEISURE TIME

Prior to the introduction of cable television, an argument used against television in the 1950s was reintroduced. It was argued that television would seduce "people into intellectual and physical passivity" (Mayer, 1984). A long list of leisure-time activities was used to determine any changes that might have taken place since the introduction of cable television (Table 9.19). With the exception of playing cards and other games, and of playing a musical instrument/making music, there is no evidence of significant changes in leisure-time behavior. General trends may also be involved in these instances, because the same pattern is also evident among non-subscribers to cable TV. Leisure time activities that demand considerable activity, such as walking, visiting friends and relatives, having people over, working in the garden, attending the theater or concerts, taking pictures or making movies, and "continuing education, attending courses" were not reduced after subscribing to cable TV.

The pattern of a decline in an activity in the test group of cable subscribers accompanied by no decline of the same sort in the quasi-control group shows up only once—for the item "devote myself to my neighbors, others." Before broadcasting of cable TV, the test group and control group did not differ on this item, whereas, 3 years later, they appeared to differ. The control group is now more active than the test group. Although the differences are slight, attention should be paid to this if future research is conducted.

Although participation in sports did not decline, attendance at sports events did drop. It is impossible to determine whether this was a consequence of increased coverage of local sports by cable TV or a general trend. Nor was there evidence that cable TV had a negative effect on community life. In autumn 1986, 21% of cable subscribers said that they were active in a club, a citizens' action group, a political party, or a labor union. This did not represent any change compared with the period prior to cable.

There have been no indications that the active use of leisure time suffered from cable TV. Nor was this really to be anticipated, given the fact that the increase in television consumption has been limited rather than extensive since the diffusion of cable TV began. The leisure-time behavior of cable subscribers essentially remained stable.

## EFFECTS OF CABLE TV ON CHILDREN

The argument that expanded television programming is detrimental to children did the most to polarize supporters and opponents of commercial television. As Table

TABLE 9.19

Leisure Time Activities

QUESTION: "There are several leisure time activities listed here. Could you tell me which of them you are involved in often--but what you do at your job doesn't count?"

| | Panel I | | Quasi-Control Group | |
| --- | --- | --- | --- | --- |
| | Before Cable Began % | 3 Years Later % | Before Cable Began % | 3 Years Later % |
| Watch television | 67 | 75 | 64 | 60 |
| Read the newspaper | 64 | 71 | 68 | 69 |
| Relax at home | 73 | 67 | 70 | 62 |
| Spend time with my family, be available for my family | 57 | 61 | 55 | 62 |
| Read magazines | 60 | 60 | 57 | 51 |
| Go for walks | 59 | 56 | 64 | 60 |
| Visit friends and relatives | 51 | 56 | 50 | 52 |
| Have company over | 51 | 50 | 50 | 42 |
| Work in the garden | 46 | 50 | 41 | 46 |
| Listen to the radio | 49 | 50 | 55 | 43 |
| Repair something, fix things up | 47 | 49 | 48 | 46 |
| Read books | 48 | 46 | 58 | 48 |
| Listen to music at home on records, cassettes or tapes | 49 | 39 | 47 | 35 |
| Excursions with the car | 39 | 38 | 35 | 39 |
| Do nothing, rest | 36 | 37 | 36 | 35 |
| Needlework | 35 | 35 | 42 | 38 |
| Do sports | 32 | 33 | 27 | 30 |
| Spend time with the children, play with children | 34 | 32 | 36 | 34 |
| Attend theatre, concerts | 23 | 26 | 27 | 28 |
| Home improvements, do-it-yourself work, such as carpentry, etc. | 28 | 23 | 25 | 21 |
| Devote myself to my neighbors, others | 25 | 22 | 25 | 28 |
| Take pictures, movies | 22 | 22 | 22 | 17 |
| Be active in a club, a citizens' action group, a party or a labor union | 21 | 21 | 24 | 24 |
| Attend sports events | 21 | 18 | 17 | 15 |
| Play cards and other games | 26 | 18 | 32 | 24 |
| Visit exhibits, museums, galleries | 19 | 17 | 19 | 21 |
| Continuing education, take courses | 17 | 16 | 21 | 17 |

(continued)

| | | | | |
|---|---|---|---|---|
| Make video tapes | 13 | 14 | 6 | 10 |
| Go to the movies | 11 | 12 | 13 | 13 |
| Play a musical instrument, make music, sing | 15 | 12 | 17 | 15 |
| Spend time with my collection | 10 | 8 | 10 | 11 |
| Make some money on the side | 10 | 8 | 13 | 9 |
| Paint, draw, make pottery | 9 | 8 | 9 | 8 |
| Play chess | 8 | 7 | 10 | 8 |
| Take train trips | 7 | 6 | 9 | 8 |
| Total | 1182 | 1163 | 1202 | 1129 |
| | | (n=620) | | (n=283) |

9.20 shows, heads of households who did not have children between the ages of 2 and 14 were less optimistic about the positive effects of cable than heads of the household with children, probably showing the effect of this argument in the political debate. After the 3-year trial period, the parents of children from 2 to 14 in the test group were increasingly convinced that television encourages children's development. The members of the control group, on the other hand, did not change their evaluations.

Although the subsample was small, including only fathers and mothers with children aged 2 to under 14, we tried to determine whether there were more problems with the children 3 years after subscription to cable than before. The comparison with the similarly limited quasi-control group is especially important because the children were maturing and that in itself gives rise to changes. These data are shown in Table 9.21.

The findings from this part of the study led Lehr and Minnemann (1987) to conclude "that no clear connection can be established between having cable, on the one hand, and children's behavioral problems, on the other. Since most of the changes determined apply to both children of cable subscribers and of nonsubscribers, developmental phenomena . . . would appear to be responsible, rather than the fact of having cable or of increased television consumption" (p. 353).

All of the pilot projects on the effects of cable television concluded that the effects feared by the public did not occur. The time spent viewing television increased only slightly, active leisure-time activities were evidently not displaced, and the influence of cable TV on children did not seem to be negative. Thus, the questions that the pilot project and communications research were expected to answer from the practical point of view of social experimentation were resolved.

In addition to this, and even more importantly, the Allensbach project determined two concrete effects that are of theoretical and practical interest. The first was reported previously in the section on "Changes in Competition Between the Media." The competition initiated by cable television has resulted in an improve-

TABLE 9.20

A Dialogue about the Effect of Cable TV on Children

QUESTION: "Two mothers/fathers are discussing whether they should subscribe to cable TV. Which of the two says more or less what you think too, the first or the second?"

Heads of Households with More Than 1 Person
(Dec. 83/Jan. 84)

|  | With Children Aged 2 to Under 14 % | Without Children Aged 2 to Under 14 % |
|---|---|---|
| **The first:** | | |
| "The many different programs make children nervous and irritable. In short, their personal development is restricted." | 41 | 47 |
| **The second:** | | |
| "The many different programs mean that children can find what is just right for them. In short their personal development is encouraged." | 41 | 32 |
| Undecided, no response | 18 | 21 |
| Total | 100 (n=192) | 100 (n=561) |

Fathers and Mothers with Children Between
the Ages of 2 and 14 at Home

|  | Panel I Before Cable Began % | 3 Years Later % | Panel II Before Receiving Cable % | 1 Year Later % | Quasi-Control Group Before Cable Began % | 3 Years Later % |
|---|---|---|---|---|---|---|
| **The first:** | 27 | 13** | 32 | 21* | 53 | 48 |
| **The second:** | 45 | 64 | 50 | 60 | 27 | 30 |
| Undecided | 28 | 23 | 18 | 19 | 20 | 22 |
| Total | 100 | 100 (n=148) | 100 | 100 (n=136) | 100 | 100 (n=81) |

* significant (5%)
** significant (1%)

TABLE 9.21

A Comparison of Problems with Children before the
Introduction of Cable TV and 3 Years Later

QUESTION: "When talking with parents you often hear complaints about
problems they have with their children. Is there anything on these cards
that you are currently worried about, that you are annoyed or upset about?"*

|  | Panel I | | Quasi-Control Group | |
|  | Before Cable Began % | 3 Years Later % | Before Cable Began % | 3 Years Later % |
|---|---|---|---|---|
| There are toys, notebooks, books, and shoes all over the apartment | 59 | 63 | 53 | 55 |
| You have to say things 10 times before anything happens | 59 | 58 | 64 | 71 |
| There's a fuss at night when it's time to go to bed | 44 | 45 | 45 | 36 |
| Stubbornness and pigheadedness | 44 | 36** | 31 | 35 |
| It is often simply too loud | 27 | 33 | 27 | 23 |
| There's often dawdling at mealtime | 39 | 31** | 41 | 23*** |
| There are too many snacks | 41 | 29*** | 32 | 32 |
| There's too much television | 29 | 28 | 33 | 33 |
| Sassy talk | 22 | 27 | 27 | 30 |
| There's usually a fuss about washing up and brushing teeth | 21 | 23 | 24 | 28 |
| There are often quarrels and fighting | 26 | 21 | 21 | 24 |
| Getting up is a problem every morning | 21 | 21 | 17 | 22 |
| Homework isn't done right; you always have to check | 20 | 19 | 15 | 15 |
| Choosiness, so many demands are made | 15 | 16 | 15 | 18 |
| There are often problems with homework | 12 | 14 | 17 | 13 |
| Money is spent for silly things, instead of being saved | 10 | 14 | 13 | 15 |
| A lack of interest and initiative, passivity | 8 | 14 | 9 | 10 |
| Endless questions | 8 | 12 | 9 | 9 |
| Lots of dawdling on the way home from school | 18 | 11 | 10 | 10 |
| Not much trust in their parents | 8 | 8 | 3 | 6 |
| I worry about all the fibbing | 3 | 8 | 4 | 4 |

(continued)

| | | | | |
|---|---|---|---|---|
| Coming home late | 6 | 5 | 4 | 9 |
| They already smoke | 5 | 5 | 1 | 3 |
| They already drink | 3 | 1 | **** | 1 |
| None of the above | 8 | 10 | 6 | 10 |
| Total | 556 | 562 | 521 | 543 |
| | (n=147) | | (n=78) | |

\* Only parents of children 14 and under.
\*\* significant (5%)
\*\*\* significant (1%)
\*\*\*\* less than 0.5%.

TABLE 9.22

Comments on Family Life

Statement about family life: "The atmosphere is often tense because of minor differences."

| | Panel I | | Panel II | | Quasi-Control Group | |
|---|---|---|---|---|---|---|
| | Before Cable Began | 1 Year Later | Before Receiving Cable | 1 Year Later | Before Cable Began | 1 Year Later |
| | % | % | % | % | % | % |
| Agree | 31 | 17* | 19 | 16 | 22 | 23 |
| | (n=336) | | (n=562) | | (n=272) | |

| | Panel I | | Quasi-Control Group | |
|---|---|---|---|---|
| | Before Cable Began | 2 years Later | Before Cable Began | 2 Years Later |
| | % | % | % | % |
| Agree | 27 | 15* | 21 | 18 |
| | (n=512) | | (n=267) | |

| | Panel I | | Quasi-Control Group | |
|---|---|---|---|---|
| | Before Cable Began | 3 years Later | Before Cable Began | 3 Years Later |
| | % | % | % | % |
| Agree | 29 | 16* | 23 | 20 |
| | (n=578) | | (n=245) | |

Note: Based on the dynamic adjustment made to changes in social reality, the samples for the quasi-test group and the quasi-control group are neither constant in size nor composition over the entire period of observation. The before and after comparions documented here in different phases of the study, however, are based on statements by the same respondents who were interviewed at the respective points in time.

\* significant (1%).

ment in the psychological position of the television medium. There has been an increase in the importance of the medium as a source of information. The second concrete effect occurred in the area of family life and was absolutely unexpected. The following section deals with this.

## AN IMPROVEMENT IN FAMILY LIFE
## DUE TO CABLE TELEVISION?

The first panel wave in winter 1984/85, at a time when the test group had been receiving the cable programming for an average of about 9 months, resulted in the surprising finding that there had been a significant decrease in the statement that the family life "atmosphere is often tense because of minor differences." There essentially had been no change on this point in the control group (Table 9.22). This finding, as the table shows, also was confirmed in subsequent surveys.

The finding was verified by analyzing the statements made by the family members. Taking a table with nine fields (see Table 9.22 as an example), we can determine the extent of the married couple's agreement on tension in the family over minor differences at the beginning of the project—prior to subscribing to cable TV (1983/84)—and at the end. In total, 238 pairs were available for this analysis, 169 of them in the test group and 69 in the quasi-control group. As Table 9.23 shows, overall there were 163 cells where there was no change in the opinions that the two partners had about tensions in the family because of minor differences. In 138 of the cases, both parties disagreed at both time points. In 53 pairs, however, there was a decrease in the opinion that tension existed. In 22 cells, there was an increase in the opinion that tension existed.

When these relational analyses were performed separately for the quasi-test and quasi-control groups, we found that, in 66% of the quasi-test group cases in panel I, there was no change in opinions about tension in the family. For the quasi-control group, the figure was 74%. There was a decrease in the opinion that tension existed in 26% of the group cases and 13% of the control group cases. An increase in opinion that tension existed surfaced in 8% of the test cases and 13% of the control.

In view of the great concern about the detrimental effect of cable TV and its commercial programming on family life, this finding was surprising and therefore—this evidently often amounts to the same thing—not credible in the view of many critics. To explain the finding, the thesis was elaborated that tension may decrease in families receiving cable TV because family life is smothered by too many entertainment programs, because conversation is limited by this, or because the family may disperse once a new television set has been acquired for cable TV

TABLE 9.23

Relational Analysis of Changes in the Atmosphere in the Family
Before Cable TV was Introduced and at the Conclusion
Of the Pilot Project

The statement: "The atmosphere is often tense in our family because of minor differences."

Panel I

In Fall 1986, Agreed With the Above Statement

| | Both Partners in Household | Only One of the Two | Neither of the Two |
|---|---|---|---|
| In Dec. 83/Jan. 84, before cable was initiated, agreed with the above statement | | | |
| Both partners in household | 10 | 11(d) | 15(d) |
| Only one of the two | 6(i) | 15 | 27(d) |
| Neither of the two | 2(i) | 14(i) | 138 |

Note: In 163 cells there was no change in the atmosphere, in the tendency toward tension; in 53 cells there was a decrease (d) in tension; and in 22 cells there was an increase (i) in tension.

and family members watch different programs in different rooms, consequently not even discussing them anymore, much less getting into arguments.

It was possible to test these explanations. The statements about family life prior to the introduction of cable TV and 3 years later did not confirm the thesis that family life had become more passive in the cable subscriber households. There were no changes in the direction anticipated in statements such as "we talk a lot" for the test group as compared with the control group (Table 9.24).

Additional verification was possible, based on statements about spending time with the children and playing with them. There was no indication of a decrease in this leisure-time activity compared with the control group 1, 2, or 3 years after the introduction of cable TV (Table 9.25).

Finally, information about activities engaged in by parents and children together was included. The findings suggest that parents and children in households with cable TV tended to watch television *together* more than they did 3 years ear-

TABLE 9.24

Indicators of Family Life And Cable TV

QUESTION put to persons in households with more than 1 person: "Which of
the things on this list apply to your family life?"

| | Panel I | | Quasi-Control Group | |
|---|---|---|---|---|
| | Before Cable Began % | 3 Years Later % | Before Cable Began % | 3 Years Later % |
| Excerpts from the replies | | | | |
| We talk to each other a lot | 67 | 66 | 71 | 66 |
| We stick together, in good times and bad | 66 | 63 | 66 | 57* |
| We talk about everything. No one hides his or her problems or views | 66 | 58** | 67 | 55** |
| We do a lot together | 63 | 60 | 65 | 64 |
| We have a lot of similar interests | 60 | 64 | 59 | 60 |
| We laugh a lot together, have a lot of fun | 53 | 48* | 58 | 50* |
| My birthday is always a big celebration in the family | 42 | 46 | 38 | 42 |
| I think we are happier than most families | 35 | 38 | 35 | 36 |
| If I tell my children something or forbid them to do something, my wife/ husband always supports me | 30 (n=578) | 26 | 26 (n=245) | 26 |

* significant (5%)
** significant (1%)

TABLE 9.25

Spending Time with Children

QUESTION: "There are several leisure time activities listed here. Could you tell me which of them you are involved in often--but what you do at your job doesn't count."

Activity: Spend time with the children, play with children.

|  | Panel I | | Panel II | | Quasi-Control Group | |
|---|---|---|---|---|---|---|
|  | Before Cable Began | 1 Year Later | Before Receiving Cable | 1 Year Later | Before Cable Began | 1 Year Later |
|  | % | % | % | % | % | % |
| Involved often | 30 | 31 | 31 | 30 | 31 | 33 |
|  | (n=359) | | (n=583) | | (n=311) | |

|  | Panel I | | Quasi-Control Group | |
|---|---|---|---|---|
|  | Before Cable Began | 2 years Later | Before Cable Began | 2 Years Later |
|  | % | % | % | % |
| Involved often | 33 | 30 | 32 | 28 |
|  | (n=544) | | (n=307) | |

|  | Panel I | | Quasi-Control Group | |
|---|---|---|---|---|
|  | Before Cable Began | 3 years Later | Before Cable Began | 3 Years Later |
|  | % | % | % | % |
| Involved often | 34 | 32 | 36 | 34 |
|  | (n=620) | | (n=283) | |

Note: Based on the dynamic adjustment made to changes in social reality, the samples for the quasi-test group and the quasi-control group are neither constant in size nor composition over the entire period of observation. The before and after comparisons documented here in different phases of the study, however, are based on statements by the same respondents who were interviewed at the respective points in time.

TABLE 9.26

Joint Activities with Children

QUESTION: "What do you do with your child/your children often, occasionally
or rarely, or almost never?"*

| | Panel I | | Quasi-Control Group | |
|---|---|---|---|---|
| | Before Cable Began % | 3 years Later % | Before Cable Began % | 3 Years Later % |
| We do this together often... | | | | |
| Watch television | 50 | 56 | 54 | 48 |
| | (n=293) | | (n=137) | |

* Asked only of persons with children at home.


TABLE 9.27

Watching Television at Different TV Sets

QUESTION: "Do you have two or three or more television sets in your
household which are used at least occasionally?" If "yes": "Are different
programs ever watched at the same time on different sets?"*

| | Panel II | |
|---|---|---|
| | Before Receiving Cable % | 1 Year Later % |
| Yes, often | 17 | 19 |
| Yes, but rarely | 20 | 23 |
| No, never | 13 | 11 |
| Not asked: There is only one TV set in the household or no response as to how many | 50 | 47 |
| Total | 100 | 100 |
| | (n=562) | |

* Asked in households where more than one person lived.

lier, before cablecasting began. The opposite situation appears to apply to the control group (Table 9.26).

A question about watching TV on different television sets, which was not included until the panel survey of fall 1985, does not provide any indications of
whether this practice might have increased under the influence of cable TV (Table
9.27).

In order to observe the intensity of conversations in the family, the question
about joint parent-child activities also included questions about 11 different topics
of conversation. Again, there are no indications of a decrease in talking compared
with the control group (Table 9.28).

TABLE 9.28

Joint Communication Activities with Children

QUESTION: "What do you do with your child/your children often, occasionally or rarely, or almost never?"*

| | Panel I | | Quasi-Control Group | |
|---|---|---|---|---|
| | Before Cable Began % | 3 Years Later % | Before Cable Began % | 3 Years Later % |
| We do this together often... | | | | |
| Talk about career and job plans | 27 | 32 | 31 | 28 |
| Talk about what is prohibited and what is allowed, what children may do and what they may not | 37 | 31 | 33 | 30 |
| Talk about vacations and vacation plans | 34 | 27** | 30 | 28 |
| Talk about other people | 19 | 27*** | 20 | 23 |
| Talk about purchases, plans to make purchases | 36 | 26*** | 30 | 29 |
| Talk about life and how you should live | 25 | 25 | 24 | 20 |
| Talk about money | 32 | 24** | 34 | 29 |
| Talk about sickness and health | 23 | 17** | 25 | 19 |
| Talk about politics | 12 | 14 | 18 | 12** |
| Talk about the boss and experiences with the boss | 8 | 12 | 12 | 12 |
| Talk about religion | 8 | 7 | 11 | 7 |
| | (n=293) | | (n=137) | |

* Asked of persons with children at home.
** significant (5%).
*** significant (1%).

Finally, the findings on additional joint activities by parents and children are included. Again, there are no indications that family life has become more passive under the influence of cable television (Table 9.29).

After the initial findings on the improved atmosphere in the family were presented approximately 1 year after the introduction of cable TV in spring 1985, the hypothesis was formulated that the increased channel options available would lead to viewing fewer political programs, which might provide less occasion for controversial debate and hence for tension in the family. This thesis is supported by changes in the number of viewers of current affairs programs that are highly controversial politically (e.g., "ZDF Magazin," "Kennzeichen D," "Monitor,"

TABLE 9.29

Joint Leisure Activities with Children

QUESTION: "What do you do with your child/your children often, occasionally
or rarely, or almost never?"*

|  | Panel I | | Quasi-Control Group | |
| --- | --- | --- | --- | --- |
|  | Before Cable Began % | 3 Years Later % | Before Cable Began % | 3 Years Later % |
| We do this together often... | | | | |
| Go for walks | 35 | 36 | 42 | 39 |
| Go shopping | 33 | 36 | 41 | 36 |
| Make large excursions on foot or by car | 30 | 28 | 29 | 34 |
| Accept invitations, visit | 29 | 28 | 29 | 21 |
| Bicycle, go on bike trips | 22 | 28** | 26 | 23 |
| Read, read to each other | 25 | 24 | 31 | 19** |
| Take care of animals | 24 | 24 | 31 | 26 |
| Attend events and parties | 21 | 23 | 18 | 19 |
| Work in the household | 24 | 21 | 33 | 18*** |
| Do homework | 21 | 18 | 20 | 17 |
| Clean, do dishes | 22 | 17 | 28 | 15** |
| Cook | 20 | 17 | 26 | 9*** |
| Play board games, card games, parlor games | 21 | 15 | 23 | 14* |
| Think up games, play with toys | 20 | 15 | 19 | 16 |
| Prepare parties, invitations, events | 21 | 13** | 18 | 10** |
| Play sports | 15 | 13 | 16 | 12 |
| Do handicrafts, home mechanics, home improvements | 15 | 12 | 19 | 10** |
| Attend church | 12 | 11 | 14 | 12 |
| Paint, draw | 10 | 11 | 11 | 6 |
| Make music | 6 | 7 | 10 | 10 |
| Attend concerts, theater | 7 | 3 | 6 | 4 |
| Go to movies | 1 | 1 | 2 | * |
|  | (n=293) | | (n=137) | |

* Asked of persons with children at home.
** significant (5%).
*** significant (1%).

"Report"). In the areas that can receive cable TV in West Germany, there was a particularly strong reduction in the number of viewers for these programs; according to electronic measurements up to 1986/87, they were roughly reduced by one quarter to one half compared with areas that did not have cable.

In trying to find explanations for the decrease in tension in families, which also was confirmed tentatively in panel II (Table 9.22), we found support for the assumption that differences of political opinions in the family might be reduced by more programs and by commercial television, which, as content analysis has shown, tries very hard to avoid a political bias.[8] As an instrument for our study, we used a test question developed in the international value systems study of 1981 (Noelle-Neumann & Koecher, 1987). This question seeks to determine in which of five different areas the respondent's values agree with those held by his or her spouse: morality, religion, attitudes toward others, political views, and sexuality. In the area of political views, agreement between partners increased significantly from 55% to 63% in households with cable TV, whereas it essentially remained the same in the control group, at 54% and 55% respectively (Table 9.30).

These findings take on increased importance in the light of the growing gap in values between parents and children in West Germany since the late 1960s. The gap is very much larger than in almost all the other countries in Western Europe and is quite large in comparison with England and the United States. It also has a negative effect on one's view of life, on the enjoyment of work, on confidence in government institutions, and on the willingness to defend one's country (Noelle-Neumann & Koecher, 1987).

This gives the findings from the study of the effects of cable TV a highly political emphasis. In the light of polarized views of such developments, we should point out again the problems encountered by social research in proving media effects. Because such effects essentially take place on an unconscious level, and thus cannot be reported in response to direct questions, the only solution is to design the study as far as possible so as to increase the probability that the findings are in fact causal. This is ensured by the pretest-posttest design and by the field experiment with a panel design, using a rather large sample and a great variety of indicators in the questionnaire.

## SUMMARY

The Allensbach research project, which was to investigate the effects of cable television in the test region, is described here in the context of a 15-year-long political debate about the introduction of cable TV and commercially sponsored television in West Germany.

TABLE 9.30

Agreement on Political Issues

QUESTION: "In which of the following areas do (did) you and your
husband/wife/partner share similar views?"

| Test Group: **With** Cable Television | Mentioned | | Fall 1986 Not Mentioned | | Total | |
|---|---|---|---|---|---|---|
| Late Fall 1985 | n | % | n | % | n | % |
| Agreement on political views mentioned | 122 | (43) | 33 | (12) | 155 | (55) |
| Not mentioned | 57 | (20) | 73 | (25) | 130 | (45) |
| Total | 179 | (63) | 106 | (37) | 285 | (100) |

Results: The diagonal cells contain 195 persons, the fluctuating cells, 90
persons. Turnover: 32 %. McNemar test: 2.42, i.e., a significant
change.

| Control Group: **Without** Cable Television | Mentioned | | Fall 1986 Not Mentioned | | Total | |
|---|---|---|---|---|---|---|
| Late Fall 1985 | n | % | n | % | n | % |
| Agreement on political views mentioned | 35 | (39) | 13 | (15) | 48 | (54) |
| Not mentioned | 14 | (16) | 27 | (30) | 41 | (46) |
| Total | 49 | (55) | 40 | (45) | 89 | (100) |

Results: The diagonal cells contain 62 persons, the fluctuating cells, 27
persons. Turnover: 30 %. McNemar test: 0.00, i.e., no
significant change.

The Ludwigshafen project represents a breakthrough for the method of social experimentation, a method seldom used in West Germany so far.

The design of the study consisted of a combination of a panel and a quasi-experiment with pre- and post-measurements (the first before the introduction of cable and several other measurements before and after subscription), based on a total sample of 1,486 persons in 881 households (interviewed repeatedly). The sample consisted of two separate panels: panel I, the so-called "innovators" and "early adopters," and panel II, the early cable majority. The effects of cable were observed over a period of 3 years in a total of six panel waves. In addition to the individual as a unit of analysis, analysis also focused on the collective, that is, all persons 14 and older in the household, and included a relational analysis (cell analysis).

Commissioned by the state government of Rhineland-Palatinate, which gave the cable pilot project in Ludwigshafen its legal base, the project was, above all, to answer the following questions: Did the population accept cable? Was there a need for cable? What were the effects on the amount of television viewed? What were the effects on family life and on children? How were active leisure-time activities affected? Which other media were used? How strong were local and regional bonds?

A strong positive change in attitudes toward cable during the 3-year trial period showed the acceptance of cable. Only a small minority (8%) of the population in the test region remained opposed. At the end of the trial period in the test region, 45% of the households subscribed to cable or had applied for a subscription.

The negative effects warned of in the public debate did not occur during the test period, but there were some indications of encroachment on the daily newspaper and among occasional readers of books. A completely unexpected finding was that family life in the cable-subscriber households became more harmonious and was characterized by stronger bonds in comparison to the quasi-control group.

## NOTES

[1] See, for example, the decisions about the design of the control group.

[2] Included here are the design of the control group and the use of electronic audience measurements.

[3] This follows the subdivision of the process of diffusion into three phases suggested by Rogers (1962): "innovators" (the first 2.5%); "early adopters" (the next 13.5%); "early majority" (the next 34%); "late majority" (the next 34%); and "laggards" (the last 16%).

[4] See, for example, the changes in the climate of opinion as a whole in the test region, Table 9.1.

[5] The method of analysis we have termed "cell analysis" represents a special type of relational analysis. See Coleman (1972).

[6] According to findings from content analyses, entertainment constitutes 81% of the overall programming on SAT1, 75% on RTL plus, 64% on ZDF, and 61% on ARD. See Faul (1987, p. 384).

[7] This is based on the results of telemetric measurements conducted by GfK for the second half of 1986 and published in Darschin and Frank (1987, p. 206). According to this evidence, the public TV networks account for 95% of overall television consumption nationwide, as compared to 70% in households with cable.

[8] Faul (1987, p. 475) comes to the following conclusion after comprehensive content analyses of cable programming: "The avoidance of value judgments which at RTL plus is practically systematic and at SAT 1 is also a very prominent feature, especially on political issues, is an important finding. Commercial operators seem to follow the business principle of refraining from taking a political stance in order to avoid losing customers."

**REFERENCES**

Bundesministerium fuer das Post- und Fernmeldewesen (Ed.). (1976). *Telekommunikationsbericht der Kommission fuer den Ausbau des technischen Kommunikationssystems—KtK* [Telecommunication report by the commission for the development of the technical communication system]. Bonn: Dr. Hans Heger.

Campbell, D.T., & Stanley, J.C. (1966). *Experimental and quasi-experimental designs for research*. Chicago: Rand McNally.

Coleman, J. S. (1972). Relational analysis: A study of social organization with survey methods. In P. F. Lazarsfeld, A.K. Pasanella, & M. Rosenberg (Eds.), *Continuities in the language of social research* (pp. 258-266). New York: Macmillan.

Darschin, W., & Frank, B. (1987). Tendenzen im Zuschauerverhalten: Fernsehgewohnheiten und Fernsehreichweiten im Jahre 1986 [Tendencies in viewer behavior: Television habits and television coverage in 1986]. *Media Perspektiven*, (4), 197-208.

Faul, E. (1987). Ergebnisse der Programmuntersuchungen [Findings from programming studies]. In Wissenschaftliche Begleitkommission (Ed.), *Versuch mit Breitbandkabel in der Region Ludwigshafen/Vorderpfalz. Die wis-*

*senschaftliche Begleitkommission zum Abschluss-Bericht an die Landesregierung Rheinland-Pfalz* (pp. 303-481). Berlin and Offenbach: VDE Verlag.

Frank, B., & Klingler, W. (1987). Die veraenderte Fernsehlandschaft: Zwei Jahre ARD/ZDF-Begleitforschung zu den Kabelpilotprojekten [The changed television landscape: Two years of ARD/ZDF research in conjunction with the cable pilot projects]. *Schriftenreihe Media Perspektiven* (No. 7). Frankfurt and Berlin: Alfred Metzner Verlag.

Infratest-Kommunikationsforschung. (1985). *Kabelpilotprojekt Muenchen: Hauptuntersuchung* [Cable pilot project Munich: Main study]. Unpublished manuscript, Muenchen.

Institut fuer Demoskopie Allensbach (1968). *Auswirkungen des Fernsehens in Deutschland: Lebensgewohnheiten, Interessen und Bild der Politik vor und nach der Anschaffung eines Fernsehgeraetes* [Effects of television in Germany: Customs, interests and picture of politics before and after the purchase of a television set]. (Rep. 1489). Allensbach am Bodensee.

Kiefer, M.-L. (1987a). Massenkommunikation 1964 bis 1985: Trendanalyse zur Mediennutzung und Medienverwertung [Mass communication 1964 to 1985: A trend analysis for media use]. *Media Perspektiven*, (3), 137-148.

Kiefer, M.-L. (1987b). Vielseher und Vielhoerer: Profile zweier Mediennutzergruppen [Heavy viewers and heavy listeners: Profiles of two media user groups]. *Media Perspektiven*, (11), 677-692.

Kutteroff, A., & Pfetsch, B. (1987). Cable television in the Federal Republic of Germany: A study of audience reactions to the introduction of a new medium. *EBU Review, 38* (4), 17-23.

Landesgesetz ueber einen Versuch mit Breitbandkabel vom 4. Dezember 1980 (1980, December 15) [State law of December 4, 1980, on a pilot project with broadband cable]. In *Gesetz- und Verordnungsblatt fuer das Land Rheinland-Pfalz*, Mainz.

Lehr, U., & Minnemann, E. (1987). Wirkungen im familiaeren Bereich [Effects in the family sphere]. In Wissenschaftliche Begleitkommission (Ed.), *Versuch mit Breitbandkabel in der Region Ludwigshafen/Vorderpfalz. Die wissenschaftliche Begleitkommission zum Abschluss-Bericht an die Landesregierung Rheinland-Pfalz* (pp. 251-302). Berlin and Offenbach: VDE Verlag.

Mayer, R.A. (1984). *Medienumwelt im Wandel: Aspekte sozialer und individueller Auswirkungen der alten und neuen Medien* [The changing media environment: Aspects of social and individual effects of the old media and the new]. Muenchen: Deutsches Jugendinstitut.

Noam, E. (1987). *The impact of market structure and entry barriers on the diverisity of television: Theory and empiricism.* Lecture presented at a symposium on guidelines for an open regulatory system for broadcasting, the Bertelsmann Foundation, Guetersloh.

Noelle-Neumann, E. (1979, April 9). Massenmedien und sozialer Wandel—Methodenkombination in der Wirkungsforschung [Mass media and social change: Combinations of methods in effects research]. *Zeitschrift fuer Soziologie,* pp. 164-182.

Noelle-Neumann, E. (1980). *Die Schweigespirale: Oeffentliche Meinung—unsere soziale Haut* [The spiral of silence: Public opinion—our social skin]. Muenchen: Piper.

Noelle-Neumann, E. (1982). Fernsehen und Lesen: Ein Werkstattbericht [Television and reading: A workshop report]. In Gutenberg-Gesellschaft (Ed.), *Gutenberg Jahrbuch 1982: Vol. 57* (pp. 35-46). Mainz: Selbstverlag der Gutenberg-Gesellschaft.

Noelle-Neumann, E. (1984, July 9). *Pressebericht: Das Kabel-Pilot-Projekt Ludwigshafen/Vorderpfalz. Ergebnisse der ersten Umfrage im Versuchsgebiet* [Press release: The cable pilot project Ludwigshafen/Vorderpfalz. Findings from the first survey in the test region]. Mainz.

Noelle-Neumann, E. (1985a). *Auswirkungen des Kabelfernsehens: Erster Bericht ueber Ergebnisse der Begleitforschung zum Kabel-Pilot-Projekt Ludwigshafen/Vorderpfalz, Materialien Vol. 1* [Effects of cable television: First report on findings from research in conjunction with the cable pilot project Ludwigshafen/Vorderpfalz, Materials Vol. 1]. Berlin and Offenbach: VDE Verlag.

Noelle-Neumann, E. (1985b, July 5). *Zweiter Pressebericht: Das Kabel-Pilot-Projekt Ludwigshafen/Vorderpfalz. Ergebnisse der ersten Wiederholungsbefragung im Versuchsgebiet* [Second press release: The cable pilot project Ludwigshafen/Vorderpfalz. Findings from the first repeat survey in the test region]. Mainz.

Noelle-Neumann, E., & Koecher, R. (1987). *Die verletzte Nation: Ueber den Versuch der Deutschen, ihren Charakter zu veraendern* [A traumatized nation: On German attempts to change their character]. Stuttgart: Deutsche Verlagsanstalt.

Noelle-Neumann, E., & Schulz, R. (1987a). Erkenntnisse zum inter- und intramediaeren Wettbewerb der Medien aus dem Kabel-Pilot-Projekt Ludwigshafen [Findings on the competition within the medium and between the media from the cable pilot project Ludwigshafen]. In W. A. Mahle (Ed.), *Intermediaerer Wettbewerb nach dem Ende des oeffentlich-rechtlichen Monopols* (pp. 79-99). Muenchen: AKM.

Noelle-Neumann, E., & Schulz, R. (1987b). *Reaktionen auf ein duales Fernsehprogrammangebot: Ergebnisse des Kabel-Pilot-Projekts Ludwigshafen/Vorderpfalz 1983 bis 1986* [Reactions to dual television programming: Findings from the cable pilot project Ludwigshafen/Vorderpfalz, 1983 to 1986]. Allensbach am Bodensee: Institut fuer Demoskopie Allensbach.

Rogers, E. M. (1962). *Diffusion of innovations.* Glencoe: Free Press.

Schmidtchen, G. (1974). Soziologische Analyse des Buchmarkts fuer den Boersenverein des deutschen Buchhandels [A sociological analysis of the book market for the Boersenverein des deutschen Buchhandels]. *Archiv fuer Soziologie und Wirtschaftsfragen des Buchhandels, 30,* 707-896.

Schulz, W. (1986). Das Vielseher-Syndrom: Determinanten der Fernsehnutzung [The heavy viewer syndrome: Determinants of television use]. *Media Perspektiven,* (11), 762-775.

Sparkes, V. (1983, November). *The people who don't subscribe to cable television: Who and why?* Paper presented at the meeting of the Midwest Association for Public Opinion Research, Chicago.

Steiner, G. A. (1963). *The people look at television: A study of audience attitudes.* New York: Knopf.

Witte, E. (1987). *Kabelpilotprojekt Muenchen. Bericht der Projektkommission* [Cable pilot project Munich: Report by the project commission]. Muenchen: Kommunalschriften-Verlag J. Jehle.

# 10

# Federal Republic of Germany: Developing the Entertainment Option

**Albrecht Kutteroff**
**Barbara Pfetsch**
*University of Mannheim*
**Klaus Schoenbach**
*Academy for Music and Theater, Hannover*

## NEW MEDIA TECHNOLOGIES IN WEST GERMANY

Unlike in other countries, the new media diversification in West Germany began relatively late. New technologies had already started to spread in many Western societies, for example in the United States, Britain, Belgium, and the Netherlands, in the early 1970s. Their actual introduction in West Germany, however, did not commence before the early 1980s. Cable television, in particular, was accompanied by heavy public discussions about its advantages and dangers (see chap. 9 in this volume). On the other hand, the spread of VCRs has been an almost noiseless process, rarely accompanied by political comments.

Hopes and fears about teletext and viewdata could be found somewhere in between. After viewdata had been introduced in 1981, it soon became clear that this medium would not revolutionize the everyday habits of the average West German. Indeed, viewdata developed, for instance, into a communication system between travel agencies and became an information tool for salespeople and mechanics working away from their company's headquarters. By the end of 1987, some 96,000 terminals were connected to viewdata's computers.

Teletext, on the other hand, is more widespread. The major controversies about its introduction were more or less history by 1987. They had dealt with a West German issue unknown to most other Western societies: by federal law, the "transportation systems" (cables, satellites, transmitters) of all new *electronic* media are under the control of the Federal Post Administration. So, no private company is allowed to wire a city without the permission of this office. In the case of the distribution of teletext, however, the postal supervision would have been legitimate only if teletext had been an electronic medium. Had it been regarded as some kind of a newspaper, the Federal Post would have had no say about its introduction. Plus, as a newspaper, it could have been commercially organized, as opposed to radio or TV, which had to be under public control until recently. The compromise found in this controversy was that the Post controls the distribution, as if teletext were an electronic medium, but the newspapers as private organizations are allowed to use it. As a result, teletext contains news provided by some newspapers and program information and subtitles by the TV stations themselves. By the end of 1986, about 11% of the West German households could receive teletext.

Similar to the controversy about teletext, the discussion about cable technology in West Germany resulted from the fact that only the Federal Post has been allowed to set up and run cable systems. So, the introduction of cable networks supposed to transport more than the few TV and radio channels already available definitely required a political decision. Before cable systems with more and new TV and radio services were permitted to operate, a federal advisory commission was set up. The experts discussed policies of implementation and, in 1976 (Bundesministerium fuer das Post- und Fernmeldewesen, 1976), decided to assess the technical, organizational and societal aspects of cable communication prior to its general introduction. As a consequence, four cable experiments, called "pilot projects," were established in 1984-1985 in the cities of Berlin, Dortmund, Munich, and Ludwigshafen (see also chap. 9 in this volume).

Among the new services to be delivered by cable, the most crucial one was the option of new television channels. Whereas, up to then, the average viewer could receive only about three to four television channels via airwaves, the cable technology easily allowed the proliferation of many more, among them—for the first time in West Germany—commercial ones. It was quite clear that the addition of new and commercial services meant the end of West Germany's split media landscape. Established by the Western Allies in 1945, the dual media system had consisted of a private press and public, nonprofit radio and television services.

Constrained and even hindered by political controversies, the pilot projects aimed to empirically examine the individual and social consequences of cable television. The findings were supposed to be a basis for decisions on state and federal policies concerning cable communication. However, in 1982, the conservative-liberal party coalition came into power in Bonn. This government was decisively procable and allowed cable systems immediately to spread beyond the boundaries of the initial cable test areas. By 1986, federal and state governments permitted the introduction of cable television on a nationwide level.

After this dam was broken, some states also saw no reason anymore to prohibit commercial, over-the-air television from broadcasting. By the end of 1987, households in some areas could get up to two new TV services without being wired. Not only had the number of TV channels increased via cable and over the air, but the number of hours of the day during which TV was offered also had expanded. In the fall of 1987, two commercial stations started to expand their daily broadcasting time and made TV available in the early morning. Other stations planned to follow by creating their own "breakfast TV."

Also a number of new—and mostly commercial—radio stations sprang up. Most of them were strictly local in scope, as opposed to the statewide stations that West Germans had been used to for almost 60 years. The new stations specialized their formats more strongly and thus forced many of the older ones to do the same.

To evaluate these profound changes in the West German media system correctly, it is important to know that, as late as in 1987, the new television and radio offerings were still to a great extent confined to some regions. In some cities, for instance, people even without cable could receive two more TV and five more radio stations than before. In other areas, however, the over-the-air offering was virtually the same as, say, in 1980. Cable, too, started to spread in some regions earlier than in others. By the end of 1987, about 34% of the 25.7 million West German households were passed by cable. Thirty-eight percent of these households (3.3 million) had decided to subscribe to it. So, cable television reached about 13% of the West German population.

As opposed to the history of cable TV and the other new media offerings in West Germany, the distribution of VCRs and their software has developed in a somewhat different fashion. After a rather hesitant growth during the introduction phase of the home video systems VHS, Beta, and Video 2000 in 1978-1980, the period from 1980-1984 can be regarded as the first boom period of the video recorder in West Germany. By the end of 1987, one can assume that VCRs reached a household coverage in West Germany of about 35%, up from about 4% in 1980 (Deutsches Video Institut, 1987).

The following analysis concentrates on the two new media for which we have the most and the most revealing audience data. We—on the one hand—examine how West Germans with video recorders and with cable TV differ in terms of their social and psychological characteristics from those without access to these media. Other foci are how the audiences use cable TV or VCRs, what particular contents they prefer, what functions are fulfilled by watching cable TV and materials on video, and what effects this behavior may have on individuals, groups, and the society.

## THE DESIGN OF THE STUDIES

### The Cable Study

The cable study was based on a quasi-experimental design. From 1985 on, about 630 households were surveyed both in the area of the cable pilot project in Ludwigshafen/Vorderpfalz and in a region in and around Mannheim, still not passed by cable. The cities—just separated by the Rhine river—possess many structural and contextual similarities. Together, they form an industrial center with about 400,000 people dwelling in the urban areas alone. Around the commercial and industrial center, there are structually mixed, rather rural areas where farmers and commuters live. Thus, it is possible in the study to differentiate between respondents living in the cities and those living on the countryside.

Cable subscribers in the test area enjoyed a television menu that had increased from the three to four public channels available before to up to 23 TV services in 1987. The new channels included 10 delivered by the two nationwide public television organizations (ARD and ZDF)—among them regional, special interest, and educational channels. Twelve services were produced by commercial corporations. Among them were RTL-PLUS and SAT1, two full-fledged channels directly competing with the major networks. Cable subscribers also got new music stations, such as Sky Channel and Music Box, and several services with local news and current-affairs programs. Besides some offerings from Britain, two French channels were distributed. Finally, there was an "open channel" that featured productions by whichever citizen was willing to participate.

The cable study—directed by Professor Max Kaase from the University of Mannheim—was funded by the German National Science Foundation (Deutsche Forschungsgemeinschaft) and the federal government (Kaase, 1986). Its purpose was to assess social but also individual changes brought about by the introduction of cable TV. The logic of the quasi-experimental design was to permit comparisons between several groups of respondents. First, in Ludwigshafen and the surrounding region, people were divided into those who had opted for cable TV, but were not yet connected, and those who did not want cable. Second, in order to control contextual effects of the pilot region, households were recruited in the structurally similar region of Mannheim, where cable services were not available at the time of the study. There, households were separated into those who wanted to subscribe to cable if available, and those who definitely did not. Third, those four groups were further divided according to whether the respondents lived in the urban or in the rural parts of the region. This makes for a total of eight groups into which the sample was subdivided (Fig. 10.1).

These different groups were—as a panel—interviewed three times: the first measurement (fall, 1985) took place when none of the households studied in the cable area that had requested to be connected to cable TV had actually received it. The second panel wave (spring, 1986) was in the field shortly after the "experimental" households had joined the cable network. The third wave of interviews (fall, 1986) was conducted to find out about the cable group after it had had cable TV for more than 6 months.

Three basic instruments were used in the study at each of the three times. In each household, one randomly selected member, 18 years old or older, was asked about the technical and media appliances in the home and about the everyday routines in the family. This instrument also included some questions about VCRs in the household. Whenever appropriate, we use these questions in our analysis of VCR behavior. In addition, every family member 14 years and older was asked to fill out a questionnaire about attitudes and evaluations of television in general and of cable TV in particular, about leisure time behavior and the amount of and the topics of conversations. The third instrument, again directed to all family members over 14, was a standardized time-use diary. For a period of 8 days, all activities from 6:00 a.m. to 1:00 a.m. were to be recorded in 30-minute intervals. Those activities were divided into media use and other activities like sleeping, eating, working, educational training, and homework. We distinguished between leisure activities inside and those outside the home.

Interviews were completed with 749 households (1,655 individuals) in the fall of 1985, with 670 households (1,470 persons) in the spring of 1986, and with 599

| Cable Area Ludwigshafen/ Vorderpfalz | | | | Control Area Mannheim | | | | |
|---|---|---|---|---|---|---|---|---|
| **Urban** | | **Rural** | | **Urban** | | **Rural** | | |
| Sub- scribers | Nonsub- scribers | Sub- scribers | Nonsub- scribers | Plan to subscribe if available | Do not plan | Plan to subscribe if available | Do not plan | |
| 103 | 95 | 105 | 87 | 61 | 51 | 61 | 69 | (Households) |
| 237 | 174 | 267 | 196 | 125 | 95 | 134 | 163 | (Individuals) |

FIG.10.1. The design of the cable study: Number of households and individuals surveyed in the two panel waves.

households (1,299 respondents) in the fall of 1986. For every wave of interviews the panel mortality was approximately 10% of the households interviewed in the previous wave. For the purpose of the following analysis, we use the first two panel waves, those in the field shortly before and after the experimental households had joined the cable. From the 670 homes reinterviewed in the second wave 632, (with 1,391 individuals) were included in our analyses. The cases dismissed were those that had changed their minds in terms of subscribing or not subscribing to cable TV.

## The VCR Study

The study from which we draw most of our results for audience responses to VCRs (see Hackforth & Schoenbach, 1985; Schoenbach & Hackforth, 1987) consisted of three mail surveys, funded by the Second German Television Channel (Zweites Deutsches Fernsehen).

In July 1983, the heads of 5,000 representatively selected households in West Germany and in West Berlin received a questionnaire by mail asking them about the structure of the household and the technical appliances in it. Some 407 of those households had a videocassette recorder. These 407 households were the subject of the following surveys. For the purpose of comparison with households of a similar structure but without a VCR, a control group of 407 households without a video recorder was selected from the 5,000 original ones according to a "matched pairs" procedure. A "statistical twin" household had to live in the same state as its VCR counterpart; its head of household had to belong to the same age cohort out of five possible; and the household's monthly net income had to be roughly the same. All three criteria had to match simultaneously.

All household members 6 years old and older in both samples were asked to keep a standardized time-use diary. From October 3 to October 30, 1983, they recorded their activities in the same fashion as in our cable study described previously. Also included in the diary were questions directed to the head of the household and/or to the four oldest persons in the household (if they were more than 14 years old). These questions dealt with attitudes toward new technologies in general, with favorite leisure time activities, with media behavior, and with attitudes toward the media. The diary was completed by 348 video households (for a return rate of 85%) and by 304 nonvideo households (75% return rate). Some 826 persons in video households and 718 in the other households had their activities recorded.

In October 1983, another questionnaire, directed only to the heads of households (males or females with the highest income of the household), was mailed to our two samples. The purpose of this special survey was to get some additional information, primarily about the use of and attitudes toward the video recorder from at least one person in the household. After 3 weeks, the return rate for the video owners was 86% ($n$=350) and for the nonowners it was 76% ($n$=390).

## DISTRIBUTION AND ACCEPTANCE OF THE NEW MEDIA

### Cable Television

When the cable test period in Ludwigshafen/Vorderpfalz had started in 1984, the number of subscriptions climbed up in a rather tedious way. Although 40,000 homes were wired at that time, only 1,200 decided to subscribe instantly (Wissenschaftliche Begleitkommission, 1987, pp. 11, 62). That at first suggested low levels of acceptance of the innovation. When the Federal Post and the cable operators started various marketing campaigns with low introductory rates, the number of cable subscriptions grew continuously. Survey data showed that, by January 1986, 25% of a representative sample in Ludwigshafen/Vorderpfalz was connected to cable and another 37% was interested in a cable subscription (Frank & Klingler, 1987, p. 25). About a year later, in December 1986, 41% (76,162) of all homes had cable or had at least applied for it (Wissenschaftliche Begleitkommission, 1987, p. 63). By fall 1987, 184,800 households were passed by cable, so that about 500,000 people had the opportunity to receive cable programs.

According to the analysis of our household interviews, those who did not want to subscribe in 1985 rejected cable because of their negative evaluation of the quality of the new programs and the high costs involved: 84% of the members of nonsubscriber households believed that commercially sponsored programs might deliver biased information on important issues. More generally, there was an 80% approval of the statement that the provision of cable systems by the federal post is a waste of tax money. Seventy-six percent of people in noncable homes agreed with the opinion that the subscription to cable is too big an investment. Depending on the date, the one-time connection fee ranged from about U.S. $50 to U.S. $300 per household, and the monthly subscription fee from U.S. $5-$10. In addition, many people needed a new television set. All the attitudes measured toward cable remained all in all stable between the first and the second wave of our interviews.

Surprisingly, some of this criticism was shared by a considerable number of subscribers even after they had cable. The fear of biased information through cable channels decreased among cable users only somewhat from 75% in 1985 to 60% in 1986, after cable had been installed in their homes. Quite naturally, there was a decrease in agreement that cable systems are a waste of tax money. Whereas 43% of people in subscriber households had agreed with that item before they had been supplied with cable, only 28% confirmed it in 1986 after their homes were actually connected.

Typical innovators (see chap. 9 in this volume) were no longer found among the cable subscribers by the time the new services had been available for about 1 year. But in the cable area, the actual cable subscribers and the nonsubscribers differed still slightly according to their age, education, and occupational levels. Cable subscribers were older, lower in education, and more likely to belong to the working class. In the control region, on the other hand, potential subscribers differed significantly from those without any intention to subscribe only in terms of their education. Also, highly skilled white collar workers were somewhat more likely to resist a cable subscription (Table 10.1).

## Videocassette Recorders

Our data about VCR owners enable us to cover a longer period of time than was possible with the cable data, and they show that, at least in the beginning, there actually was a "top-down" development from "early adopters" with a higher socioeconomic status to what Everett Rogers has termed an "early majority" resembling more closely the average citizens. According to earlier research (teleskopie, 1980), the first owners of video recorders in 1978/1979 were, compared to the rest of the population, more likely to be men, between 30 and 49 years old, with a relatively high formal education, and with a fairly high income. Among them were more white-collar workers. Video owners lived in households with many technical devices. They liked television, and their leisure time behavior was comparatively active. Single households were underrepresented among video households.

About 5 years later, in 1983, video households still differed from households without a VCR in some demographic characteristics. Video households still had an above-average income, more persons lived in them, and there were more children and adolescents. Heads of VCR households were younger and better educated than was the case in an average German household. More often, they were white-collar workers.

This was not quite true for 1985, however. Heads of video households in our cable study (28% of all households) were still younger, but their formal education was—at least in the Ludwigshafen/Mannheim area—lower than that of their counterparts without a VCR. Also, they were less frequently white-collar workers. It looks as if the video recorder had already passed owners representing the sociodemographic characteristics of the average West German and was about to

TABLE 10.1

The Socioeconomic Structure of the Subsamples

| | Cable Area | | | | Noncable Area | | | | Total | |
| | Sub-scribers | | Nonsub-scribers | | Plan to Subscribe | | Do not Plan to Subscribe | | | |
| | % | n | % | n | % | n | % | n | % | n |
|---|---|---|---|---|---|---|---|---|---|---|
| **Age** | | | | | | | | | | |
| 14-29 years | 26.4 | 133 | 35.1 | 130 | 33.2 | 86 | 28.7 | 74 | 30.4 | 423 |
| 30-49 years | 42.5 | 214 | 37.9 | 140 | 41.7 | 108 | 43.4 | 112 | 41.3 | 574 |
| 50 and older | 31.1 | 157 | 27.0 | 100 | 25.1 | 65 | 27.9 | 72 | 28.3 | 394 |
| **Education** | | | | | | | | | | |
| Low | 56.9 | 263 | 42.7 | 148 | 56.7 | 140 | 40.7 | 99 | 50.1 | 650 |
| Medium | 25.3 | 117 | 33.1 | 115 | 21.4 | 54 | 32.1 | 78 | 28.0 | 364 |
| High | 17.7 | 82 | 24.2 | 84 | 21.4 | 53 | 27.2 | 66 | 21.9 | 285 |
| **Occupation** | | | | | | | | | | |
| Worker | 33.3 | 124 | 22.2 | 63 | 31.9 | 66 | 28.4 | 54 | 29.1 | 307 |
| Employee | 41.1 | 153 | 52.8 | 150 | 45.9 | 95 | 45.3 | 86 | 46.0 | 484 |
| High position employee | 14.0 | 52 | 16.9 | 48 | 13.5 | 28 | 18.9 | 36 | 15.6 | 164 |
| Professional/ Own Business | 11.6 | 43 | 8.1 | 23 | 8.7 | 18 | 7.4 | 14 | 9.3 | 98 |

climb down the social ladder. Even lower was the formal education of that group of our respondents who had both a video recorder and cable in their homes.

Members of VCR households both in 1983 and in 1985 were generally more enthusiastic about technology than other people. For many of them, one might assume, buying a video recorder was nothing but an addition of a new device to the extensive technical equipment already available in their households. Indeed, the average video household of 1983 owned more appliances than a household without a VCR. From a list of 30 devices, including a TV set, stereo equipment, a cassette tape recorder, an electric sewing machine, a typewriter, a telephone, a deep freezer, a dishwasher, a camera, a movie camera, a slide projector, and a video disc player, video households owned 12.8, two more than non-video households (10.7) with otherwise similar demographic characteristics. This holds true for our 1985 respondents. Even after controlling for the income of our sample members, video households still owned more technical appliances than did other households.

Remarkable also is the fact that, in 1986, we found VCRs considerably more often in cable homes (34%) than in those passed by cable but not interested in the new services (23%). Also, more households had VCRs among those who wanted

TABLE 10.2

Perceived Importance of VCRs for "Modern Lifestyle"

Question: Some people say that today a video recorder simply belongs
to the modern lifestyle. What do you think? Do you completely agree,
partly agree, or disagree?

Year Video Recorder Purchased

|  | 1978-1980 % | 1981 % | 1982 % | 1983 % |
|---|---|---|---|---|
| Completely agree | 21 | 8 | 10 | 8 |
| Partly agree | 72 | 64 | 62 | 64 |
| Disagree | 7 | 28 | 28 | 28 |
| Total | 100 | 100 | 100 | 100 |
| n | 47 | 54 | 148 | 83 |

Note: Base is heads of video households, 1983.

to have cable in the non-wired area of the site of our study (45%) than among those
not passed by cable and not interested in it (20%).

As early as in 1983, however, a more sober attitude toward video surfaced
among those who had bought a VCR in 1981-1983. Compared to respondents
having purchased that device earlier (in 1978-1980), late buyers to a much less extent believed that the video recorder "simply belongs to modern lifestyle." Earlier
buyers obviously regarded their recorder still with more passion (Table 10.2). Plus,
only 4% of the buyers of 1983 said that the video recorder was their most important mass medium, as opposed to 11% of the heads of households having owned a
VCR since 1980 or earlier. Also, 38% of the early buyers "often" talked "about
topics having to do with video recorders and video movies," but only 33% of the
late buyers did so.

These results are an indication of the fading fascination that is initially inherent
in a new medium. It becomes part of everyday life. It is routinely integrated into
other leisure-time behaviors. Its particular value diminishes.

## QUANTITY AND COMPOSITION OF NEW MEDIA USE

### Cable TV

Television ranked much higher than all the other media activities among those who
had cable or planned to subscribe to it. They significantly watched more television

than people who did not go for cable TV. Already before these households had sub-scribed to cable, their members had watched TV for an average of 133 minutes per day, whereas nonsubscribers had spent only 115 minutes per day viewing television. This finding also held—analogously—in the control area. Generally, time spent on watching television was longer for older and less educated people. In all age and education groups, however, actual or planned access to cable was accompanied by at least somewhat more television time (Tables 10.3 and 10.4).

After cable television had been installed into the homes, TV time changed only for particular groups among the cable subscribers. Actual shifts emerged for subscribers between 30 and 50 years of age: They increased their TV time on an average by about 6 minutes per day, whereas during the same period of time, all nonsubscribers decreased watching TV by 10 minutes. This finding can be ex-plained by an overall decrease in TV time due to seasonal effects. Cable seems to prevent the people in the subscriber homes from following the general pattern. Those subscribers with an average educational background watched more television. Also, workers evidently increased their television exposure (about 7 minutes per day) after cable had been delivered. White-collar workers, in contrast, remained fairly stable in their television time (see also chap. 9 in this volume).

Cable subscribers in 1985-1986 also differed from nonsubscribers to a con-siderable degree in the types of television shows they liked or disliked. Generally, people in families having opted for cable in 1985 were more likely to prefer all kinds of entertainment programs. They particularly tended more than nonsub-scribers to go for western movies, detective films, entertainment serials, quiz programs, and comedies. On the other hand, there were no significant differences as to news, sports programs, and general information materials.

All groups under study used a great amount of entertainment on TV before and after the introduction of cable in Ludwigshafen/Vorderpfalz: at least 75 minutes per day. Current-affairs programs and news ranked second with an average of about 22 minutes, both in 1985 and in 1986. Exposure to high-culture materials was negligible, with generally about 5 minutes per day. Surprisingly, exposure to high culture and politics did not vary significantly among our different audience groups (Table 10.5).

Even before the introduction of cable, however, the future cable subscribers had spent up to 15 minutes more per day on entertainment shows than the nonsub-scribers. People interested in subscribing to cable had devoted also a bit more time to local information programs than had other audience members, although neither group used these extensively. When cable actually became available, it was accom-panied by even more time devoted to watching entertainment. Between 1985 and 1986, all nonsubscribers not only reduced their general viewing time, but also the time for entertainment shows (-6 minutes a day). The subscribers, however, used

TABLE 10.3

Time Spent on Television, by Age (Minutes Per Day)

| | Panel Wave | Cable Area | | Noncable Area | | Total |
|---|---|---|---|---|---|---|
| | | Sub-scribers | Nonsub-scribers | Plan to Subscribe | Do Not Plan to Subscribe | |
| 14-29 | 1 | 96 | 90 | 125 | 90 | 99 |
| years | 2 | 93 | 76 | 124 | 81 | 92 |
| Difference | | -3 | -14 | -1 | -9 | -7 |
| n | | 133 | 130 | 86 | 74 | 423 |
| 30-49 | 1 | 123 | 108 | 144 | 115 | 122 |
| years | 2 | 129 | 104 | 131 | 100 | 118 |
| Difference | | +6 | -4 | -13 | -15 | -4 |
| n | | 214 | 140 | 108 | 112 | 574 |
| 50 years | 1 | 179 | 156 | 180 | 165 | 171 |
| and older | 2 | 172 | 146 | 169 | 158 | 163 |
| Difference | | -7 | -10 | -11 | -7 | -8 |
| n | | 150 | 100 | 65 | 72 | 394 |

TABLE 10.4

Time Spent on Television, by Education (Minutes Per Day)

| Education | Panel Wave | Cable area | | Noncable area | | Total |
|---|---|---|---|---|---|---|
| | | Sub-scribers | Nonsub-Scribers | Plan to Subscribe | Do Not Plan to Subscribe | |
| Low | 1 | 146 | 136 | 167 | 149 | 149 |
| | 2 | 146 | 126 | 153 | 143 | 142 |
| Difference | | 0 | -10 | -14 | -6 | -7 |
| n | | 263 | 148 | 140 | 99 | 650 |
| Medium | 1 | 132 | 98 | 127 | 116 | 117 |
| | 2 | 134 | 92 | 127 | 100 | 113 |
| Difference | | +2 | -6 | 0 | -16 | -4 |
| n | | 117 | 115 | 54 | 78 | 364 |
| High | 1 | 111 | 109 | 119 | 94 | 108 |
| | 2 | 106 | 97 | 111 | 83 | 99 |
| Dilfference | | -5 | -12 | -8 | -11 | -9 |
| n | | 82 | 84 | 53 | 66 | 285 |

TABLE 10.5

Time Spent on Watching Specific TV Genres (Minutes Per Day)

| | Panel Wave | Cable Area | | Noncable Area | | Total |
|---|---|---|---|---|---|---|
| | | Sub-scribers | Nonsub-scribers | Plan to Subscribe | Do Not Plan to Subscribe | |
| Total TV | 1 | 133 | 115 | 147 | 122 | 129 |
| | 2 | 133 | 106 | 138 | 111 | 123 |
| Difference | | 0 | -9 | -9 | -11 | -6 |
| TV enter- | 1 | 95 | 80 | 108 | 83 | 91 |
| tainment | 2 | 98 | 75 | 102 | 77 | 88 |
| Difference | | +3 | -5 | -6 | -6 | -3 |
| News, | 1 | 21 | 21 | 23 | 25 | 22 |
| current affairs | 2 | 20 | 22 | 22 | 23 | 22 |
| Difference | | -1 | +1 | -1 | -2 | 0 |
| Local | 1 | 12 | 7 | 10 | 7 | 9 |
| programs | 2 | 10 | 6 | 10 | 5 | 8 |
| Difference | | -2 | -1 | 0 | -2 | -1 |
| High | 1 | 6 | 6 | 7 | 7 | 6 |
| culture programs | 2 | 5 | 4 | 4 | 5 | 5 |
| Difference | | -1 | -2 | -3 | -2 | -1 |

light materials more extensively, both relatively and absolutely (+3 minutes per day), after cable had entered their homes.

In other words, from the various cable services delivering not only movies, sports, and music, but also educational and local programs, only entertainment was used more extensively by cable households than by other ones (Dehm & Klingler, 1985, p. 463).

Among the cable subscribers who were the strongest entertainment aficionados, we find the typical heavy television users. People more than 50 years of age had watched 112 minutes of entertainment per day and, with cable, increased their entertainment exposure slightly. Also, blue-collar workers and those with low formal education, who had earlier watched 106 minutes per day, watched 113 minutes after they got cable TV. On the other hand, young people under 29 years of age and the highly educated respondents seem not to have been affected in their patterns of entertainment exposure. They had watched it only about 80 minutes daily before they got cable and reduced this time after they had been provided with cable, following the seasonal trend (Table 10.6).

TABLE 10.6

Time Spent on Televison Entertainment, by Sociodemographic Variables:
Cable Subscribers Only (Minutes Per Day)

| | Panel Waves | | | |
| | 1 | 2 | Difference | n |
| --- | --- | --- | --- | --- |
| Sex | | | | |
| Male | 96 | 96 | 0 | 257 |
| Female | 94 | 99 | +5 | 247 |
| | | | | |
| Age | | | | |
| 14-29 | 82 | 79 | -3 | 133 |
| 30-49 | 90 | 98 | +8 | 214 |
| 50+ | 112 | 113 | +1 | 157 |
| | | | | |
| Education | | | | |
| Low | 105 | 110 | +5 | 263 |
| Medium | 88 | 94 | +6 | 117 |
| High | 74 | 71 | -3 | 82 |
| | | | | |
| Occupation | | | | |
| Worker | 106 | 113 | +7 | 124 |
| Employee | 99 | 99 | 0 | 153 |
| High position employee/ professional | 70 | 78 | +8 | 52 |

## Videocassette Recorders

As in most other Western countries, the recording of TV programs and replaying them later at a suitable time is the primary function of the video recorder in West Germany. On workdays, in 1983, members of video households played back material from television for about 12 minutes, followed by another 9 minutes from rented or bought videocassettes. Two years later in a national survey, whole households with a VCR watched taped programs for 22 minutes on an average workday and prerecorded cassettes for 10 minutes (Wild, 1986, p. 192).

Earlier studies showed that movies were the TV programs recorded most frequently. TV series, sports programs, quizzes, comedies, and music programs ranked somewhat lower (Wiedemann, 1984, p. 709). Late in 1985, 57% of the recording time was devoted to movies, another 27% to entertainment series, and 11% to entertainment shows. The meager rest of 5% contained sports, information, and everything else (Wild, 1986, p. 189).

A second function of the VCR was to watch prerecorded movies instead of television or in addition to it. In 1982, for instance, 70% of the video households had rented cassettes at least once in a while (Burda, 1982). In 1986, revenues of sales and rentals of prerecorded cassettes for the first time surmounted the revenues of movie theaters (Zielinski, 1987, p. 509). Since about 1980, VCR owners have been able to rent or buy from a fairly manifold offer. The number of prerecorded cassettes has increased strongly. Early in 1985, about 5,800 different video programs were available. In 1986, the figure was 6,300, and in 1987 it was 7,100 (Deutsches Video Institut, 1987).

Video recorders made contents available that couldn't be watched at home even if one had been spending a lot of time in front of the TV set. As in most other countries, TV stations in the Federal Republic of Germany are not allowed to broadcast pornographic and extremely violent movies. Almost 20% of video shop revenues in 1984 were made by selling or renting erotic and horror movies (Deutsches Video Institut, 1984). When the mass marketing of video recorders began in 1979, as many as 80% of the prerecorded cassettes available were X-rated movies. In 1981, this figure had dropped to 20%, and in 1983 to 12%. In 1987, it was as low as 2% (Deutsches Video Institut, 1987). That does not necessarily mean that the number of pornographic movies watched on video has decreased tremendously, but that other genres have picked up considerably. Such genres were primarily action, horror, and adventure movies (Radevagen & Zielinski, 1982, p. 161; Zielinski, 1982, p. 191).

In the mid-1980s, cassettes with "international movie hits" became more important due to the increased involvement of the large U.S. movie companies, such as Warner, Columbia, Paramount and Twentieth Century Fox, in the video business after 1981 (Radevagen & Zielinski, 1982, 1984). A trend has developed to classic movies and to current releases away from the so-called B-pictures and those movies so often on TV that nobody wanted to see them anymore.

In our 1983 VCR study, the most important correlate of recording a lot of material from TV was having bought a VCR fairly early (in 1980 and earlier). This feature stood out in a multiple regression among all other sociodemographic and even attitude variables. We may conclude that the earlier the VCR was available, the more it was an instrument of replaying television material. Households having bought a video recorder in 1980 or earlier still stuck to that routine as late as in 1983.

VCRs were relatively often used to help their owners through those parts of the day that are still almost without television for most people in West Germany—mornings and early afternoons (Wild, 1986, p. 193). Plus, nonfictional programs on TV were "bridged" by watching entertaining material on video. This function of the video recorder may have been particularly important for Germans because West German TV had not provided as great a variety of entertainment programs as U.S. television had. Also, the average West German TV viewer was—at least in 1983—not always able at any given time to choose between at least one nonfictional and one fictional program on TV, and even less so between different enter-

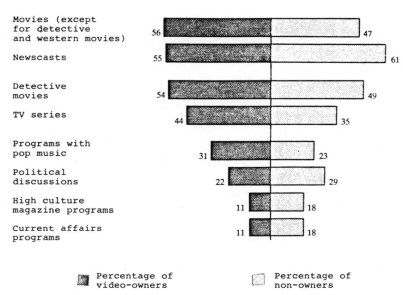

Movies (except for detective and western movies)  56 / 47

Newscasts  55 / 61

Detective movies  54 / 49

TV series  44 / 35

Programs with pop music  31 / 23

Political discussions  22 / 29

High culture magazine programs  11 / 18

Current affairs programs  11 / 18

■ Percentage of video-owners          □ Percentage of non-owners

**FIG.10.2.** Favorite programs on TV. (Shown are only those programs preferred by video owners and non-owners to a different extent.) Base: Persons over 14 years of age in video and nonvideo households.

tainment programs. There were two reasons for this: The German television system supplied the average viewer with only up to four different channels, and German TV was much more educational and political than most other TV channels in the world.

How strongly members of video households focused on entertainment is not only shown by their preferences for programs they record or of the cassettes they rent or buy. If we look more closely at the contents preferred in those media most similar to the VCR, cinema and television, this picture becomes even clearer. Relatively more video owners than other people declared entertainment programs on TV—series, movies, and music programs—their favorites. Persons without a VCR in 1983 listed nonfiction programs somewhat more often than the VCR owners as programs that they liked to watch (Fig. 10.2).

This difference between video owners and non-owners is supported by their choice of the movie genres they frequently watched in movie theaters. "Spaghetti westerns" (made in Italy), detective movies, science fiction, horror movies, Kung Fu, and pornographic and super-films were watched more often by video household members than by others. The greatest difference could be found for science fiction movies (71% of the non-owners in 1983 "never" watched those movies, but only 57% of the owners), for detective films ("never" watched by 60% of the non-owners and 47% of the owners), and Spaghetti westerns (77% vs. 65%).

Here, more than a mere entertainment orientation of those with a VCR in 1983 manifests itself. The contents preferred by people with a VCR are not only somehow entertaining but also represent genres with the strongest escape potential: the most exciting programs, programs with the greatest suspense or with a plot the farthest from reality. This also becomes clear in the answers to the following question: "There are movies that our television is not allowed to show. Is this a reason for you to have a video recorder? Would you say: a very important reason, an important reason, or not so important?"

This reason was at least "important" for almost a third of the heads of video households in 1983 (31%), but only for 1 in 20 of the non-owners (5%). We can assume that the respondents knew which movies television is not allowed to show: pornographic and extremely brutal ones.

The strong entertainment orientation of video owners was confirmed by our 1985 sample. Video households in our cable study watched fewer political programs, local affairs and high culture materials than nonvideo homes. But entertainment was watched in video homes considerably more extensively than in nonvideo homes (13 minutes more in the first panel wave; 8 minutes more in the second). When the audience also was segmented according to their cable subscription status, tremendous differences could be found. Respondents with cable and a VCR in 1986 watched 104 minutes of TV entertainment daily while those without cable or a VCR spent about half an hour less on these types of programs. As to those who use either cable or video, cable subscribers without a VCR watched 96 minutes of entertainment per day while nonsubscribers with a VCR spent 77 minutes daily on televised entertainment. This pattern is virtually the same for 1985 and 1986. In other words, audience members, in particular, who prefer and use both cable TV and the VCR are the entertainment freaks (Table 10.7).

## THE TEMPORAL DEMANDS OF NEW MEDIA USE

### Cable Use and Other Media Behaviors

As the use of each new medium requires the reallocation of time, cable television should have affected either the use of the already existing media in the home and/or other activities. Indeed, there was some tendency for cable households to use their radios less extensively than noncable ones. Moreover, cable subscribers in our

TABLE 10.7

Time Spent on TV Entertainment, by VCR/Cable Ownership
(Minutes Per Day)

| Panel Wave | Persons Who Have/Want Cable, With VCR | Persons Who Have/Want Cable, Without VCR | Persons Who Do Not Have/ Want Cable, With VCR | Persons Who Do Not Have/ Want Cable, Without VCR | Total |
|---|---|---|---|---|---|
| 1 | 109 | 93 | 80 | 81 | 91 |
| 2 | 104 | 96 | 77 | 75 | 88 |
| n | 273 | 485 | 133 | 488 | 1379 |

study somewhat reduced their reading of newspapers, books, and magazines (see also chap. 9 in this volume). Whereas there had been no difference in print media use before the homes had been supplied with cable, subscribers later on spent less time (38 minutes) reading than nonsubscribers (46 minutes) on an average day.

As to the time for listening to records and tapes, in our first cable survey there had been no difference between those applying for cable and the others. After the provision of cable, however, actual cable subscribers spent less time listening to music, at least on a weekend day (13 minutes), than nonsubscribers (22 minutes).

The level of VCR use, however, was virtually unaffected by the introduction of cable: Those with cable or at least planning to subscribe to it, did not watch video less extensively than did those who decided against a subscription.

## VCR Use and Other Media Behaviors

In 1983, those who had a video recorder at home were more likely to say that they watched television at least "several times a week" (93%) than those in households without a VCR (88%). Surprisingly, however, the duration of watching regular television was a little bit longer for persons in nonvideo households (103 minutes) on an average workday as compared to video households (92 minutes). Also, in the 1983 video study, the older the respondents, the more time they spent on TV, with the exception of people 13 years old or younger. As in the cable study, watching TV decreased with higher levels of education. But our result, that video households in general watched less regular TV than those without a VCR, held true in all of our subgroups. In 1985, however, when video had entered the lower strata of the society, people in video households in a national survey obviously spent more time on regular television: 146 minutes per average workday as opposed to 129 minutes in nonvideo households (Wild, 1986, p. 193).

TABLE 10.8

Time Spent on Television and Video,
By Education and VCR Ownership

| Education | VCR in Household | | VCR Not in Household | | Total |
|---|---|---|---|---|---|
| | Low | High | Low | High | |
| Watching television min/day | 140 | 122 | 152 | 109 | 130 |
| Watching video min/day | 22 | 16 | -- | -- | 19 |
| n | 219 | 172 | 466 | 505 | 1362 |

Even though not strictly comparable to our 1983 study and to the 1985 national survey, our cable study showed virtually no difference in the time spent on TV between video households and nonvideo households in 1986. On the average, persons in video households spent 132 minutes watching television (including cable channels), and those in nonvideo households spent 130 minutes. When we segment our respondents according to their level of education (in contrast with our 1983 study, VCR and non-VCR households were not matched demographically), an interaction effect becomes visible. Low-educated audience members in nonvideo households watched the most television in our sample, followed by low-educated persons in video households. We find the reversed proportion for those with a higher education (Table 10.8). It seems as if watching television ceased being a time resource for VCR use in the mid-1980s. Video households, then, not only watched materials on their VCRs, they also could be found among those with an equal or even more extensive consumption of regular TV.

On the other hand, as early as in 1983, we find a clear tendency for the heads of video households to spend less time on nonentertaining, educational, sophisticated books, papers, and magazines (Figs. 10.3 and 10.4). Very similar results for the reading behavior of VCR owners were revealed in the 1986 cable study. We found less local newspapers (76%), political magazines (14%), and general magazines (33%) in video households than in nonvideo homes (81%, 22%, 38%, respectively).

In contrast to our results for cable subscribers in 1986, however, video owners in 1983 were generally more oriented toward audio media. They listened to records, audio-cassettes and tapes, and to the radio more frequently and more extensively than other people.

VCR ownership does not seem to have harmed movie going. Fairly equal portions of both groups of respondents in 1983 claimed to see movies in the cinema.

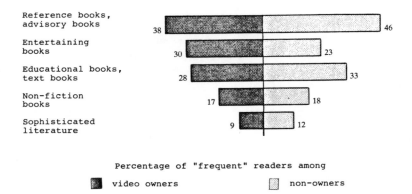

Percentage of "frequent" readers among

video owners                    non-owners

**FIG.10.3.** Book reading preferences of heads of video and nonvideo households. Question: On this card there are several books listed. Please check whether you read these books frequently, occasionally, or never.

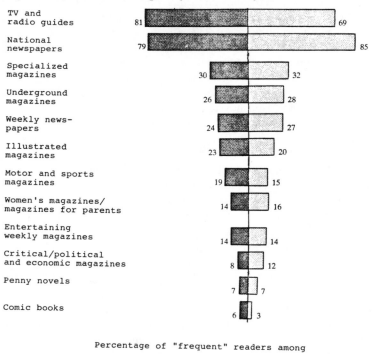

Percentage of "frequent" readers among

video owners                    non-owners

**FIG.10.4.** Newspaper and magazine preferences of heads of video and nonvideo households. Question: Here is card listing types of newspapers, weeklies, and magazines. Please check how often you read these newspapers, weeklies, or magazines.

And although video penetration was even higher in 1986, the movie theaters in West Germany boasted of having attracted more movie goers than at the beginning of the 1980s.

## Cable Use and Nonmedia Activities

It was quite obvious that cable television altered patterns of television use, particularly among specific audience segments. It also competed with other activities for time. Indications of such a dislodgement come from an examination of the winners of competition between the individual's most favorite television program and other possible activities. Interestingly enough, the respondents who had opted for cable in 1986 more often indicated a willingness to dismiss other activities than their noncable counterparts, if their favorite TV show was featured at the same time. Television was particularly strong when it competed with unorganized social outdoor activities. Seventy-four percent of the actual and potential subscribers to cable (vs. 67% of the nonsubscribers) preferred their favorite TV show to going out to a restaurant or bar. Sixty-nine percent (vs. 57% of the nonsubscribers) would skip going out for a movie. Fifty-nine percent (vs. 53% of the nonsubscribers) would cancel their "Stammtisch" (regular meetings in bars), and 57% (vs. 51% of the nonsubscribers) would not go for a walk if their favorite television show was on. Also, significantly more of those respondents who favored the new services would have cancelled a theater performance (35% vs. 28%), a sports event (42% vs. 29%) and a meeting of their social club (35% vs. 26%). More resistant are mutual visits of family or friends when it comes to a competition with television. But still significantly more cable supporters (18%) than nonsubscribers (12%) would cancel a visit with their friends.

Although cable subscribers differed from nonsubscribers in their readiness to skip other activities in favor of television, they actually had extremely similar patterns of time allocation for homework, hobbies, meals, going out, joining cultural activities, and meeting friends. Because the differences in these general categories were not significant between the groups and over time, there is no evidence that general habits were affected more than slightly by cable television. They may be in the future, however, should the hypothetical competition mentioned earlier, between favorite TV program and other pastimes, tend to translate more often than in the past into real decisions.

## VCR Use and Nonmedia Activities

At first glance, persons in video households in 1983 were not as passive in their leisure time as many media critics had assumed. First of all, the two contrasting groups only differed in 6 out of 18 leisure-time activities studied. Aside from the trivial difference that members of video households more often watched videocassettes, we found that those who had a video recorder at home were significantly more likely to say that they paid visits to other people or were visited by them frequently than did persons from non-owner households (23% to 15%). But members of video households did say that they were more likely never to go to a theater performance or to a concert. Almost half of the video group (49%), but only about one third of the people in nonvideo households (36%), gave this answer. In addition, persons without a VCR were more likely to say they went for a walk "several times a week" (36%) than those with a video recorder (29%).

According to time-use diary results, people in nonvideo households in 1983 took more time for their meals and were more often busy with their work at home than those in video households. Their "homebodiness" showed also in a greater amount of leisure time spent at home. Members of video households, on the other hand, spent some more time for work outside the home. They also had more leisure-time activities outside their homes, and visitors stayed longer at their places than at nonvideo households.

In sum, then, what these data do not show is that VCR users were less active than those without a VCR. Inspite of this, heads of video households seemed to be more often bored than those in the other group. The question used to determine that was: "There are days, when one sometimes doesn't know what to do. How about you? On which days of the week does that happen to you?" For an average of 1.7 of the 7 days of a week, video owners claimed to "frequently" or "sometimes" not know what to do. For non-owners this score was only 1.2. In spite of their activities, life obviously was not exciting enough for VCR owners. They might have sought this excitement in quite specific areas, however: in their leisure time and—as we have seen—by exposing themselves to entertaining TV programs and motion pictures.

## FUNCTIONS OF THE NEW MEDIA

### Cable TV

When people in 1985 were asked what they expected from cable TV, the most frequent answer for future subscribers was the proliferation of new programs, particularly of more entertainment programs. Also remarkably strong was the expectation that cable services delivered better information on local affairs (90% of members of cable households and 83% of persons in potential subscriber households outside the cable area). A not quite so strong argument in favor of cable TV, and probably lip service, was that more programs meant more political information. Two thirds of the respondents in subscriber homes expressed this opinion, and half of the potential subscribers in the noncable area agreed. These expectations remained stable after cable had been delivered. Thus, actual exposure to the new programs obviously did not change the audience's basic attitudes regarding the benefits of their purchase.

As to the households that were not planning to subscribe to cable, 75% of them also welcomed the addition of new channels to the television menu in general, but only about 40% liked cable because of more entertainment programs. Moreover, compared to the two thirds of the people in subscriber homes expecting more political information, just about 30% of the nonsubscribers shared this hope.

We know that those in favor and those against cable had differed from the start in their exposure to television both in terms of extent and program choice. Obviously, TV watching fulfilled different functions for these audiences. In order to describe these functions, respondents were asked to assess a battery of items representing various purposes of watching television. Based on a factor analysis of this battery, we conclude that television meets three basic functions: (a) it serves the desire for relaxation, diversion, and escape from the daily routines; (b) it provides the feeling of being well advised on all kinds of things in daily life ("personal utility"), and (c) it enhances the impression of keeping pace with the times and of being up-to-date with the latest trends ("surveillance").

Across all groups investigated, the most important function attributed to television was personal utility. Relaxation ranked second, and surveillance took the third position. Not too surprisingly, respondents who favored cable generally attributed all three functions to television more frequently than people who rejected the new medium.

As the data of our second panel survey—in 1986—suggest, the functions attributed to TV seem to have remained pretty stable over time and not to have been influenced by the actual cable treatment. The differences between subscribers and nonsubscribers had already existed before cable was provided; they were at most deepened by the actual connection to cable.

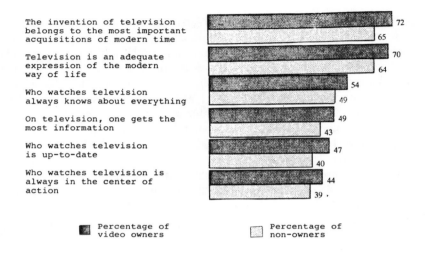

**FIG. 10.5.** The importance of the surveillance function of television. (Percent who agreed.) Question: Here are some opinions about television. Please check whether you rather agree or disagree with this opinion. Base: Person over 14 years old in video and nonvideo households.

## Videocassette Recorders

In West Germany, as noted previously, the major purpose of a VCR has been the delayed viewing of TV programs. It is certainly legitimate, then, to deduce at least some of the gratifications of VCRs from video owners' perceived functions of TV. Generally, like those connected to cable in 1986, members of video households in 1983 regarded all three functions of television more often as important than the other respondents. In none of the three dimensions, however, did video owners in 1983 differ as strongly from non-owners as in the relaxation function. The expectations of people from video households typically were "to be well entertained," "to recover," and to have "not too many problem-laden programs." In a discriminant analysis including virtually all the characteristics mentioned so far, this function showed as one of the most discriminating factors between video and nonvideo households.

Differences this great did not exist for the personal utility function of television. They did exist to some extent, however, for its surveillance function. Video owners in 1983, significantly more frequently than non-owners, claimed that

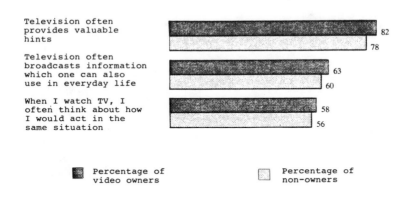

Television often
provides valuable
hints                          82
                               78

Television often
broadcasts information         63
which one can also
use in everyday life           60

When I watch TV, I
often think about how          58
I would act in the
same situation                 56

■ Percentage of          □ Percentage of
  video owners              non-owners

**FIG. 10.6.** The importance of the personal utility function of television. (Percent who agreed.) Question: See Fig. 10.5. Base: Persons over 14 years old in video and nonvideo households.

one is "up-to-date" with television, that television is "an adequate expression of the modern way of life," and one of the "most important acquisitions of modern time" (Figs. 10.5, 10.6 and 10.7).

For people who had purchased their VCR fairly late, however, television was demystified significantly. Those who had been among the first to acquire this device, in 1978-1980, more frequently than everybody else regarded television as an instrument of advice. That it provided "valuable hints" was believed by three quarters (74%) of those having bought a VCR as late as in 1983. But that was 11 percentage points less than this answer among the buyers of 1980 and earlier (85%). Similarly, only 48% of the buyers of 1983 agreed with the statement "When I watch something on TV, I often think about how I would act in the same situation." But 59% of those having bought a video recorder in 1978, 1979, or 1980 agreed.

On the other hand, later buyers of video recorders seem to have been a bit more entertainment-oriented than earlier buyers. About half (52%) of the early buyers suggested that "television should show more consideration for working people who want to relax during their leisure time," but more than two thirds (67%) of those having bought this device in 1983 said this. Consequently, only a third (32%) of the later buyers, but almost half (48%) of the earlier buyers, agreed with the statement: "I find it good that television frequently shows problem-laden programs."

Late buyers were more often members of video clubs (39%) than earlier ones (17% of those having bought the videocassette recorder between 1978 and 1980).

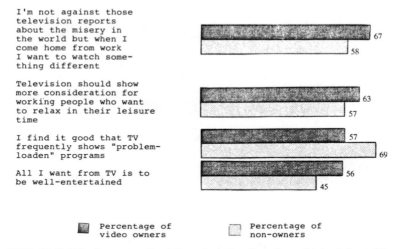

**FIG. 10.7.** The importance of the relaxation function of television. (Percent who agreed.) Question: See Fig. 10.5. Base: Persons over 14 years old in video and nonvideo households.

This may be a sign for late buyers' preference for prerecorded cassettes that allow them to circumvent the seemingly unsatisfactory TV programs. Indeed, the playing of prerecorded cassettes was the only use of TV set and video recorder that late buyers of the video recorder at least did not spend less time with than earlier buyers, as noted previously.

The overwhelming majority of the video owners in 1983 had characteristics as described in this chapter. In addition, however, we found two very specific video user groups not quite fitting into this pattern. They differed from the average video user in terms of specific functions of the VCR. A cluster analysis comprising virtually all characteristics measured in our study revealed three clusters of respondents:

Cluster 1 (comprising 56% of the total of 332 households in the 1983 analysis): Its members more or less looked like the average video owner described in the previous sections. In these previous sections, we compared video owners and nonowners as if there were one single type of video owner. Although we can now say that there is not a single type of owner, the first cluster encompasses a majority of the owners, and the persons in this cluster have the characteristics of the average owner described previously.

Cluster 2 (16%) primarily included those households that taped virtually everything on television. They were not particularly interested in movie pictures in the cinema; they were not very active in their leisure time; they themselves realized that the video recorder had reduced several of their leisure-time activities.

Cluster 3 (32%) consisted, above all, of the movie theater fans, people with a very active behavior during their leisure time, and those who thought the videocassette recorder made them free for even more activities.

The last two clusters may be called the introverted and the extraverted video user groups. The introverted cluster contained those video households with weak contacts to the outside and few activities in general. For them, the VCR—in a relatively undifferentiated fashion—increased traditional TV consumption. Their desire for convenient, fairly passive entertainment was obvious. These households were right in believing that their leisure-time activities suffered from their access to the VCR. Large households with many children belonged to this group. The head of household was fairly young and had a sub-average formal education. Women were more frequently housewives. The number of household appliances in those households was rather small. Introverted video users significantly more frequently felt bored than all the other respondents.

The opposite type was the extraverted video user. This person was very active, used the VCR more often for playing prerecorded cassettes and liked to go to the movie theater. For this group, the video recorder was an instrument of liberation. People in this cluster believed that the video recorder helped increase their leisure-time activities. Typically in these households, the head of household has an above-average formal education, women more often earn their own money, there is a somewhat higher household income, and there are relatively large numbers of household appliances.

## CONCLUSIONS

With the introduction of cable television and VCRs, a considerable portion of the West German audience is enjoying an expanded audio-visual offering. One of the most crucial aspects of this change is that both video and cable television allow the audience to individualize media use. People with access to cable and VCRs are no longer dependent on the programs and the schedules of both the movie theaters and the traditional public television stations. They have the opportunity to adapt their television use—as was the case for print media already—to their individual situations and needs (Zielinski, 1986, p. 317).

Suprisingly, though, we found that the patterns of everyday behavior have not been strongly altered by cable television or VCR use. In general, our studies suggest that television exposure has increased. But our data, so far, show that cable television and the use of the VCR have not replaced or even dangerously reduced other media activities or leisure-time behaviors. Instead, they have been added to already existing patterns, taking a little time away more or less from everything else. There are some hints, however, that reading and listening to music may have suffered a little bit more than other behaviors.

There is also convincing evidence in our data that the opportunity to receive cable services and to watch material on VCRs confirmed and expanded already existing patterns of television use. In general, those who had already watched much television watched more television when the VCR and cable became available. Those who had already watched much entertainment watched more entertainment. This rule is, to some extent, a result of averaging out interesting differences between groups of the audience, however.

True, there may be many people who use their freedom of choice for simply watching lots of televised entertainment now that it is finally available to them. On the other hand, there is a considerable portion of the audience exploiting the new flexibility in a more "emancipated," even "professional" way (Lahnstein, 1987, p. 6). These audience members now turn to their favorite audiovisual material when it suits their timetable, not the one of the TV stations or movie theaters. For these people, cable TV and VCRs do not necessarily take bites out of other leisure-time activities. On the contrary, they may even be able to spend more time on such things as activities outside their homes. Are we observing a new communication gap emerge? More flexibility, used for a variety of activities, furthers the emancipation of one segment of society, along with a rather contrasting trend for other strata of society that may become more dependent on the media to fill their leisure time.

## REFERENCES

Bundesministerium fuer das Post- und Fernmeldewesen (Ed.). (1976). *Telekommunikationsbericht der Kommission fuer den Ausbau des technischen Kommunikationssystems* [Telecommunication report by the commission for the development of the technical communication system]. Bonn: Dr. Hans Heger.

Burda. (Ed.). (1982). *Daten zum Video-Markt 1982* [Data about the video market, 1982]. Offenburg: Burda-Verlag.

Dehm, U., & Klingler, W. (1985). Programmvielfalt versus Programmnutzung [Channel plurality vs. channel use]. *Media Perspektiven*, (6), 459-463.

Deutsches Video Institut. (1984). *Der Video-Markt in der Bundesrepublik Deutschland* [The video market in the Federal Republic of Germany]. Berlin: Deutsches Video Institut.

Deutsches Video Institut. (1987). *Medienstatistik 1986/87* [Media statistics, 1986-87]. Berlin: Deutsches Video Institut.

Frank, B., & Klingler, W. (1987). *Die veraenderte Fernsehlandschaft: Zwei Jahre ARD/ZDF-Begleitforschung zu den Kabelpilotprojekten* [The changed television landscape: Two years of ARD/ZDF studies of the cable pilot projects]. Frankfurt and Berlin: Metzner.

Hackforth, J., & Schoenbach, K. (1985). *Video im Alltag: Ein Forschungsbericht ueber Nutzung und Nutzen einer neuen Medientechnik* [Video in everyday life: A research report about uses and gratifications of a new media technology]. Mainz: Zweites Deutsches Fernsehen.

Kaase, M. (1986). *Kommunikationskanaele und Freizeitverhalten im lokalen Raum: Einfluesse des Kabelfernsehens* [Communication channels and leisure time behavior in the local area: The impact of cable television]. (Grant proposal, Deutsche Forschungsgemeinschaft). Mannheim.

Lahnstein, M. (1987). Medienmarkt im Wandel [The changing media market]. *Bertelsmann Briefe, 122*, 3-9.

Radevagen, T., & Zielinski, S. (1982). Video-Software: Annaeherungsversuche an einen neuen Markt [Video software: Attempts to approach a new market]. *Media Perspektiven*, (3), 153-165.

Radevagen, T., & Zielinski, S. (1984). Video-Software 1984: Strukturen des Marktes und Tendenzen des Angebotes [Video software, 1984: Structures of the market and tendencies of supply]. *Media Perspektiven*, (5), 372-387.

Schoenbach, K., & Hackforth, J. (1987). Video in West German households: Attitudinal and behavioral differences. *American Behavioral Scientist, 30*, 533-543.

teleskopie (1980). *Personen in Fernsehhaushalten mit Videorekorder: Eine vergleichende Sekundaerauswertung der Teleskopie-Strukturerhebung Winter 1978/79* [Persons in TV households with a VCR: A comparative secondary analysis of the teleskopie structure survey, winter 1978-79]. Allensbach am Bodensee: Institut fuer Demoskopie Allensbach.

Wild, C. (1986). Die Videorecordernutzung im GfK-Meter-System [VCR use in the GfK meter system]. *Media Perspektiven*, (3), 183-193.

Wiedemann, J. (1984). Fernsehen wird durch Video erst schoen: Eine Synopse der rundfunkeigenen Untersuchungen zum Videoverhalten [Television becomes nice only with video: A synopsis of those studies about video behavior initiated by broadcasting stations]. *Media Perspektiven*, (9), 706-714.

Wissenschaftliche Begleitkommission (Ed.). (1987). *Versuch mit Breitbandkabel* [A test with broadband cable]. (Abschlussbericht an die Landesregierung Rheinland-Pfalz). Berlin and Offenbach: VDE Verlag.

Zielinski, S. (1982, September). Im Zentrum: Spielfilme von Kinoklassikern bis zum alternativen Kino: Analyse der auf dem Markt befindlichen Programme bespielter Video-Kassetten [In the focus: Movies from cinema classics to the alternative cinema: An analysis of the titles of video cassettes offered by the market]. *FUNK-Korrespondenz, 37*, 14-21.

Zielinski, S. (1986). *Zur Geschichte des Videorekorders* [On the history of the VCR]. Berlin: Spiess.

Zielinski, S. (1987). Der Heimvideomarkt im zehnten Jahr. Bestandsaufnahme und neuere Tendenzen—besonders im Hinblick auf die Software [The home video market in its 10th year: An inventory and new tendencies—particularly in terms of the software]. *Media Perspektiven*, (8), 507-516.

# 11

# Italy: A Broadcast Explosion

**Paolo Martini**
*Panorama*
**Gianpietro Mazzoleni**
*University of Salerno*

## A DECADE OF UNREST IN THE MEDIA FIELD [1]

In 1975, the average daily amount of television broadcast time in Italy was 14 hours and 2 minutes, almost completely concentrated on one public channel. A dozen years later one could count 678 private television stations; each viewer in the larger metropolitan areas had at his or her disposal more than 400 hours per day of programming, both from public and commercial channels.

Even though 515 out of 687 stations are independent, about 90% of the daily audience clusters around major TV services RAI (Radio Televisione Italiana, the public broadcasting company), and FININVEST (the biggest commercial broadcasting trust, owned by Silvio Berlusconi). The public company runs three channels: RAI-UNO, RAI-DUE, RAI-TRE; the private one runs three commercial networks (CANALE-5, ITALIA-1, RETE-4).

In short, Italian television has experienced the most extraordinary change that has ever taken place in such a short time in the field of mass media. This phenomenon actually consists of (a) an unprecedented increase in the number of broadcast channels and in their consumption; and (b) a rapid concentration of the television market in terms of ownership, audience, programming, and advertising.

This process started in a very peculiar political phase, the mid-1970s, when the country's political and social balances were facing serious challenges. It was furthered by the structural incongruities of the Italian communication market.

The "television revolution" of the last decade can thus be described on two different levels of interpretation: (a) the *political-judicial* level, referring to the long-lasting stalemate of government and party policies and to the role of the judiciary in the place of other institutions in enforcing existing (though obsolete) regulations; and (b) the level of the *advertising market* and of the *television content* offered. There was a movement from a rigid separation of the two to the transformation of the latter into a product of the former.

Until 1975, the broadcast monopoly had been reserved by the country's constitution to the state that controls it by means of a public-owned company (RAI).

In 1960, the Constitutional Court still backed the legitimacy of such a monopoly. In 1974, however, it sentenced its *partial* illegitimacy, requiring a few "minimal conditions" for a more legitimate monopoly. These requisites were translated into a reform bill by the parliament in 1975 that allowed some commercial enterprising in cable and broadcast television. Just 1 year later, these newly established stations succeeded in getting the Constitutional Court to allow their activities on a *local* scale. In 1981, however, commercial broadcasting was somewhat restricted by a further ruling that prohibited them from airing nationwide programs.

Repeatedly—but in vain—the Court has urged the parliament to come up with new and positive regulations.

The Reform Bill of 1975 freed RAI from the suffocating control of the central government and put it under parliamentary supervision. This reform was partly due to the decline of Christian Democratic hegemony in the country, while the Communist Party (PCI) was gathering new, enormous electoral support.

In this political context—with a turbulent social climate in the midst of an economic recession that was pushing the country's entrepreneurial class to seek an agreement with the communists—the instrument of state television became the object of a reform that followed the pluralistic ideas of the Constitutional Court. Key responsibilities of television were redistributed to several political organizations. This process of partitioning the RAI power reached its climax in 1986, when each of the three major political parties gained control of one of the three channels.

What actually happened was that the political forces of the coalition governments—afraid of the PCI's success—backed some anti-communist entrepreneurs' plan to establish commercial television and secured for them the greatest flexibility simply by refusing to issue new regulations. Only when the Judiciary in 1984 stopped the private broadcasters' attempt to circumvent the *localness* limitation, the parliament could not help intervening, approving a government's decree that allowed the nationwide operation of commercial networks. All this has brought about chaos in the television legislation. At the end of 1987, the policy stalemate was still far from ending.

On the "market" level, the commercial revolution is simply disruptive. Until the mid-1970s, the pressure of companies interested in advertising was contained by the centralized political control over television. Advertising resources were extremely limited, and strict censorship of the content of spot ads was exerted by RAI. In addition to this, the Sipra (RAI's advertising managing company), holding the advertising monopoly on television, controlled also the allocation of advertising to the press.

Private television channels (mainly the FININVEST trust) confined themselves to simply be the opposite of the other media, reducing the contents to a product of the advertising market, in a desperate search for the majority of consumers.

## DEVELOPMENT OF OPTIONS

### Television Programming

Between 1975 and 1985, the three public television channels increased their broadcasting time from 8 hours per day to 14 hours each, filling time slots previously neglected. This expansion of RAI's programming is mostly due to the efforts of public broadcasting to counter the fierce competition of the commercial stations, especially of the three networks of FININVEST.

FININVEST totalled 21,000 hours of transmission in 1983—not counting the broadcasting time of the 400 local stations. The FININVEST transmissions, added to the 20,000 hours of RAI, make a huge volume of television materials available to the audience.

The commercial channels "invaded" first the early afternoon, then the morning, traditionally free from television. RAI followed by introducing a sort of "breakfast television" program.

One of the most important characteristics of the commercial programming is the great amount of imported material that they rely on. At their outset, the private stations—and networks—contained almost 100% foreign material. The 1986 data of the FININVEST networks (Canale 5, RETE 4, Italia 1), however, show some efforts to produce more programs themselves. (See Table 11.1.)

In the same time span (1976-1986), the RAI networks decreased their previously very large self-production volume, from about 93% to 78%, mostly because of the need for filling the expanded transmission time.

The program types most offered by RAI channels are light entertainment (shows, quizzes, light music), serials and soap operas, films, and news. The commercial channels stand out for a heavy offering of serials and soap operas (of foreign

TABLE 11.1

Proportion of Self-Produced Versus Foreign Made Programming
of RAI and FININVEST

|                    | RAI UNO | RAI DUE | RAI TRE | TOT RAI | RETE 4 | ITAL 1 | CAN 5 | TOT FIN |
|--------------------|---------|---------|---------|---------|--------|--------|-------|---------|
| % self-production  | 82.5    | 69.0    | 83.9    | 78.2    | 10.7   | 20.7   | 44.6  | 25.0    |
| % foreign-made     | 17.5    | 31.0    | 16.1    | 21.8    | 89.3   | 79.3   | 55.4  | 75.0    |
| N (minutes)        | 5663    | 5619    | 4689    | 15971   | 6396   | 6338   | 6008  | 18742   |

Note: From RAI (1987).


TABLE 11.2

Program Types in the Weekly Offering

|               | RAI-UNO % | RAI-DUE % | RAI-TRE % | RETE-4 % | ITALIA-1 % | CANALE-5 % |
|---------------|-----------|-----------|-----------|----------|------------|------------|
| Music         | -         | .8        | 12.7      | -        | -          | -          |
| Drama         | -         | -         | -         | -        | -          | -          |
| Serials/Soap  | 10.5      | 15.4      | 6.9       | 34.6     | 50.3       | 39.8       |
| Film          | 7.7       | 15.3      | 9.0       | 30.0     | 4.9        | 6.1        |
| Children      | 3.5       | .6        | -         | 11.7     | 11.2       | .3         |
| Light Entert. | 29.3      | 20.4      | 15.7      | 6.7      | 9.8        | 25.3       |
| Cultural      | 16.2      | 11.6      | 11.7      | 1.1      | 1.3        | 5.9        |
| Educational   | 1.9       | 3.5       | 15.0      | -        | -          | -          |
| News          | 10.2      | 11.5      | 11.1      | -        | -          | -          |
| Curr. Affairs | 1.3       | .8        | .9        | -        | .6         | 2.1        |
| Sport         | 7.8       | 10.7      | 13.1      | -        | 6.7        | 2.5        |
| Political     | 2.2       | 1.4       | -         | 1.3      | -          | -          |
| Other         | 9.4       | 8.0       | 3.9       | 14.6     | 15.2       | 18.0       |
| Total         | 100.0     | 100.0     | 100.0     | 100.0    | 100.0      | 100.0      |

Note: From RAI (1987).

production), of movies, and of light entertainment. No news is broadcast by the
FININVEST networks, because they are legally prohibited to offer live nationwide
transmissions (Table 11.2).

From a diachronic perspective, one observes how the growth of broadcasting
time of RAI consisted mostly of a net upswing of fictional programs (films, serials,
series, soap operas) at the expense of information. Total time for information
decreased from 41.4% in 1976 to 26.4% 10 years later (Table 11.3).

TABLE 11.3

Program Types on RAI, 1976 and 1986

|  | 1976 | 1986 | Change |
|---|---|---|---|
|  | % | % | % |
| Fiction | 12.7 | 27.5 | 14.8 |
| Entertainment | 8.2 | 13.7 | 5.5 |
| Educational | 5.1 | 4.7 | -.4 |
| Information | 41.4 | 26.4 | -15.0 |
| Other | 32.6 | 27.7 | - 4.9 |
| Total | 100.0 | 100.0 | |

Note: From RAI (1987)

## Home Video

The enormous offering of television content, especially of feature films, has slowed the spread of VCRs in Italian homes. Only in 1986 and 1987 did the distribution pick up some speed. In 1986, 1.3 million prerecorded cassettes and 5 million blank ones were sold. Forecasts indicate the establishment of a steady rental market (video shops, video clubs) that was almost unimaginable just 2 years earlier.

## Cinema

In Italy, the decline of cinema seems inversely proportional to the spread of other media. From 1976 to 1986, the national production of feature films decreased from 233 to 114 per year. The offering of films via television has grown dramatically, however. The RAI channels broadcast 1,000 movies in 1986 (vs. only 200 in 1977). The FININVEST networks and the remaining local stations, according to media analysts, carry "thousands" of films.

## Teletext

This service, carried only by RAI, was inaugurated in January 1985 after a period of testing. At the end of 1986, it was present in 1.5 million homes. *Televideo* (its Italian name) now offers more than 800 pages of various information throughout the daytime.

TABLE 11.4

Television Viewing Time on an Average Day
(in Hours and Minutes)

| Year | Households | Individuals |
|------|------------|-------------|
| 1977 | 3:39 | 2:23 |
| 1978 | 4:05 | 2:30 |
| 1980 | 4:10 | 2:47 |
| 1981 | 4:22 | 2:48 |
| 1983 | 5:00 | 3:04 |
| 1984 | 5:10 | 3:51 |
| 1985 | (N/A) | 3:48 |
| 1986 | 5:48 | (N/A) |
| 1987 | 6:13 | 3:33 |

## NATURE OF AUDIENCE RESPONSES

The sharp increase in the television offered in the last decade has been matched by a parallel growth of TV viewing. In 1977, the TV set in an average household was on for 3 hours and 39 minutes per day. By 1986, that time had practically doubled. It then was 6 hours and 13 minutes. The individual viewing time registered an increase of about 1 hour, from 2.23 to 3.33 hours (Table 11.4).

The intensification of television viewing is indirectly demonstrated by household penetration with TV sets. In 1984, 94.4% of the households had a television set. In 1986, the figure was 97.8%. A color TV set was present in 47.6% of households in 1984, and in 66.5% just 2 years later, although color television had been introduced in Italy in 1976. In 1986, 24.1% of the homes had more than one set—a fact that may be a signal of a gradual fragmentation of TV viewing patterns.

A national survey conducted in 1984 depicts how much time different sociodemographic groups spend in front of the TV screen (Table 11.5). More than 60% of the population spend more than 3 hours per day watching television. Women watch more TV than men. The youngest and oldest segments of the population appear to be the heaviest consumers (more than 6 hours per day). Also, the unemployed and the housewives are other categories of society that tend to consume more television (over 5 hours daily).

The ISTAT survey just quoted also illustrates the preference of viewers for different program types, as shown in Table 11.6. Fiction is the most popular television fare in Italy, even more for women than for men. Movies and serials outdistance the second most viewed content, that is, television news, by 15 points. Light entertainment ranks third in the viewing menu of the Italian audience, especially of the female part.

TABLE 11.5

Television Viewing Time by Sociodemographics

| | Up to 2 | 3-4 | 5-6 | 6+ | Total |
|---|---|---|---|---|---|
| | | Number of Hours | | | |
| Gender | | | | | |
| Males | 42.4 | 45.1 | 10.3 | 2.2 | 100.0 |
| Females | 35.4 | 48.2 | 13.4 | 3.0 | 100.0 |
| | | | | | |
| Age | | | | | |
| 6-10 | 27.3 | 50.7 | 18.7 | 3.3 | 100.0 |
| 11-13 | 24.1 | 54.2 | 18.2 | 3.5 | 100.0 |
| 14-19 | 31.8 | 51.5 | 13.9 | 2.8 | 100.0 |
| 20-24 | 38.6 | 48.6 | 10.4 | 2.4 | 100.0 |
| 25-34 | 41.8 | 46.8 | 9.8 | 1.6 | 100.0 |
| 35-44 | 47.9 | 43.0 | 7.3 | 1.8 | 100.0 |
| 45-54 | 44.7 | 43.3 | 9.7 | 2.3 | 100.0 |
| 55-64 | 36.8 | 46.9 | 12.8 | 3.5 | 100.0 |
| 65+ | 38.3 | 43.5 | 14.2 | 4.0 | 100.0 |
| | | | | | |
| Education | | | | | |
| University Degree | 59.6 | 34.7 | 4.7 | 1.0 | 100.0 |
| Senior High School | 46.9 | 43.0 | 8.4 | 1.7 | 100.0 |
| Junior High School | 37.1 | 49.0 | 11.5 | 2.4 | 100.0 |
| Elementary School | 36.1 | 47.7 | 13.0 | 3.2 | 100.0 |
| No School | 35.2 | 46.6 | 14.9 | 3.3 | 100.0 |
| | | | | | |
| Total | 38.8 | 46.7 | 11.9 | 2.6 | 100.0 |

Note: From ISTAT (1986)

Before 1983, the primacy of RAI channels was unmatched as far as audience shares were concerned. RAI seized about 65% of the viewers. The competition by FININVEST took a significant slice of the national audience away from RAI. By 1987, figures for prime time television (8:30 to 11:00 p.m.) by AUDITEL, the independent and official audience research agency, showed that the television audience split into two equally sized blocks: one with RAI and the other with FININVEST (Table 11.7). Only during the time span between 7:30 and 8:30 p.m. did RAI get a larger share, thanks to its live news bulletins—of which the public company maintained the monopoly. The equal division of the audience during prime time was certainly due to the fact that, in those hours, the programming structure of public and commercial channels was little diversified and primarily offered entertainment. Viewers then had actually a small range of program types to choose from, whereas in previous years—when competition was feeble—the RAI programming offered more options.

TABLE 11.6

The Reach of Different Types of Television Programs

|          | News % | Curr. Affairs % | Cul- tural % | Sports % | Light Enter. % | Fic- tion* % | Children's Programs % |
|----------|------|-------|-------|------|-------|-------|-------|
| Gender   |      |       |       |      |       |       |       |
| Males    | 77.6 | 46.2  | 27.4  | 69.7 | 48.5  | 84.8  | 22.9  |
| Females  | 67.3 | 45.1  | 25.9  | 19.0 | 71.0  | 90.0  | 28.6  |
|          |      |       |       |      |       |       |       |
| Age      |      |       |       |      |       |       |       |
| 6-10     | 7.7  | 5.3   | 4.2   | 30.0 | 48.6  | 71.5  | 95.9  |
| 11-13    | 19.8 | 16.9  | 12.7  | 50.3 | 66.7  | 87.5  | 86.7  |
| 14-19    | 46.8 | 39.6  | 26.0  | 59.5 | 77.6  | 92.9  | 35.0  |
| 20-24    | 72.3 | 53.1  | 35.3  | 53.6 | 70.1  | 91.2  | 15.6  |
| 25-34    | 82.8 | 55.7  | 35.7  | 47.0 | 62.6  | 90.2  | 19.9  |
| 35-44    | 86.5 | 53.9  | 32.3  | 44.1 | 55.8  | 90.5  | 16.4  |
| 45-54    | 88.8 | 51.9  | 27.0  | 42.1 | 54.8  | 87.7  | 10.1  |
| 55-64    | 91.1 | 52.6  | 27.1  | 38.8 | 55.1  | 87.1  | 8.9   |
| 65+      | 89.8 | 46.0  | 21.0  | 28.3 | 54.5  | 82.3  | 9.5   |
|          |      |       |       |      |       |       |       |
| Education|      |       |       |      |       |       |       |
| Univ.    | 92.7 | 70.4  | 65.9  | 44.8 | 37.1  | 81.7  | 8.3   |
| Sr. H.S. | 86.3 | 65.0  | 50.4  | 49.1 | 56.6  | 87.9  | 13.0  |
| Jr. H.S. | 72.1 | 50.2  | 28.9  | 53.0 | 66.4  | 91.3  | 20.8  |
| Elem.    | 75.9 | 42.8  | 19.1  | 41.6 | 61.4  | 88.7  | 25.3  |
| None     | 47.2 | 20.1  | 7.5   | 26.3 | 54.3  | 79.0  | 51.7  |
|          |      |       |       |      |       |       |       |
| Total    | 72.3 | 45.7  | 26.6  | 43.6 | 60.1  | 87.5  | 25.9  |

* Includes movies and serials.
Note: From ISTAT (1986).

TABLE 11.7

Average Prime Time Shares of TV Channels
During the First Seven Months of 1987

| | | | | |
|---|---|---|---|---|
| RAI UNO | : | 25.8. | CANALE 5 | : | 23.6 |
| RAI DUE | : | 15.8 | RETE 4 | : | 8.4 |
| RAI TRE | : | 3.3 | ITALIA 1 | : | 13.7 |
| Total RAI: | | 44.9 | Total FININVEST: | | 45.7 |
| Other | : | 9.4 | | | |

Viewers are not as channel-loyal as one might infer from the share figures, however. AUDITEL in-depth monitoring reveals great mobility of viewers between channels, partly due to remote-control devices in many Italian homes.

In the last few years, two interesting signs of a more "mature" TV viewing habit of Italian audiences could be observed. After years of an increase in simple viewing time, a less quantitative approach to television consumption is emerging. First of all, there seems to be a trend toward a tailored viewing diet, a specialized, self-constructed pattern of enjoying television. Secondly, somewhat less people than in the recent past spend their leisure time in front of the TV set (Porro, 1987).

## Videocassette Recorders

The rapid—even if somewhat late compared to other countries—penetration of the VCR shows that a change is under way in the way the audience's needs for entertainment are fulfilled. Certainly, 1.5 million homes (out of 18.6 million) are still a tiny number, but the growth rate is dramatic (1984-1986: plus 300%). Also, the ownership of the VCR is not limited—as it was at the beginning—to the upper-middle class, but now is typical of the middle class. This is shown by a survey for UNIVIDEO, the National Association of Videocassettes Producers. The use patterns show that the viewer first starts recording programs and movies from television. Only later on does he or she turn to buying cassettes or to the rental market.

Preferences for TV genres differ significantly between VCR owners and non-owners, especially in the case of comedy and science fiction (Table 11.8). Two interesting facts signal rapid adaptations of the audiences of home video. On one part, in just a few years, hundreds of video clubs sprang up all over the country, and 90% of cassette circulation goes through these channels. On the other, the piracy in this field has reached extreme dimensions. It is estimated that about a quarter of the money spent on video goes to video pirates.

The saturation of television viewing and the rapid penetration of VCRs has resulted in a crisis for the movie industry. Movie attendance has dropped from about 514 million of 1975 to 123 million in 1985 (SIAE, 1985). In other words, in only 1 decade, movie consumption decreased to one quarter of what it was before. In 1985, an average Italian went to the movies only twice a year (Table 11.9).

TABLE 11.8

The Most Preferred TV Genres

| | Age Group | | | | | | | | | | | |
|---|---|---|---|---|---|---|---|---|---|---|---|---|
| | 18-24 | | 25-34 | | 35-44 | | 45-54 | | 55-64 | | 65+ | |
| | VCR | NON-VCR | VCR | NON-VCR | VCR | NON-VCR | VCR | NON-VCR | VCR | NON-VCR | VCR | NON-VCR |
| Dramas | 2 | 2 | 3 | 3 | 3 | 3 | 2 | 3 | 3 | 3 | 0 | 3 |
| Adventure | 4 | 5 | 4 | 4 | 5 | 4 | 4 | 4 | 4 | 4 | 0 | 3 |
| Comedy | 3 | 2 | 4 | 2 | 4 | 2 | 0 | 3 | 1 | 2 | 2 | 3 |
| Opera | 0 | 0 | 0 | 1 | 0 | 0 | 1 | 2 | 1 | 2 | 2 | 2 |
| Science fiction | 2 | 3 | 4 | 2 | 2 | 2 | 3 | 2 | 1 | 1 | 3 | 1 |
| Horror | 1 | 2 | 0 | 1 | 1 | 1 | 1 | 0 | 2 | 0 | 1 | 0 |
| Western | 1 | 2 | 1 | 2 | 1 | 2 | 4 | 3 | 1 | 3 | 0 | 2 |
| Cartoons | 1 | 1 | 2 | 1 | 1 | 1 | 0 | 1 | 0 | 1 | 0 | 0 |
| Comic Present. | 3 | 3 | 2 | 2 | 0 | 2 | 1 | 2 | 1 | 2 | 0 | 1 |
| Erotic | 0 | 0 | 0 | 1 | 0 | 0 | 0 | 0 | 0 | 0 | 0 | 0 |

Key: 0: up to 10% (penetration)
    1: 10-30%
    2: 20-30%
    3: 30-40%
    4: 40-50%
    5: 50%+

TABLE 11.9

Cinema: Number of Days of Showings, Number of Tickets Sold,
Expenditures of the Audience

| Year | Days of Showings (in 1,000s) | No. of Tickets Solds (in 1,000s) | Expenditure (in Millions of Lire of 1970) |
|---|---|---|---|
| 1951 | 1,616 | 705,666 | 137,768 |
| 1955 | 2,009 | 819,424 | 195,737 |
| 1960 | 2,037 | 744,781 | 177,039 |
| 1965 | 2,031 | 633,080 | 181,080 |
| 1970 | 1,831 | 525,006 | 181,896 |
| 1975 | 1,758 | 513,697 | 211,688 |
| 1980 | 1,235 | 241,891 | 108,055 |
| 1985 | 714 | 123,113 | 70,604 |

Note: From SIAE (1985).

TABLE 11.10

Content Preferences for Radio Channels

| Radio-UNO (RAI) | | Radio-DUE (RAI) | | Private Radios | |
|---|---|---|---|---|---|
| News | 45.5 | News | 44.3 | Music | 89.6 |
| Music | 14.9 | Music | 13.4 | News | 3.6 |
| Interviews | 10.3 | Interviews | 13.4 | Interviews | 2.3 |
| Variety | 9.3 | Curr. Aff. | 7.3 | Sport | 1.3 |
| Sport | 7.0 | Variety | 6.8 | Curr. Aff. | .8 |
| Curr. Aff. | 6.3 | Sport | 4.6 | Variety | .8 |
| Cultural | 2.7 | Cultural | 3.7 | Cultural | .4 |
| Drama | 1.3 | Drama | 3.2 | Drama | .1 |
| Other | 2.7 | Other | 3.3 | Other | 1.1 |
| Total | 100.0 | Total | 100.0 | Total | 100.0 |

## Radio

Radio has enjoyed a much better fate. The expansion of local radio and the amelioration of the offerings of public radio channels obviously have drawn new audience to this old medium. Unfortunately, there are no trend figures of listening rates, because reliable surveying has begun only recently. In 1986, figures from an ABACUS poll show that 42.8% of the Italians turn their radio set on every day (ABACUS, 1987).

Like the TV audience, radio listeners split equally between RAI channels and commercial ones. They listen to different types of broadcasts in those two systems, however. The RAI channels are primarily used for information, whereas commercial radio is listened to almost exclusively for music—which is the most-offered program type (Table 11.10).

## Teletext

Recent data reveal that 1.5 million of the homes have a decoder for the Italian teletext signal. The number of potential users is about 5 million. A 1986 RAI survey of a national sample (RAI, 1986) suggests that 54% of adults use the service on an average day. The service enjoys a positive evaluation by its viewers: It is considered quick, handy, and complete. Teletext viewing habits can be summarized as follows: (a) People do turn television on just to watch teletext, and (b) people turn to teletext as an alternative to advertising breaks or to unappealing programs. The most preferred contents are the latest news headlines, weather forecasts, train and plane timetables, games, and the stock exchange figures.

## CONCLUSIONS

Media options of the mid-1980s in Italy are far from being as diversified as in other major countries. There is no cable television, no pay-TV, no pay-per-view, no satellite TV, very little home video, and a scarce penetration of teletext. On the other hand, the options that are available (mostly public and private radio and TV) are among the richest.

Italy has experienced an explosion of the broadcasting sector, both through the establishment of new radio and television stations and through the strengthening of RAI's presence. This fact has actually jeopardized a harmonious growth of the media environment as a whole, as demonstrated, for example, by a total absence of cable television. The hypertrophic television offerings overshadowed for a decade other new channels, such as home video (VCR), teletext, and satellite television (DBS), and have also penalized cinema.

In recent years, however, there have been some suggestions that these other media are gaining ground. VCR growth, for example, has now begun. Overall, there seems to be a trend toward specialized use of the mass media, reflecting a certain maturity in use habits.

## NOTE

[1] Paolo Martini is author of the introductory section. Gianpietro Mazzoleni is author of the latter sections.

## REFERENCES

ABACUS. (1987). *Sondaggio nazionale sulla fruizione dei mezzi di comunicazione di massa* [National survey on media consumption patterns]. Milan: ABACUS.
ISTAT. (1986). *Indagine sulla lettura e su altri aspetti dell'impiego del tempo libero-1984* [A study of reading and other aspects of leisure time use]. Rome.
Porro, R. (1987, May 25). Sempre meno davanti alla TV [Fewer people watch television]. *Electronic Mass Media Age*.
RAI (1986). *Gli utenti del Televideo RAI dopo un anno di esercizio* [RAI teletext users]. Rome: RAI-Studi di Mercato.
RAI (1987). *Struttura della programmazione RAI/Networks* [The structure of the RAI/Networks programming]. Documentazione e Studi RAI. Rome: RAI.
SIAE (1985). *Lo spettacolo in Italia* [Drama in Italy]. Rome: Publicazioni SIAE.

# 12

# Australia: Hollywood Goes Down Under and Out Back

**R. Warwick Blood**
*Mitchell College*

*As I've been complaining in these pages for 20 years, the Global Village exists, but it's called Los Angeles. To be specific, it's a suburb of that city named Hollywood which, having hijacked cinema, has kidnapped global consciousness and turned it into an industry.*
—Phillip Adams, *The Australian*, July 4-5, 1987.

In the next decade, Australian researchers may look back to 1987 as a watershed year in mass media development. Never before had the Australian media system witnessed so much rapid change. In July 1987, a federal Labor government was reelected for an historic third term in office, and legislation radically altering media policy was presented to the new parliament and to the public.

Concurrent with the continuing debate about new policy, Australia had seen the development of a variety of new media technologies. These new technologies altered the shape of production and dissemination systems and the content of mass media. They may ultimately alter the structure of media organizations. Long-term audience responses to these new media are difficult to gauge, particularly given the lack of longitudinal audience research. This chapter focuses, nonetheless, on audiences and broadcasting and the widespread acceptance by Australians of one new media form, the videocassette recorder (VCR).

## THE CHANGING TELEVISION LANDSCAPE

Australia's first television broadcast was made by a commercial station on September 16, 1956 from the site of a former dairy in a Sydney suburb. More than 25 years later, commercial television has grown to a multibillion dollar business.

In a continent almost double the size of Europe and the United Kingdom but populated by only 16 million people, television penetration is about 98%. Approximately 97% of the population has color television and more than a third of all homes have more than one television set (Federation of Australian Commercial Television Stations, 1986). The recent acquisition of domestic satellites by the federal government means that television eventually will reach almost all of the continent.

Australia operates a dual system of commercial and government-funded broadcasting. The largest television markets are in the heavily populated eastern coastal strip, with the two largest markets in Sydney and Melbourne. Each has more than one million television homes. The major cities have three commercial television stations, whereas most country or regional centers are served by only one commercial channel. From the advent of television, regional and provincial commercial operators have enjoyed government-controlled monopoly status primarily on the basis of small advertising revenues in these markets.

The government-funded sector comprises the ABC (the Australian Broadcasting Corporation—a British Broadcasting Corporation public service model) and a unique multicultural system, the Special Broadcasting Service (SBS), which features imported television programs in several languages. This special service was designed to meet the needs of the country's large immigrant populations. The ABC has a single station in all television markets and the SBS serves the largest metropolitan cities. Following the BBC model, both the ABC and SBS are independent of government but are funded directly from federal government revenues and no advertising is allowed. Australia has yet to develop a public or community access television system, although there are several plans to do so.

Remote areas of the country receive an ABC service, on Homestead and Community Broadcasting Satellite Service, and the Remote Commercial Service, via the federal government's domestic satellite system. In late 1986, approximately 100,000 homes in the remote parts of the state of Western Australia were able to receive continuous commercial television for the first time via the Golden West Network.

In summary, the major cities have access to the national, government-funded channel and three commercial channels. The bigger cities also receive the multicultural service. Country viewers usually receive only one commercial channel and the one government-funded channel. (For a description of Australia's changing telecommunications and broadcasting industries, see Barr, 1985.)

In general, government-funded broadcasting attracts about 10% of television homes, although audiences have been decreasing. Like most national broadcasters, the ABC has had to live with decreased yearly budgets from the federal government. A similar situation exists with SBS. SBS has also seen a drop in audience partly as a result of its recent move to the UHF band.

Networking, in the usual American sense of the term, is new in Australia. Until recently, commercial television operators were linked only by ownership or agreement. Networking is only used for specific programming. Commercial stations in each capital city, for example, produce their own news and current affairs programs. Although national in concept, the ABC also has separate news and current affairs programs in each capital city.

In the mid-1960s, Australian television content was dominated by American programs. Imports from the BBC comprised the majority of ABC programs. Dizard (1964) reported that the daily schedule of a typical commercial Australian television station was "virtually indistinguishable from that of a station in Iowa or New Jersey." Following the introduction of quotas on imports, the picture has changed dramatically in the 1980s with local content comprising the majority of the top 10 rated programs. On average, local programming comprises about 50% of program schedules. Nevertheless, American formats and styles are the norm (Breen, 1979). For example, the CBS-franchised version of "60 Minutes" is always among the top-rated programs. In the government sector, budget cuts have resulted in less locally produced drama.

Legislation in effect prior to 1987 prohibited a commercial television operator from owning controlling interests in more than two stations. The new legislation will allow an owner to reach all major television markets, but it prohibits cross-ownership of television, radio, and newspapers in the same market. Certainly, the new regulations encourage widespread networking and further concentrate Australia's already highly concentrated media ownership structure (Brown, 1987; Harrison, 1987). It is important to note that the major media operators have substantial investments in other forms of publishing, telecommunications, leisure and travel industries, and in major commercial enterprises (Barr, 1985; Bonney & Wilson, 1983; Wheelwright & Buckley, 1987).

Public reactions to these major changes in the industry are interesting. Approximately 67% of respondents in one major nationwide survey report that media ownership is too concentrated. Older respondents are more concerned about media ownership and content diversity than younger respondents. Anticoncentration, prodiversity arguments are supported most by higher-income groups and by the better educated (Mayer, 1987). These groups are more likely to be light television viewers, viewers of government television, and readers of serious morning newspapers.

The federal government has, in effect, placed a moratorium on cable television until the 1990s, principally because of cost, the potential use of direct broadcast satellites, and, perhaps, pressure from existing media owners. The Bond group (owner of a new network to emerge in recent ownership shuffles) has acquired an entertainment service called Sky Channel. Using the domestic satellite system, this service is beamed into more than 700 hotels, motels, and taverns, and it provides live sporting coverage and other entertainment services. The Bond group also operates Club Superstation—a similar satellite system serving more than 1,700 hotels, motels and clubs. Live horse racing is now being transmitted on this service. Public response to these systems has been somewhat lukewarm, although it is too early to assess long-term responses.

Within the framework of a rapidly changing telecommunications system, a number of small-scale videotext services have been established, primarily in the travel, banking and finance industries (see Barr, 1985). The government body responsible for domestic telecommunications, Telecom, launched a public videotext system—Viatel—in February 1985, modelled after the British system, Prestel. Telecom, as a common carrier, operates Viatel for private or government information providers. The idea was to allow infrequent, untrained users easy access to an information system and, at the same time, to give inexperienced information providers access to a nationwide audience. Users can access the system with specially designed decoders or personal computers connected by phone lines. In June 1986, Telecom had about 16,000 users and more than 250 information providers. Telecom boasts that Viatel's growth is second only to the French system (Cox, 1987). Yet it is a difficult task to attract both information providers and information users and it is too early to state whether there will be a sufficient audience to support Viatel into the 1990s as a public service (LeGras, 1987).

Observational evidence (Nielsen, 1987) suggests that an unintended use of Viatel is for interpersonal communication via bulletin boards, some of which have restricted access. It appears that the newspaper "personal" classified advertisement has found a new home.

The major newspaper groups have been quick to realize the potential of their computerized production systems in establishing information data bases (Putnis, 1987). Whether these data base systems can become commercially viable is still problematic.

Related to these developments, the Fairfax television station Channel 7 in Sydney launched Australia's first teletext system in February 1980. Known as Seventext, it was followed by a similar service, Seventel, in Brisbane. Although initially slow to attract advertising, these systems may yet be able to provide a low-cost information service to Australians. Long-term audience reaction, of course, is impossible to gauge.

## MEDIA HABITS

Australia's television viewing habits are remarkably similar to those of the United States. From the end of the 1970s to the mid-1980s, time spent viewing commercial television has marginally increased to an individual average of about 22 hours per week. There has been a decrease in this figure during the 1985-1986 period. Time spent viewing government television has also declined during the same period. Children under 12 watch about 15 hours of television per week, with total viewing in the home averaging about 30 hours each week. In 1985, about 85% of the viewing audience reported that television was their main source of news, and about 49% said television was the most reliable and accurate medium for news and information (Federation of Australian Commercial Television Stations, 1986). Country viewers generally watch more television than viewers in capital cities.

By comparison, time spent listening to commercial radio averages about 22 minutes each day. Approximately 72% of people read a daily newspaper and about 78% read a Sunday newspaper. Whereas afternoon newspapers continue to lose readers in line with North American trends, morning newspapers are currently increasing circulation. About 3.6 million metropolitan newspapers are sold each day, and about 1.4 million women's magazines are sold each week. There are more than 1,400 magazine titles published on a regular basis (Patterson, 1986).

### A Home, A Car and a VCR

The VCR is the first major change to Australia's television landscape since the introduction of color television. For nonmetropolitan television viewers, the VCR offers a relatively cheap alternative to limited (2 channels) television broadcasting.

Ownership of VCRs has rapidly increased in Australia from about 11% penetration in 1982 to about 50% in 1986. This places Australia among the world's leading users, although international data on the penetration of VCRs are difficult to interpret, given differing times of data collection and methodologies.

The widespread acceptance of the VCR has had at least three major areas of impact: on traditional television broadcasting; on other media and leisure activities, particularly the cinema; and on television viewing patterns and habits within the home environment.

Noble (1984) argued that the VCR has shifted the psychological locus of control from the external to the internal. Broadcast television for the consumer has been controlled externally by broadcasters, whereas the VCR offers the consumer control over what is viewed, when it is viewed, and how it is viewed. Indeed, VCR technology calls into question the concept of "audience" as it relates to broadcast television.

Table 12.1 shows the percentage of homes with VCRs from 1983 to 1986 by state. During 1986, video penetration increased by about 10% nationally, in 1985 by about 7%, and in 1983 by 13% (TvB, 1985, 1986).

TABLE 12.1

Estimated Percentage of Homes with VCRs

| State | 1983 % | 1984 % | 1985 % | 1986 % |
|---|---|---|---|---|
| New South Wales | | | | |
| Sydney | 21.8 | 30.2 | 37.5 | 46.8 |
| Regional | 21.4 | 31.9 | 39.8 | 50.7 |
| Victoria | | | | |
| Melbourne | 18.5 | 28.8 | 31.6 | 44.1 |
| Regional | 9.5 | 22.2 | 30.0 | 39.7 |
| Queensland | | | | |
| Brisbane | N/A | 32.5 | 31.6 | 44.1 |
| Regional | N/A | 31.8 | 38.6 | 46.1 |
| South Australia | | | | |
| Adelaide | N/A | 33.7 | 43.1 | 54.2 |
| Regional | N/A | 38.8 | 48.9 | N/A |
| Western Australia | | | | |
| Perth | N/A | 33.1 | 47.6 | 53.6 |
| Regional | N/A | 34.5 | 35.1 | N/A |
| Tasmania | 17.3 | 28.9 | 33.2 | 40.7 |

Note: From TvB (1985, 1986). Information is compiled from omnibus surveys of more than 2,277 interviews each year. New South Wales figures include the Australian Capital Territory. South Australian figures include the Northern Territory.

On a national basis, there is no difference between VCR penetration in the city or country. But this national comparison may hide more than it reveals. For example, as Table 12.1 shows, VCR penetration in Sydney is about 47%, compared to 51% in surrounding nonmetropolitan areas. The country figure does include the federal capital, Canberra, but this city has only one commercial channel. The urban-country comparison for Melbourne and the rest of the state is less clear, although people in this part of the country have been slower to purchase VCRs than elsewhere. People in the nonurban areas of Queensland are slightly more likely to have a VCR than their urban counterparts in the capital city, Brisbane.

The two less-populated states of South and West Australia show higher-than-national-average figures for VCR penetration. The TvB has not released 1986 figures for non-metropolitan penetration in these states. In 1985 and 1984, however, penetration was higher for the outlying areas than for the city of Adelaide in South Australia. In 1985 in Western Australia, the city of Perth had even higher penetration levels than the outlying area. But Perth was served by only two commercial channels during that period. City-versus-rural data are unavailable for Tasmania.

In summary, Table 12.1 shows that, in general, nonmetropolitan viewers are more likely to have VCRs than their urban counterparts. This difference is understandable, given that country viewers have less programming choice than viewers in the cities. Interestingly, median family incomes for country viewers are less than for urban viewers, and country people watch more television.

According to the TvB reports, about one third of all respondents used a VCR during the 7-day period before the survey. The average time spent viewing a VCR was about 1 hour and 52 minutes each week. VCR owners spend about equal time viewing prerecorded tapes and tapes of recorded broadcast material. The 1986 data are similar to that reported by another market research organization, the Roy Morgan Research Centre. These data showed that more people watched prerecorded tapes than home-recorded tapes (B&T, 1987). Table 12.2 shows TvB data for VCR use for 1985 and 1986. Respondents were asked how many hours they had watched their VCRs during the past 7 days.

Table 12.2 shows a significant increase in heavy use of VCRs (5 hours or more per week) between 1985 and 1986. About 20% of respondents used their VCRs for more than 5 hours per week in 1985, and about 25% did in 1986. The TvB research suggests that although high-income groups were more likely to purchase VCRs when they were first introduced, the heaviest users in 1986 were married with children in the home, more than 35 years old, and receiving lower-than-average incomes. The parallels with cable television in North America are obvious (see, for example, Becker & Blood, 1984). Table 12.2 separates the VCR users into two

TABLE 12.2

House Watched VCR During Past 7 Days: 1985 and 1986 Surveys

|  | Own VCR | | Rent VCR | |
|---|---|---|---|---|
|  | 1985 | 1986 | 1985 | 1986 |
|  | % | % | % | % |
| No Use | 36.6 | 35.6 | 37.1 | 27.2 |
| Less than 2 hours | 22.5 | 21.1 | 17.5 | 27.3 |
| 2 to 4 hours | 20.6 | 18.7 | 16.6 | 14.9 |
| 5 hours or more | 20.4 | 24.6 | 28.7 | 30.6 |
| Total | 100.0 | 100.0 | 100.0 | 100.0 |
| N | 838 | 1116 | 55 | 105 |

Note: From TvB (1985, 1986).

groups: those who own versus those who rent a VCR. VCR renters, who have lower incomes than owners, tend to use their VCRs more than owners.

## VCRs and Television Viewing Patterns

How VCR use has changed long-term household television viewing patterns remains to be answered. Agardy and Burke (1982) showed that peoples' perceptions of the impact of owning a VCR were mixed. Convenience and flexibility were seen as the major attractions of owning a VCR. Some participants stressed that the flexibility offered by a VCR would enable television to fit better into their social life. That is, they would be able to go out and not miss favorite programs! Or, by inviting friends to their house to view taped or rented materials, they could enjoy a reasonably priced social activity. Presumably, this latter view of television as a leisure activity would be held more strongly by heavy television viewers. Many participants believed they would become more selective in television viewing if they owned a VCR. Equally, other participants expressed the concern that owning a VCR would lead to increased television viewing.

Australian Broadcasting Corporation (ABC) Audience Research (1983, 1984), in studies conducted in 1983 and 1984, showed that VCR users do not watch more television than those without VCRs, thus suggesting some displacement of time spent with broadcast television. The data also imply that heavy television users may also be heavy VCR users.

In 1984, the ABC reported that more than 80% of VCR owners rent videos on a regular basis. The earlier 1983 study showed that, in Sydney, about 44% of respondents reported hiring a video every week compared to 57% in the New South

Wales country areas of Bega and Cooma. VCR owners also make considerable use of television broadcast programs for recording.

Although the surveys are limited in scope, the data suggest a good deal of time-shifting occurs in VCR use. VCR owners tend to use a combination of recording and watching the same channel, recording one channel and watching another, and recording while not watching television. VCR users tend to record action drama, music-variety, drama serials and movies more than other program types. News and current affairs programs are rarely recorded. In renting videos, users overwhelmingly prefer movies, ranging from the latest film releases to old black-and-white classics. American films are the most favored and most accessible.

In the remote parts of Western Australia, homesteads received direct satellite transmissions for the first time in 1986. These media-poor communities had no reliable radio service, infrequent newspaper service and no television. Electricity is produced by diesel generators. In one remote community, Fitzroy Crossing, Green (1987) reported a VCR penetration of more than 60%. In another small community, Sandstone, VCR penetration was more than 75%. Preliminary evidence suggests that these pre-television-VCR communities may differ from pretelevision communities of the 1950s. Respondents say television will not interrupt their established leisure patterns, particularly outdoor activities. Respondents report using the VCR to record satellite transmissions for later use.

## VCR and Television Content

Predictably, major American film distributors and associated corporations dominate the Australian video rental market. The biggest seven videotape distributors, with more than 80% of the market, are RCA-Columbia, CIC-Taft, Warner Home Video, Roadshow, Communications and Entertainment Limited, CBS-Fox Video, and Thorn-EMI (Taylor, 1987). In 1986, the top three video rentals were "Rambo II," "The Breakfast Club," and "Return of the Jedi." One video distributor promotes its product as "Hollywood at Home!"

In the author's hometown of Bathurst, a small college town in rural New South Wales, the two franchise video rental retailers enjoy booming business despite the downturn in the rural economy. The local commercial television station frequently schedules a Sunday night movie that has been available for months at the local video rental outlets. In contrast, in the major cities, VCR impact can be seen in the change in movie release time. In recent years, there has been a marked reduction in the time between cinema release of movies and when they first appear on television.

VCR use data are being watched very closely by the major television stations and their advertisers. One controversial (and contested) study showed that VCR owners were watching about 29% less broadcast television on days when the VCR was in use. About 50% of all commercial television played back at a later time was fast-forwarded to exclude commercials. The report (Shires, 1985) said that VCRs were "having a damaging effect on the consumption of broadcast television, contrary to conclusions drawn by other analysts and commentators" (p. 20). The report concluded that "people are replacing and will replace in the future a significant proportion of live television with commercial-free taped television" (p. 20).

Table 12.3 shows that, from 1977 to 1985, homes using television during prime-time hours have dropped significantly from about 67.2% to 60.4% (Patterson, 1986). Not all of this decrease, of course, could be attributed to the use of VCRs. Qualitative audience research (focus-group interviews with several panels across the nation) suggests that television viewing may have peaked in the late 1970s and that audiences are now more selective. Mackay Research (1987) reports that older people still watch television as a deliberate act. But for younger people of the television generation, viewing has less of an appeal. Mackay argued that selective viewing stems from the "guilt" of watching too much television or the adoption of a take-it-or-leave-it approach. The research, he said, reveals that people adopt these attitudes because they have so many competing demands on their time and feel that time spent watching television can be spent another way. The report

TABLE 12.3

Homes Using Television 1977 to 1985 During 7:00 to 10:00 p.m.
Five Capital City Average

| Year | Commercial % | Government % | Total % |
|------|------------|------------|---------|
| 1977 | 54.5 | 13.2 | 67.4 |
| 1978 | 56.2 | 11.7 | 67.0 |
| 1979 | 55.3 | 11.7 | 66.5 |
| 1980 | 55.3 | 11.1 | 66.0 |
| 1981 | 53.7 | 11.2 | 64.3 |
| 1982 | 53.8 | 12.1 | 65.4 |
| 1983 | 53.4 | 10.4 | 64.2 |
| 1984 | 52.2 | 9.7 | 62.5 |
| 1985 | 51.4 | 8.4 | 60.4 |

Note: From Patterson (1986). Figures are five capital city averages and compiled from annual television audience surveys. The Special Broadcasting Service (multicultural service) is included in total HUT figures but not in government HUT figures. Multiple set usage is measured in all homes.

also says that VCRs are used as an adjunct to television—the first-preference fall-back medium, although regular patterns of VCR use have yet to be established. This research, based on group interviews, is only suggestive of television viewing trends (also see Wright, 1987). Longitudinal quantitative and qualitative audience research is needed to probe these suggestions. The available commercial research, which focuses on ratings and audience shares, cannot hope to tap these issues.

### VCR and the Cinema

When television was introduced in the 1950s, the most obvious impact was on cinema attendance. Within 5 years, most suburban cinemas had closed, and city cinemas continued to suffer declining audiences and profits. In 1950, there were about 1,600 cinemas in Australia, but, by 1970, the number had declined by 41%. In 1984, there were only 630 cinemas. In that year, 73 closed, mostly in country regions ("Media Briefs: Cinema," 1987). Since then, about a dozen cinemas have reopened. Certainly, the major city trend is toward multiscreen entertainment centers housing several cinemas and video-game rooms. Cinema attendances dropped about 38% in the mid-1980s and industry sources attribute most of this decline to VCR use (McKnight, 1986). A study by Duck (1985), however, showed that heavy VCR users tended not to visit cinemas before they bought their VCRs. Cinema audiences in 1986 are improving, but again it is difficult to assess the long-term impact of VCR use on cinema attendance.

### CONCLUSIONS

There is an indication that VCR penetration is slowing. The major manufacturers, National Panasonic, Sony, Sanyo, Phillips, Sharp, Toshiba, Akai, and Hitachi (all foreign companies) have reported slower sales during 1986 and 1987. Whereas market demand once was sufficient to keep prices high and return record profits to the manufacturers, the rapid penetration has resulted in a slowdown in overall growth and price-cutting to gain VCR sales. This trend is also reflected in the videotape rental market. During the last 5 years, the number of tape rental retailers has declined from about 4,000 to 2,000 nationally. Video rental retailers are now more inclined to offer special discounts to customers, especially for videotapes for children, where repeated viewing is an attraction.

Analyses of the impact of new media and information technologies tend to fall into three principal camps: the hypercritical-pessimistic; the uncritical-optimistic; and the "balanced" view, which, while acknowledging the first two positions, concludes superficially that, in the end, we must choose between a new information-rich, participatory society or Mr. Orwell's 1984 (Marien, 1985). Marien persuasively argued, however, that the reality of the so-called information revolution is likely to be "complex and ambiguous, requiring many critical choices, over time and incorporating elements of simultaneous euphoria and gloom that fluctuate in their balance" (p. 649).

Marien's point is that we must continually ask the right questions and, even if we have only approximate answers, we must share these answers across national boundaries. Following Marien, it is ironic that, in the era of the information and communication "revolution," so little is known about the impact of new media.

In Australia, most new media and information technologies are primarily confined to business, banking, and finance, and it is too early to assess long-term public response. But this chapter has described how the widespread use of VCRs has, at least to some extent, displaced traditional television broadcasting and changed social life. The introduction of VCRs is the first major change in the television landscape since the introduction of color television, and many Australians have certainly embraced this new technology. Given the economic constraints and structure of commercial broadcasting in Australia, what the VCR has offered in content diversity to Australians is predictable. Viewers have been given a choice of when and where they will watch but a very limited choice about what they will watch. Diversity of media dissemination has not meant greater social or political diversity. Yet, it is another thing to conclude that the VCR has produced a renewed tidal wave of American cultural imperialism with Australians adopting more and more American values and culture. To do so argues for a passive audience and ignores the social context of which watching television and using VCRs is but one part.

## REFERENCES

Adams, P. (1987, July 4-5). Adam's first law: I am a camera. *The Australian*, Magazine Section, p. 2.

Agardy, S., & Burke, J. (1982). *Extended TV services in perspective: In-depth reactions to new services and their implications.* Melbourne: Australian Broadcasting Tribunal.

Australian Broadcasting Corporation Audience Research. (1983). *Video Update No. 1*. Sydney: Author.

Australian Broadcasting Corporation Audience Research. (1984). *Video Update No. 2*. Sydney: Author.

B&T (1987, April 24). Morgan poll shows video owners higher than McNair. *B&T*, p. 3.

Barr, T. (1985). *The electronic estate: New communications media in Australia.* Sydney: Penguin Books.

Becker, L. B., & Blood, R.W. (1984, August). *Leisure time allocation and the new media.* Paper presented at the meeting of the Sociology and Social Psychology Section of the International Association for Mass Communication Research, Prague, Czechoslovakia.

Bonney, B., & Wilson, H. (1983). *Australia's commercial media.* Melbourne: MacMillan.

Breen, M. (1979). Differing views on the flow of television materials: Is Australia a test case? *Australian Scan: Journal of Human Communication, 6,* 37-54.

Brown, G. (1987). *Media ownership in Australia 1987.* Melbourne: Information Australia Group.

Cox, F. (1987, July). *Developments in telecommunications.* Paper presented to the annual conference, Australian Communication Association, Macquarie University, Sydney.

Dizard, W. (1964). American television's foreign markets. *Television Quarterly, 3,* 63.

Duck, K. (1985). *Video cassette recorders: An analysis of audience usage and effects on the mass media.* Unpublished BA honours thesis, Macquarie University, Sydney.

Federation of Australian Commercial Television Stations. (1986). *Facts 1986.* Sydney: FACTS.

Green, L. (1987, July). *The impact of satellite broadcasting upon remote communities in western Australia.* Paper presented at the annual conference, Australian Communication Association, Macquarie University, Sydney.

Harrison, K. (1987). The changing face of the television industry. *Media Information Australia, 44,* 16-17.

LeGras, C. (1987, July). *Perspectives on the human factor in diffusion of new communication technology.* Paper presented at the annual conference, Australian Communication Association, Macquarie University, Sydney.

Mackay, H. (1987). *Television.* Bathurst, NSW: Hugh Mackay Research.

Marien, M. (1985). Some questions for the information society. In T. Forester (Ed.), *The information technology revolution* (pp. 648-660). Oxford: Basil Blackwell.

Mayer, H. (1987). Public opinion and media concentration. *Media Information Australia, 44,* 18-19.

McKnight, D. (1986, March 29). The video bug that ate Australia. *The Sydney Morning Herald,* p. 7.

Media Briefs: Cinema. (1987). *Media Information Australia, 37,* 106.

Nielsen, S. (1987, July). *Videotext: A user friendly data base*. Paper presented at the annual conference, Australian Communication Association, Macquarie University, Sydney.

Noble, G. (1984). The social significance of the videorecorder. *Australian Journal of Screen Theory. 17*, 141-154.

Patterson. (1986). *86 status of the media*. Sydney: George Patterson Pty. Ltd.

Putnis, P. (1987, July). *Data in search of a problem*. Paper presented to the annual conference, Australian Communication Association, Macquarie University, Sydney.

Shires, D. (1985, February). Mistake admission fuels brawl over VCR. *Australian Financial Review, 14*, pp. 1, 20.

Taylor, M. (1987, February). VCR majors continue to lead. *Australian Financial Review, 8*, p. 48.

TvB. (1985). *1985 home video research*. Sydney: Television Bureau of Advertising.

TvB. (1986). *1986 home video research*. Sydney: Television Bureau of Advertising.

Wheelwright, T., & Buckley, K. (Eds.). (1987). *Communications and the media in Australia*. Sydney: Allen & Unwin.

Wright, L. (1987, June 18). The television set is on but viewers are switching off. *The Sydney Morning Herald*, p. 30.

# 13

## New Zealand: The VCR
## Is the Only Alternative

**Geoff Lealand**
*New Zealand Council for Educational Research*

Although its rank in the international standard of living has slipped in recent years due to persistent inflation (in 1986, 18% or more), New Zealand still shares—with those countries placed higher and lower—well developed and widely distributed electronic media systems. Broadcast television was introduced in 1960, and in the 1980s a two-channel, monopolistic television system provided near total coverage for an estimated audience of slightly less than 3 million.

Beneath the bureaucratic umbrella of the Broadcasting Corporation of New Zealand (BCNZ), Television New Zealand (TVNZ) attempted, with some success, to run the two channels as complementary, maintaining a rough-and-ready 50/50 split of the New Zealand viewing audience. Both commercial considerations and public service objectives were to be accommodated within this limited set of options. Because the annual license fee (required by law for every set owner) provides less than 17% of total revenue for the Corporation, commercial imperatives (raising money through advertising or sponsorship) dominate the decisions of television executives.

The BCNZ also oversees the operation of 64 medium-wave radio stations (both national and local), 38 of which program advertising at all times except for Sundays. Television advertising also rests on that day. Considerable competition in commercial radio comes from privately owned radio stations, both am and fm. In 1986, there were 18 of these. Such stations, led by Radio Hauraki (which broadcasts in the largest metropolitan area of Auckland), were the first to successfully challenge the state-owned monopoly of the airwaves, a control that has dated from the earliest beginnings of broadcasting in New Zealand.

Despite mounting commercial pressures, however, the public service ethos of broadcasting still permeates both radio and television structures, owing its origins to a direct borrowing of a BBC-style version of the role of national broadcasting. Broadcasting in New Zealand has a statutory obligation to "obtain, produce, commission and broadcast a range of programs (that) reflect and develop New Zealand's identity and culture." The BCNZ is further bound by law (Broadcasting Act, 1976) to act as a "trustee of the national interest" (Section 3.1).

Coupled with such high-minded social objectives, however, has been a willingness for broadcasting to be subservient to intermittent restructuring or other interference by successive New Zealand governments. In 1986, lengthy governmental hearings were held to determine who should be granted the right to operate a third television channel. This task was given to the Broadcasting Tribunal, an appointed body formed under the 1976 Broadcasting Act, and its final decision (announced in August 1987) means that, for the first time, the private sector will have an opportunity to run a television station in New Zealand. Squabbles quickly developed between the BCNZ and the new contenders over the allocation of reception frequencies.

At the same time that the Broadcasting Tribunal was conducting its hearings, another government-appointed body—the Royal Commission of Inquiry into Broadcasting and Related Telecommunications in New Zealand—was examining the future of television and radio broadcasting in New Zealand. The first task demanded of the Commission was to investigate "the opportunities presented to New Zealand by technological change for new options for the transmission of broadcasting services and the economic aspects of these opportunities" (p. 23). These new options comprised: domestic cable services carrying radio, television, and information services; direct broadcast satellite services (DBS); and videocassette recorders (VCRs). The first two options required much speculation on the possible social impact resulting from the introduction of such new methods of conveying increased information and entertainment into New Zealand homes; the third option (VCRs) was easier to report on, because such technology had already been available in New Zealand for more than 5 years and was being used by a significant proportion of the population.

## DIVERSIFICATION BEGINS

In the United States and Europe, additional sources of media diversification, such as the introduction of cable services, have accompanied the introduction of video recorders. In New Zealand, however, the VCR has been a solo actor in the process of media diversification. Its presence is now both significant and visible. Unfortunately the consequences of this have been underresearched. In 1984-1985, several in-house studies of the impact of video recorder ownership on existing broadcasting systems were undertaken for TVNZ (to be described in greater detail shortly), but these failed to investigate the social consequences of the introduction of this new technology. Little was done, for example, to investigate the impact of the VCR on existing leisure options. As a consequence, most allegations of social impact are based largely on anecdotal evidence, such as the visible proliferation of videocassette rental outlets in New Zealand towns and cities.

## Cable and DBS

Cable radio and television was unknown in New Zealand in the 1980s and was likely to remain so. This was largely due to the geographical and demographic characteristics of the country. Only one population area—the Auckland metropolitan area of 240,000 homes—would be able to meet minimum requirements for cost-effective reticulation of cable services, according to the report of the Royal Commission investigating media options in New Zealand (Royal Commission, 1986). The Commission concluded that:

> There was little evidence . . . that a large proportion of the public want cable services. Although there will always be those who are critical of present services, by and large, the BCNZ seems to have managed to satisfy most wants, at least partially, in the community. Further choice will, of course, eventuate when the third channel is operational. (p. 36)

The Commission, however, concluded that DBS distribution systems were a more likely prospect for New Zealand: "We agree that the introduction of some form of DBS is inevitable. The technology is well known and has been for a number of years. The basis for DBS has already been laid and this is largely outside the control of the New Zealand authorities" (p. 53).

Because ownership and control of DBS signals are likely to remain beyond New Zealand shores, the Commission felt that a "cultural invasion" (p. 51) across New Zealand's borders would ensue. Because New Zealand could not possibly provide any directly competitive technology, the best means (according to the Commission) of diverting potential audience interest in DBS was by ensuring "domestic broadcasting is adequately funded" (p. 54), in addition to expanding the fare of conventional, terrestrial television, using the underutilized UHF spectrum. New Zealand has normally managed to contribute little more than 30% to 35% of total programming from local sources over the last 30 years, the bulk of television programming coming principally from the United States and the United Kingdom.

Julian Mounter, Director-General of TVNZ, voiced similar fears about satellite "invasions" early in 1987 (Mounter, 1987). Noting that some New Zealand motels and hotels already sported a satellite dish (receiving signals from Australian and U.S. Armed Forces Service), Mounter warned against taking a too relaxed or blase attitude to the presence of such technology: "I am convinced that satellite technology is as significant a threat to the current broadcasting industry as broadcasting itself was to the print media many years ago . . . Pan-national satellite television will change your world as well as mine. Many of these changes will be unexpected, many will be unwelcome" (p. 13). The programming that such satellites bring is most likely to be Australian mixed with redistributed fare from the United States and Europe. Such programming could provide New Zealanders with media hardware choices previously unknown, once cheap home reception dishes became available.

The presence of receiver dishes in New Zealand homes, drawing signals from foreign-owned satellites, is still in the future. Despite Mounter's doom-saying, there is no real evidence that large numbers of New Zealanders are likely to rush out and install such devices. There may be some novelty value in the new technology and the apparent consumer freedom it brings—that broadcast television signals could be received in the home without the intervention of any agency—but there is likely to be little novelty value in the types of programming that such signals will bring.

New Zealanders have always had generous quantities of foreign television programming on their screens. For example, during November-December 1985, an analysis of television program titles on both channels in New Zealand showed that twice as much material originated outside the country as inside it (Table 13.1).

The majority of New Zealand-originated television programming tends to be "factual" television—that is, sport, news, and information and service programs. The great bulk of "fictional" television (drama, comedy, light entertainment) is imported. If, for example, feature films are added to the totals in Table 13.1, some 59 hours of Hollywood films (dating back as far as the early 1930s) would inflate the American presence on New Zealand television screens in the period analyzed. The advent of a third television channel is unlikely to alter this situation, especially as its commercial viability will rest on attracting audiences to popular programming. The production of locally made television programs in New Zealand has always been hindered by a lack of finance and resources as well as a degree of institutional neglect.

TABLE 13.1

Origins of Television Programs on New Zealand Screen
(both channels), November-December 1985

| U.S.A. % | U.K. % | AUST. % | N.Z. % | OTHERS % |
|--------|--------|---------|--------|----------|
| 39.7 | 19.1 | 5.3 | 34.9 | 1.0 |

Note: From a content analysis of the New Zealand
Listener. Theater film excluded.

## Teletext

Since 1984, a teletext service has been provided by Television New Zealand. This service, which requires a decoder, reached an estimated 60,000 households by September 1987. This service was introduced in order to supplement the information potential of broadcast television, such as news, weather, and travel information. It also provides some entertainment services, such as a children's club and film and music news. The service also provides subtitling of up to 20 hours of popular programming per week for the hearing impaired.

The service is advertised as "free" after the initial cost of the special receiver and is utilized by Television New Zealand as an adjunct to broadcast television, not as a competitor.

## Videocassette Recorders

The introduction of domestic videocassette recorders (VCRs) in the early 1980s brought the first serious challenge to the status quo of television in New Zealand. VCR ownership grew rapidly, reaching an estimated 21% to 25% of New Zealand households by mid-1985 (Royal Commission, 1986). A 1984 BCNZ audience research survey (Lealand, 1984), sampling 2,073 households in the six main metropolitan areas, revealed that 8.5% of these possessed a VCR. Only 1 year later, a follow-up sampling of 3,265 households revealed a 20.8% penetration figure. A 1987 study, conducted by the Market Research Centre (1987) at Massey University, surveyed a sample of 447 households within the city of Palmerston North (population 48,000) and found that 44% possessed a video recorder.

There is some evidence that VCRs had reached preliminary saturation in New Zealand by early 1987. In late 1986, there had been a prolonged "price war" among shops selling VCRs, with drastic discounting of many models. Prices for many models dropped below $NZ 1,000, whereas $1,500-$2,000 had previously been the norm. It is perhaps symptomatic as well that thefts of VCRs from New Zealand homes seem to have declined drastically. In 1984-1985 such thefts seemed epidemic.


## AUDIENCE RESPONSES TO CHANGE

The Market Research Center (1987) study showed a tendency for ownership to be concentrated in younger age groups (with 80% of ownership in the 15-49 age group), and more pronounced in higher income households. There was little difference, however, between owners and non-owners with respect to cinema visits. For example, 47% of owners and 48% of non-owners had not visited the cinema during the previous 6 months. The most frequent filmgoers (two or more times in the previous 6 months) were in the 15-29 age group (55%). Younger respondents also tended to rent prerecorded videocassettes more frequently than older respondents, with 49% of those aged 15-29 renting cassettes at least once or several times per week. Fewer older respondents rented such cassettes at this rate, with 30% of those aged 30-49 and 18% of those aged 50 years or more utilizing this media option.

There are problems in extrapolating from this case study to the entire New Zealand population. There are fewer competing leisure options available in Palmerston North than in larger New Zealand cities such as Auckland and Wellington, which possess more cinemas, nightclubs, and social venues. Nevertheless, Palmerston North can be regarded as a fairly typical medium-sized New Zealand city. It is situated in the lower North Island of New Zealand and services the surrounding farming province of Manawatu and possesses institutes of agricultural research and Massey University.

Despite the fact that VCR sales are no longer as vigorous as they once were, it cannot be denied that the video recorder is now an important component of the entertainment options of a significant number of New Zealand homes. In addition, it is being used as an educational tool in many schools and teaching institutions (in the absence of broadcast educational television). Anecdotal evidence encountered by the author suggests that this has led to some re-allocation of time, money, and space among New Zealanders, as well as to modifying rituals of media use and the social context of viewing. For example, group viewing of recorded or prerecorded material is becoming more common, with participants being drawn from beyond the customary family-centered structures of television viewing. Many older New Zealanders seem to be acquainting themselves with the feature films of the past 3 or 4 decades as a result of the availability of these on pre-recorded cassettes.

There is also an open acknowledgment by Television New Zealand with respect to the role of the video recorder as a mediator in television viewing. From mid-1987, for example, bar codes were printed in the *New Zealand Listener* containing information about the scheduling of programs as a service to those viewers who had VCRs capable of utilizing this time-shifting capacity.[1] The introduction of video recorders has also led to a renewed debate about the right to view, in private, violent or sexually explicit material, with lobby groups from both the moralistic Right and ideological Left demanding increased censorship of prerecorded cassettes.

Since the introduction of VCRs into New Zealand, Television New Zealand has monitored their spread with "nervous interest" (Royal Commission, 1986), anxious to learn whether such devices would fragment the viewing audience and prompt a decline in overall viewing numbers. Such fears have been subsequently allayed by the conclusions of in-house research (in particular, the 1984 and 1986 surveys) and through comparison with overseas experiences. The Lealand (1984) survey shows that most households (89%) used their VCRs to record programs, or parts of programs, from their TV sets. The most mentioned reason for recording material was to accommodate for absence from home while the program was being screened. A majority (77%) estimated that they replayed all, or nearly all, of the material they recorded. Although the Lealand (1984) study showed that respondents with VCRs at home tended to watch less broadcast television than respondents without VCRs, they did watch an average of 1 hour, 8 minutes of "nonbroadcast" TV per week, or material that they had time-shifted.

The Morton (1985) survey for the entire New Zealand population, aged 5 years or over, showed that videotape viewing accounts for a very small proportion of people's time. For example, on an average day during the survey period (May-July 1985), an estimated 1.3% of the population viewed videotapes at the busiest VCR viewing time.

These data were obtained from self-completed video recording and reply charts, with the focus on the numbers and types of programming taken off the broadcast signal. The results obtained in both surveys were not startling. Long-term analysis of audience viewing figures (obtained through conventional ratings) also tends to show that VCR ownership has not resulted in any dramatic shifts in patterns of viewing. For example, the average number of hours that viewers watched television during a Monday to Friday week changed little between July 1980 (12.6 hours) and July 1985 (13.0 hours).

Figure 13.1, utilizing ratings gathered by the BCNZ Audience Research Unit (now BCNZ IRIS Research), shows the patterns of audience behavior in the 1982-1986 period. There is an apparent downward trend in average audience size for the two New Zealand channels combined over this period (illustrated quite graphically by the trend line). Even though this apparent decline is exaggerated by the narrow range of the scale (44% to 41%), a fall of 3 rating points over a 5-year period

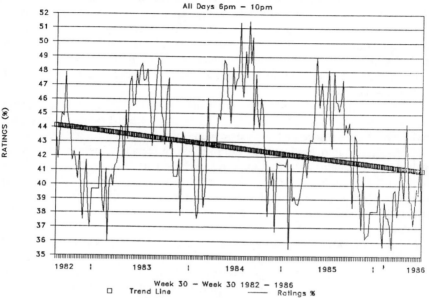

**FIG.13.1.** New Zealand Television audience behavior, 1982-1986. Based on IRIS Audience Research, Broadcasting Corporation of New Zealand.

would be disastrous for an American television network. But such an event can be more readily accommodated by a monopolistic system like Television New Zealand.

Although televison executives failed to ascribe such a fall to one single factor (such as the impact of domestic VCRs), 1986 did see some new programming strategies within Television New Zealand. There were deliberate attempts to identify each channel with a particular style of television: Television One to have an "information and quality drama" orientation and Television Two to have a more populist, "entertainment" orientation.

Although VCRs have been judged as nonthreatening to existing television systems in New Zealand, they have not been received with as much favor in other quarters. New forms of entertainment usually displace old forms and in the case of video, the availability of recent theatrical film releases on prerecorded videocassettes (available for purchase or rental) has had an impact on conventional cinema attendance. Such attendance has been in decline since the 1960s, when television was first introduced to New Zealand. In 1962-1963, for example, the average attendance per capita was 15.0. By 1972-1973 this had fallen to 4.0. Although more recent data are unavailable, the accelerated closure of movie theatres in small towns and the conversion of larger urban theatres to multiple screens in recent years suggests that video has been a significant factor in the demise of large-scale moviegoing. According to a spokesman for Amalgamated, one of the two chains monopolizing film distribution and exhibition in New Zealand, companies such as his were losing more in theatrical exhibition through the impact of video than they were making up from being in the business ("Impact of Video," 1987).

Amalgamated has become involved with its rival chain (Pacer Kerridge) in a belated attempt to share the benefits of video distribution. According to Joseph Moodabe (the Amalgamated spokesman), the video market has taken away the "action audiences" from the two chains. The films on video that "action audiences" find attractive are films like *Back to the Future*, *Rocky IV*, *The Jewel of the Nile*, *Indiana Jones and the Temple of Doom*, and *American Ninja*. All these films appeared in a list of top videocassette rentals for January 1987 ("In The Top," 1987). In addition, their release on video followed theatrical release in New Zealand.

## SUMMARY

The number of movie theaters in New Zealand and the size of the remaining venues are likely to get smaller in the next decade. Meanwhile, videocassette rental outlets will probably continue to expand, with increasing control of distribution by larger organizations. Already the smaller "Mom and Dad" rental outlets are disappearing. Although video continues to sound the deathknell for movie-house managers, the attention of television executives has shifted from a defused threat to other dangers on the horizon.

The next decade will bring a third, directly competitive, broadcast television channel, as well as the real prospect of DBS signals beaming into New Zealand homes. The greatest unnkown quantity in all this is not in what likely impact such new media choices will have on the operation and profitability of present structures, but with the use New Zealanders will make of such opportunities—how eagerly they will embrace them and what likely effects they will have on the social fabric of New Zealand. There are many large questions, but few in New Zealand seem willing to tackle them. The future remains very uncertain.

For example, in early 1987, there seemed to be a vigorously voiced section of public opinion that jumped at any chance to criticize the American cultural presence in New Zealand and would have been eager to express its distaste at the prospect of increased amounts of American television in New Zealand screens. In many ways, this was a spin-off from the testy relations between the two countries as a result of New Zealand's denial of port access to American nuclear-capable warships.

It is often said that New Zealanders are a cautious, conservative lot. If media content diversifies in New Zealand, the reaction of New Zealanders is likely to be a mixture of careful appraisal and gradual acceptance—and for many—a singular lack of enthusiasm.

## NOTE

[1] The *New Zealand Listener*, which can be described as a cross between the *TV Guide* and the British *Listener*, is the official organ of the Broadcasting Corporation of New Zealand but is required to be editorially independent. Despite its name (a hangover from pre-TV days), it is the primary source of television programming in New Zealand.

## REFERENCES

Broadcasting Act. (1976). Section 3 (1). Wellington: Government Printer.

Impact of video, good and bad. (1987, April 12). *Dominion Sunday Times*, p. 15.

In the top 20. (1987, January). *Videoscreen*, p. 3.

Lealand, G. (1984). *Video recorder ownership and use in New Zealand.* Wellington: Audience Research Unit, Broadcasting Corporation of New Zealand.

Market Research Centre. (1987). *Palmerston North omnibus: Ownership of VCRs, renting of videos, and cinema attendance.* Unpublished manuscript, Massey University, Palmerston North, New Zealand.

Morton, S. (1985). *Video recorders in New Zealand homes.* Wellington: IRIS Audience Research, Broadcasting Corporation of New Zealand.

Mounter, J. (1987). Satellite invasion. *Televiews, 87,* p. 10.

Royal Commission. (1986). *Royal Commission on broadcasting and related telecommunications in New Zealand.* Wellington: Government Printer.

# 14

# United States: Cable Eases Its Way into the Household

**Lee B. Becker**
**Pamela J. Creedon**
*The Ohio State University*
**R. Warwick Blood**
*Mitchell College*
**Eric S. Fredin**
*The Ohio State University*

In the U.S. tradition of media research, no single issue has received as much attention as the effects and potential effects of the media on their users. Concerns about media effects have been particularly prominent during periods of media change.

Certainly, the 1980s have been one such period. During this time, many were the promises of the new media or new forms of media. The new cables coming into people's homes would carry not only new types of television programming but also make possible a new lifestyle centered in the home. The home would become the locus of work, play, and other activities of daily survival. Satellites, computers, various electronic recorders and players, and other such devices would further add to the disruption of the American scene. Life in the year 2000, if not earlier, would only slightly resemble life in 1980.

This chapter is the product of research undertaken in the effects tradition in the United States. It was stimulated by the change taking place on the media landscape. The results that this research produced speak both to general issues of media effects and to the concerns and prophecies of the observers of media change in the 1980s.

The chapter begins with a brief overview of the U.S. media system. It then presents the outlines of some of the changes that have taken place in that system in recent years and places those changes within the larger context of the media scene. The major issues dealt with in the pages that follow are those of the effects of those changes in the media on the persons who use them. The content of those media and the types of effects the media might have are outlined first. Then, three different types of data drawn from national sources and a series of studies of a single community are examined in detail in an attempt to understand the true meaning of media change for those who use them.

## OVERVIEW OF THE U.S. MEDIA SYSTEM

Much has been written about the U.S. media system; yet many discussions ignore or underplay three characteristics that separate it from media systems in many other Western societies. The first is its sheer size. The second is its degree of decentralization. The third is the extent to which it is commercial.

The size of the system, of course, is in part a function of the size of the country. In 1986, the U.S.'s 241 million people living in 88 million different households were served by just under 1,671 daily newspapers, 495 semiweekly newspapers, 6,857 weekly newspapers, 1,235 television stations, and 9,924 radio stations. There were 6,238 magazines or other periodicals appearing at least monthly, 7,600 cable television systems, and 22,384 movie theaters. [1]

These numbers, however, present an artificial view of the U.S. system unless the second characteristic is taken into consideration. Individual households do not get to choose from among all of these media products. Because the U.S. system is decentralized, households can select only among the media serving their given communities. Most often, this means choosing to read or not to read the single local daily newspaper, selecting from a few weekly newspapers, picking from among a half-dozen television signals and perhaps from two dozen radio signals, and deciding to subscribe or not to subscribe to the single local cable television system.

The country has only one general circulation national newspaper, *USA Today*. The *Wall Street Journal*, a national business daily, is available throughout the country. The other U.S. prestige papers, such as the *New York Times*, the *Washington Post*, and the *Los Angeles Times*, are not readily available in many parts of the country and have most of their circulation in a single metropolitan area. Even the *national* television networks depend on *local* television stations to use their signals, and they must pay the local stations to carry the network programming. Increasingly, the local stations (called affiliates) have alternative sources of programming and can make more money by selling advertisements around that programming than by using the network materials.

This picture of decentralization can be misleading. As is the case in many other Western societies, there is tremendous concentration of ownership in the U.S. media system. Although the media organizations are locally oriented in many respects, they must also answer to major national corporations. Most daily newspapers, for example, are owned by national groups. These groups, in turn, are often parts of larger corporations with interests inside and outside of the communications industry. Gannett, one of the largest newspaper groups in the U.S. in terms of number of papers, owns 90 daily newspapers, 39 nondaily newspapers, eight television stations, 16 radio stations, and a weekly newspaper magazine insert. Times Mirror, publisher of the *Los Angeles Times* and other newspapers, also publishes magazines, operates television stations, owns more than 40 cable systems in 14 states, operates a variety of book publishing companies, and owns a land and timber company. So the local decision-making is counterbalanced by national, corporate decision-making as well.

The third relevant characteristic is that the U.S. media system is, to its very core, commercial. The media organizations are owned by persons or corporations interested in making a profit. Profits are made by amassing an audience that can be marketed to advertisers and/or by asking audience members to pay for the product through some kind of subscription fee. Even the public (government subsidized) broadcasting system, designed to be noncommercial, is dependent on a loyal audience for its revenues (either through tax subsidies or direct contributions). Increasingly, the public broadcasting system also is obtaining financial support directly from sponsors.

## CHANGES IN THE U.S. MEDIA SYSTEM

These three generalizations about the U.S. media should be treated as just that. There are clear exceptions. Some communities are served by alternative newspapers making little profit. The magazine industry is rather centralized (although there has been much growth of late in regional and city publications), and some communities are being served by more than one cable operator. But the basic patterns hold true. Observers who fail to understand that the U.S. media system is large, decentralized, and commercial will fail to understand the nature of change that is taking place in that system.

That the U.S. media system is undergoing change should be obvious (see Tunstall, 1986). The change has been most dramatic in the period of the late 1970s and early 1980s in the area of cable television.

The technology of cable, of course, has been around almost since the beginning of broadcast television in the late 1940s (Baldwin & McVoy, 1983). It was first used in the U.S. to bring broadcast signals into homes in small, isolated communities that could not otherwise receive television. The cable operator put up an antenna on high ground, grabbed distant signals from the air, and transmitted the signals via cable to subscribing homes. In the 1970s, the cable industry moved into middle-sized communities that already had local broadcasting outlets. The cable operators offered signals from independent stations in other markets to their subscribers and signals from the stations in the community of a higher quality than was available over the air. In the late 1970s, cable teamed up with satellites to deliver content particular to cable. This specialized content allowed cable to move into even the large metropolitan areas that had a large number of over-the-air signals available.

In keeping with the basic character of the U.S. media system, many decisions on cable are made at the community level. Local governments usually award a contract to a commercial operator who builds the system and provides cable services. The operators make money by charging subscribers a fee that can vary greatly from community to community. Part of the fee is passed along to the program provider. Some program providers earn additional money from advertising.

The cable companies that operate the local systems often are part of large national groups, commonly referred to as multiple system operators. In the bidding for local cable contracts during the late 1970s, these large companies and many local, smaller ones promised a wide range of services to the communities that they were seeking to wire. Included were interactivity, large amounts of local programming, and channels provided free to local governments and community organizations. Perhaps best known outside the U.S. were the experiments of Warner Amex with its interactive Qube systems (Becker, 1987; Davidge, 1987). These experiments, by and large, were commercial failures. The promises had ended by the middle of the 1980s, and cable systems largely were providing what came to be labeled "vanilla" services: simple, nonexperimental content (O'Donnell, 1986).

By 1986, cable was servicing just under half of the U.S. television homes. Three quarters of the homes were passed by cable, meaning 75% of the households could receive cable if it was wanted. Forty advertising-supported cable-only channels, five "superstations" (over-the-air stations without network affiliation), 13 non-advertising supported channels, and six pay-per-view services were being distributed by satellite. ESPN, a large sports service, was reaching 43% of U.S. homes. Other satellite services provided music, religious, news, children's, and speciality programs for women and minorities. Many had become profitable or were nearing profitability. The content of these cable services is mostly visual; cable radio has not developed in the U.S.

Cable television was not the only area of change in the U.S. media landscape in the early 1980s. Direct broadcast satellite was spreading, particularly to the rural areas of the country where cable probably will never penetrate. By 1986, 2% of U.S. homes had a home receiving dish attached. The videocassette recorder (VCR), which experienced slower growth in the U.S. than in many other countries, had penetrated 35% of U.S. homes. The compact disk player became a prominent part of audio systems, and the technology promised much more. Although teletext never developed (in part because of a lack of agreement over standards), three national viewdata or videotext services were reaching 600,000 subscribers. These national videotext services experienced much greater success than did several community-based videotext projects.

Clearly cable television was the most prominent addition to the list of options available to the U.S. consumer in the first half of the 1980s. Cable, to paraphrase the industry promoters, would pick up where broadcast television left off. The VCR was at first promoted as an alternative to cable. By the middle of the decade, however, the VCR in the U.S. had become cable's companion. Together they gave consumers control over content and use of television as never before.

## LITERATURE ON AUDIENCE REACTIONS TO MEDIA CHANGE

Reports of the impact on audiences of changes in the media environment in the United States began to make their way into the mass communications literature in the 1970s. Representative of this early work is the research of Becker, Dunwoody and Rafaeli (1983), Robinson and Jeffres (1978), and Sparkes (1983). In general this work has suggested that television viewing behaviors had been altered by the introduction of cable. The amount of time that audience members spent with television seemed to be higher in homes with cable than in those not using this service. In addition, persons living in cable households watched different types of programs than did persons living outside cable homes. In a national survey conducted in 1980, Bower (1985) found that cable subscribers had not acquired the service because of an unusually high regard for television in general, nor did they develop a greater fondness for the medium as a result. Cable subscribers said they were seeking more variety in their programming and actually watched more light entertainment than persons in homes without cable.

Despite the increased use of television in the cable households, however, there was little evidence that other media habits had been radically affected. Newspaper reading, as well as television news viewing, seemed to have decreased only small amounts, if at all, for cable subscribers (Becker, et al., 1983; Dyer & Hill, 1981).

Use of radio and movie theater attendance, however, seem to be slightly more threatened by cable (Becker, et al., 1983; Guback, 1982; and Kaplan, 1978).

More recent cable research has focused on such things as resistance to cable on the part of a significant segment of the U.S. population and program preferences and decision-making in cable households. Sparkes (1984), for example, has shown that cable has limited appeal to certain age and income groups who seem unwilling to subscribe to the service because of conflicts with their lifestyle and because of a lack of interest in the services provided. Heeter and Baldwin (1984), Heeter and Greenberg (1985) and Kahan (1983) have looked at program choices by cable subscribers and found that there is a limit to the number of channels that a subscriber will watch with regularity (at around seven), regardless of the number provided, but that, at least within that set of watched channels, subscribers do switch around from channel to channel quite a bit, often sampling from more than one program at the same viewing time. As both Kahan (1983) and Webster (1986) point out, not all cable subscribers have the same program preferences, and there is evidence of specialization of viewing not found in noncable households. Neuman and de Sola Pool (1986) have documented the increasing gap between the amount of television programming and the actual amount of program consumption during the period of early cable growth. Clearly, there is a limit to the amount of time that audience members will spend with television, regardless of the amount of programming offered.

Audience responses to the videocassette recorder in the U.S. also have come under early examination. Agostino and Zenaty (1980) and Levy (1980) showed that the audience, at least in the late 1970s, largely used the medium to record normal television programming for use at a later time. Later work by Rubin and Bantz (1987) suggested that the playing back of rental materials had become more prominent as rental outlets proliferated. Yet Levy (1987), in summarizing this research, noted that the "rental or purchase of prerecorded cassettes is an important but secondary behavior" to the watching of materials recorded from cable or television sources.

Also coming under frequent analysis has been audience interest in videotext or viewdata, represented by the work of Bolton (1983), Butler and Kent (1983), Ettema (1983), Heikkinen and Reese (1986), Paisley (1983), and Reese, Shoemaker and Danielson (1986). Given lesser attention has been teletext, studied by Elton and Carey (1983, 1984) and Henke and Donohue (1986). Summaries of some of this research appear in Aumente (1987) and Williams (1987). In general, the research and field experiences suggest that these textual services have the potential to disrupt audience media use patterns, but there is considerable resistance to these new services in their present forms (Carey & Moss, 1985; Neuman, in press). Carey (1982), drawing on parallels between videotext and the newspaper and television, argues that videotext is not likely to develop as a broad-based, public medium in this century.

## CONTENT OF CABLE AND THE VCR

When the cable industry in the U.S. blossomed in the mid 1970s, it promised to provide unlimited entertainment and information programming. By offering subscribers 24-hour-a-day movies, sports, entertainment, and news, cable's proponents promised to make it possible for people to have all of their entertainment and information needs satisfied in the home. In some sense, the promise was met. Cable did spawn the development of an all-news network, an all-weather network, a network for children, a sports network, religious networks, a network for coverage of Congress, several movie channels, and other channels providing a variety of information and entertainment packages.

Local cable operators, however, pick and choose from among the various services available to create the package of offerings that they sell to their audiences. As a consequence, it is difficult to provide a precise picture of a typical cable system in the United States. Becker and Creedon (1986), however, provide some assistance through two content-analytic studies of cable content. The first analysis was of an entire week's programming on the then 34-channel Warner Amex Qube system serving Columbus, Ohio. The second investigation was of the content of the six national premium channels (channels, usually specializing in movies, for which the subscriber pays an additional, per channel fee) with the largest numbers of subscribers. This second study was conducted for a 4-week period.

The studies showed that cable does provide a certain type of programming not available with broadcast television. For example, the analysis showed that cable contains additional community programming and public affairs and news materials not found on broadcast channels. Overall, cable programming was found to be heavily entertainment-oriented. It was dominated by movies, sports, and other forms of diversion. Even the channels that specialized in movies, however, provided at least some diversity of programming. On the other hand, it also is clear that cable has not altered the basic nature of television programming. The categories of programming offered by cable are not radically different from those provided by the broadcast channels, as the Becker and Creedon data show. In many cases, cable has offered more of the same.

A separate analysis of children's programming on cable by Siemicki, Atkin, Greenberg, and Baldwin (1986) shows that the growth of satellite cable programming has resulted in more children's fare. Yet, the authors note, no single cable system is likely to carry all of the channels available. Nonetheless, the existence of cable has resulted in specialized programming to a greater extent than before.

The available data on the kinds of content that viewers watch on their VCRs is quite consistent with the picture emerging from the analysis of cable content. Papazian (1986), based on an overview of available U.S. research, reported that the bulk of the recording done in the home is of prime-time programming, which is then played back on the weekends and other, mostly non-prime, times. Most of the recording is of shows presented by the three major, national broadcast networks. Mayer and Sweeting (1986) indicated that 92% of the rentals of videocassettes are of movies, and 84% of the purchases are movies. Rentals account for 98% of all cassettes leaving the video shops.

## THE NATURE OF EXPECTED CHANGE
## IN AUDIENCE BEHAVIOR

What kinds of change in audience behavior is a medium such as cable or the VCR likely to produce? The contents are intended to appeal to entertainment and, to a lesser extent, informational needs of consumers. To the extent that they are successful, they must accumulate resources of time and money available for these purposes.

The allocation of financial resources is, of course, important. Cable systems depend on it, as consumers are required to pay fees (making television in the U.S. for the first time a "pay" versus "free," or entirely advertiser-supported, medium). Financial resources, however, are not constant across time. As a result, the impact of a new medium such as cable on the allocation of time may be more easily isolated.

Yet both financial and temporal resources are important, and their allocation is not necessarily firmly linked. People can subscribe to cable (or purchase a VCR or even purchase or rent a cassette) without using it. The respective industries will be delighted, at least in the short run. But such a situation is likely to take place only in a situation of financial resource abundance. In a period of scarcity, it is unlikely that the financial commitment will continue without a temporal one as well. At present, in the U.S., it is difficult to commit time to these new media without also making a financial commitment, although library loans of tapes and even machines at least hide the costs in general tax contributions.

The studies reported here have focused most heavily on the impact of the new media on the allocation of time. This is done through an examination of the changes that these media have brought about in use of other media and in various other kinds of leisure pursuits. The allocation of financial resources, however, has not been ignored.

The primary focus has been on cable television because, as noted before, it has been the most prominent new medium in the U.S. in the first half of the 1980s and because, in the U.S. at least, its development has laid a path for development of the videocassette recorder. The VCR is examined here as a potential competitor to cable, although the results suggest that there is little evidence that such competition has in fact resulted.

Three kinds of evidence of adaptation as a result of cable are examined. First, U.S. national data are studied for the 1980-1986 period to determine if shifts in media use habits have accompanied the growth of cable. Second, in keeping with the observation that media systems in the U.S. are local, trends within a selected community are examined for the 1981-1986 period. Finally, specific studies within that same community are used to determine static correlates of use of cable.

## NATIONAL TRENDS IN MEDIA USE IN THE 1980S

The basic picture of cable growth in the U.S. is shown in Table 14.1. The general growth of cable is well documented, with penetration growing from 19.8% in 1980 to 46.8% in 1986. The percentage of television households passed by cable (and therefore able to subscribe) increased from 43.1% in 1980 to 76.0% in 1986. Growth in cable during this period, then, was largely the result of new wiring, as the percentage of households passed subscribing to cable increased only from 55.3% in 1982 to 57.0% in 1986. In 1980, 41.1% of the cable households purchased a premium channel, that is, a channel costing more than just the basic cable fee. That figure increased to 60.2% by 1983, showing evidence of just slight erosion after that point.

Table 14.1 also shows the penetration of VCRs into American television homes during this same period. Penetration stood at 1.1% in 1980. By 1986, it was 36.0%. Compared with the growth of 27 percentage points for cable from 1980 to 1986, then, the videocassette recorder grew by 34.9 percentage points.

It seems reasonable to expect that these new means of delivering services to a television set would disrupt the previously existing television viewing habits. National Nielsen data for May of 1980 through 1986, presented in Table 14.2, show that total weekly television usage (in terms of average hours of viewing) increased by 3.7 hours in households with premium cable services, increased by 5.4 hours in households with basic cable, and increased by only 1.6 hours in households without cable. In other words, the growth in television viewing time was attributable largely to households with cable services.

TABLE 14.1

U.S. Cable TV and VCR Growth

|  | 1980 | 1981 | 1982 | 1983 | 1984 | 1985 | 1986 |
|---|---|---|---|---|---|---|---|
| Percent of households with cable* | 19.8 | 25.3 | 29.0 | 37.2 | 41.2 | 44.6 | 46.8 |
| Percent of households passed by cable** | 43.1 | 51.2 | 59.9 | 68.0 | 72.1 | 74.5 | 76.0 |
| Percent of households passed by cable with cable** | 55.2 | 55.2 | 55.3 | 55.1 | 56.0 | 57.0 | 57.0 |
| Percent of cable households with premium services** | 41.1 | 51.3 | 55.0 | 60.2 | 59.4 | 59.0 | 56.8 |
| Percent of households with VCR* | 1.1 | 1.8 | 3.1 | 5.5 | 10.6 | 20.8 | 36.0 |

* From Nielsen Co. data reported in U.S. Bureau of the Census (1986).
** From Bortz, Wyche & Trautman (1986) for 1980-1985; National Cable Television Association for 1986.

Table 14.2 also shows that all television homes decreased the amount of time that they spent watching network affiliate stations during this time period. The size of the decrease was 2.4 hours for premium cable homes, 1.4 hours for basic cable homes, and 1.0 hours for noncable homes. Table 14.2 also shows, however, that households without cable increased their viewing of the growing number of independent stations and Public Broadcasting System (PBS) affiliates during this time period, as did (to a lesser extent) households with basic cable services. Households with premium cable services, however, showed a drop in viewing of signals from independents and PBS.

The 1986 column in Table 14.2 shows that, by the end of the period, premium homes were watching considerably more television than basic cable homes, which were watching more television than noncable homes. All three watched about the same amount of programming from non-network broadcast sources. But the cable homes were devoting fewer hours to the major broadcast network fare than the non-

TABLE 14.2

Average Hours of Household Weekly TV Usage: U.S.

| | 1980 | 1981 | 1982 | 1983 | 1984 | 1985 | 1986 |
|---|---|---|---|---|---|---|---|
| **Total TV Usage** | | | | | | | |
| Noncable homes | 41.6 | 43.7 | 41.2 | 43.7 | 43.0 | 41.8 | 43.2 |
| Basic cable homes | 43.1 | 42.4 | 40.8 | 46.4 | 46.9 | 45.8 | 48.5 |
| Premium cable homes | 50.7 | 51.7 | 55.4 | 54.1 | 55.8 | 53.2 | 54.4 |
| **Usage of Network Affiliates** | | | | | | | |
| Noncable homes | 34.2 | 34.9 | 32.4 | 34.9 | 33.1 | 32.4 | 33.2 |
| Basic cable homes | 31.7 | 30.8 | 28.5 | 31.4 | 30.6 | 29.2 | 30.3 |
| Premium cable homes | 30.1 | 28.5 | 27.5 | 29.0 | 28.8 | 26.7 | 27.7 |
| **Usage of Independents and Public Broadcasting System** | | | | | | | |
| Noncable homes | 8.1 | 10.3 | 9.2 | 10.3 | 11.3 | 11.5 | 11.7 |
| Basic cable homes | 10.9 | 10.8 | 10.5 | 12.5 | 11.9 | 12.1 | 12.2 |
| Premium cable homes | 16.0 | 15.1 | 14.4 | 13.9 | 13.2 | 12.9 | 13.6 |

Note: From Nielsen Co. data reported in Papazian (1986, 1987).

cable homes—even though the cable homes watched more television. Essentially, then, this indicates that the larger the number of choices, the lower the amount of actual attention given to the networks.

During this period of cable growth, however, the percentage of U.S. adults watching one or more early evening newscast on a network affiliate grew by a few points, according to the data presented in Table 14.3. The percentage watching a network affiliated late-night newscast, however, dropped slightly.

Shifts in viewing behavior of the sort identified in Tables 14.2 and 14.3 have had impact on the broadcast television industry, but Table 14.4 shows that, despite the changes in viewing behavior associated with the introduction of cable, the number of commercial television broadcast stations grew rather dramatically in the period of the 1980s. In 1980, 734 commercial stations were on the air. The number was 919 in 1986. Commercial radio stations also grew in that period, from 7,871 stations in 1980 to 8,593 stations in 1985. For most Americans, this growth in broadcasting signals has meant an increase in the number of channel choices even without the existence of cable.

TABLE 14.3

Percent of U.S. Adult Population Watching News on Network Affiliates

|  | 1980 | 1981 | 1982 | 1983 | 1984 | 1985 | 1986 |
|---|---|---|---|---|---|---|---|
| Watching one or more early evening newscasts | 31.5 | 30.8 | 31.3 | 32.1 | 31.2 | 30.8 | 34.7 |
| Watching one or more late evening newscasts | 28.0 | 26.7 | 23.8 | 25.6 | 23.3 | 21.8 | 24.5 |

Note: From Papazian (1986, 1987).

TABLE 14.4

U.S. Media Outlets, Circulations

|  | 1980 | 1981 | 1982 | 1983 | 1984 | 1985 | 1986 |
|---|---|---|---|---|---|---|---|
| Commercial TV stations | 734 | 756 | 777 | 813 | 841 | 883 | 919 |
| Commercial radio stations | 7,871 | 7,983 | 8,048 | 8,260 | 8,470 | 8,593 | 8,807 |
| Newspapers (Number of Titles) | | | | | | | |
| Semiweekly and weekly | 7,696 | | 7,304 | 7,363 | 7,323 | 7,328 | 7,352 |
| Daily | 1,744 | | 1,740 | 1,735 | 1,711 | 1,701 | 1,671 |
| Daily Newspaper Circulation | | | | | | | |
| Millions | 62.2 | 61.4 | 62.5 | 62.6 | 63.1 | 62.8 | 62.5 |
| Per Capita | .275 | .267 | .269 | .267 | .267 | .263 | .259 |
| Periodicals (number of titles) | 10,236 | | 10,688 | 10,952 | 10,809 | 11,090 | 11,328 |
| Motion Pictures | | | | | | | |
| Theaters (thousands) | 18 | 18 | 18 | 19 | 20 | 21 | 22 |
| Attendance (millions) | 1,022 | 1,067 | 1,175 | 1,197 | 1,199 | 1,056 | 1,030 |
| Box office receipts (billion $) | 2.75 | 2.97 | 3.45 | 3.77 | 4.03 | 3.75 | 3.83 |

Note: From U.S. Bureau of Census (1986); supplemented by additional data from sources used by Bureau.

Additional data are presented in Table 14.4 to determine the impact of changes in the content of television on other media behaviors and industries. The picture for the newspaper industry is a bit clouded, these data show. The actual number of newspaper titles decreased during the early 1980s. The number of semiweekly and weekly titles dropped from 7,696 to 7,352, although the 1986 figure is up from the 1984 and 1985 figures. The number of daily newspapers dropped from 1,744 to 1,671. In both cases, however, the decreases began long before the advent of either cable or the videocassette recorder, going back at least to the introduction of television itself.

As far as the daily newspaper is concerned, the trend represents a consolidation within the local market from more than one competing paper to a single daily newspaper. For the most part, the departing paper has been the one published in the afternoon. From 1980 to 1985, for example, the number of morning daily newspapers actually has increased, from 387 to 482 (U.S. Bureau of Census, 1986). And the 1980s also were a period in which the first truly national U.S. daily newspaper appeared, *USA Today*. Circulation for the paper, begun in 1982, had reached 1.5 million by the middle of 1987 (Nasser & Guy, 1987). Circulation for all daily newspapers, as Table 14.4 shows, actually increased slightly during the 1980-1985 period, nearly keeping up with growth in the population.

The number of non-newspaper periodicals (published weekly through quarterly) has increased during this same time period, Table 14.4 shows. So whereas the number of one form of print medium (the newspaper) has declined, the number of another (the magazine) has increased.

Table 14.4 also shows that U.S. cinema attendance increased in the 1980 to 1984 period before dropping in 1985 and 1986. Box office receipts increased overall during the period, suffering only a slight drop in 1985. The number of theaters also grew during the years 1980-1986.

In sum, then, the period of the first half of the 1980s has shown a sharp increase in the availability of cable television and in the number of homes with a videocassette recorder. It is clear, at least where cable television is concerned (which had reached the larger number of households during this period and consequently is the primary focus of this chapter), that the result has been a change in the way television is viewed. Usage of television has increased in all homes, but the increase has been most dramatic in the homes with cable. Although all television homes have decreased the amount of time that they are spending with the traditional broadcast television material, the decrease in the premium cable homes has been quite dramatic. Even in the noncable homes, it should be noted, there has been some shifting to the increasing number of non-network programming options. The premium homes have shifted from independents and public broadcasting to cable services.

Overall, there also is evidence that the viewing of late evening network-affiliate delivered newscasts decreased during this period. Many of the independents offer competing, non-news materials during this time slot, as do the cable companies. Cable, of course, also offers its own newscasts. Early evening news viewing (when the networks themselves play a stronger role in the programming) did not show this similar decrease in viewing.

Despite these changes in the way television time is allocated, there is little evidence of additional disruption in the U.S. media environment at the national level during the first half of the 1980s. The number of commercial television and radio stations grew, as did the number of periodicals, and motion picture theaters. Theater attendance ended the period slightly ahead of its level at the beginning, and box office receipts were up considerably. The number of newspaper titles decreased, but circulation grew slightly. While newspaper circulation growth and, as Guback (1987) has noted, theater attendance have not kept up with population growth, it is clear that these trends began long before the beginning of the 1980s.

## COLUMBUS, OHIO, TREND ANALYSES

Although the data presented heretofore give an overview of the changes in audience behavior during the first part of the 1980s on a national basis, they perhaps best can be viewed as setting the context for more intensive study of a select community. As argued previously, the U.S. media system is a local one, and national patterns may hide or blur changes that are best studied at the community level. At that level, it is possible to identify precise changes in audience behavior under specifiable conditions of content diversification.

Columbus, Ohio, and its suburbs were chosen because in many ways they represent the media diversification typical of the United States. Although cable had come to the community at an earlier time, it was during the early 1980s that the amount of programming on cable began to expand markedly. Columbus was a particularly attractive community for cable development because, prior to its introduction, no independent (non-network affiliated) stations were in operation. So cable, even before the introduction of satellite services in the early 1980s, could provide subscribers with a mixture of broadcast services not available to noncable households.

Columbus and its suburbs were served by four nonoverlapping and noncompeting cable companies. One of these, operated by Warner Amex, was known as a Qube system. It was the first long-term, commercially operating interactive system in the U.S., and it served as a pilot for larger systems in other cities. The Columbus Qube operation at the beginning of the 1980s was a 30-channel system; it had been expanded to offer five additional channels by 1986. Each of the three remaining systems in Columbus also offered services with at least 30 channels. The actual number of channels purchased by subscribers to all four systems could vary from about 12 to 36. In all cases, cable provided entertainment and public affairs materials that were unavailable to nonsubscribers.

The community also was served by a variety of other media, including daily newspapers, weekly newspapers, local magazines, and specialty publications. Most residents could receive approximately 20 radio signals and over-the-air television signals from three network-affiliated television stations, a local public broadcasting station, and as many as three independent stations (all of which came on the air after 1980).

Six surveys dealing at least in part with cable television were fielded in each January of 1981 through 1986. The studies employed telephone interviews with probability samples of household heads in Columbus and its suburbs, which have a combined, demographically diverse population of nearly 1 million. The interviews, which lasted approximately 10 minutes, were conducted by trained interviewers. Sex of the household head to be interviewed was predetermined randomly. Only persons 18 years old or older were eligible. A nonsexist definition of household head was used, assuming, in the prototypical situation, that each household had a head of each sex. When the household did not have a head of both sexes, the head was interviewed regardless of sex. Demographic characteristics of the sample matched known population parameters. Final sample sizes and completion rates for the six surveys were: 1981 (403, 71%); 1982 (540, 65%); 1983 (523, 67%); 1984 (656, 67%); 1985 (552, 68%), 1986 (599, 68%).

The survey instruments included items requiring respondents to provide information about their use of television and cable services as well as use of the other media. Respondents to the 1982 through 1986 surveys also were asked questions about their non-media leisure time activities.

## Results of the Trend Analyses

The data presented in Table 14.5 show the basic pattern of cable growth in the Columbus market. During the first half of the 1980s, the data in Table 14.1 make clear, cable penetration continued to grow on a national level. In the Columbus market, however, cable penetration leveled out after a significant initial growth from 1981 to 1982. By the end of 1982, construction of the cable systems in Columbus was nearly complete and most people could receive cable service if they wanted it. Table 14.5 also shows the percentage of subscribers for each of the four companies over the 6 years of study. It is an important examination because the pattern

TABLE 14.5

Cable Penetration: Columbus, Ohio

|                                    | 1981   | 1982   | 1983   | 1984   | 1985   | 1986    |
|------------------------------------|--------|--------|--------|--------|--------|---------|
| Percent subscribing                | 35.6   | 46.5   | 51.0   | 49.8   | 50.4   | 50.5*   |
| (N)                                | (403)  | (540)  | (523)  | (656)  | (552)  | (599)   |
| Percent of subscribers customer's of: |        |        |        |        |        |         |
| All American                       | 18.2   | 20.6   | 20.8   | 22.4   | 20.2   | 20.6    |
| Coaxial                            | 32.4   | 26.9   | 33.6   | 31.9   | 34.8   | 32.9    |
| KBLE                               | 6.8    | 3.2    | 3.5    | 3.4    | 2.1    | 4.0     |
| Warner                             | 39.2   | 43.9   | 40.5   | 39.9   | 41.9   | 38.9    |
| Receive fewer than 12 channels     |        |        | 29.5   | 19.5   | 16.0   | 11.3*   |
| Spend more than $30 per month for cable |   |        | 9.2    | 14.2   | 20.7   | 22.9*   |
| Receive no premium channel         |        |        | 35.1   | 36.9   | 33.8   | 36.1    |
| (N)                                | (143)  | (250)  | (261)  | (324)  | (275)  | (302)   |

* Difference between the first and final data point temporally is significant at the .05 level, one-tailed test.

of stability in evidence in the top of Table 14.5 could be caused by growth for one company, such as Warner, perhaps because of its attractive services and interactivity, and decline for another, perhaps because it didn't offer what the audience wanted. In fact, the data show, there is a nearly identical share of the audience for each of the four companies in 1981 and 1986, with the minor fluctuations between most likely due to sample error. The Warner system seems to be no different from the others in terms of audience appeal.

The 1981-1983 time period is rather significant, then, for it was during this period that cable continuned to grow in Columbus. It was also during this time that the cable systems "matured," that is, grew away from the noisy promises of the early period of cable franchise bidding to the kinds of noninteractive cable entertainment and information services later prevalent in the U.S. and described earlier. In this regard, it is interesting to note that the decision to curtail the interactive use of the Qube system in January of 1984 had no apparent effect in Table 14.5 on subscription to Warner's services. (From the beginning of 1984 on, the only significant use of Qube's interactivity was for pay-per-view services.) The evidence, as noted elsewhere (Becker, 1987), seems to have been that interactivity as practiced by Warner was of less concern to the subscribers than to the company itself.

The bottom of Table 14.5 shows that even during the period of stability in penetration of cable in Columbus, other types of important changes were taking place. For those persons with cable, there was growth in the number of channels received and growth in the amount of money spent on cable. There was no evidence, however, of change in the number of expensive, premium channels purchased. More specifically, the data show that the number of persons receiving fewer than 12 channels of cable service had declined from just under 30% in 1983 to just over 11% in 1986. The percentage of persons spending more than $30 per month on cable services (during a period of relatively low inflation overall but relatively high inflation in cable rates) went from just over 9% in 1983 to just under 23% in 1986. Although much of this growth in expenditure no doubt is accounted for by inflation, the growth in number of channels received and the lack of decline in the number of premium channels received (for which an additional fee must be paid) indicates that inflation is not the sole explanation. At a minimum, the data suggest that the added costs of the inflated services did not cause subscribers to reduce the services purchased.

The period from 1982 on also was one with a tremendous amount of growth in penetration of videocassette recorders. Table 14.6 shows that growth in videocassette recorder penetration in the Columbus market was rather consistent in the 6 years of the study. Growth was quite dramatic from 1985 to 1986, however, and that growth was most dramatic among cable subscribers. From 1985 to 1986, penetration grew from 19% in the cable homes and just under 15% in the noncable homes to just over 42% in the cable homes and 23% in the noncable homes. It was during this period that cable operators became aggressive in marketing their services as means of providing content for VCRs. The result seems to be that the technology that many argued would be most likely to threaten cable growth should be seen instead as complementary.

In contrast to the findings for VCR growth, Table 14.6 shows that penetration of computers into the Columbus market was rather slow and took place equally for cable and noncable homes. In other words, there is no evidence here that growth in these two types of products (cable and computers) are related, as would be expected if cable subscribers were simply the electronic gadget innovators.

TABLE 14.6

Media and Leisure Habits: Columbus, Ohio

| | 1981 | 1982 | 1983 | 1984 | 1985 | 1986 |
|---|---|---|---|---|---|---|
| **VCR ownership (%)** | | | | | | |
| Cable | 8.0 | 9.6 | 16.8 | | 19.0 | 42.4 |
| No cable | 1.4* | 3.1* | 8.3* | | 14.6 | 23.0* |
| | | | | | | |
| **Computer ownership (%)** | | | | | | |
| Cable | | | 8.4 | 18.0 | 17.8 | 23.2 |
| No cable | | | 4.6* | 16.8 | 11.3 | 18.2 |
| | | | | | | |
| **Hrs. weekday** | | | | | | |
| **TV viewing (mean and sd)** | | | | | | |
| Cable | | 4.0 | 3.3 | 3.2 | 4.1 | 3.5 |
| | | (2.83) | (2.38) | (2.31) | (3.75) | (2.72) |
| No cable | | 3.6* | 2.9* | 2.9* | 3.5* | 3.2 |
| | | (2.91) | (2.30) | (2.46) | (2.88) | (2.69) |
| | | | | | | |
| **Hrs. weekend** | | | | | | |
| **TV viewing (mean and sd)** | | | | | | |
| Cable | | 7.9 | 6.9 | 6.8 | 7.5 | 7.5 |
| | | (5.47) | (4.57) | (5.04) | (5.88) | (5.04) |
| No cable | | 5.9* | 4.8* | 5.2* | 6.3* | 5.5* |
| | | (4.65) | (3.76) | (4.32) | (5.56) | (3.83) |
| | | | | | | |
| **Days read** | | | | | | |
| **daily newspaper** | | | | | | |
| **(mean)** | | | | | | |
| Cable | 5.3 | 5.5 | 5.5 | 5.5 | 5.4 | 4.6 |
| | (2.50) | (2.44) | (2.47) | (2.44) | (2.65) | (2.87) |
| No cable | 4.9* | 4.7* | 4.8* | 5.2* | 5.1 | 4.1* |
| | (2.67) | (2.80) | (2.70) | (2.55) | (2.60) | (2.98) |
| | | | | | | |
| **Paid sport event** | | | | | | |
| **attendance in** | | | | | | |
| **last month (%)** | | | | | | |
| Cable | | | 21.1 | | 15.6 | |
| No cable | | | 13.2* | | 14.9 | |
| | | | | | | |
| **Movie attendance** | | | | | | |
| **in last month (%)** | | | | | | |
| Cable | | | 44.2 | | 46.0 | |
| No cable | | | 51.9* | | 42.6 | |
| | | | | | | |
| **(N)** | | | | | | |
| Cable | (143) | (250) | (261) | (324) | (275) | (302) |
| No cable | (260) | (288) | (261) | (319) | (277) | (287) |

\* Difference between Subscriber and Nonsubscriber samples is significant at the .05 level, one-tailed test.

What is the impact of this growth in cable penetration (in the early period) and growth in cable services and VCRs (in the latter period) on television viewing in Columbus households? Something of an answer is presented in the remaining entries in Table 14.6. These data are based on respondent estimates of the amount of time spent with television viewing on the average weekday (Monday through Friday) and on the average weekend (Saturday and Sunday combined). Perhaps what is most striking in this table is the variability in estimates of time spent with television, reflecting, most likely, the unreliability of the measures. Perhaps next most striking is the discrepancy between weekend viewing time for cable and non-cable subscribers. This discrepancy is nearly constant across time and consistent with the view that cable subscribers were heavy television viewers (and probably were even before cable was introduced) and used cable and even the VCR as a means of expanding what they viewed, although not greatly the amount of viewing. During the week, amount of viewing seemed to be related to cable subscription less strongly than was viewing on weekends.

Further analyses showed that television viewing time did not vary significantly among the various cable systems. In other words, the Warner subscribers did not report higher or lower levels of viewing than did the viewers of the other systems. Nor did the number of channels make a significant difference. On the other hand, respondents with premium channels, that is, pay-per-channel offerings of movies and entertainment specials, did view more television than the cable subscribers without these services.

The general strategy of examining net change across time in behaviors of cable and noncable subscribers is followed in the remainder of this section. Table 14.6 shows that cable subscribers rather consistently have been heavier users of the daily newspaper, and that discrepancy held constant across the period of analysis. The average number of days per week of newspaper readership was stable until 1985, the data show (reflecting, it would seem, higher reliability for this measure than for those of television time). The drop in readership from 1985 to 1986 for both subscribers and nonsubscribers is rather interesting in and of itself. At the end of 1985, one of the two daily newspapers in Columbus ceased publication. The consequence was a rather marked decrease in reading, taking place equally for subscribers and nonsubscribers to cable.

The 1983-1986 surveys included a variety of questions on leisure activities of the respondents. The bottom of Table 14.6 shows evidence that in 1983 cable subscribers were more likely to have reported attending a sporting event outside the home than were nonsubscribers, but by 1986 this difference seems to have disappeared. It may well be that during that time subscribers found their initially stronger needs for sports viewing being satisfied by expanded and improved sports programming on cable and no longer felt the need for attending sporting events outside the home.

There is a similar blurring of initial differences for movie attendance. In this case, an initial lower level of movie theater attendance for subscribers compared to nonsubscribers has been erased. In 1983, consistent with the expectation that cable television would serve as a substitute for movie attendance outside the home, subscribers were less likely to report having attended a movie outside the home in the last month than were those without cable service. By 1986, however, this difference had disappeared, with subscribers to cable reporting just slightly (and nonsignificantly) higher levels of movie attendance than nonsubscribers. Subscribers, in fact, showed a steady level of movie attendance between 1983 and 1986. For the noncable home, however, movie attendance dropped, as it had nationally (Table 14.4). By 1986, in fact, those homes having both cable television and a videocassette recorder reported the highest level of movie attendance in the last month (50.8%), followed by those without cable but with a VCR (45.6%), those with cable but no VCR (42.5%), and those without either cable or a VCR (41.9%).

The 1983-1986 surveys contained an open-ended question asking respondents to list their leisure activities. Based on these data, respondents were classified as having mentioned television, reading, a sport, or family activities. Multiple responses meant that persons could be classified as mentioning one of these activities (television, for example) as well as another (such as sports). The data are summarized for these four years in the top half of Table 14.7. The data show no statistically significant differences between subscribers and nonsubscribers in terms of considering reading (of any print medium) as a leisure activity during the period of analysis. Subscribers, however, rather consistently listed television viewing as a leisure activity throughout, although the difference seems to have decreased somewhat by 1986. This results from a decline in that response for cable respondents and a constant response for the persons without cable. Overall, the cable subscribers viewed television, which the other analyses show they watch quite extensively, as a more prominent part of their leisure activities than do nonsubscribers. Table 14.7 shows no evidence of any difference between the subscribers and nonsubscribers in terms of likelihood of mentioning sport or family.

The bottom of Table 14.7 shows that cable subscribers are bigger spenders for leisure activities than nonsubscribers, but there is no evidence of change in this discrepancy during the period of analysis. In contrast, there is no consistent difference between subscribers and nonsubscribers to cable in terms of the amount of time that they spend on leisure activities.

In sum, then, the Columbus trend data show that there was growth in cable and VCR penetration during the period of study. For cable, there also was a growth in the number of channels received and the amount of money being spent on the

TABLE 14.7

Allocation of Leisure Resources: Columbus, Ohio

| | 1983 | 1984 | 1985 | 1986 |
|---|---|---|---|---|
| Percent Listing Following As Leisure Activity | | | | |
| **Television viewing** | | | | |
| Cable | 33.0 | 31.1 | 28.0 | 24.2 |
| No cable | 19.5* | 20.2* | 20.7* | 19.6 |
| **Reading** | | | | |
| Cable | 40.2 | 33.8 | 34.9 | 26.5 |
| No cable | 40.6 | 34.4 | 40.7 | 31.4 |
| **Sports** | | | | |
| Cable | 22.6 | 33.2 | 24.4 | 35.1 |
| No cable | 28.3 | 31.6 | 21.9 | 31.8 |
| **Family** | | | | |
| Cable | 8.4 | 16.5 | 14.9 | 22.0 |
| No cable | 5.6 | 19.9 | 16.3 | 20.9 |
| Percent spending more than $20 per week on leisure | | | | |
| Cable | | 48.6 | 48.4 | 50.8 |
| No cable | | 39.1* | 31.4* | 39.6* |
| Mean hours per week devoted to leisure (sd) | | | | |
| Cable | | 17.4 | 16.3 | 14.3 |
| | | (14.78) | (19.54) | (11.99) |
| No cable | | 16.5 | 15.4 | 16.0 |
| | | (14.71) | (14.59) | (15.68) |
| **(N)** | | | | |
| Cable | (261) | (324) | (275) | (302) |
| No cable | (261) | (319) | (277) | (287) |

\* Difference between Subscriber and Nonsubscriber samples is significant at the .05 level, one-tailed test.

service. In fact, videocassette recorders penetrated more completely into the cable homes than the noncable homes.

As was true at the national level, there is evidence that the cable homes watch more television than the noncable homes, although there is no evidence in the Columbus data of an increase in this gap over time. The differences in the Columbus samples are mostly in terms of weekend television viewing, not weekday viewing. There is no evidence that cable has adversely affected newspaper reading or movie theater going. In fact, the presence of movies on cable may have held interest in movies high, offsetting for cable subscribers the drop in attendance in evidence for the noncable household heads. Any impact of cable on paid attendance of sporting events outside the home appears to be slight.

There also is no evidence that cable has made people less interested in reading, sports or family as a means of relaxing. Cable respondents are more likely to think of television viewing as a leisure activity than persons without cable, but there is some evidence that cable respondents have lost some satisfaction with cable in this regard over time. Cable households spend more money on leisure than noncable households, but there is no increase over time in this regard. The amount of time spent on leisure is unrelated to cable subscription.

## STATIC CORRELATES OF SUBSCRIPTION TO CABLE IN COLUMBUS

The trend data just discussed present an overall picture of adaptation and change during the period of the early 1980s in Columbus. The analyses were based on a variety of items included in the survey instruments for at least two administrations. A large number of items, however, were used only once. Yet an examination of these single-administration items to show correlates of subscription to cable television provides additional insights about how cable has been incorporated into the lives of members of this single community.

The basic strategy in these analyses was to compare, at a single time point, cable and noncable subscribers on a variety of criteria, including their use of other media, their television content preferences, their evaluations of television, their attitudes toward communication technologies, and their leisure activities. In addition, the 1986 survey was used to assess levels of satisfaction with and evaluations of cable on the part of current and past cable subscribers.

A variety of items included on the various surveys conducted between 1981 and 1986 were used for these purposes. The specific items are discussed in the results section that follows.

### Results of the Static Analyses

The Columbus studies have shown rather consistently through the period of analysis that home owners are more likely to subscribe to cable than renters. Married persons and those with children in the home are more likely to have cable than the nonmarried and those with no children in the home. Age of the household heads,

TABLE 14.8

Media Use by Cable Subscription: Columbus, Ohio

| | Cable | No Cable |
|---|---|---|
| 1981 Sample (N) | (143) | (259) |
| No. of days per week some TV news watched (mean and sd) | 5.57 (1.94) | 5.16* (2.18) |
| No. of TV movies viewed per week (mean and sd) | 2.83 (2.86) | 1.47* (1.62) |
| No. of sports programs viewed per week (mean and sd) | 1.92 (2.82) | 1.37* (1.88) |
| No. of religious programs viewed per week (mean and sd) | 0.67 (1.28) | 0.44* (0.98) |
| 1982 Sample (N) | (250) | (288) |
| No. of days local early evening TV news watched (mean and sd) | 3.73 (2.33) | 3.86 (2.40) |
| No. of days local late evening TV news watched (mean and sd) | 3.04 (2.36) | 2.79 (2.50) |
| No. of days national news program watched (mean and sd) | 3.61 (2.31) | 3.64 (2.29) |
| No of days of radio news/weather listening (mean and sd) | 4.57 (2.76) | 4.76 (2.68) |
| Regular readership of personality or fashion magazines (percent) | 34.0 | 25.3* |
| Regular readership of sports or hobby magazines (percent) | 48.0 | 37.4* |
| Regular readership of news or political magazines (percent) | 48.4 | 42.7 |

* Difference between Subscriber and Nonsubscriber samples is significant at the .05 level, one-tailed test.

on the other hand, does not seem to be related to cable subscription. Those with a high school degree or less formal schooling are more likely to subscribe to cable than those with more formal education, and Black respondents are more likely to subscribe than White respondents. Persons higher in income are more likely to be cable subscribers than persons in households with under $20,000 annual income.

In Table 14.8, comparisons are shown between the media habits of subscribers and nonsubscribers. Data are taken from the 1981-1984 studies, although only measures that are unique to the designated study are shown. In 1981, respondents were asked about their use of some of the content of television, and, as expected, subscribers report higher levels of use of each program type than nonsubscribers. Subscribers report higher levels of use of movies (the young subscribers watch more than the old subscribers, and subscribers with less formal education watch more than higher educated subscribers), sports (the males watch more than the females), and religious programs (the old watch more than the young). Subscribers report higher levels of viewing of some type of news program in the 1981 survey, although not in the 1982 survey where specific local and national news programs are mentioned. Cable subscribers at that time had access to scrolling printed news displays (i.e., continuous textual reports rotating on a fixed schedule) whereas nonsubscribers did not. It may have been this headline service that accounted for the 1981 differences. (These services were replaced in the early 1980s by traditional news programming.)

Cable subscribers, as was shown in Table 14.6, are heavier users of newspapers than nonsubscribers. There is evidence as well that subscribers are high in use of other print media, as the bottom of Table 14.8 indicates. The 1982 survey showed, however, that radio listening did not vary between subscribers and nonsubscribers, a finding replicated in the 1983 survey as well, but in conflict with earlier work (Becker, et al., 1983).

The 1983 survey contained a question designed to determine what role, if any, television played in social entertainment in the home involving people not a part of that household. Respondents were asked to indicate the last time friends came to the house of the respondent and the respondent and friends "sat around and watched something on television, such as a movie or sporting event." Table 14.9 shows that cable subscribers are more likely to report having watched television in the home with friends within the last month than nonsubscribers.

Table 14.9 shows data for another item, this one included on the 1986 survey, on the social context of viewing television. As can be seen here, respondents with cable are somewhat less likely to report viewing television alone than are respondents with no cable service (Z=1.63; a Z of 1.65 is required for statistical signficance at the .05 level, one-tailed test). This finding is consistent with an earlier report by Kahan (1983) that cable brought household members out of their separate rooms and away from their separate television sets to the set in the home connected to cable. Data not tabled here, however, show that this effect is concentrated in households without children and those of single, as opposed to married adults. The level of viewing alone is 41.4% for single respondents with cable, compared with a significantly different 56.6% for single respondents without cable. So it may be as much a case of singles inviting others into their homes to watch cable as anything else. As shown in Table 14.9, cable subscribers are more likely

TABLE 14.9

Social Context of Viewing Television: Columbus, Ohio

|  | Cable | No Cable |
|---|---|---|
| 1983 Sample (N) | (261) | (262) |
| Watched television at own mome with friends within last month | 55.6% | 43.9%* |
| Watched television at own home with friends less frequently | 44.4 | 56.1 |
| Total | 100.0% | 100.0% |
| 1986 Sample (N) | (302) | (296) |
| Mostly view alone | 27.0% | 33.1% |
| Mostly view with others | 61.0 | 54.4 |
| Both | 12.0 | 10.8 |
| Don't know | 0.0 | 1.7 |
| Total | 100.0% | 100.0% |

* Difference between Subscriber and Nonsubscriber samples is significant at the .05 level, one-tailed test.

to report watching television with friends within the last month than are persons without cable television.

Items were included in both the 1982 and 1983 surveys to determine if cable subscribers and nonsubscribers have different needs, reflected in different program preferences. In the 1982 study, respondents were asked how important it was to them that television provided various kinds of programming, such as that for children, for teenagers, and for entertainment and relaxation. The relationships were slight and below traditional significance levels, and the data are not tabled here. They did suggest, however, that those people wanting programming for children and teenagers as well as programs for their own entertainment and relaxation were more likely to be cable subscribers than persons not finding these program choices important.

In the 1983 instrument, all respondents were asked a series of questions about their television program preferences. First, the interviewers asked for favorite programs, then for programs that the respondent would like to see more of on television, and finally, for programs that the respondent would like to see less of on television. Table 14.10 provides a summary of these data, indicating that subscribers are more likely to list movies and sports as preferred programs than nonsubscribers and less likely to list news and documentaries. In general, the data are consistent with those gathered in 1982. There are no striking differences between subscribers and nonsubscribers in terms of what programs they want to have shown more frequently on television. Cable subscribers are more likely than nonsubscribers to list violent programs, police programs, or detective programs as those to be eliminated. Cable carries many movies that fit such a classification.

The 1981 and 1982 surveys contained questions about the attitudes that respondents have toward issues confronting television. Data not tabled here show that subscribers are more likely to be favorable toward the banter and glamour associated with much local news programming in the U.S. (nicknamed "Happy Talk" news), be less supportive of government censorship of adult programming on cable, and be less likely to think that there is too much sexually explicit material on television.

In the 1984 sample, questions were posed about respondent attitudes toward government and technology in an attempt to determine if cable subscription was associated with a specific attitudinal cluster. In general, there were few differences. Subscribers were slightly (and statistically significantly) more likely to think that government keeps too many records on computer files, but slightly less likely than nonsubscribers to think that interactive cable of the sort represented by Warner's Qube is a threat to privacy. Interestingly enough, Qube subscribers are slightly less likely to be concerned about government and business computer records than subscribers to the other cable systems and slightly less likely to see interactive cable as a threat to privacy. The question on interactive cable mentioned Qube by name as a type of service that allows cable operators to "know when people are watching television and just what they are watching." Experience with the system certainly didn't lead subscribers to Qube to become more concerned about the privacy issue.

The Columbus survey instruments in 1983 and 1984 contained questions to measure respondent interest in videotext services. If cable subscription were simply an index of willingness to participate in innovation, subscription would be correlated with interest in videotext. On the other hand, if cable subscription were an indicant of a disinterest in the kinds of information dominant in videotext services, it would be negatively correlated with interest in videotext. An index of interest in videotext services was created by summing the number out of five (1983) or seven (1984) listed interactive services in which the respondent reported an interest. The lists included home banking and home shopping as well as news and encyclopedic services.

Table 14.11 shows that persons subscribing to cable television do not show significantly higher levels of interest in videotext than persons not subscribing to cable. But among those with cable, subscription to pay channels is associated with higher levels of interest, at least where the 1984 data are concerned. Data not shown here on the amount paid for cable services monthly are consistent with this find-

TABLE 14.10

TV Content Preferences by Cable Subscription: Columbus, Ohio

|  | Cable | No Cable |
|---|---|---|
| 1983 Sample (N) | (261) | (262) |
| Favorite programs (percent listing) | | |
| Movies | 34.5 | 17.6* |
| News/documentaries | 21.5 | 29.0* |
| Sports | 29.1 | 17.9* |
| Comedy/situation comedies | 25.2 | 21.4 |
| Programs would like increased (percent listing) | | |
| Movies | 12.3 | 8.4 |
| Educational | 8.4 | 11.8 |
| News/documentaries | 6.5 | 10.3 |
| Programs would like decreased (percent listing) | | |
| Comedies/situation comedies | 19.2 | 24.0 |
| Violent/detective/police | 26.4 | 15.6* |
| Soaps | 14.9 | 15.6 |

* Difference between Subscriber and Nonsubscriber samples is significant at the .05 level, one-tailed test. Multiple responses were coded, so categories are independent.

TABLE 14.11

Interest in Videotext by Use of New Media: Columbus, Ohio

|  | 1983 | | | 1984 | | |
|---|---|---|---|---|---|---|
|  | Mean | sd | (N) | Mean | sd | (N) |
| Subscribe to cable | | | | | | |
| Yes | 2.58 | 1.62 | (261) | 3.37 | 2.23 | (328) |
| No | 2.49 | 1.70 | (262) | 3.28 | 2.28 | (326) |
| Have pay channels | | | | | | |
| Yes | 2.10 | 1.32 | (162) | 3.60 | 2.19 | (210) |
| No | 1.89 | 1.33 | (95) | 2.95* | 2.25 | (118) |
| Have video/computer games | | | | | | |
| Yes | 2.93 | 1.48 | (115) | 3.95 | 2.06 | (215) |
| No | 2.43* | 1.69 | (407) | 3.02* | 2.28 | (439) |
| Have tape/disk player | | | | | | |
| Yes | 2.82 | 1.65 | (33) | 3.87 | 2.33 | (82) |
| No | 2.52 | 1.66 | (489) | 3.25* | 2.23 | (572) |
| Have home computer | | | | | | |
| Yes | 3.15 | 1.42 | (34) | 3.98 | 2.00 | (114) |
| No | 2.50 | 1.67 | (488) | 3.19* | 2.28 | (534) |

* Difference within the sample is significant at the .05 level, one-tailed test.

ing. The individuals who pay $20 or more per month for cable services are more interested in videotext than those who do not. The individuals with video disk players or cassette recorders are more interested in videotext services than those who do not have access to these devices. Interest in videotext, it seems, is predicted by current spending on electronics equipment, not merely subscription to cable. Cable subscribers overall are no less interested than their counterparts without cable, but the cable subscribers already spending a large amount of money for cable are more likely to be interested in videotext than the cable subscribers making a lesser investment.

The preceding analyses have focused on what appear to be two distinct groups of people, one subscribing to cable and the other not. These groups differ demographically and in terms of such things as television program preferences. It is quite possible that these groups have simply evaluated television and cable specifically in different ways. The analyses that follow focus specifically on the decision to either reject or accept cable services. They also seek to understand what kinds of evaluations users and nonusers make of cable and television in general.

Table 14.5 showed that there was a large number of persons in each of the Columbus samples not receiving cable and that that number was relatively stable across time. Data not tabled here show that the number of persons who had tried cable but not continued service indeed increased rather dramatically in Columbus during the period of study. In fact, the number of people who were not cable subscribers but who had had experience with cable increased from just under 30% in 1984 to just under 40% in 1986. In other words, the situation in 1986 was that half of the household heads had cable, just under 20% had cable at one time but did not have it in 1986, and just over 30% never had any cable experience despite its availability in the market for several years. Whereas the first of these figures (for penetration) was stable, the last two were not, as persons experimented with cable and found that it wasn't satisfactory for them. The stability in the first figure seems to have been maintained because of this experimentation, allowing those who gave up cable for whatever reason to be replaced by new subscribers.

In 1982 and 1983, those persons not subscribing to cable were asked to provide their reasons for that decision. Over one fourth of those surveyed in each of these years had subscribed to cable at one time. The cost of cable was the most pronounced reason for not subscribing in both years, followed by two responses suggesting that, for some respondents, television was not very important or provided sufficient materials without cable. Only a small percentage of respondents indicated that they did not subscribe to cable because they did not like the kinds of programming offered. The unavailability of cable was a factor for not subscribing for nearly 20% of the 1982 respondents but less than 8% of 1983 respondents.

TABLE 14.12

Reasons for Cancelling Cable: 1986 Columbus, Ohio

| Reason | Percent of Former Subscribers |
|---|---|
| Cost | 29.5 |
| Dislike content | 23.2 |
| Moved | 23.2 |
| Poor service | 12.5 |
| Not enough time to use | 7.1 |
| Used it too much | 4.5 |
| Purchased VCR | 2.7 |
| Purchased satellite dish | 1.8 |
| (N) | (112) |

Note: Multiple responses were accepted and coded.

Respondents to the 1986 survey who were not at that time cable subscribers but who had been subscribers at one time were asked why they had discontinued service. Multiple responses were allowed. Table 14.12 shows that cost was the dominant factor for cancelling service and was cited by just under 30% of the respondents. Dissatisfaction with the content of cable was a close second, with just under a quarter of the respondents listing it. The same number of respondents indicated that a move, perhaps from one dwelling to another in the same market or from one market to another, had caused the disruption. But it is important to recognize that they had not resubscribed after the move, indicating some sort of dissatisfaction nonetheless. Service complaints were cited by 12%; 7% said they just didn't have enough time to watch cable so they thought it wasn't worthwhile to continue the service. And just under 5% said that they discontinued because they were using it too much and wanted to lessen the temptation. Two alternatives to cable—purchase of a videocassette recorder or a satellite dish—were not often listed. In fact, only three persons listed a VCR and two listed a satellite dish as a reason for cancelling.

The 1986 survey also included a number of questions on subscriber evaluations of cable and television in general. As Table 14.13 shows, satisfaction with cable in 1986 was quite high among current subscribers. Respondents were asked: "Some people say they generally have been satisfied with what is on cable television, while others say it hasn't really provided the kinds of programs they wanted. Which of these comes closes to how you feel?" Two thirds of the cable subscribers chose the first option of satisfaction. As Table 14.13 indicates, there was no relationship between length of time of subscription to cable and level of satisfaction. That is to say, there was no evidence that dissatisfaction continued to

TABLE 14.13

Satisfaction with Cable: Columbus, Ohio, 1986

| | | Length of Subscription | | |
|---|---|---|---|---|
| Percent | Total | Under 3 Yrs. | 3,4 Yrs. | 5+ Yrs. |
| Satisfied | 66.4 | 66.7 | 66.7 | 67.0 |
| Not satisfied | 27.9 | 28.1 | 29.2 | 27.5 |
| Don't know | 5.6 | 5.3 | 4.2 | 5.5 |
| (N) | (302) | (114) | (72) | (109) |

grow as the respondents' experiences with cable continued. It may have been, however, that the individuals who became dissatisfied simply already had discontinued their subscription before 5 years of service.

One way of determining how fully integrated cable was into the perspective of the cable subscriber was to ask respondents with cable to indicate how many channels of television they would receive if they were to discontinue their cable service. The correct answer was seven, if the respondent could receive the low powered television service (which many in 1986 could), or six if both independents were receivable (as they would have been in most cases), or five if only one of the independents were receivable. When all three numbers or responses are treated as correct answers, just under 45% of the cable subscribers were able to indicate the correct numbers of channels they would receive without the cable service. The majority of respondents (55%) gave an incorrect answer, most of them underestimating the number of channels they would receive without cable.

The evidence presented in Table 14.6 was that cable households watched more television (particularly on weekends) than noncable households, though it wasn't clear that cable itself brought about the increased use of the medium. From the perspective of a large number of the household heads surveyed in 1986, however, subscription to cable had increased their use of television. Respondents with cable in the 1986 survey were simply asked to indicate if they thought they were watching more television at the time of the survey than before they subscribed to cable, less television, or about the same amount. Just over 46% said they were watching more television, just under 43% said there had been no change in the amount of their television viewing, 9% said they were watching less television after cable, and 2% didn't have an answer to the question. Differences between the persons who have been subscribing for less than 3 years, those subscribing for 3 or 4 years, and those subscribing for 5 or more years were small and rather inconsistent.

Cable subscribers, consistent with these data, were more likely to report that they expected to watch television on the night after the survey, as indicated in Table 14.14. Three quarters of the cable subscribers indicated that that was their plan, whereas just under 65% of the nonsubscribers gave that response. Among those

TABLE 14.14

Tomorrow Viewing Plans, Descriptions of TV: Columbus, Ohio, 1986

|  | Cable % | No Cable % |
|---|---|---|
| Tomorrow viewing plans |  |  |
| Watch | 75.5 | 64.5* |
| Not watch TV | 24.5 | 35.5 |
|  |  |  |
| Among planned watchers** |  |  |
| Plan to watch |  |  |
| specific program | 41.7 | 38.7 |
| No specific program |  |  |
| plans | 58.3 | 61.3 |
|  |  |  |
| Consider TV |  |  |
| Exciting | 36.5 | 31.1 |
| Not exciting | 63.5 | 68.9 |
|  |  |  |
| Imaginative | 44.2 | 44.4 |
| Not imaginative | 55.8 | 55.6 |
|  |  |  |
| Having lots of |  |  |
| variety | 44.2 | 29.0* |
| Lacking variety | 55.8 | 71.0 |
|  |  |  |
| (N) | (302) | (296) |

* Difference between Subscriber and Nonsubscriber samples is significant at the .05 level, one-tailed test.
** Subgroups sizes for watchers are 228 (Cable) and 191 (No Cable)

who planned to watch, nearly equal percentages actually stated a specific program or program type when asked what they would watch. There was no evidence, from this question, that cable subscribers were any more or less directed toward specific programs than nonsubscribers. There is no evidence, then, that cable subscribers engage more in unmotivated general television watching, as opposed to specific program viewing, than do noncable subscribers.

There also is no evidence that cable subscribers find television more exciting or more imaginative than noncable subscribers, as additional data in Table 14.14 show. Subscribers to cable did, on the other hand, find television to offer more variety. For each of these questions, respondents to the survey were asked which of two words better describes most of what is on television. Approximately a third of the cable subscribers and a third of the nonsubscribers selected "exciting" rather than "dull" as descriptive of television. Among subscribers, 44.2% selected "imaginative" rather than "unimaginative" as descriptive of television; among nonsubscribers, the figure was a nearly identical 44.4%. Of the cable subscribers, 44.2%

TABLE 14.15

What Subscribers Like About Cable: Columbus, Ohio, 1986

| Response | Percent |
|----------|---------|
| Variety | 46.5 |
| Movies | 25.2 |
| Sports | 9.6 |
| News | 7.6 |
| Better reception | 4.7 |
| Children's Programs | 4.0 |
| (N) | (302) |

Note: Multiple responses were accepted and coded.

said television offers lots of variety rather than providing programming that is pretty much all the same, whereas 29.2% of the noncable household heads said television offers lots of variety.

This theme of variety is in evidence in Table 14.15 as well, which shows responses to an open-ended question asking cable subscribers what it is that they like best about cable. Variety is the dominant response among the multiple-coded options. All of the other categories except one, better reception, also reflect a variety theme. Yet, when subscribers were asked how cable television could be improved, a call for more variety was again the dominant category. Interestingly, however, none of the responses could be interpreted as calling for different kinds of services, indicating that cable's promise of at least some variety had been fulfilled, for the most part at least, from the perspective of the subscribers.

In sum, the data reviewed in this section, consistent with those reviewed in the trend analysis, show that there are differences between those persons who subscribe to cable and those who do not. There are demographic differences and there are differences in the ways that the media, particularly television, are used and evaluated. Cable subscribers are heavy users of television, including television news and various forms of entertainment. But they are also users of the print media.

Clearly, television is a prominent part of the leisure environment of the cable subscriber. They entertain around it, viewing in a social context. They prefer entertainment fare to news and documentaries and do seem to take a more relaxed view of television content generally and television news in particular than those who do not subscribe.

In general, the data reviewed here suggest that those persons with cable have found that it has met their needs. There was no evidence of a decrease in subscription to the expensive services of cable. Satisfaction was quite high and about the same for those just beginning the service as for those who had had more experience with cable. There was little evidence that cable subscribers even were aware of or interested in alternatives to cable. In fact, alternatives to cable, such as VCRs, were embraced more readily by cable subscribers than nonsubscribers.

Persons who had had cable the longest were no less likely than the new subscribers to feel that cable had had impact on their use of television. Cable subscribers were heavy television users, but they were just as likely to be motivated in their use of television as nonsubscribers. Cable subscribers were different from nonsubscribers in terms of perceptions of the variety offered by television, but no different in terms of other evaluations of television. In short, households with cable and those without seem to differ to a large degree because they have different feelings about and make different uses of television itself and the ability of cable to make television more worthwhile for them.

No attempt has been made here to eliminate through statistical control the effects of the demographic differences between cable subscribers and nonsubscribers on the correlations between cable subscription and other examined variables. Such social classifications as marital status and education are viewed here as shaping factors, directing a variety of media and leisure activities, including the decision to subscribe to cable television. Because these demographic differences temporally precede the decision to subscribe to cable, it isn't meaningful to partial out these background factors in examining the relationship between cable subscription and subsequent behaviors. The interest here is in the total impact of subscription, including that part due to the impact of demographics on the decision to subscribe. The independent effects of these demographic factors on subsequent behaviors also is not of prime concern.

It is quite another issue to raise questions about the generalizability of findings by asking if an established pattern or finding holds within all subgroups or is concentrated in only some of them. Earlier in this chapter, for example, length of subscription to cable was used to look for differences in such things as satisfaction with cable for those with varying degrees of experience with the service.

Perhaps more important is the question of any differential effects and evaluations of cable by members of different social strata, best represented in the U.S. situation by age of respondent, educational level and household income. As indicated at the beginning of this section, cable does appeal more to the less well educated than to the better educated. Those low in income (who are not always low in education in the U.S.) are less likely to subscribe to cable than those with higher incomes. Cable appeals equally to the young and the old, although cable does appeal more to those with children in the home than those without. While it isn't practical to review all of the preceding findings for members of these different strata, some of the more important findings do deserve at least brief attention.

Cable in the U.S. is not a free medium. As Table 14.5 indicated, just under a quarter of the subscribers to cable in the Columbus sample in 1986 were spending $30 or more per month for the service. That kind of an expenditure would seem to be possible for only certain segments of the community. In fact, low income respondents did report slightly lower expenditures for cable than those high in income, and they were less likely to subscribe to premium services, which result in a higher bill. An examination of the reasons given for cancelling cable (Table 14.12) by income level, however, shows that those low in income were no more likely than those high in income to give cost as a reason for discontinuing the service. It seems, in fact, that the costs of cable are an issue only with those very low in income. Those in the middle or higher brackets find a way to pay for the service if it is viewed as important to them.

Cable takes on more value to an adult if there are children in the household who can take advantage of it. In 1985, for example, 58.3% of the adults living with children under 18 subscribed to cable, compared with 44.8% of those with no children in the home. Those cable homes with children also were more likely to be the ones with premium cable services. Overall, those under 40 years in age were more likely to have these premium services than those 40 years or older. Among those who had once had it but cancelled it, however, cost was more likely to be a reason for the young than the old. Complaints about content of cable, mentioned by just under a quarter of those who cancelled cable (Table 14.12), were mentioned equally by those with and without children, by the young and the old, and, in fact, by those low and high in both education and income. Satisfaction with cable among subscribers also was equal for the young and the old, those with and without children, those low and high in education, and those low and high in income.

The evidence reviewed here is that cable has had some impact on the amount of television viewed by subscribers. The national data (Table 14.2) suggest that it is predominantly in cable homes that television viewing has increased over time. The Columbus data show generally higher levels of television viewing, particularly on the weekends, for respondents from cable homes than for respondents without cable (Table 14.6). In the 1986 Columbus survey, cable subscribers were more likely to report plans to watch television the day following the interview than those not subscribing to cable (Table 14.14). Finally, nearly half of the cable subscribers in the 1986 survey reported that they had increased their television viewing since getting cable. But the evidence also is that this increased use of television as a result of cable has not been experienced equally by all users.

Overall, it seems, cable has had its strongest impact in terms of increased television time among those low in education. In 1986, for example, hours of weekday television viewing were the same for those high in education (at least some college experience) whether or not they had cable. For those lower in education, however, television viewing was at least slightly higher when cable was present. The difference was even more pronounced for weekend television viewing time. Here, there was a 3-hour gap between the amount of viewing of television for those with and without cable in the lower education group. For those high in education, cable subscribers reported only 1 hour more viewing than those without cable. The less well educated overall watched more television than the better educated.

Consistent with these findings for hours of television viewing, those respondents low in education and with cable were more likely to report plans to view television the night following the 1986 survey than were any of the other respondents. In fact, the other respondents did not differ in this regard. Specifically, just under 85% of the cable respondents without college were likely to say television viewing was in their plans for the following night, whereas the figure was 67% for those with cable but some experience in college, 67% for those without cable and low in education, and 63% for those without cable and high in education.

Among cable subscribers, however, education is not associated with a recognition that cable has increased use of television. Of those low in education, 45% said cable had increased their use of television. Of those high in formal education, 48% gave that response. It seems that the reality is not matched by a recognition of the effect. The evidence is that cable has not led to great increases in use of television. But those increases do seem to be more pronounced among those low in education, although the effect appears not to be recognized.


## CONCLUSIONS

The findings about cable presented here can be summarized via three generalizations. First, there is no evidence of dramatic change in the lives of Americans resulting from the introduction of cable. Second, cable has been found useful by a group of people for whom television is an important part of their lives. Finally, cable has altered the way in which television itself is viewed.

These are, of course, generalizations. They also are drawn from incomplete data. Yet a case has been made here for each. There is, for example, no convincing evidence on a national basis or in the Columbus data that the introduction of cable has led people to cancel their newspaper subscriptions, stop reading magazines, or turn off their radios. The evidence that cable has adversely affected movie attendance even is contradictory. The case can be made as convincingly that cable has helped the movie industry as much as it has hurt it.

Nonetheless, cable is an important part of the lives of many people. Television itself is a more important leisure activity for subscribers than nonsubscribers. They form something of a subgroup, relying more heavily on the media, and particularly television, for rest and relaxation. Demographically, of course, they are a group constrained by family, children and home ownership. Cable seems to have provided this group of people with the means of developing and expanding use of and dependence on television for escape from work and the routines of life.

Cable also appears to be a social vehicle. It brings family members together to watch programs at the set connected to cable. Moreover, it appears to be a social vehicle for singles, with nonmarried persons with cable watching programming with others more than do nonmarried persons without cable.

The audience assessment of cable is not that of the media critic. The argument that cable has not delivered on its original promises seems irrelevant to the half of the population that subscribes. Users appear to have already integrated cable into their overall definition of television, and they are willing to pay for the increased choice that cable offers. They appear to have found it to be an adequate means to satisfy some of their leisure and entertainment needs. They are generally satisfied with its content or variety of programming and generally willing to pay additional fees for premium channels or more choice.

The evidence that cable has resulted in increased use of television is a bit mixed. Many of the subscribers themselves, however, think that cable has increased their use of the medium. Logic seems to be on their side. Yet so is the argument that these were the people who always used a lot of television and cable has merely allowed an expansion—and not an overly great one—in use of the medium. The evidence is that the increased use of television as a result of cable is most pronounced among those low in education.

That cable has altered the kinds of television watched is rather clear. The viewing of materials from the three main broadcast networks has been cut in cable homes as other, cable-delivered services have been judged more valuable. Cable households watch more of what cable delivers, such as movies and sports. But they also watch news, and don't seem to have necessarily abandoned the network versions of this type of programming, at least not in the early evening. Cable has freed the subscriber from the constraints of network programming. The cable subscriber can get national news, weather, and sports summaries throughout the day on specialty channels and is not dependent on network scheduling for these materials. The evidence of a slight drop in late night, network-affiliated news programming may reflect the exercising of this choice.

It is worth noting that there has been a decline in the number of hours of household viewing of network programming even in housholds without cable. These noncable households, however, show an increase in the viewing of broadcast signals from stations not affiliated with the networks. The point is that there is evidence of modification of viewing behavior resulting from the increases in programming choices, whether delivered by cable or, in this case, over-the-air non-network-affiliated stations.

It is wrong to conclude that cable has had no effects, just as it wrong to conclude that the effects are dramatic in their social consequences. Once again, the conclusion seems to be that the effects are greatest where the audience is receptive to the media delivering them.

Harris (1987), in a recent summary of research findings from the 1980s, portrayed Americans as a people increasingly lacking time for rest and relaxation. Since 1973, the number of hours worked by Americans, according to Harris, has increased by 20%, whereas the amount of leisure time available to the average person has dropped by 32%. Between 1980 and 1985, available leisure hours dropped from 19.2 to 17.1 hours per week. The number of hours worked per week increased from 46.9 hours in 1980 to 48.8 hours in 1985. The people most squeezed for leisure time are small business people, professionals, those with incomes of $50,000 or more per year, and women.

Fifty-six percent of adult women work outside the home, and 71% of those not so employed wish that they were. Personal development and experience, not finances, are the motivation. In 41% of the households in the U.S., both the husband and the wife are engaged in work outside the home. Half of those households are home to children under the age of 18. These are changes in the ways Americans live their lives. And they have had impact on many things. On any given day, more than one in three American adults will eat at least one meal away from home. Eleven percent buy take-away food on any given day. By 1985, 45% of U.S. homes had a microwave oven, and, on any given day, 12% bought food for use in the microwave. When doing their grocery shopping, over half of the consumers buy food prepared for immediate consumption at home.

The impact of lifestyle changes on leisure time is quite dramatic. People must consider carefully how to allocate their leisure time. But, according to Harris, the decisions on time commitment are being made not in terms of cost of leisure activities but on the basis of the most desirable way to spend scarce hours. In the future, Harris says, if people want to spend time on something badly enough, they will be likely to find the money to do it. Up to now, the assumption has been that if people had the money to do something and wanted to commit to it, they would find the time.

The evidence assembled here is that money is not the real issue with such things as cable and the VCR. It is a matter of the appeal of the service. If there is an interest in the service, people are willing to spend. There is little evidence that the service has lured people without that initial interest. And there is little evidence that those who decided to increase their television offerings then abandoned their other habits or activities. The appeal of these services seems to be that they make what the people were already doing—watching television—a more enjoyable experience. And they did that *without* necessarily requiring much more time.

In a little more than a decade, nearly half of American homes have subscribed to cable, and more than a third have purchased at least one VCR. Cable and the VCR have blended into the environment with little apparent disruption to leisure and information habits. The potential for dramatic change nonetheless remains. In the late 1980s and beyond, cable operators may find the content to deliver on some of those early promises. The battle for the finite commodity of audience time is not over.

## NOTE

[1] These figures are drawn from the U.S. Bureau of the Census (1986), excepting the number of radio stations, taken from *Television and Cable Factbook 1986*, and the number of theaters, taken from Gertner (1987).

## REFERENCES

Agostino, D., & Zenaty, J. (1980). *Home VCR owners' use of television and public television: Viewing, recording & playback*. Washington, DC: Office of Communication Research, Corporation for Public Broadcasting.

Aumente, J. (1987). *New electronic pathways*. Beverly Hills: Sage.

Baldwin, T., & McVoy, S.D. (1983). *Cable Communications*. Englewood Cliffs, NJ: Prentice-Hall.

Becker, L. B. (1987). A decade of research on interactive cable. In W. Dutton, J. Blumler, & K. Kraemer (Eds.), *Wired cities: Shaping the future of communications* (pp. 102-123). Boston, MA: G. K. Hall and Co.

Becker, L. B., & Creedon, P. J. (1986). Cable television in the United States: Content and consequences. *Rundfunk und Fernsehen, 34*, 387-397.

Becker, L. B., Dunwoody, S., & Rafaeli, S. (1983). Cable's impact on use of other news media. *Journal of Broadcasting, 27*, 127-140.

Bolton, T. (1983). Perceptual factors that influence the adoption of videotex technology. *Journal of Broadcasting, 27*, 241-253.

Bortz, P. I., Wyche, M. C., & Trautman, J. M. (1986). *Great expectations: A television manager's guide to the future*. Washington, DC: National Association of Broadcasters.

Bower, R. T. (1985). *The changing television audience in America.* New York: Columbia University Press.

Butler, J. K., & Kent, K. E. (1983). Potential impact of videotext on newspapers. *Newspaper Research Journal, 5*, 3-12.

Carey, J. (1982). Videotex: The past as prologue. *Journal of Communication, 32* (2), 80-87.

Carey, J., & Moss, M. L. (1985). The diffusion of new telecommunication technologies. *Telecommunications Policy, 9*, 145-158.

Davidge, C. (1987). America's talk-back television experiment: Qube. In W. Dutton, J. Blumler, & K. Kraemer (Eds.), *Wired cities: Shaping the future of communications* (pp. 75-101). Boston, MA: G.K. Hall and Co.

Dyer, J. A., & Hill. D. B. (1981). Extent of diversion to newscasts from distant stations by cable viewers. *Journalism Quarterly, 58*, 552-555.

Elton, M., & Carey, J. (1983). Computerizing information: Consumer reactions to teletext. *Journal of Communication, 33* (1), 162-173.

Elton, M., & Carey, J. (1984). Teletext for public information: Laboratory and field studies. In J. Johnston (Ed.), *Evaluating the new information technologies* (pp. 23-41). San Francisco: Jossey-Bass.

Ettema, J. S. (1983, November). *Self-reported vs. system-monitored uses of videotex.* Paper presented at the meeting of the Midwest Association for Public Opinion Research, Chicago.

Gertner, R. (Ed.). (1987). *International motion picture almanac* (58th ed.). New York: Quigley.

Guback, T. H. (1982). Die neuen Medien und die Zukunft der Filmtheather in den USA [The new media and the future of film theaters in the USA]. *Media Perspektiven*, (11), 166-177.

Guback, T. H. (1987). The evolution of the motion picture theater business in the 1980s. *Journal of Communication, 37* (2), 60-77.

Harris, L. (1987). *Inside America.* New York: Vantage Books.

Heeter, C., & Baldwin, T. F. (1984, November). *Movies and news on cable: Patterns of use.* Paper presented at the meeting of the Midwest Association for Public Opinion Research, Chicago.

Heeter, C., & Greenberg, B. (1985). Cable and program choice. In D. Zillmann & J. Bryant (Eds.), *Selective exposure to communication* (pp. 203-224). Hillsdale, NJ: Lawrence Erlbaum Associates.

Heikkinen, K. J., & Reese, S. D. (1986). Newspaper readers and a new information medium: Information need and channel orientation as predictors of videotex adoption. *Communication Research, 13*, 19-35.

Henke, L. L., & Donohue, T. R. (1986). Teletext viewing habits and preferences. *Journalism Quarterly, 63*, 542-545, 553.

Kahan, H. (1983). *The cable subscriber speaks: Channels, choice or chaos.* Unpublished paper. Advertising Research Foundation.

Kaplan, S. J. (1978). The impact of cable television services on the use of competing media. *Journal of Broadcasting, 22,* 155-165.

Levy, M. R. (1980). Home video recorders: A user survey. *Journal of Communication, 30* (4), 23-27.

Levy, M. R. (1987). Some problems of VCR research. *American Behavioral Scientist, 30,* 461-470.

Mayer, I., & Sweeting, P. (1986). Videocassettes: 24,000 shops on Main Street. *Channels 1986 Field Guide,* p. 76.

Nasser, H. E., & Guy, P. (1987, June 17). USA TODAY posts profit 6 months early. *USA TODAY.* p. B1.

Neuman, W. R., & de Sola Pool, I. (1986). The flow of communications into the home. In S. J. Ball-Rokeach & M. G. Cantor (Eds.), *Media, audience, and social structure* (pp. 71-86). Beverly Hills: Sage.

Neuman, W. R. (in press). *The future of the mass audience.* Cambridge: Harvard University Press.

O'Donnell, F. (1986, March). No frills cable. *Channels,* p. 47.

Paisley, W. (1983). Computerizing information: Lessons of a videotext trial. *Journal of Communication, 33* (1), 153-161.

Papazian, E. (Ed.). (1986). *TV dimensions '86.* New York: Media Dynamics Inc.

Papazian, E. (Ed.). (1987). *TV dimensions '87.* New York: Media Dynamics Inc.

Reese, S. D., Shoemaker, P. J., & Danielson, W. A. (1986). Social correlates of public attitudes toward new communication technologies. *Journalism Quarterly, 63,* 675-682, 692.

Robinson, J. P., & Jeffres, L. W. (1978, November). *Cable television: Who subscribes and what happens.* Paper presented at the meeting of the Midwest Association for Public Opinion Research, Chicago.

Rubin, A. M., & Bantz, C. R. (1987). Utility of videocassette recorders. *American Behavioral Scientist, 30,* 471-485.

Siemicki, M., Atkin, D., Greenberg, B., & Baldwin, T. (1986). Nationally distributed children's shows: What cable TV contributes. *Journalism Quarterly, 63,* 710-18, 734.

Sparkes, V. M. (1983). Public perception of and reaction to multi-channel cable television service. *Journal of Broadcasting, 27,* 163-175.

Sparkes, V. M. (1984, April). *The half wired nation: Cable television's fifty-five percent barrier.* Paper presented at the meeting of the Broadcast Education Association, Las Vegas, NV.

*Television and cable factbook 1986.* (1986). Washington, DC: Television Digest Inc.

Tunstall, J. (1986). *Communications deregulation: The unleashing of America's communications industry*. New York: Basil Blackwell.

U.S. Bureau of the Census. (1986). *Statistical abstract of the United States: 1987*. Washington, DC: U.S. Government Printing Office.

Webster, J. G. (1986). Audience behavior in the new media environment. *Journal of Communication, 36* (3), 77-91.

Williams, F. (1987). *Technology and communication behavior*. Belmont, CA: Wadsworth.

# 15

# United States: Changing Perceptions of Television

**Vernone M. Sparkes**
*Syracuse University*
**Jeffrey P. Delbel**
*Cayuga Community College*

It is arguable whether cable television should be considered "new technology," because the beginnings of this medium are tied in with the earliest days of broadcast television in the United States. It was because of delays in broadcast spectrum allocation that the earliest Community Antenna Television (CATV) systems were set up in 1949. The fact that this fledgling industry did not disappear once "free" broadcast television service became widely available is largely due to the fact that the technology kept changing to meet new market conditions. The technology is in fact still evolving and its potential is still unfolding. The steady expansion of channel capacity (close to 60 channels per coaxial cable by 1985), the increasing availability of satellite interconnection, the spread of computer-controlled digital interactivity, and the proliferation of not just video programming services but also data and information services together present a medium that is indeed new, as tomorrow's systems with high definition screens, stereo sound, video interactivity, and "smart" modems will be new.

The focus of this chapter is on behavioral changes associated with the spread of cable television service in the United States, as such had evolved in the period 1980 to 1986, a time of dramatic expansion of the industry. The primary basis of our observations is a broad data set collected in Syracuse, New York, a middle-sized television market with considerable demographic diversity. We offer what might be characterized as an in-depth site study with considerable generalizability.


## BACKGROUND

With the beginning of serious public discussion of cable television (Sloan Commission on Cable Communications, 1971; Smith, 1970) there appeared a rather steady stream of reports and studies seeking to broadly project the direction of technological and social change. Government- and foundation-sponsored studies dominated in the early to mid-1970s (Cabinet Committee on Cable Communications, 1974; Committee for Economic Development, 1975; Land, 1968; Mitre Corporation, 1972; National Science Foundation, 1976; New York State Senate, 1972; Tate, 1971) supplemented by discussions from other critical sources (Gerbner, Gross, & Melody, 1973; Scott, 1976; Steiner, 1972). Indicative of the attention stimulated by this emerging technology is the early interest from urban planners, in particular Kas Kalba [1], Mandelbaum (1972), and Dakin (1972).

Early planners and researchers seemed to assume that cable would have an effect on the overall media scenario similar to the effect that television had in the 1950s. Bogart's (1956) consolidation of early television studies indicated an increase (self-reported) in total time spent with mass media (from 3 hours 10 minutes to 4 hours 27 minutes). Television was also reported to decrease time with radio, books, magazines, and newspapers along with decreasing attendance at college sports events. Himmelweit, Oppenheim, and Vince (1958) provided similar reports on televisions's effect on English children. Here, a field experiment indicated some displacement of reading fiction along with other activities that were of little value to the child. Schramm, Lyle, and Parker (1961) provided evidence of television's displacement of movies and radio, and Steiner (1963) indicated a rise in television's perceived level of overall importance when compared to other media. Comstock, Chaffee, Katzman, McCombs, and Roberts (1978) could subsequently observe that "television's absorption of leisure time naturally occurs at the expense of other activities" (p. 8).

So it was logical to suppose that if cable were a major media innovation it would begin to displace at least broadcast television services and would intensify the effect that video services generally were having on other media and leisure activities. Further, whereas the development of commercial broadcast television was largely laissez faire, cable was being subjected to a fair amount of experimental manipulation for purposes of expanding its social utility (National Science Foundation, 1976).

From the perspective of 1987, many of these studies look naively optimistic about when and how the projected changes were to come about. There has not been a displacement of the printed newspaper, even though publishers are hedging their bets through continued experimentation with electronic text services. The emergence of a new electronic political system with instant referenda and electronic town hall meetings via two-way cable is still primarily a matter of speculation. Certainly, the anticipated demise of the commercial broadcast networks was simplistically premature at least. Finally, actual penetration of cable television has not reached the expected levels. Far from the 80% to 90% penetration projected for the end of the 1980s, it more likely will be around 60% (Sparkes, 1984).

The problem, however, does not necessarily lie with the content of the projections, but perhaps instead with the process of adoption and behavioral change assumed. Even if an economic recession and restrictive regulations had been anticipated, most forecasts still did not allow for the rather complex route by which such social changes come about.

By the end of 1987, cable television in the United States had evolved to the point were 50% of all television households had some level of cable service, with the average market penetration hovering around the 55% level. The normative system for 1987 is a one-way, 36-channel system with converters (receiving devices) in the homes addressable by the cable operators. These systems are filled with a fair degree of program diversity, but interactivity is still largely experimental. For a typical service, excluding pay or premium channels, the subscriber pays approximately $18 per month. The range of charges goes from as low as $5 for a 12-channel tier, to close to $50 per month when several pay or premium channels are added to the basic service.

## USEFUL CHANGE MODELS

Two behavioral models in particular have informed the research subsequently reported in this chapter—one drawn from the diffusion of innovation literature, and the other from work on consumer information processing.

Basic to diffusion theory and research is a concern with mapping the processes by which perceptions of innovations are formed and the relationship of these perceptions to behavioral change. This research has clustered around three emphases: adoption rate, adoption motivation, and adoption process. It is the analyses of the adoption process that offer the most helpful insights for studying public responses to cable television.

The notion that an innovation can change during diffusion is central to what Brown (1981) and others have labeled the "economic history" perspective. Not only the form of an innovation, but also the environment into which it is introduced can be modified throughout the life of an innovation. In what Rogers (1983) called reinvention, individual consumers experience the same innovation from unique perspectives and contexts. Further, early adopters are not always the true innovators, and their premature action often leads to "disenchanted discontinuance" (Rogers, 1983, p. 186). On the other hand, Brown suggests, late adopters might actually be very attuned to an innovation, waiting for specific improvements before making their move (Brown, 1981, p. 177).

Critical to intentions to adopt are perceptions by the target public of the attributes of an innovation. Rogers (1983) settled on a list of five dimensions that he believed were most important in evaluation by consumers. The *relative advantage* of the innovation will be weighed. The innovation's *compatibility* with existing factors such as other equipment, social values, or self-image will be judged. How *difficult* the innovation is perceived to be, or how complex and demanding of special learning it is, will be influential on adoption, as will the possibilities of *trial* without full commitment. And finally, the existence of *observable characteristics* will be important. (You cannot evaluate what you cannot see.)

Trialability and observability are clearly strong attributes of cable television, as attested to by the high subscriber turnover in the industry (called "churn"). Complexity of use could be a deterrent to subscription for some people, particularly the elderly. Finally, judgments about relative advantage over functionally equivalent sources of entertainment, news, and so on, will influence consumer willingness to redirect resources and attention.

Consumer information-processing models seek to plot how a potential customer sorts out the benefits and disadvantages of a new product or service like cable television. Several different selection rules can operate in consumer decision making, depending on the characteristics of the product and the individual making the decision. In the disjunctive rule, consumers choose an alternative simply because it does one thing very well, whereas, under the conjunctive rule, a choice is made because of no particularly bad reports on the product. The lexicographic decision rule involves choice based on one criterion that was the single most important for the decision maker, whereas the compensatory decision rule involves an aggregate of all individual category ratings (Hawkins, Best, & Coney, 1983, p. 527).

Consumer information-processing research has provided indications of which rules operate most frequently with which kinds of products. For example, a study by Reilly and Holman (1977) reported that lexicographic decision-making accounted for over 60% of consumer choices in automobiles, with compensatory decision-making accounting for 32%. How the consumer comes to the decision on cable television is a point of some speculation. Early researchers seemed to anticipate adoption on compensatory decision-making rules (based on the overall advantage of cable). However, the success of specialty channels (HBO, CNN, ESPN) may indicate that some lexicographic decision-making is operating either independently or as a major part of the total evaluation. (Cable provides more sports. I want more sports. I want cable.) To the extent that the lexicographic rule accounts for decisions to subscribe to cable, it may indicate that consumers have not seriously considered the total programming package before adoption. Experience with the total service, however, may lead to compensatory evaluations.

One additional aspect of consumer decision-making that is crucial to cable is the post purchase dissonance that may follow subscription. Following the initial novelty of cable, the consumer may begin to ask if it is used enough to warrant the expense, or if it is a sufficient improvement over the available broadcast service. With service products like cable television, the consumer has the opportunity to reevaluate purchase continuously.

For cable television in the United States, it seems clear, the current level of adoption/purchase has been arrived at in a very halting manner, with numerous false starts and even some stillborns. There have been some surprising spurts and breakthroughs. Indeed, we suggest that the development of cable television in the United States is best understood and therefore best studied as a process of *dynamic interaction amongst incremental changes on different fronts*— technological, economic, regulatory, and, of course, behavioral. The model in Fig. 15.1 seeks to express this process.

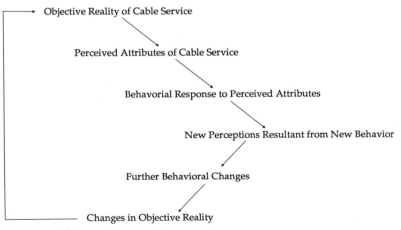

**FIG.15.1.** Model of development of cable television in the United States.

One current development in the United States illustrating this point is pay-per-view (PPV). Actually PPV cable is hardly new; it was offered in Columbus, Ohio, as early as 1975. But the service was not well received, and the industry abandoned PPV in the 1980s for the pay channel or premium channel arrangement offered by Home Box Office (HBO) and others. (Cable subscribers purchase a whole, distinct channel of offerings, usually movies, and usually without advertisements, on a flat-fee basis rather than per-program or per-view.)

So what changed that PPV should be regarded as a promising new frontier for cable operators in the late 1980s? First of all, addressable converter technology spread throughout the country at a steady pace, thus allowing convenient product control. Interestingly, this change itself was not triggered by a desire to develop PPV service, but rather the need to combat signal piracy. Second, upstream capability (from home to operator) was being made available by the telephone companies, providing many older systems with the capacity to process last minute or impulse orders of pay-per-view materials. Third, there has emerged a new type of competition for cable, the home videocassette recorder (VCR). And finally, both PPV and VCR services benefit from the fact that consumers have by now become more appreciative of greater program diversity and more accustomed to paying for home television service.

## METHODOLOGICAL CONSIDERATIONS

When we try to measure behavioral change in a shifting environment, some unique methodological problems arise, not the least of which is the matter of operationalization. We could ask people how they might respond to a hypothetical situation (self- projection) but it is clear that validity rests upon the respondent's accurate understanding of the proposed hypothetical scenario. In the area of new communications technology, such understanding cannot safely be assumed, a point insufficiently appreciated by some early studies (Hart, 1979; Mitre, 1972). Alternatively, we can ask people to reflect on changes that actual experience has brought about (self-reporting). However, this approach presupposes respondent ability to sort out the effect of a single variable existing within a complicated media environment, or assume a self-awareness of motivations for behavior that might not exist. Best of all would be direct observational measures, but such measures are often difficult to obtain.

A second methodological problem in this type of research is that of self-selection of subjects. In a field study, we must work from people's self-categorization, leaving us much of the time wondering whether differences between groups were caused by the independent variable or are simply correlates of it. If there is a difference in mean television viewing time between cable subscribers and nonsubscribers, do we conclude that subscribing to cable leads to increased viewing, or that heavy viewers are more likely to subscribe to cable television? The fact that the cable industry has experienced subscriber churn rates from 30% to 50% per year adds special weight to the self-selection problem, raising the prospect of shifting criteria and perceptions. There could also be unique interaction effects related to self-selection. This prospect is particularly important to the extent that adopters of a new service turn out to be demographically different from nonadopters.

Third, not only might a target medium like cable television itself be undergoing change, so might other fronts in the television field, including the spread of such alternative delivery technologies as the VCR, Direct Broadcast Satellite (DBS), and Multipoint Multichannel Distributions Systems (MMDS). Further, established services will be adjusting to better confront new competition. So whereas changes in cable television might affect only subscribers, changes in other areas could affect both subscribers and nonsubscribers. A change in frequency of movie theater attendance could be related to pay cable subscription, but it could also be related to VCR use, or even an improvement in broadcast television programming. To control for these other potential sources of variance, we must either have measures of all possible causes or find some other means of control, such as a noncabled community with similar characteristics to our test community.

Finally, there is the matter of measuring the change *process* itself. Time $X$ versus time $Y$ measures often assume a linearity of change that does not exist. Indeed, there could be many detours and trials along the way. A cable subscriber, for example, might actually drop the service and then resubscribe. Or, there might be a change from one level of service to another. Or, for that matter, what looks like the same behavior at times $X$ and $Y$ could actually be different (e.g., subscribing to cable for more movies, but keeping the subscription because of the quality of children's programming).

Further, there is the matter of public maturation. Trial and experience with a complex technology can lead to new perceptions and evaluations. Anticipated changes might not show up for several years, so even panel measures taken, say, during the first year or so of a cable system's operation might not show us much user change. It is simply too early for subscribers to make major adjustments in old habits.

## DATA BASES

The findings presented in this chapter came from several data bases. (See Fig. 15.2.) The primary set came from a 5-year panel study of a new, 36-channel system in

Syracuse, New York, involving two panels with two measures for each. This study measured media behavior and cable perceptions, beliefs, and evaluations. The first measure was taken just as the new system was beginning to hook up its first subscribers and an older system was dramatically upgrading its service.

The panel data have been augmented by several smaller studies done in the same market during the same time period. One series used company records to examine the nature of disconnections, looking at economic status, level and length of service, and type of dwelling. Another study investigated households in the middle income range ($15,000 to $30,000 annually) that were not cable subscribers. This study examined perceptions and levels of knowledge about cable. A third study, of cable subscribers, examined channel awareness and use and program selection methods.

Two additional data sets were also drawn upon. One is a two-wave panel study in the Boston, Massachusetts, area (hereafter called the Boston study), which also looked at the effects of cable subscription. The measures taken were patterned after the Syracuse panel study, with the first measure just prior to the start-up of the

| Study | Sample N | Field Date | Procedure |
|-------|----------|------------|-----------|
| **Syracuse Panel** | | | |
| Panel 1,T1 | 180 | 1979 | Telephone random |
| Panel 1,T2 | 117 | 1981 | Telephone random |
| Panel 2,T1 | 300 | 1982 | Telephone random |
| Panel 2,T2 | 220 | 1984 | Telephone random |
| **Subscriber Churn** | | | |
| Study 1 | 500 | 1981 | Random, company records |
| Study 2 | 500 | 1983 | Random, company records |
| **Nonsubscriber Study** | | | |
| | 250 | 1981 | In-house, random |
| **Cable Viewing Study** | | | |
| | 400 | 1984 | Telephone random |
| **PTV Study** | | | |
| | 575 | 1986 | Telephone random |
| **Boston Panel** | | | |
| Time 1 | 180 | 1983 | Telephone random |
| Time 2 | 180 | 1984 | Telephone random |

**FIG.15.2.** Studies drawn upon.

community's first cable system, and the second a year later. The second supplementary data set is from the first phase of what is to be a panel study of the impact of cable television and VCRs on the viewing of public television and on viewer donations to public television. This first sampling was taken in mid-1986 in the same community (Syracuse) as the primary panel study, provides more recent information on many of the factors measured in the original panel study, thus extending the time factor.

## ADOPTION BEHAVIOR

The adoption of cable television in a community is hardly a linear process. First of all, it is clear that there is a considerable amount of trial, including what Rogers (1983) has called "disenchanted discontinuance" (p. 186).

This first shows up in an analysis of subscription patterns in the Syracuse panel studies. A stepwise discriminant analysis (with .05 level of probability for inclusion in the function) at Time 1 in the first panel study identified education as the only significant, but negative, demographic predictor of cable subscription (standardized coefficient [$SC$]= -.88). Income was an initial negative component ($SC$= -.41), but it did not survive the stepwise analysis. In a similar discriminant analysis for the second panel at Time 1, education was a less impressive predictor of subscription, whereas income emerged as the strongest of the three variables included in the function: income ($SC$= .69), household size ($SC$= .61), and education ($SC$= -.41). By Time 2 of panel 2, 4 years after the first measure, this pattern continued, resulting in the elimination of education as a predictor, the reduction in importance of household size ($SC$= .48), and the strong dominance of income ($SC$= .87). [2]

It appears that early low education adopters were slowly replaced by others, primarily with higher household incomes. A series of attitude measures taken across the panel helps explain the dynamic of this behavioral pattern. At the first measure, it was found that cable subscribers (all new subscribers, remember) were considerably more positive in their evaluation of cable services than were nonsubscribers. This is not a surprising result. The surprise came in the second measure of this first panel, where it was found that the attitude gap between subscribers and nonsubscribers had greatly narrowed, and even reversed for some services (Sparkes, 1983; Sparkes & Kang, 1986). As these were repeated measures, it was clear that we were tapping changes within persons. Table 15.1 illustrates the kind of attitude change that occurred across the period of the study. Clearly, subscribers changed considerably over the test period in the cable services that they ranked as most important to them. Most notable is how the top two services changed for subscribers. News and health programs replaced education and cultural materials. For

TABLE 15.1

Top-Rated Types of Cable Programming Channels

| Group | Panel 1<br>Time 1 | Panel 2<br>Time 1 | Panel 2<br>Time 2 |
|---|---|---|---|
| Subscribers | | | |
| | Education (3.68) | Health (3.44) | News (3.73) |
| | Culture (3.61) | Imports (3.37) | Health (3.64) |
| | Imports (3.44) | News (3.36) | Educ. (3.54) |
| | Pay Cable (3.34) | Childrens (3.35) | Imports (3.40) |
| | Information (3.30) | Educ. (3.20) | Info. (3.30) |
| | (n=110) | (n=192) | (n=140) |
| Nonsubscribers | | | |
| | Educ. (3.89) | Culture (3.65) | Culture (3,62) |
| | Culture (3.89) | Health (3.54) | Educ. (3.62) |
| | News (3.50) | Children (3.38) | Health (3.52) |
| | Info. (3.47) | Educ. (3.36) | Child. (3.45) |
| | Local Progs (3.28) | Local P.(2.77) | Info. (3.07) |
| | (n=62) | (n=99) | (n=75) |

Note: Channels were rated on a 5-point scale (5=highest value.)
Numbers in parentheses are mean ratings. "Imports" are out-of-town
broadcast television stations.

nonsubscribers, there is less evidence of change across the 5-year period. Cable did seem to alter program preferences.

So the composition of the subscribing population changed rather dramatically during the first 4 to 5 years of the cable system's operation. We might expect similar types of changes, albeit on a smaller scale, as adjustments are made in rate structures and channel line-ups in the future. Further, subscribers go through a degree of perceptual change over time, first from high expectation to disappointment, and then a change in what they perceive as cable's attraction. And with changed perceptions comes behavioral change (continued subscription versus cancelling the service), which is here reflected in the discriminant analysis and which the cable industry experiences as subscriber churn.

## VIEWING BEHAVIOR

Several areas of potential change in viewing behavior were examined, including average viewing time, channels used, program selection methods, and viewing context.

No long-term differences were found between cable subscribers and nonsubscribers in average weekly viewing time (Table 15.2). A rather major increase in viewing by cable subscribers was found between *T*1 and *T*2 for the first panel members, who started at nearly equal levels of viewing. The lower part of the table shows, however, that this change occurs only among the low-education panel members. As noted earlier, during the first 2 years of the system's operation, a high proportion of low-education households subscribed to cable, and then subsequently dropped, to be replaced by more upscale households. The more striking difference, as Table 15.2 shows, is between levels of education, not subscription status. [3]

If there is no medium term impact on amount of television viewed, is there change in channels or program types viewed? Here, there is little doubt that the new services introduced through cable television are slowly but steadily picking up audience. Indeed, commercial audience measurement firms have found that the commercial broadcast network share of the viewing audience drops to below 50% in households with full service (36 or more channels) cable systems. [4]

In the Syracuse panel study, panel 2 (*T*1) subscribers were asked to indicate the three channels that they watched most often. Only 30% indicated the three local network affiliate stations, another 30% indicated a mixture of local stations and cable services, and almost 40% indicated cable services alone. Further, when the actual channels named were examined, it was clear that a variety of cable services were involved, and not just the pay (largely movie) channels. Clearly, the "chan-

TABLE 15.2

Television Viewing Time (Self-Estimated in Hours Per Week)

|                  | Panel 1 | | Panel 2 | |
|                  | T1 | T2 | T1 | T2 |
|------------------|---------------|-----------------|---------------|--------------|
| Subscribers      | 19.10 (110)   | 25.45* (75)     | 19.25 (192)   | 20.51 (140)  |
| Nonsubs.         | 18.29 (63)    | 19.42 (40)      | 19.10 (99)    | 20.13 (75)   |
| Low-Ed. subs.    | 19.55 (51)    | 29.63** (33)    | 21.50 (85)    | 23.76 (60)   |
| Hi-Ed. subs.     | 16.38 (59)    | 17.16 (42)      | 17.30 (107)   | 16.50 (80)   |
| Low-Ed. non.     | 21.60 (28)    | 20.32 (18)      | 19.60 (42)    | 21.11 (36)   |
| Hi-Ed. non.      | 14.00 (35)    | 15.11 (22)      | 16.50 (57)    | 17.12 (39)   |

* Difference for subscribers between T1 and T2 significant at the .01 level (repeated measure t test).
** Difference between T1 and T2 significant at the .001 level.

Note: All unmarked T1-T2 differences are not statistically significant. Values in parentheses are the number of cases.

nel repertoire" phenomenon is operating here. Different subscribers settle on different groupings of "favorite" channels from the selection of 36 or more that the system actually brings into the home.

The Boston study found little change in the amount of viewing in several traditional categories of programming. Subscribers did report a decrease in viewing of soap operas, suggesting that new daytime alternatives were having some impact. The Boston panel study, however, spanned only 1 year surrounding the introduction of cable service. Results from the longer Syracuse study warn us that it takes time for subscribers to integrate new types of programming into their viewing.

We postulate that subscribers first use the new cable channels to find more satisfactory examples of programming types that they already favor and only subsequently pick up on new types of programming as they slowly become acquainted with the alternatives.

Two other behavioral changes that seemed logical to expect were in program selection methods toward greater planning, and in viewing context towards greater privatization. The former change was anticipated as a natural response to cable's greater variety of programming. The latter was thought likely as different members of a household found themselves in conflict over program selection, again due to the broader menu made available through cable.

These changes were not found, however, within the time frame of the data reported on here. In both the Syracuse panel study (Table 15.3) and the Public Television study, cable subscribers were found to do less planning in their television viewing than the nonsubscribers. In fact, other analyses not shown here indicate that subscribers rely heavily on periodic checking of the telecast program listings and their ability to conduct impulse channel searches through use of remote control devices in making their program selections. (See Greenberg, D'Alessio, Heeter, & Sipes, 1983, for a discussion of channel selection procedures.)

TABLE 15.3

Use of Program Guides for Program Selection

| Program Guides Are Used | Panel 1, T1 | | Panel 2, T1 | |
|---|---|---|---|---|
| | Subs. | Nonsubs. | Subs. | Nonsubs. |
| For advanced planning | 23.4% | 19.0%* | 7.0% | 11.2%** |
| When ready to watch TV | 41.5 | 57.0 | 72.5 | 50.5 |
| Hardly or not at all | 35.1 | 24.1 | 20.5 | 38.3 |
| Total | 100.0 | 100.1 | 100.0 | 100.0 |
| n | 98 | 80 | 185 | 107 |

* Panel 1, T1: no significant association found.
** Panel 2, T1: Gamma = .20, p less than .002.

This suggests that although cable subscribers eventually come to differ from nonsubscribers in the channels they use, the approach to program selection remains largely a matter of habit and convenience rather than purposeful exploitation. Thus, although trial might lead to some new perceptions and behavior, there are clearly limits on how much exploration viewers engage in. Once a person subscribes to cable television, awareness and discovery of different or unfamiliar programming services is retarded by the failure of subscribers to systematically explore or investigate the offerings available.

Neither was any trend towards greater privatization of viewing found within the time frame of these studies. First of all, subscribing to cable television did not increase the likelihood of purchasing additional television sets. However, multiple-set owners were significantly more likely to become cable subscribers (for panel 2, Gamma = .31 and with probability at the .05 level). Nor were households with multiple television sets more inclined to use the other sets after subscription to cable television than before. Television viewing yet remains a largely social or collective activity.


## RESOURCE ALLOCATION

The two basic resources that the audience has to allocate towards the different media are time (attention) and money. As far as commercial television goes, time is the critical factor, and we have shown evidence that cable television indeed has claimed a notable share of viewer attention, and further, there is indication that this share is increasing, as programming services on cable improve and viewers become more aware of their availability and more accustomed to utilizing them. (See also Chap. 14 in this volume.)

The situation for noncommercial Public Television (PTV) in the United States is a little more complex. On the one hand is the matter of competition for viewing time. Cable increasingly offers programming that is competitive with the types of programming that PTV has traditionally thought of as uniquely theirs. Secondly, PTV goes directly to the viewing public for financial support and must worry about the possibilities that discretionary consumer dollars will be siphoned away from PTV to various cable services.

Numerous studies have taken note of this potential impact (Agostino, 1980; Frank & Greenberg, 1982; LeRoy & LeRoy, 1983), but the possibility of impact did not really become serious until the mid-1980s when competitively positioned cable services such as Lifetime, Arts and Entertainment, and Discovery began to attract meaningful audiences and generally to mature in identity and profitability.

The evidence collected from these earlier studies did not indicate a negative impact on PTV. In fact, the LeRoys argued just the opposite, suggesting that cable extended the reach of PTV considerably, thus increasing overall audience sizes regardless of what was happening to share figures. The one exception to these findings of no impact was in the area of pay cable subscription, with some evidence that such was associated with lower levels of donating to PTV.

At the time that this chapter was under preparation, our panel study of PTV had just gotten underway, and so we can unfortunately only report on the findings of the first wave, with all the interpretive limitations attending thereto. With that in mind, however, our findings indicate that there is indeed the makings of a shift in resource allocation from PTV to cable television.

Previous research in this area did not find impact from either basic cable subscription or pay subscription, but largely failed to control for household income. This would be essential, however, inasmuch as both PTV donators and cable subscribers have been found to be upscale. So actually, a "no association" hypotheses would predict cable penetration amongst PTV members to be higher than for nonmembers. The fact that these studies found similar levels of basic cable and pay subscription between PTV members and nonmembers was actually a signal that there was something going on here.

When household income is controlled for, we do indeed find a negative association between subscribing to both basic and pay cable and donating to PTV, although only in trend. [5] Sixty-two percent of high-income households ($40,000 plus) with basic cable donated to PTV. Amongst noncable high-income households, 68 % donated. The trend is somewhat stronger for pay versus nonpay households, with 60% of pay/high-income households donating to PTV, and 67% of the nonpay households (sig.=.25).

So there is some indication of impact at this time on tendency to donate to PTV. However, the matter of self-selection looms here. We really cannot say yet that subscribing to cable *causes* lower donating. It could be that persons less inclined to donate to PTV are more interested in subscribing to cable television.

As far as allocation of viewing time, there is an even stronger association, as summarized in Table 15.4. Cable subscribers report viewing PTV less frequently than do persons without cable.

These figures are supported by other information from the same study, in which 71% of nonsubscribers said that they had increased their viewing of PTV, whereas only 55% of cable subscribers so indicated (Cramer's $V$=.18, $p$=.1).

Also of considerable significance in this study were the results of a series of questions dealing with the use of alternative sources for preferred types of PTV programming. Traditionally, Public Television has been the primary source in the United States for so-called "cultural" and educational programming, including

TABLE 15.4

Public Television Viewing Levels By Cable Subscription

| Group | 3-4 Times Per Week | 1-2 Times Per Week | 1-2 Times Per Month | Total |
|---|---|---|---|---|
| Cable subs.* (n=357) | 62% | 28% | 10% | 100% |
| Non subs. (n=193) | 79% | 15% | 6% | 100% |

* Chi square between subscribers and nonsubscribers significant at the .05 level.

educational programming for children. With the advent of cable television, however, several new channels or services began to offer similar kinds of programming. The Discovery Channel, for example, is an alternative source of nature and science programming, whereas the Arts and Entertainment Channel offers concerts, dance, art appreciation, and foreign films. For children, both the Nickelodeon service and the Disney channel offer a wide range of programming that has received the praise of advocacy groups such as Action for Children's Television.

When we examined persons who were regular PTV viewers and subscribed to cable, we found that a full 40% of these subscriber-viewers judged an alternative cable channel to be as good as or better than PTV for the particular type of programming involved. The specific cable channels named, and the percent of viewers-subscribers rating them so highly are: Cable News Network (17%); Arts and Entertainment (14%); WTBS (and some other general channels) (14%); Disney and Nickelodeon (6% each); Discovery (4%), and "cable channels" in general (14%).

These results seem to indicate moderate to good awareness on the part of PTV viewers that there were alternatives available. It will be most important to watch how these figures change over the next few years. It will also be important to find out how people who neither give to nor watch PTV are using these special cable services.

As far as influence on the other broadcast media, there is some evidence of impact. Possible effects on radio were detected by Becker, Dunwoody, and Rafaeli (1983) and by Reagan (1985). Both suggested a shift from radio's role in news and weather information. McDonald (1979) also detected a negative relationship between radio listening and cable subscription. As single-measure studies, however, their findings leave the matter of cause open. In our Boston study, no significant decrease in actual listening to radio was detected following subscription to cable television (see Table 15.5). Nor was there a change in judgments of radio's "importance" to subscribers (although the trend in both measures was supportive of the earlier findings). We caution again, however, that the Boston panel covered only the first year of cable service in the community measured.

TABLE 15.5

Changes In Utilization of Other Media

| Medium | Subs., T2-T1 | Nonsubs., T2-T1 | Prob. Level* |
|---|---|---|---|
| Use of radio** | 11.74 | 5.81 | .78 |
| Importance of radio*** | -.18 | -.13 | .78 |
| Attend movie theater**** | -.35 | .11 | .08 |
| n | 69 | 69 | |

* Probability levels associated with a "t" test of difference between the subscriber and nonsubscriber change scores.
** Self estimated minutes per day.
*** Five-point Likert type scale, where 5=very important and 1=very unimportant. Figures for "Importance of radio" and "attend movie theater" are change scores.
**** Number of times in the past month.

As far as impact on the nonbroadcast media, there was only one point of negative change. The Boston study revealed a notable decrease in movie attendance amongst cable subscribers as opposed to nonsubscribers. The Boston study also looked at subscriber behavior related to attendance at plays, concerts, and sports events. No behavioral changes occurred within the year following cable's arrival in the test community. Finally, neither panel study found that cable was significantly affecting usage levels for books, magazines, or prerecorded music.

## SUMMARY AND CONCLUSIONS

In this chapter, we have documented the indirect, even circuitous manner in which audience members integrate complex new technologies like cable television service into their daily lives. Indeed, development of such a service is itself limited by the speed and pattern of this integration.

We have found changes in viewing behavior, but nothing terribly radical to date. Nevertheless, a progression of adjustments can be seen over the 5-year time period covered by our data, and there is no reason not to assume that this incremental change process will continue.

As of yet, changes do not appear to have occurred in the areas of *how* people watch television. The predetermined repertoire of local broadcast stations has been replaced by repertoires somewhat fortuitously tailored by subscribers from the array of channels that their cable service provides. In behavioral terms, then, cable television is not 36 or 54 channels, but rather differing and even changing sets of 5 to 7 channels.

Beyond viewing behavior, little evidence of behavioral change was found. The two possible exceptions—the evidence is not firm—are related to Public Television and movie theaters. There is preliminary evidence that subscribing to cable does pull people away from PTV, both as viewers and as supporters. We also found a negative association between cable subscription and movie theater attendance, but causality is still unclear here.

What about the next 5 years? We expect the channel repertoire approach to continue. We also expect increasingly frequent excursions by viewers to other channels, as utilization leads to familiarity and the industry finds better ways to guide the audience through the potpourri of viewing alternatives. We do not foresee much further displacement of other media or leisure activity until the content on "the cable" is quite different from what it is now. The most likely sources of near future behavioral change will be the electronic shopping channels and pay-per-view, both of which were in 1987 just becoming widely available.

Early evidence from a new study in a large urban market suggests an additional dimension of cable use that needs to be investigated. One of the central themes of this chapter, and the research it reports on, is that cable television in the United States today is a complex service that takes some effort to explore fully. Indeed, there is evidence that the failure or inability of subscribers to fully utilize the available services is a major cause of disconnection. In relation to this finding, there is a possibility that high-activity people and low-activity people are less likely to be subscribers to cable than others, but for quite different reasons. We suggest the following scenario.

Low activity people, those with few, if any, hobbies or outside interests, do tend to subscribe to cable television when it first becomes available. Television viewing is an attractive pastime for persons with few other interests. Cable television seems to offer diversion in abundance. However, the very passivity that attracts these folks to cable television also appears to mitigate against full utilization. This limited use of the medium subsequently makes it difficult to justify the monthly payment for cable service, then, leading subsequently to disconnection. This and other aspects of cable use can be understood only with continued investigation of the service as it develops and as users become more accustomed to making use of it.

## NOTES

[1] Somewhat overlooked today is a rather remarkable newsletter published under the direction of Kas Kalba in the early 1970s. Contributors to these early issues or *Urban Telecommunications Forum* were concerned deeply with what they

perceived to be far-reaching implications of cable for social patterns and city planning.
[2] These results were replicated in the cable subscription rates derived from both the panel study and the PTV effects study for the different income categories. From the Panel 1 Time 1 sample we find the following: For households with annual incomes of less than $15,000 it is 46%; for households between $15,000 and $40,000 it is 66%, and for households in the over $40,000 category it is 75%.

[3] This largely null finding is at variance with those from several other studies in which a positive association was found between cable subscription and television viewing. We note that these differences in results might be explained by the fact that many of the earlier studies did not employ panels and were commonly at the start-up of cable services.

[4] Figures reported by the A.C. Nielsen company over the past few years have indicated broadcast network shares from 44% to 60%, depending on the level of cable service available to the reference population.

[5] The term "trend" is used here to describe a result that, although not statistically significant, is still of a direction and magnitude to deserve attention. In this case, when the sample was broken down first by income and then by cable subscription, the size of the groups was sufficiently small as to make achievement of statistical signficance difficult. The absolute sizes of the differences are still notable.

## REFERENCES

Agostino, D. (1980). Cable television's impact on the audience of public television. *Journal of Broadcasting, 24,* 347-365.

Becker, L. B., Dunwoody, S., & Rafaeli, S. (1983). Cable's impact on use of other news media. *Journal of Broadcasting, 27,* 127-140.

Bogart, L. (1956). *The age of television.* New York: Ungar.

Brown, L. A. (1981). *Innovation diffusion: A new perspective.* London: Methuen.

Cabinet Committee on Cable Communications. (1974). *Report to the president.* Washington, DC: U.S. Government Printing Office.

Committee for Economic Development. (1975, April). *Broadcasting and cable television, policies for diversity and change: A statement on national policy.* New York.

Comstock, G., Chaffee, S., Katzman, N., McCombs, M., & Roberts, D. (1978). *Television and human behavior.* New York: Columbia University Press.

Dakin, J. (1972). *Telecommunications in the urban and regional planning process.* Toronto: University of Toronto Press.

Frank, R. E., & Greenberg, M. G. (1982). *Audiences for public television*. Beverly Hills: Sage.

Gerbner, G., Gross, L., & Melody, W. (1973). *Communications policy and social change*. New York: John Wiley and Sons.

Greenberg, B., D'Alessio, D., Heeter, C., & Sipes, S. (1983). *The cableviewing process*. Unpublished manuscript, Michigan State University, Department of Communications, East Lansing.

Hart, P. D. (1979). *A survey of attitudes towards cable television*. Washington, DC: National Cable Television Association.

Hawkins, D. I., Best, R. J., & Coney, K. A. (1983). *Consumer behavior: Implications for marketing strategy*. Plano, TX: Business Publications Inc.

Himmelweit, H. T., Oppenheim, A. N., & Vince, P. (1958). *Television and the child*. London: Oxford University Press.

Land, Herman W., Associates, Inc. (1968). *Television and the wired city*. Washington, DC: National Association of Broadcasters.

LeRoy, D. L., & LeRoy, J. M. (1983). *The impact of the cable television industry on public television*. Unpublished manuscript, Fort Lauderdale, FL.

Mandelbaum, S. J. (1972). *Community and communications*. New York: Norton.

McDonald, D. (1979, August). *Cable television subscription and conceptions of social problems*. Unpublished paper presented at the meeting of the Association for Education in Journalism and Mass Communications, Houston, TX.

Mitre Corporation. (1972). *Urban cable systems*. Washington, DC.

National Science Foundation. (1976). *Social services and cable TV*. Washington, D.C.: U.S. Government Printing Office.

New York State Senate. (1972). *Cable communications and the states*. Albany, NY.

Reagan, J. (1985). *The impact of cable television on radio use: A comparison of nonsubscriber, basic subscriber and pay subscriber households*. Washington, DC: National Association of Broadcasters.

Reilly, M., & Holman, R. (1977). Does task complexity or cue intercorrelation affect choice of an information processing stategy: An empirical investigation. In W. D. Perrault (Ed.), *Advances in consumer research* (pp. 185-190). Chicago: Association for Consumer Research.

Rogers, E. M. (1983). *Diffusion of innovation* (3rd. ed.). New York: Free Press.

Schramm, W., Lyle, J., & Parker, E. (1961). *Television in the lives of our children*. Stanford, CA: Stanford University Press.

Scott, J. (1976). *Cable television: Strategy for penetrating key urban markets*. Unpublished manuscript, University of Michigan, Graduate School of Business Administration, Ann Arbor.

Sloan Commission on Cable Communications. (1971). *On the cable: Television of abundance.* New York: McGraw-Hill.

Smith, R. L. (1970). *The wired nation: Cable TV—The electronic communications highway.* New York: Harper & Row.

Sparkes, V. M. (1983). Public perceptions of and reactions to multi-channel cable television. *Journal of Broadcasting, 27,* 163-175.

Sparkes, V. M. (1984, April). *The half wired nation: Cable television's fifty-five percent barrier.* Paper presented at the meeting of the Broadcast Education Association, Las Vegas, NV.

Sparkes, V. M., & Kang, N. J. (1986). Public reactions to cable television: Time in the diffusion process. *Journal of Broadcasting, 30,* 213-229.

Steiner, G. (1963). *The people look at television.* New York: Knopf.

Steiner, R. L. (1972). *Visions of cablevision.* Cincinnati, OH: Stephen H. Wilder Foundation.

Tate, C. (1971). *Cable television in the cities: Community control, public access, and minority ownership.* Washington, DC: Urban Institute.

# 16

## The Audience Copes with Plenty: Patterns of Reactions to Media Changes

**Klaus Schoenbach**
*Academy for Music and Theater, Hannover*
**Lee B. Becker**
*The Ohio State University*

The media scenes of the Western world experienced change in the 1980s. As expected, the research reports in this volume have shown considerable variety in audience responses to this change. Yet a closer examination shows some striking consistencies. As a result, four general conclusions are possible.

*First*, for the most part, there is surprisingly little evidence of dramatic, long-term reduction of time devoted to nonmedia behaviors as a result of the new media. The exceptions seem to be in those countries where television content had been severely restricted in the past. *Second*, we find little reason to conclude that audience members have *radically* reduced the amount of time devoted to or money spent on auditory and print media. The evidence for impact even on movies (an audio-visual medium similar to many of the new media forms) is inconsistent. *Third*, there is rather consistent evidence of increasing specialization in the uses of all the media, not only the new ones. Television, for example, has become even more of an entertainment medium than before and, within the general category of entertainment, offers materials appealing to even more specialized interests. Consistent with this specialization is an apparent dependence by the audience on the local product for information about one's own political scene and culture. *Finally*, we find no evidence that the new media, at least initially, create new audience interests; rather, they seem to provide the means via which existing interests or needs can be played out or satisfied. To put this more simply, the new media allow people with interests in areas such as entertainment to act on those interests, making the media seemingly more effective and satisfying for them. The media, in this way, may reinforce these interests.

## COUNTRY-BY-COUNTRY REVIEWS

These are the general patterns. They can be best understood by a brief review of the situations in the various countries in our study. The review follows the schema used in chapter 1 to organize countries in terms of the amounts of and types of changes being experienced in the media content of those countries.

We begin our review with the countries that are, so far, experiencing relatively little new material, almost all of which, however, is from abroad. *New Zealand* within this group is closest to the "ideal." The major feature of its media scene is its isolation. Audience members, for example, have few alternatives to the two television channels. The only real alternative at present is the videocassette recorder. Not surprisingly, the VCR is popular there, with an estimated 40% of the homes in at least some markets having one. What has been the effect? A slight, but constant decrease in the viewing of the two national channels is in evidence and seems to be one outcome of the spread of the VCR. Another is new programming strategies on the part of these channels to offset this decline. And finally, there is evidence of a decrease in patronage of movies.

The situation is somewhat similar in *Australia*, although there is considerably more television available there, at least in the large cities. What is interesting are the striking differences between the two sides of Australia: the sophisticated urban centers and the remote "outback." There, as well, the VCR has enjoyed considerable success, reaching over half of the country's homes. Not surprisingly, the VCR is even more popular in the remote regions than in the urban centers. In the remote regions, the VCR is being used to record programs arriving via satellite, which for the first time has made television itself available. Overall, the VCR seems not to have resulted in increased viewing, but rather the displacement of older habits. As a consequence, viewing of the broadcast channels has decreased. Entertainment is the dominant form of preferred video material. Rented cassettes are mainly from the United States. Convincing evidence of the impact of the VCR on movie attendance, nonetheless, is lacking. Movie attendance was even on the upswing by the end of the study period.

As in New Zealand and Australia, the VCR has played an important role in *Sweden*. About a third of the homes there have such a device. Where cable and satellite services are concerned, almost all of the new material comes from outside the country. There is a strong feeling of the need to protect the society and the culture and to educate the people to deal with the new media in a proper fashion. There is little evidence, however, that changes in the media environment already have had strong impact on audience behaviors.

Our second cluster is represented by The Netherlands, Belgium, and Switzerland. This cluster is made up of countries with considerably more change in content than has taken place in Australia, New Zealand, and Sweden but less than in countries to follow. Yet the bulk of the new content in these three countries is foreign.

*The Netherlands* is a good beginning point for the description of this cluster because discussion there of media options has been extensive and, indeed, experimentation, particularly in the area of viewdata, teletext, interactive cable, and cable delivery of newspaper-like text, has taken place. For our purposes, perhaps the most important feature of the Dutch media landscape is the high level of cable penetration. More than 70% of the households in the country are connected to cable. To a large degree, the content of cable is foreign programming, but, even without cable, many television sets in the Netherlands can receive foreign broadcasts over the air. The video recorder also has made significant inroads, with a third of the households having one.

The consequences of the change in the Dutch media content have been increased use of television, both foreign and domestic. This is largely due to increased viewing of such things as video clips on the part of young people who previously seem not to have found relevant or interesting materials on television. Television also became available at times of the day when it wasn't available before. The effect of VCR use on total television time has not been found to be great, but the VCR has brought about a shift toward entertainment viewing. There is no evidence that newspaper services delivered over cable are replacing conventional newspapers. During the period of study, there were hints of a decline in book sales and cinema attendance, but it isn't clear that changes in the availability of other media produced this.

The Dutch analysis also shows that Dutch viewers stay loyal to their own broadcast organizations for news and documentary materials and even give them increased attention. They turn to foreign materials largely for entertainment. This is a finding that is replicated in Belgium, as well as in Switzerland.

*Belgium* is another very extensively wired country, with over 80% of the households connected to cable. It also is a country whose borders are much crossed by foreign materials. Videocassette recorders are in about 15% of the households.

Some effects stand out in the Belgian case. First, there is very little use of Belgian television in one language by speakers of the other language. Second, similar to the Dutch case, there is a strong preference among the Belgians for their own news and documentaries rather than for materials from abroad, even though many of the foreign programs are in the languages of the country. Third, the amount of viewing of entertainment has increased as these foreign materials have become available.

Because of its geographic features, cable is needed for many households to receive a clear television signal in *Switzerland*. More than half of the households are connected to cable. In the Swiss case, these cable services bring in many foreign materials in languages used by the four different Swiss language groups. For example, the Italian-speaking section of the country receives not only Swiss signals in the various Swiss languages but also signals originating in Italy. The consequences, at least in the Italian sector of Switzerland, have been rather dramatic. Only a third of the viewing time there is of Swiss-originated programs. In the French- and German-speaking sectors, 40% of the viewing is of Swiss materials. Whereas in the Italian section even the viewing of Swiss news and documentaries seems to have been hurt by foreign materials, this is not the case in the German-speaking sector. Here, there seems to be more loyalty to the Swiss product.

The new means of delivering television content in Switzerland (cable and VCRs) have increased the frequency of television watching, but only among the younger segments of the population. As in most of the countries studied, the video recorder is used most extensively for viewing of entertainment recorded from television.

The Swiss have experimented with local radio as well as with the specialization of the national radio signals. The result has been increased fragmentation of the radio audience as listeners turned away from the general appeal, national signals to ones with differentiated programming, much of it youth-oriented. Also as a result of these changes, the Swiss listeners have returned to Swiss signals from foreign ones.

Our next cluster of countries consists of West Germany, Italy, the UK, and France. Much new material has come into being in these countries. In *West Germany*, cable penetration was only about 13% in 1987, but it was consistently increasing. The two channels that were most successful in drawing large numbers of audience members were different from public service television, largely in that they were fully commercial and somewhat more entertainment-oriented. VCR penetration was approximately 35% by the end of 1987. Teletext and viewdata were not particularly important for the German mass audience by the end of the period of study.

Increases in viewing as a result of cable and the VCR generally were not dramatic. More entertainment was watched than earlier as a result of both cable and the VCR. People seemed rather open in acknowledging that these new devices have allowed them increased opportunities for escape and relaxation. It also is quite clear that those who watched a lot of television even before cable and the VCR were available were most interested in these devices. In other words, cable and the VCR allowed them to do with television what they had wanted to do. The greater competition within television due to the new commercial operations seemed not to have resulted so far in replacement of the traditional programming. There also was no evidence that cable viewers turned away in great numbers from news when more entertainment became available.

The German data on cable television provided an important suggestion of a long-term effect not yet in final form. Once cable came into the home, the newspaper was not regarded as indispensable as before. Although there was no immediate evidence that newspaper reading dropped, over time this might well be the consequence of the change in assessment of the medium's importance. The German data also provided preliminary evidence of another, somewhat unexpected, effect of cable. It seems that households able to select the materials from television that they were most interested in experienced less tension, presumably as a result. The finding is consistent with other work showing positive effects of television on family life (Gunter & Svennevig, 1987). As such, it deserves further examination.

The situation in *Italy* is one of the most interesting. The explosion in content provided by the changed broadcasting situation has resulted in increased use of that medium. The new media, such as cable, have been closed out of the system by this phenomenal growth in broadcasting. The evidence of a decline in cinema attendance during the period of broadcast explosion is quite dramatic.

The *United Kingdom* is not a heavily cabled country, but it is a country that in the 1980s experienced growth in broadcasting both in terms of number of channels and amount of time of broadcasting, extensive experimentation with teletext (broadcast) services as well as with viewdata, and high levels of penetration of the videocassette recorder. Nearly half of the homes in the UK had a VCR by the end of 1987, and one in five had a teletext decoder. Teletext was used most often for weather reports, news, and sports. The VCR was used for viewing of movies taped from television, followed by the viewing of soap operas.

One result of the use of the VCR seems to have been a decreased use of broadcast television signals. Also, those homes with cable obviously experienced growth in the amount of television viewing. During several times of the day in cable homes, viewing of signals available only on cable is much more extensive than viewing of the traditional signals. In contrast, despite the introduction of new over-the-air signals, the amount of television-watching done by the noncable viewer has not expanded. In other words, those parts of the audience most interested in television (evidenced by their subscription to cable) increased their use when cable became available, but all other people's viewing was not particularly changed by expanded offerings. Only the introduction of early morning television has adversely affected radio listening at that time of the day.

Evidence from the UK suggests that the audience is not so much channel loyal as content loyal. As a result, merely increasing the number of channels does not make a difference to the audience. Increasing the offering of a certain type of programming, in contrast, can lead people to watch more television. (The Swiss data are consistent with this position as well.) The UK data specifically suggest there that is great interest in serial materials, and this interest has not yet been matched by supply.

*France* has experienced growth in broadcast materials, particularly entertainment. Most of these are transmitted over the air. The videocassette recorder is not particularly important. Viewdata has experienced considerable success, however, due to government measures to encourage use. The viewdata services that are most consulted are not the services of information but rather those of communication, such as games and messaging.

The *United States* differs from the UK, France, West Germany, and Italy in that cable penetration is quite extensive (with just under half of the homes reached) and the VCR has experienced rather dramatic growth after a slow start. More than a third of the U.S. households had such a device by the beginning of 1987. The number of over-the-air television and radio signals had also increased dramatically. In contrast with the UK (and other European countries) teletext does not exist in the United States other than in experimental forms. Viewdata also is still largely experimental or of limited appeal.

Growth in television viewing occurred in the first half of the 1980s most in cabled households; cable and noncable households differed most in terms of their viewing time on weekends. There is little or no evidence, however, that this increased time with television resulted in less reading of newspapers, decreased listening to radio, or even in decreased movie theater attendance.

The growth in both broadcast and cable signals, however, has resulted in reduced viewing of programming from the three major television networks. The exception has been the local evening newscasts, which have remained popular with audiences despite growth in the alternatives. There also is evidence that cable has adversely affected publicly funded broadcasting. It seems that the audiences were making more selective use of the media options to better suit their own—rather than programmer—purposes. Cable subscribers watched more movies, more sports, more news, and even more religious programs than nonsubscribers. Nonsubscribers, it seems quite clear, assigned television a lesser role in their lives than did cable subscribers.

This overview of the most significant results from the 11 countries studied brings into question the fruitfulness of our original scheme of clustering them in terms of changes in their media systems. In chapter 1, we ordered the countries according to the amount and the diversity of their new media offerings. Amount is clearly an important dimension. It can explain, for example, the role of the VCR as a supplement (as in the United States) or as an alternative to television (such as in New Zealand). Diversity, in terms of the range of offerings from escapist material to thorough current affairs information, determines the specialization of media use that we encountered in so many countries.

Because alternatives were lacking when we started our project, we chose the amount of *foreign* materials as an indicator of this diversity. This proportion certainly is helpful in explaining the dependency of a country's media industry on outside supplies and even in forecasting to what extent the authenticity of a national culture may be endangered (see Baer & Winter, 1983; Payne, 1978; Payne & Caron, 1982; and Pingree & Hawkins, 1981). The reports in this book suggest, however, that, in Western capitalist societies, most audience members, even if they are aware of the origin of the entertainment materials they watch, do not regard the proportion of foreign programming as an issue in their responses to changed media landscapes. To put it bluntly, it seems that people are more interested in whether a program is entertaining than in whether it was produced in their country or elsewhere. On the other hand, there is considerable loyalty to the news programming of their own country.

In general, then, the country of origin, at least of the entertainment programs, does not seem to be very decisive for the audience members. What could be a more important dimension along which to order the cases of this book is how much a society stresses the information and education functions of the mass media, as opposed to their distraction function. A tradition of media systems that are primarily expected to make people more knowledgeable, even enlightened, does seem to determine both the comparatively low speed and the nature of new media developments in countries like Sweden, West Germany, Switzerland, and New Zealand. In contrast, where the major function of the media legitimately is entertainment, where the media are taken less "seriously," we find both more and more widespread new offerings and relatively more channels exclusively devoted to entertainment. The United States and Italy seem to be representative of this approach.

## MEDIUM-BY-MEDIUM COMPARISONS

The studies assembled here did not reveal a clear international front-runner in terms of how successful or important a specific new medium has become. Depending mostly on a country's media system and its history, cable television proved to be more widespread and/or disruptive than, for example, the VCR. In other cases, the reverse was true. What we have found, however, are some fairly general patterns of what people do with the new media and what use of the new media does to other media and nonmedia leisure-time behaviors.

A significantly *expanded television offering*—in most countries via cable, in some also over the air—seems to have been accompanied by a relatively and unexpectedly small but stable expansion of time spent on television. In most countries, there is evidence that people do increase the amount of time spent with television as the content expands. But after an initial fascination had faded, people with access to the new television offerings watched relatively little more television per day on the average. As an overall pattern, this increase seems to be considerably less than an hour each day, and is often more like a quarter or half that amount. There are exceptions, with Italy seeming to stand out. At present, we do not know how much of the Italians' greatly extended television viewing time is accounted for by the novelty of their experience and the former scarcity of appealing materials.

The television content that the general audience prefers to spend more time with seems to be common in all the societies examined in this book. The greater the television offer, the greater the portion of viewing time that is—even in absolute terms—devoted to entertainment, primarily movies. This changed pattern of TV use, however, does not necessarily hurt television newscasts. Viewers do not give up watching them. They simply add more entertainment viewing to their daily television routine.

We also note the audience's increasing preference for more specialized TV services, such as movie and sports channels. There is a slight but remarkable movement away from the TV stations—often the traditional ones—that try to cater to many different interests and thus make the individual viewers wait for the content they really want to watch. It is possible that, over time, television watching for more and more specific interests will increase the attention paid to the media (if not necessarily the time), making time spent on television increasingly less available for simultaneous activities such as conversation and household tasks.

In the countries where there is a lot of foreign materials on television, domestic programs seem to be preferred over foreign ones—if the domestic services offer the types of content viewers are interested in receiving. This is consistent with Tracey (1985), who found a preference for home-produced television of all sorts, and Winston (1986), who argued that national channels can develop strategies of survival in the face of competition. Channel loyalty, in general, seems to be weaker than program or even genre loyalty. We should not forget that, in contrast with communications scholars or media politicians, most audience members probably do not discriminate completely between cable, over-the-air, and satellite channels. What these channels *offer* is important to the audience member, not how they were distributed. For them, most likely, it is all simply "television."

The distribution of *videocassette recorders*, the time spent with them, and the materials watched on them seem heavily dependent on what television without the VCR has to offer. In the countries studied here, household penetration rates range from 8% to 50%. In some of these countries, rental cassettes are the only alternative to television, and the VCR does seem to reduce the time spent watching traditional television. In others, the VCR is just a supplement to an already manifold television offering. Where VCRs play a more supplementary role, their central function often seems to be the one of shifting the viewing of content. They allow the audience members to watch TV material that they would have missed otherwise. VCRs are overwhelmingly used for entertainment purposes.

Both new television offerings and the VCR do not seem to have changed other media or leisure time behaviors to a great extent. So far, people with access to more television and video materials generally have not stopped reading, going out, or playing with their children. What seems to be the case, however, is that those not particularly interested in reading, for instance, are more inclined to the new television offerings.

These results do not preclude, of course, long-term changes in leisure time behavior. One might speculate, as an example, that those adolescent cohorts watching more television now may stick to that routine even when they are adults. Also, there may be some groups of audience members who stopped leaving their homes for outside entertainment, such as is found at the movie theater. Others, however, somehow may have balanced the new media habits and the existing leisure activities. Some may even have developed more activities outside their homes because the new media technologies allowed them to organize their television schedules more flexibly.

*Teletext* is a new medium that, where it exists, serves mostly as a headline service, a quick program guide, or a subtitling device. All services, with the possible exception of subtitling, do not seem to be overly dramatic in terms of impact. Although audience members use them, there is little evidence that they could not do without them. As far as our studies show, teletext has not changed media habits or other leisure time behaviors in any dramatic fashion.

*Viewdata* is probably the only really *new* mass medium developed in the period of the early 1980s. It allows users to interact with a central data base and with each other. Its success in terms of adoption has varied by country. In most countries, it is mainly a new instrument of business communication. Only in France, it seems, has viewdata experienced a real breakthrough into the realm of the "mass" media. The major reason for this seems to be that, from the start, it was designed to replace another medium, the telephone book, also in wide circulation. Where no such substitution has been engineered, the medium has not enjoyed public support and adoption.

## CONCLUSIONS

In the introductory chapter of this book, we identified four different ways in which audience members could respond to the new media. One is rejection, whereas the remaining three are some form of adaptation and integration.

It is clear that the new media offerings do not appeal to everyone. In each of the countries studied, significant numbers of people, given the choice, opt for the old and reject the new. In the United States, for example, only 50-60% of those passed by cable actually subscribe to it. Even in New Zealand, where the television offerings are very restricted, the videocassette recorder has penetrated only 40% of the homes. The audience in general has not yet warmed to viewdata, although France, in particular, is an exception. Teletext seems to be more favorably received than viewdata. Although there is no doubt that some people have rejected these new offerings because of their costs, it is clear that many who can afford them reject them anyway.

One form of adaptation to the new media is a reallocation of the resources of attention, time, money, and space. Another is modification of behavior combined with or following this reallocation of resources. There is little evidence of dramatic changes in these two types of audience behaviors as a result of changes in media content and delivery systems during the first half of the 1980s.

The final type of adaptation is bound to the content of the media. Audience members, for example, might change their world views as a consequence of use of the new media (see chap. 1 in this volume). Unfortunately, this topic has not yet been dealt with in the research assembled here or in that reviewed for this volume. Consequently, the plausibility of such effects remains.

In addition, evidence of long-term effects on audience behaviors of the first and second type might still come forward. Although none of the studies reported on in this book relied exclusively on single time-point designs, it remains the case that the media changes examined have been in existence for relatively short periods of time. Data from the German situation, particularly, are suggestive of long-term effects of cable television on such things as newspaper reading.

The studies that we have examined have concentrated on the consequences of changes in the media scene for the audience members. This was a conscious decision to limit the focus to the individual. This limitation in perspective here in no way denies what may be dramatic changes in the media organizations. For instance, advertising revenues for the older media are clearly harmed by the introduction of the new. The old broadcast organizations in many countries, as a result, have had to find ways to adapt to the new competition for advertising revenues. In addition, we can see that movie producing companies in various countries have experienced changes in distribution economics as a result of the new alternatives of cable and the videocassette recorder.

Another limitation to our project is that we have restricted ourselves to a group of countries that are relatively similar in a variety of ways, such as in terms of press freedoms, political stability, economic development, and prosperity. Had we looked elsewhere, we might have found evidence of dramatic changes even at the individual level. Some of these might have transferred to significant organizational and media structural adaptation as well.

As one example, we can consider the situation in Malaysia. In that country, where the Chinese-Malay citizenry had been denied access to programs from the Chinese worlds of Hong Kong and Taiwan, the VCR drew away from "TV Malaysia" significant numbers of Chinese viewers. The result has been a destabilization of the existing political assumptions behind the national broadcasting system, and shifts in communication policy to accommodate (Karthigesu, 1987).

It is not the goal of this project to develop media policy or argue the merits of the various options societies have to deal with the new media. Although an important activity, it simply isn't the focus of this undertaking. Others, such as de Bens and Knoche (1987), Ferguson (1986), McQuail and Siune (1986), and Rogers and Balle (1985), have laid the groundwork for much of this discussion.

Nonetheless, we caution against simply taking the point of view that the appropriate response to our findings is no change in policy, because there is little evidence of dramatic modification in audience behavior. This begs the question. Policy can be intended to restrict, to liberalize, or to maintain the existing order. The UK and West Germany, for example, have embarked on programs of privatization in an effort to increase content options. This is based on the assumption either that change is needed or that whatever change will take place is not harmful. Other countries may feel that a strategy of maintaining the existing order is appropriate until additional evidence is available. Our data do not argue against this position. If anything, the existing data would seem to argue against further constraint at this time.

At this point, by way of analogy, we would like to talk about alcoholism. Many people argue that alcohol must be restricted so as not to harm the population. Their argument is twofold. The first is that people who are inclined to alcohol should be kept from it. The second is that even those not inclined will find it so attractive if it is readily available that they will use it even without the initial inclination. As a result, most societies, in an appropriately paternalistic manner, restrict access on the part of children to this product. Some restrict access on the part of adults. Often in the case of alcohol, this is done via pricing schemes, which particularly restrict access on the part of poor adults.

The point of the analogy is that some social critics make the same arguments against access to new media entertainment fare as are made against alcohol. The implicit argument is that simple availability will lead to deviant behavior of various sorts because of the attractiveness of the product. In other words, even people who have no initial interest in the product will use it nonetheless because of its appeal. Those with an initial interest will become addicted to it. The deviant behaviors feared are lowered political participation, less interest in public affairs and high cultural products, and personal impoverishment.

What is the evidence here of the ability of the new media material to attract audience members not initially interested in the product? The answer, at least from what is available here, is "not much." In other words, we have no real evidence that significant numbers of people who might otherwise be reading and really preferred to read a Thomas Mann novel have turned to "Dallas" as a result of cable.

It remains possible, nonetheless, that some people have watched significantly more entertainment than before as a consequence of the new media. We simply may not have been able to find them because the activities of this group were balanced by the activities of others whose usage decreased. Such a result could not be identified because of the "averaging of effects" that took place in most of the designs employed in the studies used here.

All of this aside, we must confess that the only way to actually determine this question of the new media's potential to produce this negative effect is to introduce true experimental situations where those people who receive new media services are actually randomly determined. This would solve the problem of self-selection, that is, those who are favorably inclined toward the new media opting for them. No such experiments have been carried out. Rather, the data that exist show that indeed these new media appeal to certain types of people who are clearly fond of the product. They are the ones we are speaking of when we say they have added these behaviors to their daily lives without great disruption.

No cohesive theoretical perspective could be used to guide the project. We see the results, however, as consistent with a general view of an active audience, making use of materials to suit individual needs. This audience defines a behavior according to needs, perceived costs, and resources available to cover those costs, not according to whether the behavior is media-centered or not. Such a view of an active audience is consistent with much recent writing in the field (Zillmann & Bryant, 1985).

Our evidence of audience responses to new media offerings in the 11 countries examined contains two basic patterns. One may be called a *hedonistic* pattern of use of the new media. To a considerable extent, these new offerings fulfill entertainment functions that are important to the audience members. As Zillmann and Bryant (1986) noted, a certain amount of such entertainment consumption is probably essential for normal functioning in modern society. The notion of a totally hedonistic use of the new offerings, however, is misleading. The audience does not necessarily abandon information programs. What it does is segregate entertainment and information as a consequence of the expanded and more specialized materials available. This is the second pattern, one of *specialization*. In the future, multifunction television channels may dissolve into more and more clearly distinctive services. Such services enable individuals to decide whether and when they want to be optimally entertained or optimally informed. The days of restricted offerings seem to be numbered. There is no evidence that the audience member is unprepared or in overly serious danger as a result.

## REFERENCES

Baer, D., & Winter, J. (1983). American media and attitudes regarding government in a Canadian border community. *Canadian Journal of Communication, 10,* 51-86.

de Bens, E., & Knoche, M. (Eds.). (1987). *Electronic mass media in Europe: Prospects and developments.* Dordrecht: D. Reidel.

Ferguson, M. (Ed.). (1986). *New communication technologies and the public interest.* London: Sage.

Gunter, B., & Svennevig, M. (1987). *Behind and in front of the screen.* London: John Libbey.

Karthigesu, R. (1987, June). *Commercial competition to government monopoly in television.* Paper presented at the meeting of the Asian Studies Association, Penang, Malaysia.

McQuail, D., & Siune, K. (Eds.). (1986). *New media politics: Comparative perspectives in western Europe.* London: Sage.

Payne, D. (1978). Cross-national diffusion: Effects of Canadian TV. *American Sociological Review, 43,* 740-755.

Payne, D., & Caron, A. (1982). Anglophone Canadian and American mass media: Uses and effects on Quebecois adults. *Communication Research, 9,* 113-144.

Pingree, S., & Hawkins, R. (1981). U.S. programs on Australian television: The cultivation effect. *Journal of Communication, 31* (1), 97-105.

Rogers, E. M., & Balle, F. (Eds.). (1985). *The media revolution in America and western Europe.* Norwood, NJ: Ablex.

Tracey, M. (1985). The poisoned chalice? International television and the idea of dominance. *Daedalus, 114* (4), 17-56.

Winston, B. (1986). Survival of national networks in an age of abundance. *Inter-Media, 14* (6), 30-34.

Zillmann, D., & Bryant, J. (Eds.). (1985). *Selective exposure to communication.* Hillsdale, NJ: Lawrence Erlbaum Associates.

Zillmann, D., & Bryant, J. (1986). Exploring the entertainment experience. In J. Bryant & D. Zillmann (Eds.), *Perspectives on media effects* (pp. 303-324). Hillsdale, NJ: Lawrence Erlbaum Associates.

# Author Index

367

# Subject Index